D0891729

Agriculture on the Road to Industrialization

Other Books Published in Cooperation with The International Food Policy Research Institute

Agricultural Change and Rural Poverty: Variations on a Theme by Dharm Narain
Edited by John W. Mellor and Gunvant M. Desai

Crop Insurance for Agricultural Development: Issues and Experience
Edited by Peter B. R. Hazell, Carlos Pomareda, and Alberto Valdés

Accelerating Food Production in Sub-Saharan Africa
Edited by John W. Mellor, Christopher L. Delgado, and Malcolm J. Blackie

Agricultural Price Policy for Developing Countries
Edited by John W. Mellor and Raisuddin Ahmed

Food Subsidies in Developing Countries: Costs, Benefits, and Policy Options
Edited by Per Pinstrup-Andersen

Variability in Grain Yields: Implications for Agricultural Research and Policy in Developing Countries
Edited by Jock R. Anderson and Peter B. R. Hazell

Seasonal Variability in Third World Agriculture: The Consequences for Food Security
Edited by David E. Sahn

The Green Revolution Reconsidered: The Impact of High-Yielding Rice Varieties in South India
By Peter B. R. Hazell and C. Ramasamy

The Political Economy of Food and Nutrition Policies
Edited by Per Pinstrup-Andersen

Agricultural Commercialization, Economic Development, and Nutrition
Edited by Joachim von Braun and Eileen Kennedy

Agriculture on the Road to Industrialization

EDITED BY JOHN W. MELLOR

Published for the International Food Policy Research Institute

The Johns Hopkins University Press
Baltimore and London

The Johns Hopkins University Press
2715 North Charles Street
Baltimore, Maryland 21218-4319
The Johns Hopkins Press Ltd., London

ISBN 0-8018-5012-6

Library of Congress Cataloging-in-Publication Data will be found at the end of this book.

A catalog record for this book is available from the British Library.

Contents

Tables and Figures

Tables

Figures

Foreword

According to World Bank standards, almost one-quarter of the countries of the world and one-half of its population fall in the "low-income" category. The hope of all these countries is to raise their people's standard of living through economic development. But to do this they must choose a development strategy that is suited to their particular situation and needs. Although there is no model that can be universally applied to the great variety of subjective and objective conditions in the less advanced countries, the development experience—both the successes and the failures—could perhaps yield a number of concrete variables that they could use to formulate their own economic development strategies. Since agriculture is the mainstay of the economies of most developing countries, and it is also the foundation for their future economic development, the discussions in this volume concentrate on the role of agriculture in industrialization.

In most successful cases of economic development, such as the widely acknowledged "Taiwan experience," agricultural development was the main concern in the early period. The growth of agriculture laid a firm foundation for industrialization, which in turn led to broader economic development. Indeed, the Republic of China made a point of fostering a close and mutually complementary relationship between agriculture and industry. It adopted a policy of "building up industry through agriculture and using industry to develop agriculture" in order to attain a balanced development of both. Agriculture made three major contributions to development in the Republic of China. First, it satisfied the increased demand for agricultural products created by the rapid growth of both the economy and the population. This served to stabilize commodity prices and keep wages low. Second, it provided the labor that the industrial sector needed to proceed with economic development. Third, it provided a portion of the capital needed for industrialization.

The first step in developing agriculture in this case was to institute land reform. This policy was implemented in three phases: farmland rents were reduced by 37.5 percent, public lands were released for farming, and a project was launched for transferring "land to the tiller." In addition, landowners received reasonable compensation for their losses. Resistance to the policy was therefore reduced to a minimum, and land was smoothly transferred into the hands of those who tilled it. Once farmers were able to enjoy the full fruits of their labors, their motivation to increase production rose.

Production was also boosted by introducing methods of labor-intensive industries and refined farming, coupled with innovative technologies and infusions of capital and equipment. As a result, farming income and farmer demand for industrial products both went up. This growth in domestic market demand enabled industrialists to develop export markets. At the same time, the export of agricultural products and processed agricultural products helped the Republic of China accumulate foreign exchange and thus provided basic capital for the machines and equipment required for industrial development. Industry received further capital through transfers from agriculture, made possible by a number of taxation measures. This strategy of first stimulating agricultural growth and then using the resources of agriculture to aid in industrial development is in striking contrast to the methods employed by a number of other countries. The pattern there was to squeeze agriculture for all it was worth, without upgrading production technologies and investing in scientific-technological research and development. The outcome of their approach has been imbalanced economic development.

Despite its success in expanding agriculture and then gradually moving from import-substitution industries to manufacturing products for export, and finally to capital-intensive heavy industry, the Republic of China saw a number of problems emerge in the agricultural sector, which have still not found a solution.

- With the rapid development of industry and commerce, the growth of farming incomes began to decline. As a result, agricultural income is now relatively low.
- Since the pressure for economic liberalization is growing, it will eventually be necessary to change the current structure of agriculture.
- Because the agricultural sector is aging, it will have an increasing difficulty staying on its feet.
- As threats to the environment and pollution continue to increase, they will have an adverse effect on agricultural and fishery production.

These are the same problems that other newly industrialized economies face. They cannot be resolved without a clear understanding of the role of agriculture in industrialization. The need for such an understanding makes the studies described in this volume all the more timely. I am confident that these studies will help pave the way to successful development for other countries and thereby create a brighter tomorrow for the peace and welfare of all humanity.

Lee Teng-hui
President, Republic of China

Preface

The International Food Policy Research Institute (IFPRI) holds a central position in worldwide research on the interrelationships between food and agriculture, poverty, and the environment. John W. Mellor, who was director of the institute for thirteen key years, was among the earliest and most persuasive exponents of a set of influential ideas that are epitomized in the provocative and perhaps counterintuitive opening sentence of his introduction to this volume, borrowed from a book he published in 1966: "The faster agriculture grows, the faster its relative size declines." For thirty years he has argued that agricultural growth, particularly if it is broadly based and associated with technical progress at the level of small- and medium-size farms, is the best route to development in low-income countries. Linkages between agricultural growth and more rapidly expanding nonagricultural activities, notably via the rising consumption demands of farmers, had previously been greatly underestimated and even misunderstood. Nowhere have these linkages seemed clearer than in Taiwan.

John Mellor and IFPRI were ahead of their time. These ideas are now more widely shared. (I count myself among those who were gradually persuaded of their plausibility.) Yet the detailed mechanics of how the relevant linkages actually worked—and might still work in many poor countries in Sub-Saharan Africa and elsewhere—often remained elusive. It was for the purpose of trying to pin down some of the key issues, made clearer by the experience of a sample of developing countries that had achieved rapid agricultural growth in the period after World War II, that John Mellor assembled the authors whose deployment of hard data, detailed institutional knowledge, and cross-country comparisons appear in this volume and, I believe, epitomize the IFPRI style of research.

As chairman of the board of trustees, I would like to express not only my thanks and those of other members of IFPRI's board and staff for John Mellor's years of dedicated leadership but, if I may presume to speak on their behalf, the thanks of the Consultative Group on International Agricultural Research and the wider agricultural development community for the inspiration, energy, and intellectual guidance he has provided, as exemplified by the publication of this book.

Gerry Helleiner, Chairman
Board of Trustees
International Food Policy Research Institute

Acknowledgments

The idea for this book grew out of a conference in Taipei that allowed the authors to interact not only among themselves but with a group of senior people who participated actively in various ways in the discussions. Taiwan's political and economic leaders played a vital role in this process. I am especially grateful to President Lee Teng-hui; Terry Yu-hsien Yu, chairman of the Council of Agriculture; Shirley W. Y. Kuo, deputy governor of the Bank of China; Sam Hsieh, governor of the Central Bank of China; and their many helpful colleagues for the intellectual assistance and hospitality that was so important to this effort.

Agriculture on the Road to Industrialization

1 Introduction

JOHN W. MELLOR

"The faster agriculture grows, the faster its relative size declines." That quotation from *The Economics of Agricultural Development* (Mellor 1966) still captures the essence of agricultural growth and its causal relationship to the structural transformation and aggregate growth of an economy.

The quotation suggests that agriculture has a potential for accelerated growth. This suggestion arises from the concept that technologies capable of increasing agricultural yield can also defeat the debilitating effects of a growing population and income where the land area is fixed. It implies a relationship, rooted in Engel's Law, whereby the proportion of total expenditure on food declines with rising income even while total food consumption and the proportion of expenditure on important subclasses of food increases. The underlying assumption here is that agriculture is a large component of economies in their early stages of development. To achieve structural transformation in such economies, it is necessary to increase agricultural income and expenditure and rapidly increase labor productivity in agriculture, which will further accelerate structural change in the employment distribution of the labor force. These processes by which agriculture becomes less dominant yet paves the way for development are the primary concern of this volume.

The Relationship between Agricultural and Nonagricultural Growth

The relationship described in the opening quotation can be illustrated by comparing the agricultural and nonagricultural growth rates of countries in each of the world's three major geographic regions (figures 1.1 through 1.3).

The relationship between the two variables appears to be strong in all the countries of Asia (figure 1.1). Simple observation, however, indicates that other forces are at work besides this relationship. Note that four economies lie far outside the line of simple fit in figure 1.1: Singapore, the Republic of Korea, Burma, and the Philippines.

Singapore is, of course, a city-state. Its agricultural sector is inconsequen-

1

FIGURE 1.1 Growth rates of per capita agricultural and nonagricultural GDP, various Asian countries, 1960–1986

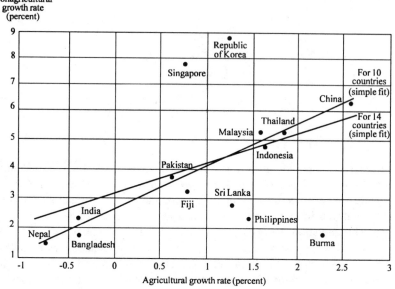

Source: World Bank (1989).

Note: Descriptive variables for simple fit of 10 countries (excluding Burma, Philippines, Republic of Korea, and Singapore): R-square, 0.91; value of coefficient of agricultural growth rate, 1.43; t-statistic of agricultural growth rate, 9.33; and standard error of agricultural growth rate, 0.15. Descriptive variables for simple fit of 14 countries: R-square, 0.23; value of coefficient of agricultural growth rate, 1.07; t-statistic of agricultural growth rate, 1.92; and standard error of agricultural growth rate, 0.56. Constant 1980 GDP at market prices in local currency.

tial. The Republic of Korea is a more interesting outlier. Its nonagricultural sector has experienced an extraordinarily rapid rate of growth whereas its agricultural sector has done less well. Here industrial growth seems to have proceeded independently of agriculture. In fact, the growing demand from the rapidly expanding nonagricultural sector pulled the lagging agricultural sector into faster growth—which is quite the reverse of the situation described in most of the cases in this book. In Korea industrial development depended heavily on large-scale industry, rather than small- and medium-scale industry, was concentrated in a few urban centers, and relied on very large inflows of private capital. Most important, the effective demand for increased output came not from domestic sources but from foreign sources. It is doubtful that developing countries generally could rely on foreign demand for the bulk of their incremental output. That is why the contributors to this volume emphasize growth in agriculture as a focus for incremental domestic demand.

FIGURE 1.2 Growth rates of per capita agricultural and nonagricultural GDP, various Sub-Saharan African countries, 1960–1986

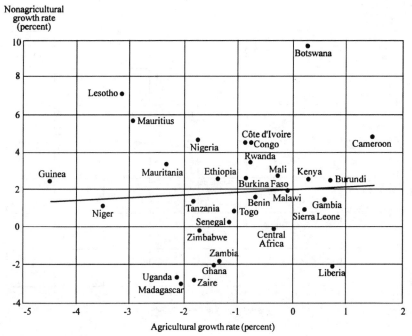

Source: World Bank (1989).

Note: Descriptive variables for simple fit: R-square 0.0029; value of coefficient of agricultural growth rate, 0.025; *t*-statistic of agricultural growth rate, 0.29; standard error of agricultural growth rate, 0.085. Constant 1980 GDP at market prices in local currency.

In Burma and the Philippines the relationship between agricultural and nonagricultural growth is somewhat different. Burma's policy environment has not been favorable to agricultural or nonagricultural growth. Thanks to an extraordinarily strong physical resource, agriculture nevertheless grew rather well. But with a hostile policy environment, agriculture failed to pull the nonagricultural sector into accelerated growth.

The situation in the Philippines is somewhat more complex. Although agriculture grew at very high rates, owing to technological advances, the non-agricultural sector lagged behind, largely because of policies at the national level. As explained in chapter 5, those policies also affected many aspects of the economy and society, notably the incidence of poverty and the pattern of urbanization.

Apart from these four outliers, the remaining economies in figure 1.1 found 91 percent of the growth in one sector associated with growth in the other.

FIGURE 1.3 Growth rates of per capita agricultural and nonagricultural GDP, various Latin American countries, 1960–1986

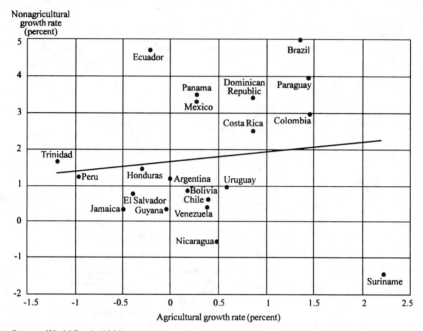

Source: World Bank (1989).

Note: Descriptive variables for simple fit: R-square 0.0170; value of coefficient of agricultural growth rate, 0.2714; *t*-statistic of agricultural growth rate, 0.57; standard error of agricultural growth rate, 0.47. Constant 1980 GDP at market prices in local currency.

The slope of the line of that relationship suggests that for each 1 percent of acceleration in per capita agricultural growth, there is about a 1.5 percentage point acceleration in per capita nonagricultural growth.

These observations from the Asian context suggest that two broad questions need to be addressed in exploring agriculture's role in the structural transformation of the economy: What accounts for the variations in the impact of accelerated agricultural growth on nonagricultural growth? And, what policies might increase the efficiency with which accelerated agricultural growth moves the structural transformation forward? In view of the outliers' demonstration of the reduced effect of agricultural growth on nonagricultural growth, it would not be unreasonable to suppose that highly effective policies might provide a much larger multiplier than the 1.5 indicated by the cross-sectional data. Yet another important question to consider as a result of these multiplier effects is how can agricultural growth be accelerated to obtain growth in other sectors? All three of these questions are treated at length in the following chapters.

The authors are careful, however, to avoid simplified answers, such as the neoclassical position that accelerated growth in agriculture, presumably based on increased productivity in the agricultural sector, proceeds at the expense of other sectors, drawing resources from them and hence slowing their rate of growth. Rather, they find the data support the view that developing economies are replete with underemployed labor, opportunities for scale economies, and market imperfection—all of which create the potential for improved productivity in one sector to have a positive impact on the growth of other sectors.

That a relationship exists between agricultural and nonagricultural growth rates is certainly less evident in Africa and Latin America, as can be seen from figures 1.2 and 1.3. In Africa, the growth rates have been notoriously slow, particularly in agriculture, and what growth has occurred seems by and large the product of external forces—weather in the case of agriculture and oil and large foreign assistance flows in the case of the nonagricultural sector. Oil and foreign assistance have typically boosted urban growth rates to unusually high levels and been responsible in part for the "Dutch disease" and associated exchange rate phenomena that have had such an adverse effect on agriculture in Africa. Some useful lessons may be gleaned from the case study of Kenya, which was somewhat more successful in achieving agricultural and overall growth than the other countries of Africa.

In the higher-income countries of Latin America, structural transformation has, of course, already proceeded much further than in Africa or in Asia, and hence agriculture's effect on other sectors is bound to be lower. In addition, a wide range of policy regimes in the region have been particularly deleterious to agriculture.

Needless to say, one should not draw continent-wide implications from the evidence presented in figures 1.1–1.3. One cannot say, for example, that in Asia agricultural growth stimulates nonagricultural growth, whereas in Africa and Latin America it does not. One can simply say that economic policy, physical resources, and external shocks have an influence on the growth of various sectors and the extent to which accelerated growth in one sector stimulates accelerated growth in the others. The purpose of this book, and its case studies, is to explore the complex relationships that cause such stimulation and to examine them under a wide range of conditions. That is the only basis on which it is possible to draw conclusions as to how public policy can reinforce those relationships and thereby meet society's objectives at a faster pace.

The Importance of the Size of Agriculture

Agriculture plays an important role in structural transformation because of its preeminent size, not its preeminent growth rate. It is innately a relatively slow-growing sector. Economists debate the resource requirements and the policies that may accelerate agricultural growth from the lower end of the normal range of growth to the upper end—an increment of two to four percentage points. Growth at the low end tends to be 2 or 3 percent a year and is driven mainly by the rate of population growth. Even with a relatively fixed land area, increases in the population and hence in the labor force combine with human ingenuity to provide the slow accretion of technological and physical improvement that normally allows agricultural production to grow at a rate comparable to or perhaps only slightly slower than the rate of population growth.

At the other end of the growth spectrum, the disciplined, structured organization of human ingenuity and accumulated scientific knowledge accelerate technological change beyond the rate of population growth. Productivity is further increased by the specialization made possible by reduced transaction costs and expanding trade. Increased trade and rising incomes make it possible to change the composition of output and thereby boost productivity still further. These forces combined move agricultural growth toward the upper ranges. But even there, it rarely exceeds, on a sustained basis, 4 to 6 percent. Short spurts of agricultural growth beyond this level do occur, of course, in areas that have experienced the sudden application of modern technologies on a broad scale. But as a whole, "accelerating" agricultural growth normally refers to a more or less doubling of the growth rate from 2 to 3 percent to 4 to 6 percent.

In contrast, the nonagricultural sector frequently grows at a rate of 8 to 10 percent for sustained periods and on occasion even exceeds that. In a traditional society, the lack of systematic technological innovation and the small local markets tend to keep nonagricultural growth down around 2 or 3 percent and thus closer to agriculture. But once modernization is fully under way, the growth rate nearly triples, while that of agriculture, at best, doubles.

Thus, as development accelerates, the economy undergoes a natural transformation from one dominated by a slower-growing agricultural sector to one with a faster-growing nonagricultural sector. Furthermore, as the non-agricultural sector—with its greater potential for high rates of growth—increases its weight, the growth rate of the entire economy accelerates toward the fast rate of the nonagricultural sector, even though the respective sectoral rates do not change.

From their observations of these patterns, many economists have concluded that the nonagricultural sector requires the most attention in development strategies, often at the expense of the agricultural sector, whether advertently or inadvertently. Why, then, do strategies that emphasize the nonagricultural sector generally end up with rather slow rates of growth for both sectors and indeed lag far behind countries that emphasize both sectors or even seem to focus primarily on agriculture? That question is at the heart of this book.

As already mentioned, agriculture is important in the early stages of growth because of its size, which helps it overcome its tendency for modest growth rates. Typically, in low-income countries the agricultural sector accounts for about 80 percent of the labor force and 50 percent of the gross national product (GNP). Add to this the problems many such countries have with overvalued exchange rates, statistical counting in the widely dispersed agricultural sector, and other forms of undercounting, it may be that their labor force distribution comes closer to representing the distribution of economic weight than does the distribution of GNP. The economic implications of an emphasis on the agricultural sector should now become clearer. Agriculture may be a slower-growing sector, but it has large mass. That large mass implies a large output, but also large economic inputs. In the early stages of development, agriculture does indeed contain most of the land, labor, and capital of a low-income country. Perhaps more important, agriculture's economic weight makes it a potential source of effective demand for consumption goods. And, precisely because of the large numbers of people involved and their modest incomes, their consumption patterns tend to favor domestically produced, labor-intensive products.

The pioneering analysis of the sources of growth in developed countries by Nobel prize winner Robert Solow (1956) and by Edward Dennison (1985) and others provides a cogent economic reason for concentrating on agriculture in the early phases of development. Technological change that increases output per unit of input in this massive existing sector could boost national income substantially and thereby hasten economic transformation and the shift to the potentially faster-growing sectors. Conversely, if the technological change begins in the smaller nonagricultural sector, it will have to proceed at a much higher rate than a given rate in the agricultural sector to achieve as much effect on national income. Moreover, in view of the great diversity of the non-agricultural sector, it may be more difficult to achieve accelerated technological change across the entire sector than it would be in agriculture.

It is no good, however, to argue that agriculture can play an important role in development and then to focus attention on only a part of the sector. Broad agricultural development is necessary if the sector is to play its role effectively. This does not mean that every subregion and every farmer must participate, which in any case would not be economic owing to the variability in the physical conditions of agriculture and in the talents of farmers. Early in development, when incomes are low and capital is particularly scarce, hard choices must be made concerning the allocation of resources within agriculture. Nevertheless, the bulk of agricultural production must be brought into accelerated growth if the desired economic transformation is to take place. Thus small farmers or tenants who operate a large proportion of the total resources must not be left out. Similarly, if only a portion of the land area is devoted to a particular crop, the technology effort should not be restricted to that crop.

Whatever the growth in specific subsectors of agriculture, the uppermost concern must be the breadth of coverage of the development efforts, as is emphasized throughout this book. That concern should pervade all such efforts, whether in the area of asset and income distribution, the regional distribution of various types of agricultural production activities, or export versus food crop production. In as many as five of the cases presented in this volume, major structural problems within agriculture substantially reduced the participation of agriculture in growth and hence the size of the agricultural multipliers.

Beyond Growth

Development, it should be added, is not just a matter of achieving growth, even though low-income countries find substantially accelerated growth is necessary before they can address other developmental concerns. But these other concerns should not receive all the attention, either. That is why the case studies here have made a point of examining the interaction of growth with other aspects of development: such as the pace and structure of urbanization, the distribution of the benefits of growth (especially as they help reduce poverty), and the role of the private sector together with the effects of market orientation. A question of particular interest is how these issues relate to massive numbers of small entrepreneurs and the role of national policies in agriculture-led growth. Democracy, with its strong ideological and humanistic traditions and current wave of support, is treated in a few of the cases, but for the most part the discussions are concerned with the institutions and the breadth of participation required for rural development.

Urbanization

The alarming rate of growth and concentration of population in a few capital cities of the developing world has unfortunately diverted attention from the rural sector. After all, the next generation of problems is expected to converge on the urban areas. On the surface, agricultural growth would appear to be a natural antidote to these problems, in the sense that it would keep people down on the farm and away from the bright lights of Dakar. In Africa, where external resources have generated a great wave of urbanization, that argument may have some merit at this particular juncture. As already pointed out, however, agricultural growth also accelerates nonagricultural growth and therefore will not automatically eliminate the problems of urbanization.

Accelerated agricultural growth may play a positive role nonetheless if the urbanization problem is viewed in terms of the degree of concentration and the structure and level of urban real wages and unemployment, rather than the proportion of the population in urban centers. In that case, redirecting public resources toward the existing megalopolises and away from agriculture would be counterproductive, as the following chapters demonstrate. That urbanization per se is not the problem becomes self-evident when cities are seen as the repositories and, indeed, the source of civilization. It is enhanced agricultural productivity that makes possible such conglomerations with their specialized inhabitants, who in turn provide the science and the arts for a prospering, civilized society. Thus, the relationship between agricultural growth and urbanization has important implications for all aspects of development.

Poverty Reduction

The case studies pay particular attention to the extent of participation of the poor in development and the progress in eliminating the worst forms of absolute poverty. The relevance of agricultural growth to this issue is obvious.

Although not all poor people are in rural areas, they are predominantly so. In Africa, some 80 percent of those living below the absolute poverty line, as it is generally defined, are located in rural areas. In Asia, where the proportion of the population in the rural sector has declined somewhat in comparison with Africa, and where urban concentrations are greater, the proportion of those living in absolute poverty in rural areas is 75 percent. Even in Latin America, the absolute poor in rural areas account for 50 to 60 percent of the population. Much of urban poverty represents a flight from rural poverty. The treatment therefore lies in economic growth in rural areas. Furthermore, any effort to treat urban poverty without tackling rural poverty is destined to be overwhelmed by the increased migration of the poor prompted by urban poverty reduction programs.

It is now well known that poor countries need to achieve accelerated economic growth before they can substantially reduce absolute poverty. The relationship between the distribution of income—as, for example, described by a Gini coefficient—and growth is less clear, with some weight on both sides. The case studies examine both income distribution and the incidence of absolute poverty, especially in countries where the poor do not even have an adequate supply of the basic nutrients for an active healthy life.

The interesting question here is whether accelerated agricultural growth, owing to its structure, decreases absolute poverty more rapidly than alternative strategies of growth. The answer depends on the extent of the multipliers between agriculture and nonagriculture. Because of the nature of yield-increasing processes, agricultural production, even when it grows rather rapidly, has a limited capacity to absorb rapidly increasing quantities of labor in a productive manner. Where poverty declines rapidly, this result is associated with accelerated agricultural growth. But the increases in employment that lift the poor out of poverty are related to the expansion of the rural nonagricultural sector. Thus the relationship between agricultural and nonagricultural growth also needs to be examined for its implications for employment.

Growth of the Private Sector

In the first few decades after the demise of colonialism, most development strategies were based on ideologies that favored the large-scale, capital-intensive public enterprise and showed little interest in developing agriculture or assisting the small farmer. That era gradually gave way to one in which private enterprise was championed, government regulation was opposed, and market forces were considered the best regulators of the economy. Throughout this postcolonial period, development strategy has been in tune with the changing political climate.

Privatization, too, has caused some concern, however, because it could bring unbridled power to large-scale multinational corporations. An alternative ideological and power framework that has recently emerged is organized around small- and medium-scale private enterprises rooted in the domestic economy of developing countries. That strategy has its own ideological cohorts, some of whom take a conservative stance on distributive issues and market orientation.

Clearly, an agriculture-led strategy with its concomitant of vigorous growth in the small and medium rural enterprises breeds massive numbers of small entrepreneurs at a high rate. That group, in turn, requires and encourages increasing market orientation. These two issues are treated at length in the case studies.

Democratization

Another issue of concern here is the extent to which democratization includes rural people or is largely an urban phenomenon. A country with more than 50 percent of its population in rural areas is a restricted democracy indeed if it excludes rural people from its development plans. Perhaps because of their colonial background and the influence of the urban intelligentsia in the processes of decolonization, the governments of today's developing countries are more urban-based and less oriented to rural areas than was typical of countries that went through a similar stage of development earlier in their history, such as Japan and the countries of Europe and North America. That is why it is important to learn more about the implications of development for local government, cooperatives, and other democratic institutions in rural areas. The cases give little explicit attention to this issue, although their intensive coverage of rural institutions does shed some light on it, particularly in the exposition on Taiwan.

The Conceptual Framework

As the preceding discussion suggests, the contributors to this volume had three principal concerns in mind as they explored the role of agriculture in the structural transformation of the economy: how productivity is affected by technological change in the agricultural sector, how the increased income is spent, and what other sectors of the economy undergo expansion as a result of the changes in agriculture.

Technology

The agricultural practices of countries at an early stage of development are technologically backward. Such circumstances carry the potential for a large increase in factor productivity. Because land is limited in area and the wage rate for labor is low in these countries, any technological innovation they attempt must be largely of a biological nature and must raise yields per acre. Note, however, that increased yields per unit area of land greatly increase the productivity of labor as well as of the land. Note, too, that the demand for labor is inelastic with respect to the output derived from such innovation, a circumstance that has important implications to the structural transformation of the economy.

By and large, the efforts to transfer applied technologies from the very different agroecological conditions of developed countries to developing countries have met with little success. The story is quite different where developing countries have drawn on the accumulated scientific knowledge from developed countries and the patterns of their institutional structures to generate appropriate technology in situ. In view of the institutional structures that have evolved in developed countries in the past century and their immense accumulation of knowledge in both basic and applied biological sciences, the pace of technological change can proceed much more rapidly for the developing countries of today than was the case for those earlier on the scene. This circumstance is particularly fortunate, and important, given the much higher rates of population growth at present. Countries must therefore develop complex institutions if they are to achieve their scientific potential.

This is not the only way to accelerate the growth of agricultural output, of course. The land area can also be expanded, although this approach holds less promise if the best land has already been brought into cultivation, in which case factor productivity will decline as additional land is cultivated. The processes of interest here are those that cause factor productivity to increase. In any case, land frontiers can only be expanded up to a point, which has already been reached in essentially all developing countries.

Furthermore, land expansion is often accompanied by one or more of three kinds of technological innovations: mechanization to increase the land area per worker; new crops; and new techniques for increasing yields of traditional crops, raising factor productivity on new land, and thereby raising the profitability of marginal land. These points should be kept in mind in the cases of Thailand and, to some extent, Costa Rica.

Changing the output mix is obviously an important means of raising factor productivity. For all the successes recorded in the case studies, this change contributed significantly to their increases in factor productivity. The dynamics of that process are an important part of the agricultural story.

Expenditure Patterns

When factor productivity in agriculture increases, real net national income rises substantially, and the expenditure of this income serves to stimulate other sectors of the economy. This is decidedly not a Keynesian process. The expenditure stimulus is derived from real resources, not monetary expansion, so there are real goods to be purchased as factors of production are mobilized in other sectors by the increased expenditure.

The process can be readily understood by comparing an economy with unemployed labor whose employment has an inflationary effect when stimulated by Keynesian expansion in the money supply (since labor will spend that money on a static supply of food) with an economy in which labor is mobilized by expenditure that is backed by the very supply of food (wage goods) that it demands. One need not think entirely in such simple barter terms, although food as wage goods is a particularly apt illustration. This example drives home the point that agricultural growth must be based on processes that increase factor productivity.

From a public policy point of view, it is important to know whether the increased expenditure will stimulate the growth, in rural areas, of commodities for which the supply will be highly elastic, and particularly whether they will be labor-intensive activities. If the stimulus takes place in rural areas, the case for expenditure on rural infrastructure and education will be strengthened. If the supply is highly elastic, it strengthens the case for providing public goods to stimulate agricultural growth because, in effect, the returns are increased by the multipliers on other sectors. If labor-intensive production processes are also stimulated, it further strengthens the case for making appropriate public allocations to agricultural growth—because of the positive effects on income distribution, as well as on growth and because of the large increase in demand for food that will occur. That demand can be met either through agricultural expansion or through foreign exchange allocations from the increased agricultural exports.

Beyond these broad questions, the details of the expenditure patterns and their precise impact on specific subsectors are irrelevant to public policy. That is because the stimulus is felt by large numbers of activities that are carried out by the private sector and that can only be regulated efficiently by market processes. Consequently, macroeconomic policy looms large in the strategy proposed in this book. Nevertheless, the nature of farmer expenditure patterns can be used to make this broad point. In all the cases studied, except the Philippines, rapid growth of the agricultural sector was associated with a sufficiently rapid increase in employment to cause real wages to rise. In many instances, this was followed by a rapid increase in the demand for cereals, which necessitated an increase in net cereal imports. But it was market processes and not central planning that precipitated these phenomena. Statistics and measurement are not critical to such processes. Perhaps that explains the difficulty the studies have experienced in corroborating the relationships, particularly in Punjab and Thailand, for which detailed data are not available.

Agricultural growth often requires a substantial increase in operating expenditure, particularly for fertilizer and other chemicals. These are typical intermediate products produced most efficiently by large-scale, capital-intensive processes. They are best imported and, hence, this linkage to domestic growth is weak. Some form of increased mechanization occurs very early in agricultural growth, at least to deal with seasonal bottlenecks in labor supply, and eventually mechanization grows rapidly. Those domestic linkages are powerful. And almost without exception, those forms of capital are readily produced at low cost in small machine shops in rural areas, by firms that are particularly well-suited to gaining a life of their own, beyond the local market. Agricultural processing varies considerably in its optimal capital intensity and in the extent of its comparative advantage in rural areas. The case studies provide a wealth of detail on this subject.

However, it is the consumption linkages that are most important. The savings rate of rural people receiving increments to their incomes tends to be high but rarely exceeds 30 percent. Thus they will spend at least 70 percent of their incremental income on consumption goods. Albert O. Hirschman's widely quoted statement that agriculture has very poor linkages to other sectors and thus is not a sector to emphasize reflects a common tendency of development economists to ignore the stimulative role of effective demand for consumption goods and services.

Empirical analyses show that in contrast the producers of agricultural commodities spend little of that incremental income on increased consumption of the basic food staples, such as cereals and root crops, even though the production of those goods may provide a substantial portion of incremental income. Among small, peasant farmers, the expenditure seems to run to some 20 percent on labor-intensively produced agricultural commodities that have high income elasticities of demand, such as livestock and horticultural commodities. This subsector merits some attention. It is not really like agriculture, since land accounts for only a small part of the input structure and demand tends to be quite elastic. It is more like the nonagricultural sectors. Some 40 percent of incremental expenditure goes to locally produced nonagricultural goods and services, which are also quite labor-intensive. The Thailand case is particularly interesting in this regard, in that it provides detailed expenditure data, all of which clearly point to place-specific expenditure patterns.

The Stimulated Sectors

Someone arguing from a simple neoclassical position would say that if agriculture benefits from increased factor productivity in comparison with other sectors, it will expand at the expense of those other sectors by drawing resources from them. That, as Bruce Johnston explains in chapter 8, is not the reality. What many economists tend to overlook here is the function performed by labor markets in poor countries. First, these countries almost inevitably have a large slack in their rural labor markets. This may well be the product of colonial regimes that certainly did not allow their colonies to operate according to neoclassical principles! In particular, population growth and the high productivity of labor on excellent land provided "surplus" labor that, according to neoclassical principles, should have gone into nonagricultural production—but that was substantially barred from doing so by the colonial regimes.

Whatever the explanation, the supply of labor in rural areas is highly elastic; a substantial labor force is working at very low levels of productivity. That labor can perform tasks that have a substantially higher productivity if effective demand is provided. Why does it not produce those goods for export? One problem is that when goods are initially produced, the quality is such that they are not exportable, although they are in demand locally. There are scale economies in exports that are difficult to reach without a local base of consumption. The point here is that producers can learn by doing, which is facilitated by expanded local demand, and that as the process proceeds, a wide range of opportunities open for meeting existing demand in distant markets. The advantage of domestic demand from rural people is that the level of sophistication of the goods need not be as high as for export markets, and hence, learning by doing can proceed before producers enter the export market. The Taiwan case is particularly interesting from this point of view, but the other cases also shed light on those processes.

A similar point can be made in a somewhat more neoclassical fashion. All developing countries have a substantial disequilibrium in their capital allocations. A high proportion of capital is allocated to a small proportion of the labor force in capital-intensive activities, and a small proportion of capital is allocated to a large proportion of the labor force in very labor-intensive activities. As a result, there is a large departure from the equalizing of marginal products of labor and of capital across activities. Some of this is inevitable—for example, a nontradable good such as electric power is innately capital-intensive but essential to the bulk of labor-intensive activities. Much of the misallocation is the product of wrong policies, including excessive import substitution policies. The point is that capital intensity is strongly determined by the output mix, and the choice of technique within any given product is often very limited. The consumption patterns from agriculture-led growth provide a structure of demand that is oriented toward products for which the efficient production processes are highly labor intensive. That change in the structure of demand brings about large increases in efficiency. A pure neoclassicist would say, "Never mind—let foreign demand provide the appropriate structure of output," but that approach, as indicated above, creates many practical problems.

It is important to remember that food is a wage good that accounts for some

80 percent of the total expenditure of the laboring classes. The expansionary processes described earlier do depend on a highly elastic supply of labor. In poor countries labor supply is no more elastic than the supply of food. Accelerated growth in the food sector, which dominates agriculture in most developing countries, automatically takes care of this problem. With rapid technological change in food production, the labor supply becomes highly elastic. If the agriculture sector is not dominated by food production, then agricultural exports are dominant. In that case, rapid technological change in agriculture will expand the aggregate of exports rapidly and hence the foreign exchange for importing food, and again the labor supply can prove to be highly elastic.

In an open economy, however, just as in a closed economy, food prices will generally go up rapidly whenever employment grows rapidly and domestic agricultural production does not. With such a large aggregate, a rapid growth in imports, except in cases where a dominant base of agricultural exports expands rapidly, will change the real exchange rate and raise domestic food prices even while international food prices are unchanged.

The expansion of small- and medium-scale rural firms can only take place in an environment of freely operating markets. If capital is constraining, prices should rise, increasing the rate of return, attracting capital, and increasing retained earnings that can be reinvested. Eventually, however, a well-integrated national financial market will become important to the movement of some of these firms to medium- and larger-scale production. Furthermore, these firms will tend to make use of increasing and soon large quantities of intermediate products such as plastics, synthetic fibers, and metals, which are produced by capital-intensive, large-scale processes inappropriate to low-income economies. International trade regimes should continue to be freely operating.

An implicit assumption of this discussion has been that agricultural prices will not decline or will decline little in the face of increased production. That is an empirically defensible position. Typically, low-income countries that attain high growth rates in agriculture increase their food imports, because the employment stimulus is so great that the demand for food shifts faster than supply, increasing food imports and maintaining domestic prices. If the process is driven only by agriculture, then food prices will decline (see Lele and Mellor 1981), but the agricultural stimulus will usually be accompanied by growth endogenous to the other sectors. The empirically observed result is rising food prices and increasing imports. Note that in an unusual case such as the Philippines, in which accelerated growth in agriculture is not accompanied by high nonagricultural growth, agricultural prices do indeed decline. Here, the agricultural stimulus to other sectors is likely to be less, partly because of the extent of benefits to the poor, through lower prices and the concentration of their expenditure on food, and partly because urban expenditure patterns will not be as likely to push up the demand for the products of labor-intensive industry. Thus the increased expenditure from prospering agriculturalists typically stimulates the growth of labor-intensive industries, which then stimulates a large increase in the demand for basic food staples.

The critical question is what if land, the principal recipient of increased returns from yield-increasing technological change, is held in large holdings by wealthy people? Such wealthy people usually do not even live in the rural areas and their consumption patterns can be expected to have a large import content, either because they invest abroad, travel abroad, purchase capital-intensive goods from abroad, or purchase domestically produced, capital-intensive goods that have a high import content. Thus the distribution of income within the agricultural sector may clearly have an important effect on the nature of the linkages between agricultural and nonagricultural growth. The case studies in this volume raise this and a number of other issues pertaining to the role of agriculture in structural transformation.

The Eight Cases

The relationship between agricultural and nonagricultural growth rates is examined in eight case studies compiled for a cross section of countries. With one exception (Argentina), countries were selected for their high agricultural growth over a protracted period in recent years and for the growth in the national economy. The seven cases, excluding Argentina, had an average agricultural growth rate of 4.4 percent over a broad period (see table 1.1). Developing countries as a group averaged 3.1 percent for the period 1965 to 1988.

The countries selected also illustrate different methods of achieving accelerated growth in the agricultural sector. These varying circumstances can be investigated to determine if the means of agriculture's growth affects the size and manner of its stimulus to other sectors.

Both Thailand and Argentina grew substantially through the expansion of the land area, by using land at low intensity relative to its innate capacity. In sharp contrast, Taiwan and Punjab, largely, and the Philippines, to a substantial extent, experienced very little agricultural growth as a result of the expansion of the land area and very much growth as a result of improved, yield-increasing technology.

In the cases of Kenya, Costa Rica, and Colombia, accelerated agricultural growth derived largely from the changed composition of production, and in particular, from the rapid growth in agricultural exports. This does not mean that increased agricultural exports were unimportant to Taiwan, Punjab, and Thailand, but simply that they formed the basic engine of growth in Kenya, Costa Rica, and Colombia, while playing a more subsidiary role in the other economies.

The Philippines was considered a country that did well in achieving agricultural growth but poorly in converting that growth into accelerated growth in the nonagricultural sector. Argentina performed poorly in both sectors, despite

TABLE 1.1 Eight studies—selected data, specified periods of relatively rapid agricultural growth

	Argentina 1960–73	Colombia 1964–79	Costa Rica 1960–73	Kenya 1963–78	Philippines 1965–80	Taiwan 1960–75	Thailand 1970–87	Punjab 1968–88
Macroeconomic environment								
GNP per capita (US$) in 1987	2,360.00	1,230.00	1,550.00	330.00	590.00	5,050.00	840.00	422.41
Growth rates (%)								
Real GDP	4.26	5.67	6.34	7.33	5.79	9.25	6.43	5.34
Real GDP per capita	2.66	3.17	3.12	3.70	2.71	6.31	4.00	3.03
Real GNP	4.21	5.74	6.20	7.22	5.80	9.23	6.30	n.a.
Real GNP per capita	2.62	3.24	2.98	3.59	2.77	6.29	3.81	n.a.
Savings (real) growth rate (%)	6.94	7.73	10.43	11.39	7.67	13.75	7.50	n.a.
Percentage of GDP								
Beginning	20.00	16.40	17.50	12.90	20.80	15.30	25.60	n.a.
Ending	20.90	19.90	17.90	20.00	16.90	26.60	23.90	n.a.
Investment (real) growth rate (%)	4.37	6.34	9.01	12.30	8.15	15.71	5.63	n.a.
Percentage of GDP								
Beginning	20.00	16.40	17.50	12.90	20.80	15.30	25.60	15.7
Ending	18.00	18.20	24.00	29.80	13.90	28.90	23.90[a]	22.7
Public consumption government expenditure (% of GDP)								
Ending	14.10	1.10	15.40	18.60	9.00	21.40	17.30[a]	21.56
Growth in public consumption (%)								
Ending	2.80	-1.10	-0.50	-4.20	-2.20	-1.30	0.90	0.97
Trade[b]								
Real export growth	5.63	5.47	10.74	3.70	5.68	18.35	10.30	n.a.
Real import growth	2.13	4.88	9.00	5.76	6.49	16.10	6.30	n.a.

(continued)

17

TABLE 1.1 (*continued*)

	Argentina 1960–73	Colombia 1964–79	Costa Rica 1960–73	Kenya 1963–78	Philippines 1965–80	Taiwan 1960–75	Thailand 1970–87	Punjab 1968–88
Agricultural growth								
Output (%)								
Growth of output (value added in %)	2.02	4.26	5.54	5.10	4.69	3.31	3.74	4.52
Growth of output per capita	.50	1.80	2.40	1.60	1.70	0.30	1.40	2.21
Share of GDP (%)								
Beginning	20.20	31.42	29.30	41.54	28.29	28.54[a]	29.10	59.69
Ending	15.80	24.01	21.41	36.92	23.35	15.74	18.20	51.59
Share of agricultural employment (%)								
Beginning	21.04	45.78	51.20	87.62	58.00	50.20	72.28	62.16
Ending	25.54	37.00	38.00	81.76	51.80	30.40	58.03	50.40
Inputs								
Growth of arable land per capita (%)	0.77	−2.12	−3.07	−1.83	−3.35	−2.83	−0.12	−2.16
Growth of nutrient consumption (%)	14.38	5.69	13.39	8.67	10.33	3.50	2.40	10.58
Nutrient consumption (kg/ha)	2.60	38.20	145.20	24.70	47.70	225.00	16.70	89.10
Growth of area under irrigation (%)	2.89	3.21	0.00	7.03	3.35	−1.85	4.50	3.68
Irrigated as percentage of arable land	(5.40)	(7.80)	(9.10)	(1.70)	(20.40)	(59.08)	(18.20)	82.07
Beginning	5.23	8.82	9.12	0.98	15.21	60.46	15.30	63.66
Ending	5.61	6.86	9.19	2.23	21.18	56.25	22.44	92.50
Rate of growth of yields (%)	3.80	3.40	2.70	.50	3.00	3.88	1.20	3.14
Nonagricultural growth								
Growth rate of manufacturing output (%)	5.12	3.49	9.00	10.21	7.23	14.80	8.30	9.04
Growth rate of services (%)	4.23	6.34	5.79	7.02	5.22	9.72	7.11	5.98

Basic social indicators

Population								
End of period (millions)	25.20	25.40	1.90	15.40	49.30	16.20	53.50	19.33
Growth rate (%)	1.55	2.42	3.14	3.50	3.00	2.77	2.40	2.11
Rural as percentage of total								
Beginning of period	25.90	41.10	63.30	91.80	67.90	49.80	86.70	76.30
End of period	20.30	36.50	59.40	85.20	63.50	35.80	78.80	72.30
Life expectancy (years)								
Beginning of period	66	56	61	47	56	64	58	57
End of period	68	63	68	54	61	76	64	65
Infant mortality (rate per thousand)								
Beginning of period	58	96	76	112	72	31	73	98
End of period	47	60	45	86	52	13	39	64

SOURCES: World Bank, *World Tables Tapes* (1988); Social Indicators of Development (1989), FAO Production and Fertilizer Yearbooks, Punjab, calculated by G. S. Bhalla from *Abstract of Punjab*, various issues.

NOTES: Growth rates are the simple arithmetic mean of annual growth rates for the corresponding periods. Variables in parentheses are period averages. Data for Taiwan are from tables supplied by the author, unless otherwise indicated.

n.a. Not applicable.

a For 1985.

b Exports and imports of goods and nonfinancial services. Exports are FOB and imports CIF. Growth rates calculated from values denominated in local currencies.

the fact that it had perhaps the most favorable physical environment for agriculture of any of the countries studied. Several lessons are drawn from these failures in the following chapters, particularly in the context of the better-performing countries.

Although they pursue the same subjects, the authors differ greatly in their approach to development economics, what they think important, their perceptions of the world, and their ideological stance. In five of the eight cases, the authors are nationals of the country analyzed. The other contributors have conducted intensive work in the country over a long period, normally in close collaboration with nationals who have been studying the country themselves. The authors differ most noticeably in their methodological approach. Those who have presented modeling exercises have shed a different light on the issues than those whose approach is more broadly descriptive. Thus some of the cases are narrower in range than others. The Taiwan and Punjab cases, for example, cover a broader territory than the others, particularly with respect to the institutional aspects of development, whereas those concerned with the countries with the least favorable macroeconomic environments are devoted largely to those environments and pay little attention to the institutional structure. In a sense, if macroeconomic policy is bad, it matters little what one does on the institutional side, and so there is no reason to cover it. When policy has been conducive to growth, the authors have described the situation and then rushed on to an in-depth analysis of the institutional structures that could be effective in such a favorable environment.

As will become apparent, there are immense problems in analyzing data on the relationship between agricultural and nonagricultural growth. To begin with, some of the important data are simply unavailable. Furthermore, some of the sectors important to this analysis—the small- and medium-size sectors stimulated by rural nonagricultural growth—are the least represented in the national statistics. In other words, we are trying to measure the effects of variables that are normally not measured. A further complication is that there are complex lags in response to the various stimuli that themselves must be the product of changing relationships. Even so, the analyses help to identify what is important and what is not and what needs to be done in the future to improve everyone's understanding of the development experience. It is hoped that such an understanding may lead to more refined statistical analysis and eventually to improved policy.

The cases are arranged in a specific order, beginning with the more classic cases (Taiwan in chapter 2 and Punjab in chapter 3), in which agricultural production was increased through accelerated technological change and then was converted into accelerated growth in the nonagricultural sector. In both cases, there is ample information and so the processes can be described in considerable detail. Although Punjab is still in midstream, it provides a snapshot of the process in action, while Taiwan has moved on to later stages and thus provides a glimpse of a more or less complete development process, as well as an inkling of the next round of problems.

Chapter 4 moves to the Philippines, which did exceptionally well in agriculture, particularly through yield-increasing technological change, but did rather poorly in converting that into accelerated growth in the nonagricultural sectors. That failure of conversion shows up in the country's poor employment growth, the increase in absolute poverty, and the unusually high concentration of population growth in the capital city. The Philippines also failed to parlay an exceptionally strong educational base into an equally admirable growth rate. The reasons for these failures bring to light some issues that previous success stories masked.

Thailand and Argentina are examined in chapters 5 and 6, respectively. Each country has favorable agricultural land bases and a potential for growth through expansion of the land area. Agricultural growth has been more rapid in one than in the other, however. The policies responsible for this difference are discussed, along with the reasons for the different patterns of nonagricultural growth.

Kenya, which is the subject of chapters 7 and 8, demonstrates very rapid population growth and a heavy reliance on agricultural growth in building a dynamic, small-farmer, agricultural, export-commodity subsector. The last two countries examined, Costa Rica (chapter 9) and Colombia (chapter 10) also expanded their agricultural exports but ran into problems with the bimodal distribution of assets in the agricultural sector, as did the Philippines and to some extent Kenya. Since Taiwan and Punjab avoided these problems, it is possible to explore the implications of various distributions of income and assets in the case studies.

It is perhaps the Taiwan study, more than any of the others, that adds immeasurably to our understanding of development processes. Taiwan is the sine qua non of rapid development based on successful agricultural projects and vigorous growth among small- and medium-size private enterprises despite a highly interventionist government. The fact that poverty has declined drastically, as has the Gini coefficient, reflects a vast improvement in the overall distribution of income. President Lee Teng-hui is the author of the award-winning analysis of intersectoral resource flows in Taiwan that is without doubt the most careful and scholarly work available on intersectoral relations analyzed over a long period of economic development. That work was the foundation for the Taiwan case presented in chapter 2.

References

Dennison, Edward F. 1985. *Trends in American Growth, 1929–1982*. Washington, D.C.: Brookings Institution.
Lele, U. J., and John W. Mellor. 1981. "Technological Change, Distributive Bias, and

Labour Transfer in a Two Sector Economy." *Oxford Economic Papers,* n.s. 33:426–41.

Mellor, John W. 1966. *The Economics of Agricultural Development.* Ithaca, N.Y.: Cornell University Press.

Solow, R. M. 1956. "A Contribution to the Theory of Economic Growth." *Quarterly Journal of Economics* 70:65–94.

World Bank. 1989. *World Tables.* Baltimore, Md.: Johns Hopkins University Press.

2 Agricultural and Industrial Development in Taiwan

YU-KANG MAO AND CHI SCHIVE

Over the past four decades Taiwan's economy has experienced significant structural change. At the outset of this period, Taiwan was just recovering from the ravages of World War II, and the economy was heavily dominated by the agricultural sector, which accounted for one-third of the net domestic product, more than half (56 percent) of total employment, and 92 percent of total exports. By 1988 agriculture's share of the net domestic product (NDP) had dropped to 6 percent, its share of total employment was down to 13.7 percent, and the sector accounted for only 6.1 percent of the total exports, including processed foods. These were years of high and stable economic growth: the real gross national product (GNP) grew at an average rate of 8.8 percent from 1952 to 1989, and two oil crises of the 1970s seemed to have little negative impact.[1] Between 1952 and 1987, per capita GNP, at 1981 constant prices, increased more than seven times, for an annual increase of 6.2 percent. In view of this growth, Taiwan is likely to be classified as an industrial economy by the turn of the century (Klein 1986).

In the period since 1952, Taiwan's economy has also become increasingly dependent on trade. Total trade as a percentage of gross domestic product at current prices grew at a steady pace, from an average of 24.6 percent in the 1950s to 101 percent in the 1980s. Since 1970 the trade balance has been positive except for 1974, 1975, and 1980, when Taiwan was hit by the oil crises and economic recession. Taiwan has exported more than half of its GNP since 1978, and its trade surplus was equivalent to 9 percent of GNP in the 1980s.

The impact of high economic growth on the distribution of wealth has been equally impressive. The ratio of the income of the highest fifth of households to that of the lowest fifth was less than 5 during the 1970s and 1980s. This ratio is comparable to the rates recorded by Japan and some European countries, whose income distribution is the most equitable in the world.

1. The growth rate by decades was 8.3 percent (1952–1959), 9.1 percent in the 1960s, 10.2 percent in the 1970s, and 7.7 percent in the 1980s.

This pattern of growth in Taiwan lends substantial support to the view that accelerated growth in the agricultural sector can promote development in the nonagricultural sector and therefore should be of considerable interest to other countries seeking to promote development. As the largest sector in the economies of underdeveloped nations, agriculture can provide savings as well as labor for nonagricultural development. Part of the agricultural surplus can be exported to finance the import of much needed foreign capital goods. Such exports can help alleviate the foreign exchange constraint. In addition, an expanding agricultural sector, accompanied by rising farm family income, can represent a major market for consumer goods produced by domestic manufacturers. The agricultural sector would share in the heavy protection costs related to the import-substitution strategy widely pursued in the developing world. By providing an adequate food supply, agricultural growth can help stabilize general prices and thereby mobilize and reallocate domestic resources more effectively. Furthermore, the existing agricultural infrastructure can be used by the nonagricultural sector. In all these ways, agriculture can contribute substantially to economic development.

To make such a contribution, agriculture must undergo growth, which cannot be achieved without the strong support of public policy, particularly in the area of physical investment, technological upgrading, and institutional arrangements for distribution and credit. During this process, the agricultural sector must adjust to changes in the economic environment. For example, it may be necessary to raise farm wages because incomes in general are rising, surplus agricultural labor is disappearing, or food demand is changing. Another important point about agricultural-led growth is that it does not mean agriculture would hold an increasing share in the economy, or that resources would flow only one way between the agricultural and nonagricultural sectors. Instead, the growing agricultural sector would pave the way for a more balanced pattern of development through stable prices, more equitable income distribution, less regional dualism, and probably a higher degree of social stability. As a result, the role of agriculture in development would change over time, as would the interaction between the agricultural and nonagricultural sectors. It is vital to understand that policy issues will shift once agriculture takes on this role in development.

Agricultural Development

Taiwan's agricultural development can be divided into two distinct periods: the colonial years from 1895 to 1945 and the postwar years from 1945 on.

The Colonial Period, 1895–1945

During the colonial period from 1895 to 1945, Taiwan was under the rule of Japan and became an important part of its agricultural sector. The principal goal of the colonial government was to make Taiwan's subsistence agriculture more productive so that large supplies of food could be exported to Japan to support its industrialization effort. In this report, the history of Taiwan's agricultural development differs from that of other economies, most of which exported only a small part of their agricultural output. The fact that agricultural output, particularly food, was not limited by domestic demand, is important in understanding its development process.

In the 50 years of Japanese occupation, agriculture accounted for about 40 to 45 percent of Taiwan's NDP and about 65 to 70 percent of the total labor force. In 1946, soon after Taiwan was returned to the Republic of China, the farm population was 3.52 million, cultivated land area was 832,000 hectares, and the average farm was 1.58 hectares. In 1937, about 50 percent of the rice and nearly all of the sugar produced in Taiwan were exported to Japan. Sweet potato was the main food of the local people.

In the period from 1913 to 1921, the average annual growth rate of total agricultural production was 2 percent, and that of gross value added was only 1.4 percent. The main factor contributing to the increase was the expansion of cultivated land area, from 687,187 hectares in 1911 to 752,800 hectares in 1921, an increase of 1 percent per year. The yield of rice and sugarcane did not increase significantly. That of sugarcane seldom exceeded 30,000 kilograms per hectare. Labor inputs measured in terms of total working days increased moderately as a result of a rise in the number of average working days per worker per year. Production techniques were labor intensive and relied on farm-produced fertilizer.

From 1921 to 1936, a period of agricultural transformation, total production increased at an annual rate of 4.2 percent and agricultural output at the rate of 4.3 percent (Chen and Wang 1980). Crop yields and multiple cropping also increased, as did the land under cultivation. Improved varieties of crops and the use of chemical fertilizers helped raise crop yields significantly. Over the 1920s and 1930s the yield of rice increased from 1,435 kilograms per hectare to 2,217, and the yield of sugarcane from 25,481 kilograms per hectare to 70,883. In addition, the area of irrigated land increased from 364,100 hectares to 528,000 hectares, and the irrigated portion of cultivated land from 48.4 to 61.6 percent. With improvements in irrigation, the multiple cropping index rose from 120 in 1921 to 137 in 1937. The rapid adoption of high-yielding ponlai rice from Japan and new farming techniques greatly contributed to these increases. Livestock production also rose significantly in this period.

Taiwan's success in applying new agricultural technology was due to the efforts of rural institutions, particularly agricultural research stations, farmers' associations, and rural credit and extension services. In the mid-1920s experimental stations developed improved seeds and modern inputs as part of a labor-intensive package and made them available to farmers. This activity explains the sharp increase in labor productivity, growth, and employment up to the beginning of World War II. The experimental stations continued to play a significant role in the postwar restructuring.

During the war, agriculture suffered a serious decline. Production decreased by 36 percent from 1937 to 1946 as a result of both typhoon and war damage. Per hectare yields dropped 30 percent as both crop area and cultivated land decreased slightly. And livestock production fell an average of 7.8 percent per year. Nevertheless, because traditional agriculture had already begun using modern inputs, by the end of the war Taiwan was also in a position to have agricultural development take off. That is to say, it had a labor-intensive technology that relied on modern inputs; an improved physical infrastructure, particularly irrigation and drainage facilities and rural roads; and rural institutions that could disseminate knowledge, provide extension and credit services, and create markets for both inputs and outputs.

Despite the transformation of agriculture in the colonial period, Taiwan was still a predominantly agricultural economy at this time. At the end of World War II about two-thirds of its labor force was employed in agriculture, but the sector generated only about 40 percent of NDP. It was not yet possible to convert rapid agricultural growth into nonagricultural growth because agricultural development had been geared to providing a surplus for export to Japan.

Agricultural Development in the Postwar Period

Taiwan's economy was in disarray when it was returned to the Republic of China in 1945. Agricultural production in that year was less than half the prewar peak, and industrial output less than one-third. The situation continued to deteriorate in the immediate postwar years, which were marked by high inflation, grave shortages of food and other necessities, a heavy defense burden, and a large influx of people from the mainland as a result of the social and political instability there. The government therefore gave the highest priority to economic stabilization, food production, and the repair of war damage. To alleviate the intense population pressure on limited land, it decided to grant incentives to farmers. The most effective incentive was the land reform program implemented between 1949 and 1953, which helped improve both agricultural production and farmers' income. In addition, war-damaged irrigation and drainage facilities were repaired, supplies of fertilizers and other farm inputs made available, and farmers' organization strengthened.

GROWTH OF AGRICULTURAL PRODUCTION. During the runaway inflation in the immediate postwar years, food prices in relation to general prices rose quickly. With high farm prices and a steady supply of inputs, agricultural production increased 19.2 percent annually between 1946 and 1950, and by 1951 output surpassed the prewar peak (table 2.1).

Three groups of factors contributed to the rapid agricultural recovery and rehabilitation during the 1946–50 period: (1) a rapid increase in labor input,

TABLE 2.1 Agricultural production, 1946–1988 (index, 1986 = 100)

Year/Period	Total	Crops	Livestock	Fisheries	Forestry
1946	10.9 (100.0)	24.1 (—)	3.6 (—)	4.1 (—)	15.7 (—)
1950	22.0 (100.0)	49.4 (63.8)	6.8 (19.1)	6.7 (10.6)	66.5 (6.5)
1953	28.9 (100.0)	59.4 (71.9)	11.5 (15.7)	10.4 (7.4)	74.6 (5.1)
1955	29.7 (100.0)	57.2 (66.2)	12.4 (15.7)	14.2 (9.4)	78.8 (4.8)
1960	37.1 (100.0)	68.9 (64.1)	15.9 (20.9)	19.3 (9.6)	128.1 (5.5)
1965	48.7 (100.0)	88.5 (64.7)	21.6 (21.2)	26.3 (8.7)	192.9 (5.5)
1970	61.5 (100.0)	98.8 (57.2)	34.1 (24.1)	45.2 (13.5)	187.4 (5.2)
1975	69.5 (100.0)	103.7 (57.9)	39.4 (25.0)	61.5 (14.2)	145.9 (3.0)
1980	90.4 (100.0)	108.9 (47.2)	70.6 (29.0)	84.5 (21.6)	103.2 (2.3)
1985	100.3 (100.0)	105.5 (47.0)	96.8 (27.3)	94.3 (24.8)	90.3 (1.0)
1988	109.6 (100.0)	105.6 (43.1)	110.0 (27.7)	118.2 (28.1)	60.1 (1.1)
Growth rate (percent)					
1946–50	19.2	19.7	17.2	13.1	43.5
1950–55	6.2	3.0	12.8	16.2	3.5
1955–60	4.5	3.8	5.1	6.9	10.2
1960–65	5.6	5.1	6.3	6.4	8.5
1965–70	4.8	2.2	9.7	11.4	−0.9
1970–75	2.5	1.0	2.9	6.4	−4.9
1975–80	5.4	1.0	12.4	6.6	−6.7
1980–85	2.1	−0.6	6.5	2.2	−2.6
1985–88	3.0	0.0	4.3	7.8	−12.7
1950–70	5.3	3.5	8.4	10.0	5.3
1970–88	3.3	0.4	6.7	5.5	−6.1
1950–88	4.3	2.0	7.6	7.8	−0.3

SOURCE: Taiwan (1989a).
NOTE: Figures in parentheses are percentage shares.

crop area, and multiple-crop diversification; (2) the introduction of better production techniques, rehabilitation of irrigation facilities, and reorganization of farmers' associations; and (3) the implementation of a land-rent reduction program in 1949 that induced tenant farmers to increase production. With the increase in crop area—from 832,000 hectares in 1946 to 874,000 in 1951 for cultivated land, and from 975,000 to 1.5 million for total crop area—the multiple cropping index rose from 117 to 172 over this period.

Total agricultural production grew 4.3 percent annually from 1950 to 1988, but the rate of increase declined sharply. In the 1980s crop production fluctuated with no growth, mainly because of the declining returns on crops and the government program to reduce the rice production in the wake of a drastic decline in consumption per capita.

A comparison of the production data for 1970 to 1988 clearly indicates that all major crops were being produced in smaller amounts except sugarcane, corn, and citrus. The liberalization of corn and soybean imports and depressed international price for most agricultural products, particularly sugar, had put great pressure on domestic farmers, even for corn and sugarcane growers.

Forestry production has shown a similar trend since 1970, when national forestry policy changed its emphasis from cutting timber to preservation. Livestock and fishery made up the loss from crops in total agricultural production. Stimulated by a rising demand in domestic and foreign markets, products in these sectors grew 7.6 and 7.8 percent per year from 1950 to 1988, respectively (table 2.1). On one hand, the increased use of feedgrains on large farms improved the efficiency and profitability of Taiwan's hog industry, and on the other, deep-sea fishing along with fish culture expanded fishery production. Nevertheless, both industries began having a difficult time in the 1980s because of environmental concerns, rising labor costs, and worldwide restrictions on fishing in coastal waters.

TRENDS IN AGRICULTURAL INPUTS AND PRODUCTIVITY. The cultivated area remained fairly constant during 1952–82. The number of agricultural workers and man-days of agricultural labor rose until about 1965 and then started falling. The number of draft cattle reached a peak in 1958 but fell substantially thereafter. The consumption of chemical fertilizer rose steadily (table 2.2). The decline in inputs of the late 1960s was a reflection of the increasing use of mechanical energy in place of human and animal energy.

From 1952 to 1960 capital productivity increased only 13 percent; it more than doubled during 1960–70 and then declined by 27 percent during 1970–80 (Chen and Wang 1980; Chen 1986). Land and labor productivity continued to rise rapidly in the early stage of agricultural development in Taiwan, when land resources were limited and farm labor was abundant, since the increase in capital investment could raise both land and labor productivity, particularly the former. In 1960–70 and thereafter, the rapidly growing industrial sector absorbed a great deal of farm labor, which helped improve labor productivity further. Consequently, the annual growth of labor productivity (5.7 percent) exceeded that of land productivity (4.9 percent). In the same period, capital productivity grew only slightly and from 1970 to 1982 exhibited negative growth because capital investment was constrained by the limited land area and farm labor.

In summary, the remarkable gains in Taiwan's agricultural output in the postwar period was attained through a rapid increase in capital investment and a reduction in surplus labor. As a result, the capital-land and capital-labor ratios rose significantly, making it possible to increase land and labor productivity.

Demand Shifts

In the 1950s agricultural products accounted for about 90 percent of the island's total exports. Although agricultural exports continued to increase after 1965, their share of total exports decreased once the industrial sector began growing.

TABLE 2.2 Agricultural inputs, 1952–1982

Year/Period	Cultivated Area (thousands of hectares)	Crop Area (thousands of hectares)	Multiple Cropping Index	Agricultural Workers[a] (thousands)	Total Man-Days (thousands)	Draft Cattle (thousands)	Chemical Fertilizer in NPK (thousands of metric tons)
1952	876	1,521	173.6	1,535	263	382	104
1955	873	1,508	172.7	1,556	266	410	130
1960	869	1,600	184.1	1,621	290	417	149
1965	890	1,680	188.8	1,622	300	370	198
1970	905	1,656	183.0	1,559	289	275	244
1975	917	1,659	180.9	1,493	261	196	371
1980	907	1,400	154.4	1,152	210	84	435
1982	891	1,380	154.9	1,149	197	n.a.	347
Growth (percent)							
Annual	0.1	-0.3		-1.0	-1.0		4.1
Total growth	1.7	-9.3		-25.1	-25.1		233.7
1952–55	-0.1	-0.3		0.5	0.1		7.7
1955–60	-0.1	1.2		0.8	2.1		2.8
1960–65	0.5	1.0		0.0	2.2		5.9
1965–70	0.3	-0.3		-0.8	0.3		4.3
1970–75	0.3	0.0		-0.9	2.0		8.7
1975–82	-0.4	-2.6		-3.7	-3.9		-1.0

SOURCE: Chen (1986).
n.a. Not applicable.
[a]Workers in crop and livestock farming only.

CHANGES IN AGRICULTURAL TRADE. From 1952 to 1965 agricultural imports amounted to about one-third of total imports. The most serious constraint on economic development in this period was the amount of available foreign exchange. The agricultural share of total imports subsequently declined and by 1988 accounted for only 12 percent of total imports.

The composition of Taiwan's agricultural exports has changed considerably since 1952. In that year sugar and rice accounted for 81 percent of total agricultural exports. By 1988 the leading agricultural exports were fishery products, hogs and pork, preserved vegetables, poultry feathers, preserved fruits, bamboo products, timber, fresh vegetables, and bananas. Fishery products alone accounted for 40 percent of agricultural exports. Over the years, several nontraditional agricultural exports were developed and are now performing well. These include asparagus and mushrooms, introduced to Taiwan in the early 1960s, and the aquaculture of eel and shrimp, introduced in the 1970s. In addition, there has been a steady flow of new technologies and vigorous promotion of foreign market opportunities. This diversification has been due largely to adaptations by a well-educated, highly motivated farm population to changing demand patterns and cost relationships.

The years from 1952 to 1988 also saw a greater than seventyfold increase in agricultural imports. Up to 1960 the main agricultural imports were soybeans, wheat, and cotton, but by 1970 lumber, corn, wool, dairy products, tobacco, and barley had become important. After 1970 imports of corn and fish meal increased rapidly in response to the growth in the livestock and aquaculture industries. The remarkable increase in the import of dairy products and beef can be attributed to the improved standard of living in Taiwan.

Japan was by far the most important export market for Taiwan's agricultural products in 1988, accounting for about 64 percent, far exceeding the United States and the European Common Market. The United States was the main supplier of agricultural imports. It provided about half, while Malaysia came in second with 22 percent.

CHANGES IN FOOD CONSUMPTION PATTERN. Since the early 1950s the population of Taiwan has increased at an annual rate of 2.5 percent and agricultural production at a rate of 4.3 percent. Daily per capita calorie intake has risen from 2,078 to 3,017 and protein intake from 49 to 90 grams. By all accounts, agriculture in Taiwan has been able to provide adequate food at reasonable prices to meet the rising per capita demand. That demand has shown some interesting trends.

Since 1970, there has been a significant decrease in the per capita consumption of sweet potatoes and rice, and a remarkable increase in the consumption of meat, sugar, vegetables, fruits, and milk (table 2.3). This change was mainly due to increased per capita income. The increase in meat consumption provided a market for the local livestock industry and pushed up the demand for imports of feedstuff. In turn, the higher production of vegetables and fruits to

TABLE 2.3 Per capita annual food consumption, selected years (kilograms)

Food	1952	1960	1970	1980	1988
Cereals					
Total	138.1	159.7	164.1	138.8	110.6
Polished rice	126.1	137.7	134.5	105.5	73.6
Wheat flour	11.3	20.0	25.4	23.6	32.1
Sweet potatoes	59.9	65.4	18.4	4.1	0.9
Sugar	9.4	9.4	15.0	24.0	25.2
Pulses, nuts, and seeds	9.9	11.4	18.3	18.8	23.1
Vegetables	61.7	61.1	84.8	129.6	122.1
Fruits	16.8	22.1	45.8	70.2	104.3
Meat	16.8	16.2	25.3	39.6	57.8
Eggs	1.6	1.6	4.1	8.0	10.9
Fish	15.1	21.7	34.2	38.7	45.8
Milk	1.2	3.2	11.0	27.6	41.1
Oil and fats	3.5	4.7	7.7	10.8	18.9

SOURCE: Taiwan (1989b).

meet the growing consumer demand greatly increased the intensity of agricultural production and farmers' income.

Significant changes in the level and pattern of food consumption and the slower growth in agricultural production have made Taiwan less self-sufficient in food in recent years. Before 1968 domestic food production was about equal to domestic requirements. But the food self-sufficiency rate dropped to 93 in 1988, as is evident from Taiwan's dependence on imports to satisfy the domestic demand for wheat, corn, soybeans, other feedgrains, and dairy products.

Institutional Framework for Agricultural Development

Many institutions, both public and private, contributed to the successful development of agriculture in Taiwan (Mao 1984, 1985). The government played a particularly important role because it got development going. Among the more influential institutions was the Sino-American Joint Commission on Rural Reconstruction (JCRR), established in Nanking in 1948, which served as a nonpermanent agency for the postwar rural reconstruction of China. With the transfer of the JCRR to Taiwan after the fall of the mainland to the Communists in 1949 and the reactivation of U.S. economic aid in 1951, the JCRR became the agricultural arm of the U.S. Mission to Taiwan. From 1951 to 1965 the United States provided a total of $1.465 billion in aid. Approximately one-third went to agriculture and was used to build infrastructure and foster agriculture and human resources. Industrial development was left by and large to private enterprise. The main source of funds was the local counterpart funds generated through aid-financed imports. Many financial experts consider Taiwan an outstanding example of the efficient use of U.S. aid for economic development (Jacoby 1966).

From the beginning, the JCRR was allowed to work with any level of government to carry out its projects. Thus bureaucratic red tape was reduced to a minimum and assistance extended directly to end users. This system made it possible for government agencies to be of real service to the people. The JCRR's role in agricultural development was that of a catalytic agent. By providing technical and some financial assistance, it was able to give direction to agricultural policies, promote new technologies and complex projects, and, most important, generate a spirit of self-help among local agencies. It supported the upgrading of agriculture in Taiwan; supplied conceptual leadership in identifying problem areas and in planning remedial measures; provided support for facilities, equipment and personnel; furnished support and coordination for nationwide research projects; and also coordinated research, education, and extension activities.

The JCRR was the only agency that attempted to combine the planning and implementation of research, extension, and irrigation through the revitalization and strengthening of farmers' associations. It is no exaggeration to say that the JCRR was promoting "integrated rural development" long before the concept was discussed in the literature and espoused by such development agencies as the World Bank (Thorbecke 1979). From the outset, planners and actors interacted in identifying general objectives, specific targets, and the best means of achieving them at the local level without the interference of a cumbersome central bureaucracy. With local farmers involved in planning and implementation, objectives could more easily be translated into specific local actions.

Taiwan's agricultural planning targets were more than mere projections. Annual production goals in each four-year plan were adjusted annually to meet the changing market conditions. Regional goals were also established by provincial and county agricultural production conferences held at the beginning of each year. Consultations between the provincial and county levels enabled farm leaders as well as officials at all levels to participate in the development process. At such meetings, farmers' representatives could express opinions and make suggestions regarding the annual plans and regional goals and indicate the support they needed from the government.

LAND REFORM PROGRAM. In the immediate postwar years, the farm population in Taiwan was more than half of the total, but many farmers did not own their own land. Tenant farmers paid high rents—at least 50 percent of the crop harvest—and social unrest was widespread in the rural areas. Consequently, it was difficult to motivate farmers to improve their farming techniques. The land reform program initiated in 1949 and completed in 1953 was the first measure taken by the government to remedy this situation and promote rural development.

This program was geared toward reducing rents, selling public lands, and giving land to the tiller. The program was carried out gradually and focused first on rent reduction. The farm rental rate was set at 37.5 percent of the annual yield of the main crop, and the lease was to cover a period of six years, but could be extended after it expired. The next step was to sell off a large area of public lands. The government thought it was unfair to ask landlords to sell their holdings to tenants while the government itself held large estates. To set an example, the government sold public lands to the incumbent cultivators. The price was fixed at 2.5 times the annual yield of the main crop, to be paid in 20 semiannual installments.

In the third, land-to-tiller phase of the program, each landlord was allowed to keep three chia (about 2.91 hectares) of medium-grade paddy field or six chia of dry land. Holdings in excess of these amounts were purchased by the government and resold to incumbent tenant farmers. Again, the price was set at 2.5 times the annual yield of the main crop. The landlord was paid 70 percent of the land price with land bonds and the rest with shares of government-owned industries. This arrangement forced some landlords to shift their investment from land to industry.

Nevertheless, farmers benefited greatly under the program. Families owning all or part of the land they farmed increased from 61 percent to 88 percent of the total, and farmers were motivated to work longer and harder and to adopt various agricultural improvements. As a result, the index of multiple cropping shot up from 170 in 1953 to 190 in 1964. Farmers became better fed and clothed, and many started to repair their houses or build new ones. The income redistribution resulting from the land reform brought social justice to the rural areas. Equally important, farmers began to participate in community activities, and many ran for public office at the local level.

AGRICULTURAL ADAPTIVE RESEARCH. From the outset, the authorities recognized that Taiwan would not be able to increase agricultural production without using new technologies and modern farm inputs, whether introduced from abroad or developed locally (see Schultz 1964). Thus they hastened to establish a number of agricultural research institutes in Taiwan. At the national level is the Botanical Institute of the Academia Sinica, which concentrates on basic scientific research. At the provincial level is the Provincial Agricultural Research Institute, which also engages in basic research, and six district agricultural improvement stations, which carry out regional adaptive experiments. In addition, Taiwan has various research institutes specializing in tobacco, sugar, tea, forestry, fisheries, livestock, sericulture, bananas, and food processing. As a result of the efforts of these institutes, Taiwan has successfully produced hybrid hogs, reduced the incidence of livestock disease, and developed many high-yielding varieties of rice, sugarcane, corn, and sweet potatoes. The successful breeding of fast-maturing varieties crops contributed to Taiwan's multiple-cropping system and gained worldwide attention in the early stages of its development. To facilitate the spread of these new technologies, experimental results are made known to farmers through demonstrations conducted by the district agricultural improvement stations and by the extension network of farmers' associations.

FARMERS' ORGANIZATIONS. Taiwan relied not only on technological progress to solve its rural problems but also on rural organizations. These were carefully designed to implement rural development policies and had the support of political and administrative leaders. Four main types of rural organizations were established: farmers' associations, irrigation associations, fishermen's associations, and agricultural cooperatives (primarily fruit-marketing cooperatives).

Farmers' associations. The most important organization in rural Taiwan is the farmers' association, which is a multipurpose cooperative. Its primary goal is to help members solve their farming, financial, and marketing problems. It also serves as a bridge between farmers and the government. At present, Taiwan has 291 farmers' associations at three levels: provincial (1), city (20), and township (270). Their total membership in 1988 was 1,094,000. Of this number 80 percent were regular members and 20 percent associates. The former are bona fide farmers with the right to elect and to be elected to any office of the association, and the latter are residents in rural areas who are not engaged in full-time farming. Associates have no right to vote but can be elected to the post of supervisor.

Irrigation associations. Paddy rice is the most important food crop in Taiwan and a reliable water supply is essential to its production. The irrigation association was formed to operate irrigation facilities, maintain orderly water distribution, and assist the government in planning and implementing new irrigation projects. There are now 16 irrigation associations in Taiwan.

Fishermen's associations. The fishermen's association is a cooperative patterned on the farmers' association. There are 37 district and 1 provincial fishermen's associations in Taiwan with a total membership of 185,000. Revenue comes from membership fees, service charges, contributions, and government subsidies for the improvement of fishing techniques, storage and marketing, and social welfare.

Fruit-marketing cooperatives. The principal activity of fruit-marketing cooperatives is the export of bananas, the most important fruit crop in the south, and oranges, the main crop in the north. Only growers of these fruits are eligible for membership. The cooperatives also supply production inputs, credit, and technical services.

METHODS OF DELIVERING SUPPORT SERVICES. New techniques developed through agricultural research are disseminated to farmers primarily by extension agents affiliated with farmers' associations. Each association has an average of six agents. These are experienced people who have been working closely with the district agricultural improvement stations since 1952. They transmit information to farmers through study groups, audiovisual aids, reference materials, training courses, demonstrations, and farm and home visits.

Farmer credit is another important support service. Before the land reform program, landlords were the main source of high-cost, short-term loans in rural areas. Afterward, the landlords withdrew from the rural financial markets, and the farmers' associations began providing loans for production and marketing, using the deposits of members as the main source of loanable funds. The rest comes from the government and banks. Most of the loans do not require collateral but must have two or more guarantors. The ceiling rates for lending are based on central bank interest rates. The Taiwan Cooperative Bank, Land Bank of Taiwan, and Farmers' Bank of China and their branches also provide loans for rural areas. But farmers usually feel more at ease in dealing with their associations than with banks. As a result, some bank loans are channeled through the associations.

RURAL INFRASTRUCTURE INVESTMENT. The investment in rural infrastructure has focused on irrigation and rural roads. Irrigation has received considerable attention because an abundant water supply is indispensable for the production of paddy rice, particularly the high-yielding varieties. In Taiwan, the yield of the year's first rice crop is always higher than the second, because the first is for the most part irrigated while the second depends more on rainfall.[2] More than 60 percent of Taiwan's farm land is irrigated by means of 1,200 structures for transporting river water and by 30,000 kilometers of canals, laterals, and ditches. These various facilities are managed by irrigation associations, and the projects financed with government subsidies, long-term and low-interest loans, and the assessments collected from farmers.

Rural development has also depended on roads to connect farms to major highways and railway stations for the transport of farm products and inputs. The construction of farm roads is coordinated with irrigation and land consolidation programs. Except in mountain areas, it is rare to see a village without paved roads.

Macroeconomic Policies

Two aspects of Taiwan's macroeconomic policy in the postwar years had a profound effect on agriculture: the move to stabilize prices and the taxation of farmers.

PRICE STABILIZATION. Prices in Taiwan rose about fivefold from 1946 to 1948 and then jumped about thirtyfold in early 1949. At the same time, two million soldiers and civilians were added to the population, and there was a continuing threat of a communist invasion. The urgent need for price stabiliza-

---

2. A regression analysis indicates a high relationship between average rice yield and area irrigated during 1922–38 and 1950–60. The correlation is similar to that of Thailand and the Philippines.

tion led to the new Taiwan dollar reform in mid-1949. The old currency was devalued by a factor of 40,000, and a highly conservative full-reserve system was established.

To further fight inflation the government introduced a high-interest policy for preferential interest savings deposits. At the beginning, the interest rate was set at 7 percent per month, which was equivalent to 125 percent per year. This rate was lowered later when prices came down. In the next nine years this policy absorbed an enormous amount of idle capital and thus contributed greatly to price stabilization. The policy also helped promote savings and investment.

In addition, the government made determined efforts to curtail public expenditures and increase tax revenue. The timely arrival of U.S. economic aid in 1951 greatly facilitated postwar rehabilitation and fiscal management. Aid-financed imports in the 15 years before 1965 accounted for about 30 percent of total imports. Equally important, the local currency generated by the sale of U.S. aid-financed commodity imports reduced inflationary pressures and helped offset government budget deficits before the budget was balanced in the early 1960s.

Substantial imports of U.S. aid-financed commodities and increases in domestic production, especially of food, helped relieve the pressure on demand. Rice was frequently used as a wage good to hedge against inflation. Financial transactions were made in terms of, or in relation to, rice. Under such circumstances, fluctuations in the price of rice could have had an adverse effect on the prices of other commodities and services. For example, it was argued that a rise in rice prices would increase labor costs and thereby raise the cost of production, which would in turn weaken the international competitiveness of many industries. To maintain stable rice prices, the government collected and stocked large amounts of rice and continued to do so right up to 1973. Collections were made through paddy land taxes in kind, compulsory purchases of paddy from landowners, rent on government-owned farmland, proceeds in kind from the sale of public farmland, the barter of fertilizers for rice, sales proceeds collected from former tenants who received land under the land reform program, and the repayment of rice production loans provided by the government. These policies were implemented under the slogan of "more food for the people and the military" and thus met with little challenge (Chen, Hsu, and Mao 1975).

The government's regulation of rice marketing has kept rice prices in Taiwan very stable, except for brief surges in 1953, 1960, and 1974, when supplies dwindled because of bad weather. In addition, the price spread between producers' prices and consumers' prices has been narrow. Seasonal rice price variations in normal years were also small.

Under Taiwan's stabilization and fiscal policies, inflation dropped from an average of 8.8 percent in the period 1952–60 to only 3 percent in 1961. This success in fighting inflation during most of the 1950s was the foundation for the development of a labor-intensive industry and for the sustained and rapid growth in the years that followed.

TAXATION OF FARMERS. Two important taxes imposed on Taiwan's farmers are the farm land tax and the hidden rice tax carried out through compulsory purchases and the rice-fertilizer barter system. The land-tax unit (Y) is determined on the basis of the productivity of the land and ranges from Y1.2 to Y49.0 for each of the 26 grades produced. Land-tax collections were adjusted seven times between 1946 and 1947, and in this period the amount of paddy collected per tax unit increased from 8.85 kilograms to 22 kilograms.

The compulsory purchase of paddy from landowners at official prices is another source of government-provided rice. Any parcel of paddy land was subject to the paddy land tax plus compulsory purchase of rice. Collections made on top of the paddy land tax were calculated on the basis of the tax unit, which, as just mentioned, depends on the productivity of the land. In 1974 the amount to be purchased was increased from 12 to 35 kilograms per unit to offset the decrease in government-collected rice after the bartering of fertilizer for rice was discontinued. The government typically paid only 70–80 percent of the prevailing market price for compulsory purchases. The difference between the official and market prices thus constituted an additional, but hidden, tax on the paddy landowners. The difference, however, was abolished in 1973 in order to increase farm incomes.

The bartering of fertilizer for rice began in 1948. About 40 percent of the fertilizer was obtained through spot barter, while the remaining 60 percent was loaned to the rice growers, to be repaid in rice after harvest. On the whole, farmers found the exchange unfavorable. In 1950, for instance, the amount of rice required for 1 kilogram of ammonium sulphate was 1.2 kilograms for the first crop of 1950, but by 1972 it had fallen to 0.53 kilogram. This policy never won the full support of rice growers, yet rice collected by the government through this system constituted the bulk of government-controlled rice until the system was abolished in 1973.

Under the land reform program, payment for the land was made in paddy if the land produced paddy. Rice collected under the land-to-the-tiller program amounted to 50,000 metric tons in the peak year of 1959 but has decreased since then. Rice collected under the public land sale and leasing program amounted to 38,000 metric tons in the peak years of 1964 and 1965. In addition, the government provided rice production loans to needy rice growers in order to encourage rice production. Rice farmers were overcharged under the rice production loan program, and it has never been popular with them.

The government's rice collection by all of these methods averaged 50 to 60 percent of the total amount of rice marketed off the farm during 1950–70. By 1973, however, this share had declined to 20 percent. In subsequent years it increased again because of the guaranteed rice price policy. The total hidden rice tax was greater than Taiwan's total income tax in the entire period before 1963 and was more than twice the farm land tax every year before 1961, except in 1954. After 1969, the hidden rice tax decreased rapidly. The ratio of the hidden rice tax to the total income tax dropped to only 8.5 percent in 1971 (Kuo 1975).

Industrialization and Export-led Growth, 1952–1988

In the 1950s and 1960s Taiwan's industrial sector performed better than the agricultural sector. In 1968 it generated more gross domestic product (GDP) than the agricultural sector for the first time and has continued to do so ever since.

Industrial Development: Growth and Structural Change

Taiwan's modern economic development began in 1953. By then, economic output had recovered to prewar levels in most sectors, and the government was about to implement its first four-year economic development plan. Over the next two decades, Taiwan changed from an agricultural to an industrial-based economy. Between 1952 and 1972 agriculture's share of NDP dropped from 36 to 14 percent, while manufacturing's share increased from 11 percent to 32 percent (table 2.4). The labor force in the agricultural sector fell to only 33 percent in 1972, while that in manufacturing rose to 25 percent. This decline in agriculture continued through the 1970s and 1980s, but the transformation of Taiwan's economy from an agrarian to an industrialized one was essentially complete by the early 1970s.

The traditional economic structure and trading patterns of the colonial era had already begun shifting during the postwar reconstruction, when Taiwan came under the Chinese Nationalist government and its trading relations with Japan were interrupted. Up to then, Taiwan's economy had been based largely on exporting agricultural products to Japan, in exchange for manufactured goods. This pattern altered somewhat in the 1930s when Japanese manufacturers set up factories in Taiwan, mainly in food processing, cement, paper, and some chemical fertilizers. Industrialization proceeded slowly, however, and by 1950 manufacturing still accounted for less than 8 percent of total employment; moreover, the majority of industry's technical and managerial staff were Japanese (Chang 1980, table 5).

After 1945, mainland China provided a market for Taiwan's exports and became a source of manufactures, but this pattern was disrupted after the Communist takeover of the mainland in 1949. After the end of World War II, the production of nondurable consumer goods, processed food, and textiles all increased rather quickly, as did bricks, paper, and cement. In the early 1950s food processing was the fastest-growing industry: it accounted for about 40 percent of the increase in manufacturing and nearly a fourth of total manufactur-

TABLE 2.4 Net domestic product and employment by kind of activity, 1952–1988 (percent)

Net domestic product

Year	Total	Agriculture	Industries				Services				
			Subtotal	Manufacturing	Construction	Electricity, Gas, and Water	Subtotal	Commerce	Transport, Storage, and Communication	Government	Finance, Insurance, and Business
1952	100.0	36.0	18.0	10.8	4.4	0.6	46.0	18.7	3.9	10.9	9.0
1956	100.0	31.9	22.4	14.5	4.9	0.8	46.0	17.0	4.0	12.7	9.8
1960	100.0	32.9	24.9	16.8	4.5	1.3	42.2	14.3	4.1	12.6	9.0
1964	100.0	28.3	28.9	20.9	4.4	1.8	42.8	15.1	4.4	12.4	9.1
1968	100.0	22.1	32.6	24.0	5.1	1.7	45.4	15.1	5.7	13.5	9.4
1972	100.0	14.2	40.3	32.3	4.6	2.1	45.5	14.9	6.1	12.6	9.6
1980	100.0	9.2	44.7	34.0	7.3	2.3	46.1	14.6	6.2	11.6	11.6
1988	100.0	6.1	46.2	38.1	4.9	2.6	47.7	15.7	5.5	11.3	11.2

Employment

Year	Total	Agriculture	Industries				Services			
			Subtotal	Manufacturing	Construction	Utilities	Subtotal	Commerce	Transportation	Other
1952	100.0	56.1	16.9	12.4	2.4	0.2	27.0	10.6	3.4	13.0
1956	100.0	53.2	18.3	13.2	2.8	0.3	28.5	10.0	4.1	14.4
1960	100.0	50.2	20.5	14.8	3.1	0.3	29.3	10.0	4.4	14.9
1964	100.0	49.5	21.3	15.4	3.3	0.4	29.2	9.6	4.6	15.0
1968	100.0	40.8	25.4	18.6	4.4	0.4	33.8	13.0	4.8	16.0
1972	100.0	33.0	31.8	24.6	5.6	0.4	35.2	14.0	5.2	16.0
1980	100.0	19.5	42.4	32.6	8.5	0.4	38.1	16.0	5.9	16.2
1988	100.0	13.7	42.6	34.5	7.3	0.4	43.7	19.0	5.3	19.4

SOURCE: Taiwan (1989b).

TABLE 2.5 Distribution of industrial production by ownership 1952–1988 (percent)

Year	Total Private	Total Public	Mining Private	Mining Public	Manufacturing Private	Manufacturing Public	Construction of Building Private	Electricity, Gas, and Water Public
1952	43.4	56.6	71.7	28.3	43.8	56.2	100.0	100.0
1956	49.0	21.0	73.5	26.5	51.7	48.3	100.0	100.0
1960	52.1	47.9	75.8	24.2	56.2	13.8	100.0	100.0
1964	46.3	43.7	79.5	20.5	31.3	28.9	100.0	100.0
1968	68.9	31.1	76.9	23.1	75.3	24.7	100.0	100.0
1972	78.7	21.3	84.2	15.8	86.0	14.0	100.0	100.0
1980	79.1	20.9	52.0	48.0	85.5	14.5	100.0	100.0
1988	81.9	18.0	48.5	51.5	88.9	11.1	100.0	100.0

SOURCE: Taiwan (1989b).
NOTE: Based on value added at 1981 prices.

ing production. The textile industry also demonstrated high growth (16 percent), particularly after the introduction of export promotion measures. Other strong performers were wood and furniture (7 percent), cement and bricks (8 percent), and paper (7 percent). In the late 1960s the product mix of manufactures changed significantly as metals, machine tools, and electronic consumer products began to take advantage of export opportunities and the expanding domestic market. The domestic market accounted for more than 60 percent of growth from 1956 to 1966, when export expansion became increasingly important.

Transition from Inward-looking to Export-oriented Development

Taiwan's success in industrialization can be attributed in part to its large, fairly well-educated, rural labor force. Rural workers began moving into industry under the impetus of the import-substitution policies of the 1950s and the export-promotion strategy of the 1960s, which enabled Taiwan to make the best use of its comparative advantage through trade. As a result, manufacturing's share of employment increased from one-quarter in the period 1940–66 to one-half in 1966–74.

IMPORT SUBSTITUTION. Taiwan sought self-sufficiency through import-substitution strategies for a number of reasons: the loss of its traditional trading partners in the late 1940s, its unfamiliarity with other foreign markets, a shortage of foreign exchange, and the government's desire to strengthen Taiwan's economy so it could be a base for the recovery of the mainland. To this end, the government decided to develop three important industries: electric power, fertilizer, and textiles. The first two were vital to the continued expansion of industry and agriculture, while textiles were the largest import item at the time.

Because of the high investment they required, the electric power and fertilizer industries were run by the government, whereas textiles were left to private investors. In large part, transportation and other public infrastructure were also developed by the government.

The measures introduced to encourage the domestic development of import-substitution industries in the early 1950s focused on nondurable consumer goods for which demand in Taiwan was strong, notably textiles, apparel, wheat flour, wood, and leather products. Import-substitution was quickly achieved in industries that used rather simple technology. Textile production, for example, surpassed its prewar peak of 2.5 million meters and by 1953 was effectively satisfying domestic demand. Although the growth in exports caused a rapid expansion of output from the mid-1950s on, import substitution did less well in this respect. The main reason was that imports shifted to capital goods in the 1950s and the growth of the export industries in the 1960s offset the effect of import substitution, (see Schive 1987; Schive and Majumdar 1990).

EXPORT ORIENTATION. It did not take long for Taiwan's import-substitution policies to saturate the small domestic market with consumer products. Production exceeded capacity in the other industries as well, both because of the lack of demand and a multiple foreign exchange rate, which created a barrier to export. Furthermore, policy reforms implemented by the government gave industries more incentive to produce exports of light industry products. Virtually all manufacturing industries increased their exports after these reforms. Textiles, wood and wood products, and nonmetallic mineral products were especially successful. Foreign firms, attracted by the improved environment of the mid-1960s, invested in electronics, mainly for export. This prompted investment by local entrepreneurs, which precipitated a change in the structure of Taiwan's manufacturing sector, as explained in the next section.

The Engine of Growth: Trade Development

Taiwan's dependence on trade has fluctuated somewhat over the past fifty years, although trade was already an important component of the economy in the colonial period (Lee 1971a).

GROWTH INDICATORS AND PATTERNS OF TRADE. Between 1951 and 1953 Taiwan concentrated on its import-substitution policy, with the result that trade declined to 23 percent of GNP. It rose modestly to 30 percent in 1960, but then doubled during the next 10 years and surpassed 100 percent by 1980. The composition of trade also changed significantly. In 1956, 82 percent of all Taiwan's exports were primary products or processed foods, and only 17 percent consisted of industrial products. After the export-orientation policies were implemented in the late 1950s and early 1960s, agriculture's share of exports fell to 67 percent and that of industrial products rose to 32 percent. As traditional agricultural exports declined, new export-oriented agricultural products, such as canned mushrooms and asparagus, took their place. At the same time, the share of manufactures continued to increase, reaching 68 percent in 1968 and 83 percent in 1972. Whereas textiles had been the leading exports in the 1960s, electrical equipment and electronics gained in importance in the 1970s. These changes reflected a fundamental change in the structure of Taiwan's economy.

The composition of imports also changed significantly. In 1952 two-thirds of all imports were agricultural and industrial raw materials, such as raw cotton. Under the import-substitution policies, the share of consumer goods in total imports dropped from 20 percent in 1952 to 7 percent in 1956. In addition, the demand for capital goods was still low since rapid industrialization was still some years away (Ho 1978, 133) and the savings rate was low and foreign exchange limited at this time. By the mid-1960s, however, these restraints were largely gone, and in 1968 imports of capital goods increased to a third of the total.

Exports have made vital contributions to Taiwan's development in different periods. During the 1950s and early 1960s, agricultural exports, primarily rice and sugar, provided the foreign exchange for at least half of Taiwan's imports. The remainder was financed primarily by U.S. aid. These imports consisted largely of raw materials and capital goods necessary for development. The export-oriented policies that followed greatly boosted economic growth: in the early 1970s export expansion accounted for nearly two-thirds of all economic growth.

COMPARATIVE ADVANTAGE. These trade promotion policies greatly benefited Taiwan's industries because they emphasized its comparative advantage in labor-intensive products, which quickly became competitive in international markets. These included radios, bicycles, sewing machines, and machine tools. Taiwan's experience demonstrates that foreign firms tend to use a much more labor-intensive technology in producing for export than for the domestic market. This was the case for all industries in Taiwan except textiles, for which a few large industries exporting artificial fiber dominated the result. Thus market orientation appears to be a crucial factor in determining the "appropriate" technology used by foreign firms (Liang and Liang 1988; Schive 1990b).

Taiwan's strategy was to increase exports of inexpensive manufactured products to developed countries in the West where labor costs were rising and to also export both capital- and skill-intensive goods to less-developed countries with few technical skills. In this way, Taiwan made full use of its comparative advantages in different export markets (Lin 1973). However, the exports of labor-intensive products were far more important to Taiwan's economy.

Export-led development eventually exhausted Taiwan's surplus agricultural labor. The wage rate of workers had been fairly stable in the 1960s, although there was a slight rise in industrial wages in response to the boost in agricultural real wages related to rising agricultural productivity (Ranis 1979, 255). By the late 1960s wages had begun to rise more steeply, and agricultural labor to decline in absolute terms. Higher wages for unskilled labor gradually led to a more capital- and skill-intensive industrial output in the 1970s. This phenomenon, known as secondary import substitution, is a further indication that the economy is responding to continuing changes in factor endowments and demand patterns (Schive 1987, 1990c).

Organization of Taiwan's Manufacturing Sector

In the early 1950s most of Taiwan's larger firms were under government control. Many of them were former Japanese enterprises.[3]

EXPANSION OF THE PRIVATE SECTOR. Private ownership gradually expanded, however. In 1952 public industries produced 57 percent of total manufacturing output. The government's basic policy toward the ownership of industry was to retain direct control of utilities; natural monopoly industries that were considered vital to the country's defense (such as the railroad and highway buses); and industries held for revenue purposes, such as the Monopoly Bureau of Wine and Tobacco. Others were left in private hands. This policy reflected in part the government's lack of capital to finance large-scale investment, and in part the support of some government officials and the U.S. economic advisory group for the development of the private sector (Commonwealth 1984, 26). As a result, the private sector gained strength in the 1950s and thus was in a position to expand at full steam in the 1960s, when the export market boomed.

The total share of the public sector in manufacturing was at its peak in 1952 but two decades later was down to 14 percent (table 2.5). Some industries, such as electrical products and wood and wood products, were dominated by the private sector from the very beginning. The government saw its share in food processing decline, but retained tight control over much of the sugar sector. Government ownership in petroleum and coal products remained high throughout the period.

GROWTH OF SMALL AND MEDIUM ENTERPRISES. Small and medium enterprises (SMEs) played an important role in Taiwan's economic development. In 1961 nearly all manufacturing firms were SMEs (defined as having fewer than 100 employees) and their average size was 8 persons. They contributed 61 percent of total manufacturing employment. By 1971 their average size had increased to 28, but it has gone done slightly since the mid-1970s. However, the percentage share of SMEs in total manufacturing firms has increased. As table 2.6 shows, the contribution of SMEs to manufacturing employment has dropped well below the 1961 peak, but the value has risen.[4]

---

3. In 1932, up to 90 percent of Taiwan's industrial capital was in the hands of Japanese enterprises. Capital participation by local business was allowed only in mining, tea-making, and sugar industries (Chang 1980).

4. According to Bruch and Hiemenz (1984, table 2.1), 1971 SME data for country comparisons did not indicate an unusually large share for Taiwan's SMEs. If data from a much later period had been used, the concentration of SMEs in Taiwan's manufacturing sector would have been similar to that of Japan and Norway.

TABLE 2.6 Share of small and medium enterprises in the manufacturing sector, 1954–1986

| | | Share of SMEs (1–99 employment) | | |
| | | Total Number | | |
Year	Average Size of Firms (number of persons)	of Firms (percent)	Employment (percent)	Value Added (percent)
1954	—	99.4	—	—
1961	8.4	99.1	61.0	—
1966	21.3	97.2	42.7	—
1971	28.2	95.4	35.6	21.6
1976	27.4	95.3	38.6	28.2
1981	24.3	95.9	41.3	31.8
1986	24.2	96.0	47.9	39.9

SOURCE: *Census Report of Taiwan District, Republic of China,* Directorate General of Budget, Accounting and Statistics, Executive Yuan, various years.
NOTE: Value-added figures for 1986 are based on gross value added.

Structural changes have occurred in both SMEs and large firms. For instance, in the 1960s employment in the largest firms (those employing more than 500 persons) grew fastest. Larger SME firms (employing 50 to 99 persons) also increased their share. The rapidly growing shares of large firms coincided with the export market boom and the inflow of the export-oriented direct foreign investment. No doubt the smallest also grew bigger but were reclassified into larger size groups. When the labor surplus dwindled in the 1970s, employment in the largest firms declined, while the employment shares of the smallest firms and firms employing 100 to 499 persons stabilized. The medium SMEs employing 10 to 99 persons became increasingly competitive in the labor market.

In the early 1950s government leaders preferred to see larger companies developed because they believed smaller ones were unable to take advantage of economies of scale and modern production and management methods (Yin 1954, 1). Consequently, the government granted most of its low-cost loans and other resources to firms attempting to develop fertilizer, cement, and sugar industries, none of which were SMEs. Small companies were tolerated, however, because they provided employment and goods for local people. Although the JCRR provides some financial and technical assistance to rural enterprise, the SMEs rely primarily on the informal money market for finance and make no demands on the government. Some government officials believe that competition would force out the least efficient firms, and that many of the remaining smaller enterprises would combine to form larger conglomerates.

Despite this lack of attention, the SMEs thrived since they were flexible enough to adjust to rapidly changing circumstances. During the 1960s and 1970s, the SMEs benefited from policies that encouraged exports. They were able to manufacture products that made use of Taiwan's abundant labor supply and of simple technologies that absorbed excess labor. Because of the small size of these firms, other small entrepreneurs could enter the various industries rather easily. As a result, competition remained keen. Some SMEs became subcontractors of large export-oriented foreign firms. The share of SMEs in total production of manufactures grew from 27 percent in 1971 to 48 percent in 1984, and SME exports as a share of their total products also grew, from 55.7 percent in 1972 to 66.7 percent in 1980, 75.9 percent in 1982, and 71.8 percent in 1984 (Chou 1989). SMEs dominated the manufacture of textiles, apparel, leather goods, wood and bamboo products, metal products, machinery equipment, and miscellaneous industrial products for which export demand was strong.

SMEs also contributed to equitable income distribution. Since many such enterprises were outside the main urban areas, they gave rural families an opportunity to supplement their incomes with nonagricultural employment. This was especially the case for lower-income farm families that relied heavily on nonagricultural income. By locating in rural areas, SMEs also helped prevent overurbanization, which has been a problem in many developing countries. Most prevalent among the SMEs were food-processing enterprises and those that produce rubber, leather and fur products, electronics and related equipment, and metal products. As the terms of trade grew increasingly in favor of manufacturing in the late 1960s, the government encouraged the establishment of local handicraft industries and other industries in rural areas. By 1966 the government had invested in 17 rural industrial districts covering an area of almost 1,600 hectares (Ranis 1979, 226). JCRR provided financial and technical support for some projects, especially food processing. The SMEs have certainly had a far-reaching and multifaceted impact on Taiwan's economy.

Economic Policies

Taiwan's policymakers endeavored to strengthen the economy in the postwar years through protectionist measures, export promotion, direct foreign investment, an export processing zone, and improvements to the infrastructure.

PROTECTION AND EXPORT PROMOTION. In the late 1940s the government placed restrictions on imports and the use of foreign exchange with a view to improving the balance of payments and promoting import substitution. The package included tariffs, import controls, quotas, and multiple exchange rates. These policies stimulated domestic production, although efficiency probably suffered. By 1954 domestic industry was supplying about 83 percent of the domestic market for manufactured goods. The share for textiles and apparel was 94 percent, although in some more sophisticated industries (such as machinery and electrical equipment), more than half of the available supply was still imported (Lin 1973, 66).[5] These policies put a dampener on the export of Taiwan's industrial goods. In addition, the overvalued NT dollar encouraged capital-intensive production and thus prevented Taiwan from making the best use of its comparative advantage (Ho 1978; Lee and Liang 1982).

At the same time, the protectionist policies enabled Taiwan's industries to meet basic needs in short order. By the late 1950s, however, Taiwan's market was becoming saturated with light industrial products, mostly consumer goods, and in some enterprises capacity and prices had begun to fall (Ho 1978, 222). Rather than attempt to develop heavy industry (which was to be the second phase of import substitution), the government decided to promote exports for which light industry enjoys comparative advantage. Initially, some were hesitant to take such a step for fear that Taiwan's textiles and other manufactured goods would not be able to compete with Japanese manufactures. Also, the Taiwanese were unfamiliar with foreign markets. But the low rates of economic growth in the late 1950s and, most important, the knowledge that U.S. economic aid was not unlimited persuaded officials to change their strategy.[6] They recognized that foreign exchange was essential for continued economic expansion, but that they could no longer rely on sugar exports, which had suffered a setback in 1958 as a result of a drop in sugar prices.

To further promote exports, Taiwan simplified the multiple exchange rate in 1958 and finally unified it in 1961, relaxed controls on imported manufacturing inputs, and introduced the landmark 19-Point Program to improve the investment climate, liberalize controls on industry (such as the restrictions on the establishment of new factories), and encourage exports. It is doubtful that Taiwan would have liberalized so early and so thoroughly without the support and encouragement of the U.S. aid mission (Jacoby 1966). Subsequent measures provided low-interest loans for exporters, a rebate of indirect taxes and tariffs on imported inputs for exports, and partial exemption from corporate income tax on export earnings of some products (Galenson 1979; Scitovsky 1986).

5. In the mid-1950s, imports of certain chemical fertilizers, wheat, flour, plywood, leather and leather products, cement, paper, rubber products, sewing machines, bicycles, soap, cotton, woolens, and man-made yarn and fabrics were suspended or controlled. Also, tariffs were high on many consumer goods. The nominal rate of protection for import-substitution industries was measured by comparing domestic prices for commodities with international prices, weighted by domestic sales. The nominal rate was 0.535 in 1961 but dropped to 0.300 in 1971 (Kuo, Ranis, and Fei 1985, 52). These tariff and nontariff protection schemes combined with foreign-exchange controls caused a widening of the differentials between the prices of imports or import substitutes and the CIF costs of comparable imports. In 1953 these differentials ranged from 41 to 48 percent for wheat flour, powdered milk, peanut oil, cotton yarns, and steel plate; but rates rose more than 300 percent for woolen yarn (Lin 1973, 50). As a result, it is not difficult to estimate the loss of efficiency from protection (Lee et al. 1975).

6. Large trade deficits in the 1950s were financed primarily through U.S. aid, which was equivalent to about 35 percent of all imports in 1958.

Beginning in the early 1960s, the government required a certain percentage of production to be exported, which in the case of new cement factories amounted to their entire output. It also removed all restrictions on textiles after they had successfully entered foreign markets. These restrictions included suspensions on production licenses, limits to the expansion of production, specific export requirements, and required ratios of local content (Hsing 1970, 202–4). In addition, industry trade associations were allowed to regulate output, prices, and sales of products. Also, limits were placed on the amount firms could sell in the domestic market; to further expand, they were obliged to export. The environment for export grew even more favorable as the price differentials between domestic and foreign markets helped subsidize exports from domestic sales (Lin 1973, 109–110), and incentives such as preferential loans were introduced (Lee and Liang 1982).

Regulations pertaining to the local content of inputs were first aimed at foreign firms but then in 1963 were also applied to local producers. Under these regulations, producers were required to increase their local content by ten percentage points a year, from an initial 40 percent to a maximum of 70 percent of product value. The aim was to further stimulate domestic-related industry, but exceptions were made so as to safeguard exports. More important, the strong backward linkages created by the quickly expanding export sector fostered the development of secondary import-substitution industries (Schive 1987, 1990b).

DIRECT FOREIGN INVESTMENT AND ESTABLISHMENT OF AN EXPORT PROCESSING ZONE. Direct foreign investment in Taiwan began in 1952, but did not reach significant levels until the mid-1960s. Since then, its contribution to gross capital formation has remained below 5 percent, although it did rise to 7 percent of the total investment in manufacturing during 1969–72. From 1974 to 1982 foreign firms accounted for about 20 percent of the country's total exports and generated 15 to 17 percent of the total employment in manufacturing (Schive 1990a).

Because they were concentrated in the labor-intensive exporting industries, foreign firms in Taiwan used more labor-intensive technology than national firms and thus helped improve the allocation of resources. Foreign parent firms also provided export-marketing assistance to their local subsidiaries. By 1972 about four-fifths of these subsidiaries were using their parent companies' international marketing network. Far more important, this marketing assistance abroad allowed local firms to start off with a large scale of production (Schive 1990a).

With the aid of foreign investment, firms were also able to introduce new products, modern marketing techniques, and new technology. Local managers, technicians, and workers trained at foreign firms gained new skills, which they subsequently put to use in starting their own firms or in hiring on at domestic firms. In this way, the new technology or skills spread to the domestic industry. Another important development was that foreign firms were now purchasing domestically produced inputs (Schive 1990a; Schive and Majumdar 1990). Econometric analysis indicates that the inflow of direct foreign investment in Taiwan was positively related to capital formation, with a significant coefficient of 2.84. In other words, every dollar of direct foreign investment from 1958 to 1987 induced $1.84 in capital formation. Although the impact is difficult to calculate precisely, these figures clearly suggest that this investment has stimulated capital formation in Taiwan (Schive and Tu 1991).

Because many foreign investors were unfamiliar with the government's procedures and thus were hesitant to open factories, the authorities decided to establish an export processing zone in Kaohsiung, Taiwan's largest port. It opened in 1965, and two more such zones were set up in 1969. Government regulations were simplified and coordinated to make it easier for foreigners to take advantage of Taiwan's favorable policies. These zones provided industrial sites, standard factory buildings, plentiful energy, and storage and transportation facilities at reasonable prices. Between 1966 and 1970 the zones attracted $33 million in direct foreign investment, which amounted to 23 percent of total investment of this kind. By the late 1970s almost 80,000 people were employed in the three zones, about 80 percent of whom were women.

In the mid-1960s the government also established policies for bonded factories. Factories established for the production of exports enjoyed the same tax benefits as those in the export processing zones but were not restricted to any particular location. Foreign firms were therefore allowed to take advantage of the labor supply available in many areas and to avoid undue competition for labor around the zones.

INFRASTRUCTURE. In the 1950s the republican government began to improve and expand the infrastructure that had already been built by the Japanese. In preparation for economic development, Taiwan invested large amounts in irrigation, land development, road construction, communication, and the electric power industry. It continued the expansion and modernization of paved roads, communications, and postal establishments into the 1980s. In addition, it modernized and improved the efficiency of its railways.

Throughout the past four decades the electric power industry has played a particularly important role in Taiwan's development. By introducing standard urban and rural power rates, the Taiwan Power Company, a government enterprise, has not only raised rural living standards but also facilitated the growth of industries in rural villages. These enterprises absorbed labor from agriculture and helped maintain greater equality between rural and urban incomes and development. As a result, regional development of industry was well balanced between 1951 and 1971. This would not have happened without adequate investment in the rural regions.

Contributions of Agriculture to Nonagricultural Sectors

As mentioned throughout this volume, agriculture contributes to the growth of other sectors by providing labor, capital, agricultural goods, and a market for nonfarm goods and services. As nonfarm sectors expand, the demand for agricultural products increases, job opportunities open up for farm families, and excess agricultural labor becomes absorbed by the job market. These interrelationships were particularly important during 1950–60, when newly developed import-substitution industries precipitated a structural change in Taiwan's economy.

Labor Flows

From 1952 to 1964 agricultural labor increased from 1.64 million to 1.81 million, although its growth rate was much lower than that of the total labor force. During this period, more than 200,000 agricultural workers migrated to nonagricultural sectors, at the rate of about 19,000 a year. The annual rate of outflow ranged from 0.3 to 2.3 percent, which was low compared with that in later periods. Thus agriculture still absorbed a large portion of the increased rural labor at this time. After 1965 agricultural labor migration accelerated owing to rapid industrialization in the nonagricultural sector. Between 1965 and 1973 an average of 93,522 persons a year migrated from agriculture to nonagricultural sectors, which was five times the 1953–63 average. In the early period the most important forces behind this migration were push factors, such as the rising per capita income and industrial wage. Pull factors, such as employment opportunities and urbanization, became significant later. The migration continued in the 1970s, in response to Taiwan's growing economic prosperity, but then slowed as economic growth moderated, only to surge upward again in 1987 and 1988, when the economy regained its vitality.

There were only three years of negative migration during the 1952–88 period. The first occurred in 1964 but was insignificant.[7] The second and third occurred in 1974 and 1982, when the oil crises hit. Thus during the economically depressed years, agriculture was a buffer for unemployed nonagricultural labor and contributed greatly to social stability. The cushion effect was much less pronounced in 1982, however, owing to the shrinkage of the agricultural sector.

Farm labor also contributed to Taiwan's economic development indirectly in that the children raised on farms were educated in schools subsidized by farm taxes. The nonfarm sector did not pay for the rearing of those who migrated to cities after finishing school. An adequate and basically balanced elementary system in the countryside helped improve the quality of migrants absorbed in the nonfarm sector.

7. The growth rates of GNP, agricultural production, and industrial production in 1964 were 12.3 percent, 9.5 percent, and 21.1 percent, respectively.

Capital Flows

According to studies on the flow of resources and funds from agriculture to nonagricultural sectors in Taiwan (Lee 1971a, 1971b), the net sectoral outflow of real capital from agriculture was positive throughout the period 1895 to 1969 and contributed significantly to capital formation of the nonagricultural sector (see table 2.7). This outflow was determined from both net real agricultural surplus (or visible net capital outflow) and changes in the sectoral terms of trade.

The net intersectoral capital flow was unfavorable to agriculture through-out the period under review. The outflow from agriculture trended upward in the prewar period, declined in the early postwar period, but picked up again in 1961-69. An invisible outflow caused by the terms of trade against agriculture accounted for more than 50 percent of the total outflow in the postwar period. Financially, land-rent payment and government taxing accounted for the lion's share of agricultural surplus transferred to nonagriculture in the prewar period, and the direct transfer of farmers' savings became a significant factor in 1966–69. The magnitude of the intersectoral capital flows was influenced by govern-ment policy and the stage of development.

Market for Nonfarm Products

The agricultural sector had a fairly large population and income share at the beginning of industrialization and had the potential of being a good custom-er for industrial goods. From 1950 to 1970 Taiwan's agricultural production grew 5.3 percent annually, which was reflected in increased agricultural in-comes. As a result, the agricultural sector's effective demand for industrial goods rose significantly. In addition, a series of land reform programs helped improve the purchasing power of farm families through income redistribution.

The relative importance of agriculture in stimulating the industrial devel-opment can be verified in two ways. First, the domestic market accounted for more than 60 percent of the growth of the manufacturing sector from 1956 to 1966. After 1966 export expansion became increasingly important. Second, from 1950 to 1955, 58 percent of the agricultural production was sold to the nonagricultural sector. In the same period, farmers' purchases from the non-agricultural sector amounted to NT$1.1 billion of working capital goods, NT$0.1 billion of fixed capital goods, and NT$2.1 billion of consumer goods.

From 1956 to 1960, 60.3 percent of the agricultural production was sold to the nonagricultural sector. Farmers in return spent NT$8.7 billion to purchase the nonagricultural products. A similar pattern occurred during 1961–65 and 1966–69, although the share of consumer goods declined while the shares of working capital and fixed capital goods steadily increased. Thus the prosperous agricultural sector clearly provided an attractive local market for the manufac-turing sector during the crucial initial period of industrial development.

TABLE 2.7 Intersectoral capital flows between the agricultural and the nonagricultural sectors (five-year average), 1931–1969 (NT$, 1935–37 constant prices)

Item	1931–35	1936–40	1950–55	1956–60	1961–65	1966–69
Total agricultural production	290,597	507,819	7,210,674	16,028,408	30,701,164	42,224,656
Total sale of agricultural products	208,470	362,474	4,183,722	9,664,662	18,606,946	26,138,740
Total sale ratio	71.70	71.40	58.00	60.30	60.61	61.90
Total outflow of agricultural products to	208,470	362,474	4,183,722	9,664,662	18,606,946	26,138,740
Nonagricultural production	88,287	163,606	2,013,044	4,925,649	9,681,331	12,872,047
Nonagricultural household	48,356	81,858	1,941,976	4,177,284	7,554,053	11,114,156
Foreign countries	71,827	117,010	228,702	561,729	1,371,562	2,152,537
Total inflow of nonagricultural products	145,886	260,692	3,267,665	8,716,325	17,260,910	24,059,808
Working capital goods	47,053	82,407	1,052,583	2,594,395	5,636,389	8,569,460
Fixed capital goods	8,201	9,462	107,100	1,196,321	1,1789,079	3,757,021
Consumer goods	90,632	168,823	2,107,982	4,925,609	9,835,442	11,733,327
Net commodity outflow	62,584	101,782	916,057	948,337	1,346,036	2,078,932
Gross outflow of fund	75,853	134,818	1,337,180	2,616,115	6,270,108	10,600,574
Land rent and interest	55,828	98,299	531,969	738,790	591,937	1,042,141
Taxes and fees	16,985	30,141	711,555	1,452,694	1,894,607	2,348,434
Transfer of funds through financial institutions	3,040	6,375	93,656	424,631	3,783,564	7,209,999
Gross inflow of funds	13,269	33,036	421,123	1,667,777	4,924,072	8,521,642
Public investment and subsidy	1,026	2,147	26,154	71,432	919,590	1,362,657
Investment by nonagricultural sector in agriculture	3,101	5,343	11,625	44,171	—	—

(*continued*)

TABLE 2.7 (*continued*)

Item	1931–35	1936–40	1950–55	1956–60	1961–65	1966–69
Income received from the non-agricultural sector	9,142	25,546	383,344	1,552,174	4,004,482	7,158,985
Net outflow of fund	62,584	101,782	916,075	948,338	1,346,036	2,078,932
Terms of trade	106.90	102.10	125.70	119.80	119.03	118.51
Agricultural price index (1935–37 = 100)	80.40	120.20	1,404.90	2,483.50	3,830.00	4,041.00
Nonagricultural price index (1935–37 = 100)	85.90	122.70	1,766.00	2,974.90	4,559.00	4,789.00
Visible net real capital outflow	77,841	84,677	65,204	38,136	35,145	51,446
Invisible net real capital outflow	11,618	4,519	47,559	58,003	72,064	92,995
Net real capital outflow	89,459	89,196	112,763	96,189	107,209	144,441

SOURCE: Lee (1971b).

In summary, during Taiwan's early postwar industrialization agriculture played an important role in providing labor, capital, and a reliable and expanding market for the nonagricultural sector. An important lesson from Taiwan's experience is that the resource flows between agriculture and the nonagricultural sector were an active two-way transfer. In 1966–69, for instance, annual sales by the agriculture to nonagriculture were 2.2 times the 1950–55 level after price adjustment, while sales in the opposite direction were 2.7 times the 1950–55 level. In the meantime, the financial outflow of capital from agriculture was NT$10.6 billion, and the inflow from nonagriculture was NT$8.5 billion (see table 2.7). The intersectoral capital flows were significant only when the relations between agriculture and nonagriculture were close.

Social Impact of Agriculture-led Growth

Taiwan's economic expansion was notable not only for its rapid industrialization but also for its improved income distribution and more balanced industrial growth among regions. With the development of many labor-intensive foreign firms and SMEs, Taiwan was able to make use of its comparative advantage and provide geographic diffusion for industry. In addition, the government's effort to maintain a rough parity of incomes between the agricultural and industrial sectors helped prevent the urban flight common in many industrializing countries.

Urbanization

Although the population of Taiwan's larger cities increased, the rate was slow in relation to the rate of industrialization. In 1951–72 the population of the five largest cities rose from 18 percent to 27 percent of total population (Ho 1968, 139). However, the proportion of industrial establishments in these cities was only slightly more than one-third in both 1951 and 1971. Between 1956 and 1966 the percentage share of industrial employment in the cities fell from 43 percent to 37 percent. This pattern is distinctly different from that of most developing countries (Ranis 1979, 222).

Taiwan's relatively slow urbanization reflected the diffused patterns of industrialization. Although substantial intersectoral migration took place from agriculture to the industrial sector, this was often not accompanied by a corresponding geographic migration. Other factors affecting Taiwan's slow polarization of population were its well-developed transportation and communication systems, which, along with Taiwan's small size, reduced transportation costs and facilitated growth in rural and semirural areas. Enterprises producing labor-intensive, light industrial goods often did not need large plants and were able to take advantage of less expensive land and surplus labor in rural areas. The increase in demand for light industrial goods was abetted by export-oriented policies that allowed these enterprises to expand rapidly. In 1971, 61 percent of all consumer goods were produced outside of the five largest cities, in comparison with only 39 percent of producer goods (Ranis 1979, 229).

With this expansion, nonagricultural income became increasingly important to farmers: it accounted for 34 percent of total farm family income in 1966, for example, and 54 percent in 1975 (Fei, Kuo, and Ranis 1979). As industries spread in rural areas, farm people were able to take advantage of the higher wages in manufacturing without leaving home, and a large number (57 percent) did so on a seasonal basis. Slightly more than half commuted to work, but only 17 percent actually left the rural area. By 1968 about one-fourth were engaged in long-term employment elsewhere (Thorbeke 1979, 189–90), but most of them probably had found jobs in the large foreign companies established in the late 1960s.

Many of those who switched from agricultural to nonagricultural activity were young (two-thirds of the laborers in manufacturing between 1966 and 1972 were under the age of 24), and 79 percent were female (Kuo, Ranis, and Fei 1985, 105). It was said that "the flow of relatively cheap labor that attracted foreign investors to Taiwan would have ended much sooner had women decided to remain at home" (Galenson 1979, 395). They were able to enter the manufacturing work force so readily because industry was widely diffused and transportation facilities were well developed.

Income Distribution

Between 1952 and 1972 real income for all population groups in Taiwan rose and was distributed more equally. The Gini coefficient declined from 0.56 in 1953 to 0.32 in 1964 and 0.29 by 1972. The rapidly expanding, labor-intensive manufacturing industries provided wage income to large numbers of surplus rural laborers. By 1979 wage income had risen to 61 percent of total income, while income from property had decreased. Without doubt, the greater increase in wage income helped reduce income inequality in Taiwan (Fei, Kuo, and Ranis 1979, 314–16).

The land reforms immediately after the war, which reduced the rents of tenant farmers by 37.5 percent, also created a shift in the relative position of landlords. This move stimulated agricultural productivity. The combination of lower rents and increased production boosted the average income of tenant farmers 81 percent from 1949 to 1952 (Kuo, Ranis, and Fei 1985, 50). In addition, farmers benefited from the redistribution of wealth from higher-income landlords to the lower-income tenants, which in 1952 amounted to about 13 percent of GDP (Ho 1968, 166). Income equity improved even further under the government's policies of promoting labor-intensive industries together with universal education (Ranis and Schive 1985).

Despite the change in income distribution, the gap between the income of farm families and nonfarm families increased between 1964 and 1972, because the former rose more slowly than the latter (Fei, Kuo, and Ranis 1979, 203).

Although decreases in the terms of trade for agriculture have been mitigated somewhat by the promotion of higher-priced agricultural goods, on the whole agricultural growth rate has lagged behind that of industry. Moreover, the productivity of agricultural labor increased by 79 percent between 1952 and 1970, whereas that of industrial labor increased by 132 percent. This difference and the continued expansion of the industrial sector have prompted more and more agricultural workers to move into other sectors. To help equalize farm income with that of the industrial sector, the government offered loans and subsidies in aid of further mechanization of farms, which it hoped would raise farmer productivity.

Farm family income was also boosted by farm women entering the formal work force in large numbers in the 1960s. While the absolute numbers in agriculture between 1965 and 1975 remained stable, the women entering the manufacturing sector increased by 400,000. The number of women employed in the service sector also increased, but the relative share remained fairly stable (Galenson 1979, 33). Since most of the women entering the manufacturing sector were probably paid higher wages than they had been receiving, the movement of female labor contributed to a more equitable distribution of income.

Postindustrialization Adjustment of the Agricultural Sector

The turning point in agricultural development occurred in the mid-1960s, when industrial production overtook agriculture in its contribution both to net domestic product and to exports.

Difficulties in Agricultural Development

One of the difficulties for agriculture at this time was that the growth rate of production had begun to slow down in response to a changing emphasis on livestock and fishery products and high-value export crops. As already mentioned, industrial employment had also begun pushing up the costs of labor and other production inputs, labor productivity in agriculture was lagging behind that in the industrial sector, and the gap between farm and nonfarm per capita incomes was increasing. These and the other ensuing problems in the agricultural sector were similar to those that many other industrial countries have experienced at a comparable development stage.

LOSS OF FARMLAND AND LABOR. Farm labor reached a record level of 1.8 million persons in 1964 but by 1988 was down to 1.1 million. In other words, 0.7 million young laborers had left agriculture. This aging of farm labor is expected to become an even more serious concern in the future.

Another concern is that little unused farmland is left on the island yet the demand for land is growing in the face of rapid industrialization, population growth, and rising incomes. Since nonagricultural use generally produces more income than farming, the conversion of farmland to nonfarm purposes is inevitable. Indeed, the process is already in full swing: from 1952 to 1988, the total area of paddy fields decreased by 50,129 hectares; and the use of land for buildings increased 77,300 hectares, for roads and irrigation facilities 57,215 hectares, and for fishponds 15,670 hectares. A large portion of this conversion involved farmland in the fertile plain. Only 69,000 hectares were added to dry farmland by reclamation and development of slope and wild land. It should also be pointed out, however, that rural industries can only be established in the planned industrial zones or in locations exempt from agricultural use.

RIGID FARMLAND SYSTEM. Under the constraints imposed on the land tenure system by Taiwan's land reforms, many part-time farmers left their land to overseers working on their behalf rather than leasing it to other farmers for fear that the government might force them to give up their landownership. Consequently, it is now almost impossible for a full-time farmer to rent additional land, and the system originally designed to prevent land concentration actually prevents more productive use. This has created a serious bottleneck to Taiwan's agricultural development. Since 1960, the government has encouraged group farming, along with mechanization, to improve the efficiency of small units and to realize economies of scale and eliminate labor shortages. Small landowners have been urged to take full-time nonfarm jobs. Unfortunately, there is no legal basis for implementing this measure, and the results have been unsatisfactory.

To address the problem, the Council of Agriculture is drafting a law to provide more flexibility in farmland transactions and the tenancy system. Under existing land laws, only the bona fide farmers are qualified to purchase farmland. The proposed new law would allow agricultural school graduates and other young people with training in farming, agribusiness, and agricultural production cooperatives to buy farmland. The proposed law would also free all tenancy contracts, except those signed under the 37.5 percent Rent Reduction Act. In addition, the proposal would put more restrictions on conversions of farmland to nonagricultural uses after a master plan of land use has been formulated. This measure is expected to prevent land speculation in rural areas and to enlarge the size of farms.

DETERIORATION OF RURAL ENVIRONMENT. Because rural industrialization has raised the income and standard of living of rural labor, it has received widespread support in Taiwan. However, industry has become the major source of pollution in rural areas and has affected agricultural production. Rivers and streams in western Taiwan have been polluted by industrial wastes in various degrees, and industrial wastewater has been discharged into rural irrigation and drainage canals without treatment. In a few cases, industrial wastes have contaminated the soil to such an extent that farmland has had to be abandoned.

Some responsibility for the deteriorating environment also falls on the agricultural sector, whose overuse of fertilizers and chemicals has polluted both surface and groundwater. Wastes from livestock farms have caused water and air pollution, and the extensive use of groundwater on aquacultural farms has produced heavy sedimentation along the southern coast. As a result, aquacultural farms have been encouraged to raise fish that tolerate brackish water, and livestock farms are not allowed to discharge the animal wastes freely. These measures are expected to improve the rural environment in the near future.

RAPID CHANGES IN FOOD DEMAND. The increase in per capita income has had a marked effect on food consumption patterns. The challenge for Taiwanese farmers has been to adjust production to the changing domestic demand while also competing with foreign producers in both the domestic and foreign markets. If Taiwan is to meet this challenge, agricultural policy must focus on the income and welfare of full-time farmers while improving their production and management practices. Part-time small farmers should either maintain their small-scale farming through group farming or participate in large-scale operations under new institutions. Either option would, of course, need strong support from the government.

SMALL-SCALE FARM OPERATION. The small farm system is likely to prevail in a country where cultivated land is limited and population density is high. The average size of a farm in Taiwan fell from 1.29 hectares in 1952 to 0.97 hectare in 1972, but then went up to 1.21 hectares in 1988 following the loss of farm households. The latest agricultural census in 1985 indicates that 73 percent of all farm households owned less than 1 hectare. In the early days, small farms were able to compete because labor-intensive farming did not provide an opportunity for significant scale economies. However, a 1-hectare farm is too small to operate efficiently when farm machinery substitutes for manual work. As the steady decline in Taiwan's multiple-cropping index indicates, land use has become less intensive.

LOW FARMERS' INCOME. Until the mid-1960s the real income of farm and nonfarm families rose at about the same steady rate. In 1970, however, the per capita income of farm families dropped to 60 percent of nonfarm income and to 70 percent of that of workers' families. Although various government support policies boosted farm income in the late 1980s, many farmers were still forced to take part-time work off the farm. The proportion of farm family income that came from net agricultural income ranged from two-thirds in 1966 to less than one-third in 1980.

INCREASE IN PART-TIME FARMING. Since the average farm size has remained small, it has become increasingly difficult for farmers to raise their income from agriculture. Many farms have therefore become sideline operations in which one or more family members have taken a job outside agriculture. In 1980 such operations accounted for 55.5 percent of total farm households, in comparison with 9 percent for full-time farms and 35.3 percent for part-time farms. Subsequently, several measures were introduced to reverse this trend, including nucleus farm projects and the creation of new farm business for rural youth. By 1985 the number of part-time farm households had dropped to 21.6 percent and full-time farm households had increased to 21.6 percent, but the sideline farm households had changed little at 63.6 percent. At present, the majority of rice farms are either sideline or part-time operations. Most full-time farms produce horticultural or livestock products.

DECLINING INTERNATIONAL COMPETITIVENESS. Largely because of the surge in wages and other farm production costs, many Taiwanese farm products have lost their competitive edge in the world market, and imports have risen. Imported corn, for example, has replaced sweet potatoes as the major feedstuff. Rice and sugar are no longer profitable for export. And Taiwan's large share of canned mushrooms, asparagus, and pineapple has been lost to other countries.

Policy Changes and Challenges

In November 1969, in response to the mounting pressure for change in agriculture, the government issued policy guidelines designed primarily to accelerate agricultural modernization and maintain a balance between the agricultural sector and the rest of the economy. Several action programs were then developed to reduce the price of fertilizer, establish the Agricultural Finance Coordinating Committee, improve the agricultural marketing system, promote farm mechanization, and reduce the tax burden on farmers. Unfortunately, funds were not provided to implement these policies, except for the reductions in the price of fertilizer and tax burden on farmers.

Under the Accelerated Rural Development Program announced September 27, 1972, the government moved to abolish the rice-fertilizer barter system, abolish the educational surtax on farm land tax, ease the terms of agricultural credit, improve agricultural marketing, strengthen the rural infrastructure, accelerate the improvement of cultivated techniques, establish specialized agricultural production areas, strengthen agricultural research and extension, and promote industrial parks in rural areas.

In the next two years the government appropriated NT$2 billion to implement these measures. From that time on, agriculture played a "supported," as opposed to "supportive," role in development. The program was originally designed to terminate at the end of 1974 but was extended to 1978 with regular financial support. From 1973 to 1978 a total of NT$22.9 billion (including NT$13.6 billion of the Food Stabilization Fund) was committed to the program.

In 1973 and 1974, in the face of a world food shortage and a dwindling rice surplus in Taiwan, the government made self-sufficiency in rice a national policy. To increase rice production and improve farmers' income, it also adopted a rice price guarantee and established a food stabilization fund. This represented a sharp switch in policy. In principle, the floor-support price for rice provided for a 20 percent profit margin above production costs. Rice production reached a record 2.7 million metric tons in 1976. From 1974 to 1977 no limit was set on the quantity purchased from rice growers. Because of its heavy financial burdens, however, the government later limited its purchases to a maximum of 970 kilograms per hectare per crop. When rice prices were falling, the government also purchased it at a price a little above the market price.

The rice-support price program created problems in the long run. Per capita consumption fell from 140 kilograms per year in 1968 to 74 kilograms in 1988. As expected, rice stockpiling became a serious problem. In order to reduce production, farm extension workers encouraged farmers to shift rice fields to other crops, but no economic incentive was provided and the program failed. A six-year rice-crop substitution plan implemented in 1984 gave direct subsidies of 1 metric ton of paddy rice per hectare to farmers who shifted their rice fields to corn or sorghum, or 1.5 metric tons of paddy rice per hectare to farmers who shifted to crops other than corn and sorghum. In addition, corn and sorghum were to be purchased by the government at guaranteed prices. Under the program, rice production declined to 1.84 million metric tons in 1988, which was 0.9 million metric ton below the 1976 peak. The paid-in-kind subsidy was changed to a cash payment in 1988 to improve management of the program. Starting in 1989, rice purchased at the guaranteed price was increased to 1,400 kilograms per hectare, and the quantity purchased at higher-than-market prices was set at 1,000 kilograms per hectare. The purpose of the new policy was to increase the income of rice growers.

The new policy had some inconsistencies, however, as a result of which the Food Stabilization Fund lost NT$81 billion in the buying and selling of rice in the period from 1974 and 1989. For one thing, the guaranteed price encouraged overproduction even though the purpose of shifting from rice to other crops was to reduce rice production. For political considerations, however, the government was reluctant to make any immediate change. Policymakers are now giving some attention to a direct payment scheme linked to farmers' income and land use.

After the Accelerated Rural Development Program came to an end, the government launched two new programs: one to enhance farm income and strengthen rural reconstruction, and the other to develop basic infrastructure. The two were merged in 1982 in an effort to coordinate and integrate long-term rural development projects. A six-year program to adjust crop production by substituting higher-value crops for rice, enlarging farming operation, improving agricultural marketing, and strengthening agricultural research and extension was begun in 1985. From fiscal 1979 to 1989, a total of NT$125.7 billion (including NT$39.8 billion of the food stabilization fund) was spent on these programs. For an area the size of Taiwan, an investment of this size over an 11-year period was no small achievement. By 1988 Taiwan had 895,000 hectares of cultivated land, 739,000 farm families, and a farm population of 3,819,000. The average expenditure of public funds on the farm economy over this period was NT$140,447 per hectare of cultivated land, NT$170,095 per farm family, and NT$32,914 per farm person. Public spending in the agricultural sector is expected to grow as the economy expands. The challenge at present is how to make the best use of public resources to develop new technology, increase the scale of farming, and improve the efficiency of agricultural production.

Conclusions and Policy Implications

During the colonial period from 1921 to 1937, Taiwan made great strides in agricultural development as output expanded and resources flowed into the sector. In the period of recovery after World War II, agriculture experienced sustained growth but with significant structural changes. The second half of the 1960s can be considered the turning point of Taiwan's agricultural development.

Several institutions contributed to this rapid development, particularly the Sino-American Joint Commission on Rural Reconstruction. Its agents worked with the government and various organizations in identifying problems and developing policy recommendations, and in providing technical and financial assistance. By merging planning and implementation and striving for "integrated rural development," the JCRR helped generate a spirit of self-help among local agencies.

The land reforms of 1949–53 produced further changes. Immediately after the war, most Taiwanese farmers were tenants and received less than half of their crop harvests. Under the land reform program, rents were reduced, public lands were sold off, and land was given to the tillers. These measures redistributed assets, provided incentives for land improvement, raised the social status of farmers, released land capital for nonagricultural purposes, and helped create small and medium enterprises. In short, the land reform program supplied an indispensable social infrastructure for the successful development of the agricultural and industrial sectors. Last but not least, research institutes and associations in Taiwan introduced, developed, and diffused agricultural technologies. Farmers' and fishermen's associations also engaged in market promotion and provided financial services to their members. These associations helped implement government policies.

Greater economic stability in the 1950s facilitated agricultural and industrial development. The rampant inflation between 1946 and 1949 was gradually brought under control by introducing the new Taiwan dollar with full reserves in 1949, along with preferential interest savings deposits and tight government budgets. The timely arrival of U.S. economic aid provided much-needed financial support. In addition, several steps were taken to stabilize rice prices as a hedge against inflation. These prices in turn helped stabilize wages, production costs, and commodity prices. In order to keep the market stable and the rice stockpile at a safe level, the government collected rice by all means, including paddy land taxes in kind, the compulsory purchase of paddy rice from paddy landowners, rent on government-owned farmland, and the bartering of fertilizers for rice. The means used in collecting rice often did not reflect the market price and hence became a hidden tax on rice growers, which by 1963 was in excess of the total income tax.

From 1952 to 1972 Taiwan changed from a primarily agricultural to an industrialized economy. This was largely due to government policies of import substitution in the early 1950s and export promotion in the late 1950s and 1960s. At the beginning of this period, Taiwan had an inward-looking economy with a heavily protected domestic market. By the early 1970s, however, Taiwan had become heavily dependent on the world's economy. To promote exports, it relaxed industrial regulations, provided various tax incentives for exports and investment, and established export processing zones and bonded factories. As part of this strategy, the government provided an adequate supply of power, land for industry, and transportation facilities. Direct foreign investment was encouraged. The key to the success of the export scheme, however, was Taiwan's ability to make the best use of its abundant labor. Because of the labor-intensive nature of small and medium enterprises and their ability to make a quick response to external changes, they exported 56 percent of their total production in 1972. Foreign companies also engaged actively in export and created a significant number of jobs.

Agriculture contributed to Taiwan's industrialization and economic growth by providing labor, capital, agricultural goods, and a sizable market for nonfarm products. Higher industrial wages and nonfarm job opportunities led to outflows of farm labor. Moreover, farm taxes paid for the education of migrant farm laborers, which constituted a subsidy for the nonfarm economy.

Between 1931 and the outbreak of war, capital outflows from agriculture increased. They declined in 1950–60 but then picked up again in 1961–69. Changes in the terms of trade against agriculture accounted for more than half of the total net real capital outflow in the postwar period. This was a considerably higher share than before the war, when land-rent payment and government taxes accounted for the lion's share of the agricultural surplus transferred to nonagriculture. Government policies clearly have played an important role in determining the speed of flow and the means of transferring farm capital.

The relatively large and booming agricultural sector provided an important market for consumer goods, farm machinery and various intermediate inputs such as fertilizer and chemicals. Purchases of nonagricultural products by farmers accounted for about 55 percent of the total value of agricultural production, or about 90 percent of the total sales of agricultural products. This sizable and easily accessible market facilitated Taiwan's industrialization, especially in the 1950s but also in the 1960s.

Despite rapid industrialization from the 1950s through the 1970s, Taiwan's population was slow to pursue urbanization, in large part because of the balanced development of the agricultural and nonagricultural sectors and the pattern of industrial development. A prosperous agricultural sector can slow down outmigration of farm labor by providing a competitive wage. Good transportation, widely spread industrial sites, and relatively small-scale operations with low capital intensity all helped to keep farm labor employed in rural areas.

Almost every factor favorable to more balanced regional development also helped equalize income distribution. When family income from agriculture lagged, that from nonagriculture made up part of the loss and slowed the widening income gap between farm and nonfarm households. A significant increase in female labor in nonfarm jobs also benefited low-income farm families.

After the surplus labor became absorbed, however, agriculture began experiencing numerous difficulties. In 1965 the number of farm laborers started declining, and wages in rural areas then went up. As a result, farm labor developed an aging problem. Furthermore, the farm sector was unable to compete with nonfarm sectors for land. Meanwhile, the supply of fertile land was shrinking, and the land regulations originally designed to prevent land concentration stood in the way of more productive land use by increasing farm size. Farms thus became smaller, and the number of part-time farmers increased because farming income had become inadequate and abundant job opportunities were available elsewhere. In addition, rural areas have suffered environmental problems because of the pollution caused by both industry and farming. Finally, rising incomes have changed food consumption patterns, and thereby the structure of domestic farm production. At the same time, agricultural imports have provided strong competition for domestic products.

In order to cope with structural changes in agriculture, the government initiated a series of policies to alleviate the burden of taxes, reduce fertilizer prices, and eventually abolish the rice-fertilizer barter system. These policies promoted new investment in agricultural infrastructure and research and development. They also encouraged institutional arrangements for zoning and marketing. After the first oil crisis, a rice price support policy was adopted to encourage rice production for food self-sufficiency and to improve farmers' incomes. As expected, this policy caused an overproduction of rice and caused a heavy drain on the government's budget. The policy was modified to limit the amount of rice purchased and provided subsidies to encourage a shift from rice to other crops.

As this chapter has explained, Taiwan's successful economic development over the past four decades has been due to many factors, beginning with a strong and growing agricultural sector. It provided savings, foreign exchange, and labor for nonagricultural development and a large market for industrial products. Agriculture shared the heavy cost of import protection beneficial to industry. Resources supplied by agriculture enabled the industrial sector to expand quickly, and agricultural growth helped maintain a balanced development between agriculture and nonagriculture and among regions. This, in turn, led to a more equitable distribution of income.

The growth of the agricultural sector depended on investment both in "hardware" and in "software." Land reform in Taiwan in the early 1950s created a social infrastructure favorable for development. The JCRR and other civil organizations then played a decisive role in policymaking and implementation. The manner in which these institutions have functioned provides a valuable lesson for those seeking to integrate agricultural and industrial development. A stable price level also seems crucial for the effective reallocation and mobilization of resources. In the case of Taiwan, a stable price for rice helped maintain price stability in general. Without doubt, a properly designed taxation system can transfer agricultural resources to nonagriculture along with changes in the terms of trade between these sectors. Nonetheless, an expanding agricultural sector with continuous investment is essential for releasing its resources in the long term.

As far as industrialization is concerned, a limited role for public enterprises in selected areas, fewer regulations on entry, certain export promotion measures, and an open policy toward foreign investment can all contribute to a more efficient use of resources and an expansion of trade. The great problem in a small economy such as Taiwan's is that a growing industrial sector will quickly emerge as a strong competitor for resources and create pollution and farm income problems. It will take both academic wisdom and practical experience to resolve these problems.

References

Bruch, M., and U. Hiemenz. 1984. *Small- and Medium-scale Industries in the ASEAN Countries.* Boulder, Colo.: Westview Press.

Chang, Chung-han. 1980. *Taiwan's Industrialization during the Colonial Period.* Taipei: United Press.

Chen, H. Y., W. F. Hsu, and Y. K. Mao. 1975. "Rice Policies of Taiwan." *Food Research Institute Studies* 14 (4).

Chen, Y. E. 1986. *Agricultural Productivity of the Republic of China.* Taipei: Council of Agriculture.

Chen, Y. E., and Y. T. Wang. 1980. "Secular Trend of Output, Inputs, and Productivity—A Quantitative Analysis of Agricultural Development in Taiwan." In *Proceedings of the Conference on Agricultural Development in China, Japan, and Korea.* Taipei: Institute of Economics, Academia Sinica, Republic of China.

Chou, T. C. 1989. "Assisting the Development of Small and Medium Enterprises." Report of the conference on national development strategy on commerce and industry (Chinese). Taipei: Ministry of Economic Affairs.

Fei, John C. H., Shirley W. Y. Kuo, and Gustav Ranis. 1979. *Growth with Equity: The Taiwan Case.* England: Oxford University Press.

Galenson, Walter. 1979. "The Labor Force, Wages, and Living Standards." In *Economic Growth and Structural Change in Taiwan,* ed. Walter Galenson. Ithaca, N.Y.: Cornell University Press.

Gold, Thomas B. 1986. *State and Society in the Taiwan Miracle.* Armonk, N.Y.: M. E. Sharpe.

Ho, Samuel P. S. 1968. "Agricultural Transformation under Colonialism: The Case of Taiwan." *Journal of Economic History* (September).

———. 1978. *Economic Development of Taiwan, 1968–1970.* New Haven: Yale University Press.

Hsing, Mo-huan. 1970. "Taiwan Industrialization and Trade Policies." In *Taiwan and the Philippines, Industrialization, and Trade Policies,* ed. John H. Power, Geraldo P. Sacan, and Mo-huan Hsing. London: Oxford University Press.

Jacoby, Neil H. 1966. *U.S. Aid to Taiwan.* New York: Praeger.

Klein, L. R. 1986. "Introduction." In *Models of Development,* ed. L. J. Lau. San Francisco, Calif.: Institute for Contemporary Studies.

Kuo, Shirley W. Y. 1975. "Effects of Land Reform, Agricultural Pricing Policy, and Economic Growth on Multiple Crop Diversification in Taiwan." *Philippine Economic Journal* 14 (1 and 2).

Kuo, Shirley W. Y., Gustav Ranis, and John C. H. Fei. 1985. "Causes and Roles of Export Expansion in the Republic of China." In *Foreign Trade and Investment: Economic Development in the Newly Industrializing Countries,* ed. Walter Galenson. Madison: University of Wisconsin Press.

Lee, T. H. 1971a. *Intersectoral Capital Flows in the Economic Development of Taiwan, 1895–1960.* Ithaca, N.Y.: Cornell University Press.

———. 1971b. "Strategies for Transferring Agricultural Surplus under Agricultural Situations in Taiwan." Report of the Sino-American Joint Commission on Rural Reconstruction (July).

———. 1972. "Wage Differential, Labor Mobility, and Employment in Taiwan's Agriculture." Proceedings of the Sino-American conference on manpower in Taiwan.

——— 1974. "Agricultural Contributions to Economic Growth in Taiwan." JCRR Report.

Lee, T. H., and Y. E. Chen. 1975. "Growth Rates of Taiwan Agriculture, 1911–1972." JCRR Economic Digest Series No. 21 (January).

Lee, T. H., and Kuo-shu Liang. 1982. "Development Strategies in Taiwan." In *Development Strategies in Semi-industrial Economics,* ed. B. Balassa et al. Baltimore, Md.: Johns Hopkins University Press.

———. 1973. "Process and Pattern of Economic Development." *Economic Essays* 4.

———. 1974. "Process and Pattern of Economic Development." In *The Development of East and Southeast Asia,* ed. Shinichi Ichimura. Honolulu: University Press of Hawaii, pp. 296–299.

Lee, T. H., K. S. Liang, C. Schive, Ryh-song Yeh. 1975. "The Structure of Effective Protection and Subsidy in Taiwan." *Economic Essays* 6 (November).

Li, K. T. 1976. *The Experience of Dynamic Economic Growth on Taiwan.* Taipei: Mei Ya Publications.

Liang, Kuo-shu, and Ching-ing Hou Liang. 1988. "Development Policy Formation and Future Policy Priorities in the Republic of China." *Economic Development and Cultural Change* 36 (April).

Lin, Ching-yuan. 1973. *Industrialization in Taiwan, 1946–1972*. New York: Praeger.

Mao, Y. K. 1984. "Agricultural Development Policy and Performance in Taiwan, R.O.C." In *Industry of Free China* (November).

———. 1985. "Agricultural Development Policy and Performance in Taiwan, R.O.C." In *Industry of Free China* (January).

———. 1987. "Current Land Problems and Policies of Taiwan, The Republic of China." *Industry of Free China* (June).

———. 1987. "Role of Agriculture in the Economic Development in Taiwan, R.O.C." Proceedings of Economic Development in the Republic of China on Taiwan.

———. 1988. "Analysis of Changes in the Type of Farm Households under Rapid Economic Growth in Taiwan, R.O.C." Proceedings of the conference on directions and strategies of agricultural development in the Asia-Pacific Region. Taiwan: The Institute of Economics, Academic Sinica.

Mellor, John W. 1966. *The Economics of Agricultural Development*. Ithaca: Cornell University Press.

Myers, Ramon H. 1986. "The Economic Development of the Republic of China on Taiwan, 1965–1981." In *Models of Development*, ed. Lawrence J. Lau. San Francisco: Institute for Contemporary Studies.

Ong, Shao-Er. 1984. "Development of the Small Farm Economy in Taiwan, A Program of World Significance." Taiwan: The Council of Agriculture, Executive Yuan.

Rada, E. L., and T. H. Lee. 1963. "Irrigation Investment in Taiwan." Economic Digest Series No. 15. JCRR (February).

Ranis, Gustav. 1979. "Industrial Development." In *Economic Growth and Structural Change in Taiwan*, ed. Walter Galenson. Ithaca, N.Y.: Cornell University Press.

Ranis, Gustav, and Chi Schive. 1985. "Direct Foreign Investment in Taiwan's Development." In *Foreign Trade and Investment: Economic Development in the Newly Industrializing Countries*, ed. Walter Galenson. Madison: University of Wisconsin Press.

Schive, Chi. 1987. "Trade Patterns and Trends of Taiwan." In *Trade and Structural Change in Pacific Asia*, ed. Colin I. Bradford and William H. Branson. Chicago, Ill.: University of Chicago Press.

———. 1990a. "Linkage: Do Foreign Firms Buy Locally?" *Asian Economic Journal* 4 (March).

———. 1990b. *The Foreign Factor: The Multinational Corporation's Contribution to the Economic Modernization of the Republic of China*. Stanford, Calif.: Hoover Press.

———. 1990c. "The Next Stage of Industrialization in Taiwan and Korea." In *Development Strategy between Latin America and East Asia*, ed. D. K. Wyman and G. Gereffi. Princeton, N.J.: Princeton University Press.

Schive, Chi, and Badiul Majumdar. 1990. "A Direct Foreign Investment and Linkage Effects: The Experience of Taiwan." *Canadian Journal of Development Studies* 11 (2).

Schive, Chi, and Cheng-hwa Tu. 1991. "Foreign Firms and Structural Changes in

Taiwan." In *Direct Foreign Investment in Developing Economics and Structural Change in the Asia-Pacific Region,* ed. Seiji Naya and Eric D. Ramstetter. Boulder: Westview Press.

Schultz, T. W. 1964. *Transforming Traditional Agriculture.* New Haven, Conn.: Yale University Press.

Scitovsky, Tibor. 1986. "Economic Development in Taiwan and South Korea, 1965–1981." In *Models of Development,* ed. Lawrence J. Lau. San Francisco, Calif.: Institute for Contemporary Studies.

Scott, Maurice. 1979. "Foreign Trade." In *Economic Growth and Structural Change in Taiwan,* ed. Walter Galenson. Ithaca: Cornell University Press.

Shei, S. Y. 1988. "Agricultural Foundation for Industrial Development." Proceedings of the conference on economic development experiences of Taiwan and its new role in an emerging Asia-Pacific area. Taiwan: The Institute of Economics, Academia Sinica.

Shen, T. H., ed. 1974. *Agriculture's Place in the Strategy of Development: The Taiwan Experience.* JCRR (July).

Taiwan, Council of Agriculture. 1989a. *Agricultural Production Statistics Abstract, Taiwan District, the Republic of China.* Taipei.

———. 1989b. *Taiwan Statistical Data Book.* Taipei: Council for Economic Planning and Development, Executive Yuan.

Thorbecke, Erik. 1979. "Agricultural Development." In *Economic Growth and Structural Change in Taiwan,* ed. Walter Galenson. Ithaca, N.Y.: Cornell University Press.

Wang, Y. T., and H. H. Chen. 1981. "Strategies of Technological Progress in Taiwan's Agricultural Development." Proceedings of the conference on experiences and lessons of economic development in Taiwan. Taiwan: The Institute of Economics, Academia Sinica.

Wu, R. I., and C. F. Wanglian. 1988. "Economic Evaluation of Rice Policy in Taiwan." Proceedings of the conference on directions and strategies of agricultural development in the Asia-Pacific region. Taiwan: The Institute of Economics, Academic Sinica.

Wu, T. C. 1988. "Directions and Strategies of Agricultural Development in Taiwan." Proceedings of the conference on directions and strategies of agricultural development in the Asia-Pacific region. Taiwan: The Institute of Economics, Academic Sinica.

Yin, K. Y. 1954. "A Discussion on Industrial Policy for Taiwan." *Industry of Free China* 1 (5).

Yu, Y. H. 1978. "The Accelerated Rural Development Program in Taiwan." Agricultural Economic Research Papers, Economic Digest Series No. 23. Taiwan: JCRR, October.

3 Agricultural Growth and Industrial Development in Punjab

G. S. BHALLA

Punjab has achieved remarkable growth since independence and is now the richest state of India. This growth and prosperity are primarily the result of Punjab's adoption of new technology in agriculture. Its cultivators were the first to adopt the Borlaug seed-fertilizer technology during the mid-1960s, and within a few years the state became the symbol of a green revolution in India.

From 1960/61 to 1987/88, the net state domestic product (NSDP) grew at 5.3 percent per year, compared with 4.3 percent for the country as a whole. Over this period, per capita income rose by 3 percent annually compared with 1.97 percent for India (India CSO, various years). Income from crop production grew at an annual rate of 3.6 percent and that from animal husbandry at a remarkably high rate of 7.3 percent (table 3.1). Punjab has also experienced labor force diversification. According to the forty-third round of the National Sample Survey (NSS), the share of Punjab's labor force in agriculture declined from nearly 60 percent in 1977/78 to 50 percent in 1987/88 (India 1990a). Unlike the rest of India, where the average per worker income in agriculture during 1987/88 was only 35 percent of the average income in the non-agricultural sector, Punjab recorded much the same per worker income in both the sectors, because of much higher productivity growth in its agricultural sector.

The rapid growth of agriculture has had a large impact on the entire economy, especially the agroindustries that supply both current and capital inputs and that process agricultural produce. The emergence of large market surpluses in agriculture stimulated an unprecedented increase in trade and transport. And the rapid increase in the per capita incomes of the rural and urban population widened the market for consumption goods and services. In short, by raising the income of a large proportion of rural workers, rapid agricultural growth not only made a deep dent in rural poverty but also led to development of other sectors.

Over the years, agricultural price policy helped Punjab farmers sustain and further develop new technology. The Agricultural Prices Commission (re-

67

TABLE 3.1 Net domestic product at factor cost, by industry of origin and growth rates in Punjab and India, 1967/68, 1980/81, and 1987/88

Industry	Punjab at 1970/71 Prices (millions of rupees)			Growth Rates[a] (1967–68 to 1987–88)	
	1967/68	1980/81	1987/88	Punjab	India
Agriculture	6,432	8,235	12,755	3.6	—
Livestock	1,233	2,976	4,746	7.3	—
Agriculture and livestock	7,665	11,180	17,501	4.5	2.8
Forestry	29	57	53	4.8	−1.1
Fishery	5	8	18	7.9	3.6
Mining and quarrying	1	3	8	21.2	4.8
Primary	7,700	11,248	17,580	4.5	2.8
Manufacturing	914	2,618	3,592	7.6	5.2
Registered	456	1,272	1,911	8.0	6.0
Unregistered	458	1,345	1,682	7.3	3.9
Construction	835	1,133	1,222	2.3	2.7
Electricity	103	285	583	10.4	8.5
Secondary	1,852	4,035	5,397	5.9	4.7
Transport and storage	377	992	1,424	7.3	6.5
Trade and hotels	1,505	3,803	5,337	7.0	5.1
Banking and insurance	172	548	992	10.1	9.5
Real estate and dwellings	225	321	413	3.4	4.4
Public administration	239	806	1,538	10.7	9.6
Other services	617	1,107	1,239	3.8	3.4
Tertiary	3,136	7,576	10,943	6.8	6.1
Net state domestic product	12,687	22,859	33,920	5.3	4.3
Per capita SDP (rupees)	1,002	1,374	1,755	3.0	1.9

SOURCES: For Punjab, *Statistical Abstract of Punjab*, various issues; Chandigarh Economic and Statistical Adviser. For India, Ministry of Planning, *National Accounts Statistics*, various years.
[a]Growth rate is the average of annual variations, 1960/61 to 1987/88.

named the Commission for Agricultural Costs and Prices in 1986) and the Food Corporation of India created in 1966 played crucial roles in augmenting agricultural output by ensuring highly remunerative prices to farmers, which encouraged large investments in tubewells, pumpsets, and other farm assets.

During the postindependence period, farmers in Punjab also were helped by a large inflow of resources from the national government for both rehabilitation and infrastructural investment. India assigned the public sector a crucial role in the development of rural and urban infrastructure. This enabled Punjab to make substantial investments in infrastructure, primarily in irrigation, power, roads, and communications. These investments were financed by large central plan transfers and the internal resources of the state. With a well-developed infrastructure, Punjab was able to adapt the Mexican seed-fertilizer technology to local conditions, whereupon it spread rapidly and was successfully exploited by Punjab farmers. Furthermore, administered prices for most crops ensured the profitability of the new technology, which encouraged farmers to invest heavily in their operations.

Punjab also benefited from specialization and comparative advantage in the context of a constrained open economy. Demand and supply constraints did not operate with the same rigor as would have been the case in a small closed economy. The state received large grants from the center. Since the state generated large surpluses in agricultural production, these were increasingly invested in the rest of India. Note, too, that many agricultural laborers continue to migrate to Punjab from Bihar and other less developed states.

The growth rate in the secondary and tertiary sectors in Punjab, although creditable, seems rather slow compared with that of Taiwan and other economies of Southeastern Asia. Why has this happened? Why has the state not been able to translate the agricultural growth into rapid growth of the entire economy?

There are several possible reasons: an inappropriate macroeconomic policy framework; an inadequate resource base, particularly in basic raw materials; a large outflow of funds; and insufficient investment in domestic industry. The dearth of domestic investment may be due to several factors. For one thing, entrepreneurs may have been reluctant to invest in a border state. For another, trained and skilled labor was not available and few people had the necessary entrepreneurial skills. In addition, the recent disturbances and instability caused by terrorism might have caused the flight of capital. Finally, increased demand for both inputs and consumption could easily be satisfied from outside the state.

Development of Agriculture Before Independence

Agriculture before independence was greatly affected by the physical features of the land, land utilization patterns, the country's cultural unity, and the colonial regime.

Physical Features and Land Utilization Patterns

The state of Punjab is composed of a submontane strip, alluvial plains, and an arid southwestern region. The submontane strip in the foothills of the Shivalik range covers nearly one-fifth of the total area of the state and is inhabited by one-fifth of its population. Average rainfall is 87.2 centimeters. Because tubewells are difficult to dig in mountainous areas, only about 60 percent of the cropped area is irrigated in this part, compared with more than 90 percent for the state as a whole.

The central plains, which cover 55 percent of the total area and are home to 55 percent of the population, are composed of new and old alluvium. More than 90 percent of the gross cultivated area is irrigated from three perennial rivers, numerous canals, and a large number of tubewells. The average rainfall in this area is 57.4 centimeters. Agriculture in the plains is more developed than in other parts of the state.

The southwestern region of Punjab is sandy, although there is some flood-plain (*bet*) area along the river. Underground water is unfit for irrigation in most parts. More than 85 percent of the area is irrigated, mostly from canals. The rainfall averages only 26.7 centimeters per year.

Wheat, rice, and sugarcane are extensively grown in the submontane strip and the central plains. Wheat and cotton are the main crops in the southwestern region. Land is intensively used in Punjab. Nearly 83 percent of the total area was cultivated during 1987/88, and there is no permanent fallow. Forests constituted a mere 4 percent of the area.

The net sown area increased rapidly during the 1950s and the 1960s but has stagnated in recent years. However, the gross cropped area increased at an annual rate of 1.64 percent between 1960/61 and 1987/88 because of an increase in cropping intensity.

The People

Until recently, Punjab enjoyed a great deal of cultural unity despite the diversity of its physical conditions, religion, customs, living habits, dialects, and racial characteristics. This unity was the product of living conditions, the predominance of agriculture, and the traditions of village life. Unfortunately, the rise of religious fundamentalism in recent years has placed cultural unity under severe strain.

Like the rest of India, Punjab is a land of villages. Even after 40 years of independence, only about 30 percent of the population lives in urban areas, and the rest still live in 12,000 or so villages. Population density in Punjab in 1991 was 401 per square kilometer, far above the national average of 267.

Agricultural Growth during the Colonial Period

Punjab was the last province to be annexed by the British, who took over in 1849. At that time, the major sources of water for agriculture were rainfall and many wells, which provided fresh underground water.

Production technology in Punjab agriculture began to change in the late nineteenth and early twentieth centuries when the British made large investments in canal irrigation in the state. Capital outlay on productive irrigation canals in Punjab was 40 percent of the total made by the British government in India up to 1919/20. Consequently, the share of irrigated acreage in Punjab was 50 percent of the total for agricultural acreage (Hirashima 1978, 22–35).

Attempts were also made to improve agricultural husbandry. The government established agricultural colleges and encouraged the production of new crop seeds and leguminous fodder.

With the coming of the canals in the first half of the twentieth century, the production of cereals and commercial crops started increasing. The output of wheat increased from 0.87 million tons in 1904/5 to 1.17 million tons in 1944/45, maize from 0.28 to 0.33 million tons, cotton from 70,000 bales to 196,000 bales and sugarcane from 124,000 tons to 279,000 (India, Ministry of Agriculture, 1976).

. Despite the increases, the balance between Punjab's food supply and demand continued to be precarious during the first half of the twentieth century. The surplus, if any, was confined to commercial crops like cotton and sugarcane. While the Punjab population grew—from 7.55 million in 1901 to 9.60 million in 1941, a compound growth rate of 0.60 percent per year—agricultural production in the state increased by only about 0.70 percent per year from 1904/5 to 1944/45.

In spite of a huge investment in canal irrigation, institutional barriers inhibited the performance of agriculture in Punjab during the colonial period. The widespread prevalence of tenancy severely constrained agricultural growth. The control of credit by moneylenders also limited the ability of the peasantry to invest for modernization. Consequently, the full potential of irrigation technology could not be tapped.

Rural Institutional Structure

During the Mughal and Sikh periods, Punjab inherited the Mahalwari system of land settlement which conferred land rights on the cultivating class in the village community. After the British annexed Punjab on March 30, 1849, the system changed somewhat.

Changes in Land Relations: Preindependence Period

In 1887 the British passed the Land Revenue Act, which retained most of the rights conferred under the earlier Mahalwari settlement system. These rights benefited a large proportion of the peasantry. Since land could now be freely bought or sold, however, the rights also paved the way for moneylenders to acquire the land of cultivators who defaulted on their loans. The number in default rose to such a level that in 1901 the British government had to enact legislation on land alienation pertaining to noncultivating castes (Punjab 1901). Nevertheless, until the late 1930s, many Punjab peasants became heavily indebted during periods of both prosperity and depression and gradually lost their only asset, land, through alienation or mortgage (Darling 1925).

Belatedly, the British passed acts to provide some legal security to the cultivators. For example, The Restitution of Mortgage Land Act of 1938 passed under the stewardship of Sir Chottu Ram returned mortgaged land to the cultivators during 1939. Despite these legislative attempts, land relations in Punjab remained fairly archaic.[1] There were a large number of absentee landlords, and tenancy was widespread in British Punjab, and even more so in the princely states. Furthermore, the big landlords had complete control of economic and political life in most of rural Punjab. It was one of the few provinces in India that had a noncongress Zamindara (Landlord) League government during the late 1930s. The predominance of landlords, a high incidence of tenancy, and inadequate investment in rural infrastructure limited agricultural growth during the colonial period.

Change in Land Relations: Postindependence Period

The independence of India brought a new momentum to land reforms. The Congress party was committed to radical changes, and several important reforms were enacted during the 1950s and the 1960s.[2] The main objectives of this legislation were to abolish intermediates (those standing between the land operator and the land), safeguard the security of land tenure, impose land ceilings, and consolidate holdings.

Only part of this legislation was implemented. The most significant achievement was the abolition of intermediaries in large parts of Punjab, particularly in the Patiala and East Punjab States Union (PEPSU), where the peasant movement was strong. However, many big landlords were able to keep their landed property intact by self-cultivation tactics. Thousands of tenants were dispossessed under the guise of "voluntary surrenders."

The rural vested interests were also able to evade the reforms involving ceilings and security of tenure. The ceiling legislation had serious loopholes. For example, the ceiling was fixed at 30 standard acres and applied to individual landowners instead of families. Large exemptions were allowed for orchards and specialized dairy, poultry, and sugarcane farms. Consequently, only 174,122 standard acres could be declared surplus and available for distribution during the mid-1950s. Another adverse consequence was the large-scale evictions of tenants. The Land Reforms Act of 1972 reduced the ceiling to 7 hectares for a family of five for lands irrigated for at least 2 crops in a year. The

1. Some of the important legislation on debt relief that was passed included the Punjab Alienation Act, 1901; the Punjab Preemption Act, 1913; the Redemption of Mortgages Act, 1915; the Usurious Loans Act, 1918; the Relief of Indebtedness Act, 1934; Debt Protection Act, 1936; the Restitution of Mortgages Lands Act, 1938; and the Registration of Money Lender's Act, 1939.

2. Among the main acts passed by the Punjab Legislative Assembly, those pertaining to the abolition of intermediaries were the Punjab and PEPSU Occupancy Tenants (Vesting of Proprietary Rights) Act, 1953; and the Punjab and PEPSU Abolition of Ala Malkiyat and Talukdari Rights Act, 1952 and 1954. Those that covered the security of tenure were the Punjab Security of Tenure Act, 1953; and the PEPSU Tenancy and Agricultural Lands Act 1955. Those that covered land ceilings were the Punjab Land Ceilings Act, 1955; and the Punjab Land Reforms Act, 1972. And those pertaining to the consolidation of holdings were the East Punjab Holdings (Consolidation and Prevention of Fragmentation) Act, 1948; and the Utilization of Land Act, 1950.

ceiling limits were graduated upward for poorer-quality land. Since the owned area had already been subdivided, this act also provided little surplus land for distribution.

The acts relating to the security of tenure and regulation of rent also met with the same fate. In the early 1950s, the landlords began fearing that the lands they owned that were being cultivated by tenants might be lost, and they ejected many tenants on the plea of "self-cultivation." In any case, the tenancy legislation failed to provide full security to tenants but instead tended to drive tenancy underground. Nor was the legislation able to regulate rents, which were being determined more by market force rather than by legislation.

The institutional structure that has emerged in the state both as a result of the implementation of land reforms and the nature of agricultural development has several distinctive features, as explained in the next section.

Distribution of Ownership and Operational Holdings

As a consequence of the unsatisfactory implementation of land-ceiling acts, the distribution of owned and operational holdings has continued to be highly unequal. Furthermore, because of demographic pressures and the lack of occupational diversification, the extent of marginalization has increased sharply over time, and there has been a marked increase in the concentration of both ownership and operational holdings in the lowest two categories. In 1953/54, 51 percent of cultivating households owned less than 5 acres of land and accounted for only 9 percent of the total owned area. By 1982, the proportion of those owning less than 5 acres had swelled to 75 percent, and they accounted for 16 percent of total owned area. At the other extreme, in 1953/54, only 11 percent of households owning more than 20 acres accounted for 47 percent of the total area. By 1982, their proportion had dropped to 4 percent, and they had claim on 28 percent of the owned area. The distribution of operational holdings, though less unequal, also continues to be highly skewed (table 3.2).

In another development, the proportion of farmers cultivating 10 to 20 acres has increased both with regard to land owned and land operated. At the same time, the proportion of area held by big farmers owning and operating more than 20 acres has dropped by about 40 percent. An important feature of the agrarian structure is the preeminent position of middle- and upper-middle peasantry who own and operate 5 to 20 acres of land. They constitute nearly one-fourth to one-third of the owning/operating households and now have two-thirds of the total land area. Their prosperity in the wake of the green revolution has had a far-reaching impact on the political economy of the state (India NSSO, 1975, 1986).

The inequalities in land distribution implies that income is bound to be distributed in an uneven manner. Furthermore, the gains in income through the adoption of new technology also are going to be inequitably shared among the peasantry.

TABLE 3.2 Changes in the percentage distribution of ownership and operational holdings in Punjab, 1953/54 to 1982

Farm Size	Proportion of Holdings (%)		Proportion of Area (%)	
	1953/54	1982	1953/54	1982
Ownership holdings (acres)				
<2.49ᵃ	36.01	64.62	3.28	5.59
2.50–4.99	14.71	10.78	6.23	10.76
5.00–9.99	21.59	12.42	17.29	22.87
10.00–19.99	16.57	8.96	26.00	32.43
20.00–29.99	6.40	2.23	17.21	13.97
>30.00	4.72	0.99	29.99	14.39
All sizes	100.00	100.00	100.00	100.00
Operational holdings (acres)				
<2.49	20.78	57.03	1.64	3.91
2.50–4.99	14.30	10.89	4.72	8.92
5.00–9.99	23.63	14.65	15.28	21.76
10.00–19.00	25.22	12.89	30.53	36.71
20.00–29.99	8.54	3.01	17.76	15.27
>30.00	7.53	1.54	30.07	13.45
All sizes	100.00	100.00	100.00	100.00

SOURCES: For 1953/54, India, Cabinet Secretariat (1955); for 1982, India, Cabinet Secretariat (1983).
NOTE: Figures for 1953/54 and 1961/62 relate to erstwhile Punjab.
ᵃ0.00-acre class has been ignored.

Changes in the Incidence of Tenancy

Of all the states in India, Punjab had, until recently, the highest incidence of tenancy. The percentage of pure and mixed tenant households decreased from a high of 53 percent in 1953/54 to 43 percent in the early 1970s but then fell to 25 percent in 1982. The total area leased by tenant households declined from 40 percent in 1953/54 to 19 percent by 1982. Tenant households and the share of area leased by them have declined in all size classes (India, NSSO, 1986).

Tenancy is also becoming commercialized. An overwhelming majority of very small farms (less than 1 acre) and large ones (between 20 and 50 acres) lease in on a fixed rent basis. Those between 2.5 and 8.0 acres lease in primarily on a crop-sharing basis. For farms of 8 to 20 acres, leasing-in is almost equally divided between fixed-rent and crop-sharing practices (India, NSSO, 1986).

Small cultivators operating on 5.0 acres or less account for only 13.0 percent of the total area leased. In contrast, nearly one-fifth is being leased in by cultivators operating on 25 acres or more. The small farmers who augment their holding through leasing in do so to optimize the use of surplus family labor, but large farmers with tractors lease in to make more optimum use of their capital assets. According to one research study, the extent of such leasing is quite high in the southern part of the state, where the holdings and numbers of tractors are relatively large. The production efficiency of the area leased by large farms was found to be as good as that of the area owned (Singh 1985). The land and credit markets in Punjab are linked, although much less than in Bihar. Nearly 14 percent of the tenants in Punjab reportedly borrow money from their landlords, in comparison with 30 percent in Bihar (Bell and Srinivasan 1989).

A recent study suggests that production efficiency is no lower on fixed-rent leased areas than on self-cultivated areas but is significantly lower on crop-sharing leased areas (Chadha 1979; Singh 1985).

Land reforms combined with rapid technological innovations have brought about important changes in the rural institutional structure in Punjab, as in many other states. For example, self-cultivation has become the dominant mode of production in Punjab, but because of the failure of land-ceiling acts, big and middle farmers work most of the land. They led the way in adopting new technologies and were the main beneficiaries of the green revolution. Consequently, their economic and political clout has increased tremendously. They are now able to resist any attempts to mobilize the surplus through increases in rural taxation or in the supply prices of highly subsidized inputs such as power, fertilizers, irrigation, and credit. In addition, they are able to exert immense pressure to get higher procurement prices for major crops.

Successive governments have found it politically expedient to respond positively to these pressures. Thus, the power of big and middle farmers is gradually becoming a barrier to accelerated capital formation, both inside and outside agriculture. Even so, increased demand has enabled agricultural laborers to obtain higher wages and remove the age-old shackles of Jajmani (the traditional system). Their emergence as free labor has increased their political consciousness and enabled them to bargain for higher wages and assert their right to human dignity. Consequently, a sharp division now exists between agricultural laborers as employees and cultivators as employers.

The rich farmers use various methods to resist the demands of agricultural laborers for higher wages. These include coercion, efforts to attract cheaper labor from poorer states like Bihar, and mechanization. As a result, real wage rates in Punjab are going through a period of very slow growth, if not stagnation, and the elasticity of employment with respect to output is also declining (Bhalla 1987; Jose 1988; Bhalla and Tyagi 1989, 41).

To sum up, archaic land relations created a barrier to rapid agricultural growth during the colonial period. Land reforms in the postindependence period abolished intermediaries and absentee landlords and thereby helped remove this barrier. The ceilings on landholding failed to eliminate large inequalities in land distribution, however, and thus led to an unequal sharing of the benefits of new agricultural technologies.

Growth and Productivity of Punjab Agriculture Since Independence

West Bengal in the east and the present Punjab bore the brunt of the partition of India in 1947. Large-scale riots and the migration of millions of refugees precipitated a serious economic crisis. Despite this shattering experience, the state was able to rehabilitate its economy in a few years. Thanks to large investments in infrastructure, its agricultural economy started on a steep growth path.

According to the available data for Punjab of that period (now Punjab and Haryana), agricultural output grew at the rate of 4.6 percent per year between 1952/53 and 1964/65 (India, Ministry of Food and Agriculture, 1968). Area increased at the rate of 1.9 percent, and yield at 2.6 percent (table 3.3). After the adoption of new seed-fertilizer technology in the mid-1960s, yield increased more rapidly than output. The first notable change came in wheat yield. This was followed by a large increase in the yield and output of summer rice in the 1970s. Consequently, wheat and rice became the state's leading crops, accounting for nearly 60 percent of gross cropped area. In contrast, the area under gram declined sharply and that under oilseeds also recorded a moderate decline. The unprecedented growth in area and output of wheat and rice reflected technological, price, and profitability advantages.

Another important development was the dramatic rise in income from animal husbandry. Between 1960/61 and 1987/88 income grew 7.3 percent per year, and livestock generated nearly 27 percent of the income in the primary sector compared with only 14 percent in 1960/61 (table 3.1). This rapid growth was due to a technological breakthrough in fodder production, the import and development of pure and hybrid cows that could produce high yields of milk, a decline in the demand for draft animals as a result of rapid mechanization and, most important, a big increase in the demand for milk and milk products because of the higher per capita income of agricultural households.

The Nature of Production Technology

Irrigation was the key to the unprecedented increases in wheat and rice yields and output. Large investments in canal irrigation during the colonial period had given Punjab an initial advantage in adopting the new seed-fertilizer technology. Subsequent investments in tubewells and pumpsets not only vastly increased the irrigated area but also helped improve it structurally. From 1950/51 to 1989/90 the net area irrigated by government canals declined from 59 to 40 percent, but that irrigated by tubewells increased from 36 to about 60 percent (Punjab, Economic and Statistical Adviser, various years).

The replacement of traditional seed by high-yielding varieties was made

Table 3.3 Area, output, and yield of principal crops, 1950/51 to 1987/88, and their growth rates

Crop	1950/51	1960/61	1964/65	1967/68	1984/85	1987/88	Growth Rates (%)	
							1952/53 to 1964/65	1967/68 to 1987/88
Rice								
Area	120	227	287	314	1,644	1,720	6.82	10.15
Output	107	229	351	415	5,054	5,442	6.68	15.56
Yield	892	1,009	1,223	1,322	3,074	3,164	1.74	4.91
Wheat								
Area	1,137	1,400	1,563	1,790	3,094	3,131	3.34	2.54
Output	1,024	1,742	2,360	3,335	10,176	11,084	5.38	4.91
Yield	901	1,244	1,510	1,863	3,289	3,540	1.98	2.67
Gram								
Area	851	838	744	530	102	66	1.11	−8.02
Output	511	681	666	452	60	29	1.11	−10.17
Yield	600	813	895	853	588	439	—	−2.34
Oilseeds								
Area	128	185	239	399	198	224	3.27	−3.66
Output	55	121	222	314	199	210	6.13	−3.02
Yield	430	654	929	987	1,004	938	4.68	0.67
Sugarcane								
Area	91	133	122	137	79	106	4.61	−2.48
Output	257	486	444	480	492	582	6.72	0.34
Yield	2,824	3,654	3,639	3,507	6,226	5,491	2.01	2.89

(*continued*)

TABLE 3.3 (*continued*)

Crop	1950/51	1960/61	1964/65	1967/68	1984/85	1987/88	Growth Rates (%)	
							1952/53 to 1964/65	1967/68 to 1987/88
Cotton								
Area	255	447	487	419	472	621	4.68	2.17
Output	43	121	136	132	210	316	7.06	2.86
Yield	191	271	279	315	445	509	2.28	0.65
Gross crops area	4,224	4,723	5,113	5,441	7,013	7,172	1.90	1.84
Agricultural index[a]								
Output	44.63	77.65	77.56[b]	97.41	219.33	244.34	4.56	4.90
Yield	47.89	73.75	74.49[b]	94.30	169.59	178.17	2.61	3.14

SOURCES: Ministry of Food and Agriculture (1968), 203, for growth rates for the period 1952/53 to 1964/65. For the period 1967/68 to 1987/88, statistical function of the type $Y = AB^t$ was fitted to time series of yearly data, drawn from the *Statistical Abstract of Punjab* (various years).

NOTE: Area is in thousand hectares; output in thousand metric tons; and yield in kilograms per hectare.

[a]Base: triennium ending 1969/70 = 100.

[b]Relates to year 1965/66.

possible by the research of agricultural scientists who adapted the Mexican and International Rice Research Institute (IRRI) varieties of wheat and rice to local conditions. By the end of 1970s, almost all of the cultivated area under wheat and paddy was planted with high-yielding varieties.

The rapid expansion of fertilizer application after 1965/66 was another important component of the new technology. Fertilizer use per hectare of cropped area increased from a mere 19 kilograms in 1965/66 to 51 kilograms in 1970/71 and 155 kilograms in 1989/90. Wheat and rice seemed to be the predominant users of fertilizers. There were also large increases in the use of other modern inputs such as insecticides, diesel oil, and electricity, whereas the use of traditional inputs such as organic manure and bullock feed declined steeply, especially after the mid-1960s. Consequently, the relative share of purchased inputs increased from about 30 percent in 1960/61 to more than 87.0 percent in 1980 (Bhalla et al. 1990).

Among the other technological changes in Punjab agriculture was an increase in mechanization, accompanied by changes in factor proportions. The number of tractors increased more than twentyfold between 1966 and 1987, and the average net area sown per tractor declined from 356 hectares in 1966 to only 19 hectares in 1987. Similarly, the number of tubewells increased fifteenfold between 1966 to 1987. There was a tubewell for every 83 hectares of net area sown in 1966, and one for every 6 hectares in 1987.

As the importance of bullocks declined, threshing became almost completely mechanized. Notable inroads were made by harvester combines. As a result, the capital structure in Punjab agriculture changed significantly. It is no wonder that Punjab's share in the national distribution of capital and other modern production assets is now disproportionately high.

Several factors were responsible for this rapid mechanization. To begin with, the highly profitable new technology in wheat and rice could not be adopted without irrigation, which accounts for the spurt in tubewell installation. But the drive toward mechanization was caused mainly by the relative scarcity of labor and a sharp rise in wages, particularly during peak agricultural operations. Tractors were increasingly used for plowing and transport and soon became a status symbol that led many small and medium farmers to purchase one, although the investment was not economically justified. Large-scale investment in tubewells, tractors, and other farm mechanization was facilitated by the ready availability of cheap institutional credit and large remittances from outside.

Agricultural Modernization and the Growth of Factor Productivities

With rapid modernization and changes in factor proportions, significant changes took place in the shares of various factor incomes in value added during the process of agricultural production. These changes are evident from data on the cost of cultivation for wheat, paddy, and cotton (India, ESA, various years).

With the technological breakthrough in wheat and rice, the output per

TABLE 3.4 Capital, employment, output, and value added in unregistered sector in Punjab and India, 1984/1985

		Punjab				India			
Code	Industry Name	Fixed Assets (Rs lakhs)	Employees (numbers)	Output (Rs lakhs)	Value Added (Rs lakhs)	Fixed Assets (Rs lakhs)	Employees (numbers)	Output (Rs lakhs)	Value Added (Rs lakhs)
20–21	Food products	43,395 (80)	78,312 (61)	18,777 (14)	6,534 (32)	624,206 (75)	6,560,714 (86)	793,810 (36)	220,541 (54)
22	Beverages, tobacco, and products	266 (18)	4,854 (53)	1,768 (18)	488 (20)	51,488 (70)	2,448,857 (87)	85,485 (30)	46,414 (48)
23	Cotton textiles	14,231 (79)	37,121 (68)	1,548 (7)	714 (20)	309,151 (60)	6,279,415 (87)	259,848 (27)	120,468 (43)
24	Wool, silk, and synthetic fiber textiles	665 (5)	11,192 (22)	3,045 (7)	820 (8)	28,756 (19)	843,644 (75)	91,712 (20)	33,778 (28)
						1,181 (6)	139,103 (32)	12,445 (8)	2,892 (7)
26	Textile products	32,805 (96)	121,367 (95)	6,308 (30)	3,703 (64)	846,776 (98)	5,567,223 (98)	277,831 (68)	168,724 (85)
27	Wood and wood products, furniture	2,241 (97)	49,856 (98)	6,410 (94)	4,209 (98)	423,032 (98)	4,944,295 (98)	260,507 (85)	149,184 (93)
28	Paper and paper products	375 (6)	6,393 (49)	996 (15)	425 (27)	45,880 (19)	390,458 (57)	75,673 (20)	29,668 (25)
29	Leather and fur products	22,232 (97)	15,781 (90)	2,816 (57)	958 (73)	98,985 (89)	759,383 (92)	102,080 (54)	41,845 (73)
30	Rubber, plastic, petroleum, and coal products	143 (9)	1,973 (19)	4,198 (24)	3,778 (63)	22,130 (10)	189,849 (50)	64,452 (5)	17,630 (13)
31	Chemicals and chemical products	225 (1)	2,573 (21)	1,824 (5)	274 (3)	29,045 (5)	359,396 (41)	85,900 (6)	18,991 (6)
32	Nonmetallic mineral products	468 (35)	16,741 (93)	2,196 (72)	946 (87)	151,722 (46)	2,598,148 (86)	107,196 (22)	60,943 (33)

33	Basic metal and alloys industries	569 (8)	5,007 (17)	3,537 (6)	417 (7)	10,211 (1)	140,920 (17)	54,840 (4)	13,799 (5)
34	Metal products and parts	915 (35)	15,571 (57)	10,275 (52)	6,858 (82)	199,226 (82)	1,036,019 (84)	164,688 (43)	81,550 (60)
35	Machinery, machine tools, and parts	11,016 (73)	20,985 (50)	7,476 (28)	2,268 (37)	47,856 (25)	284,904 (39)	76,371 (11)	28,552 (13)
36	Electrical machinery, apparatus, appliances	139 (2)	976 (14)	272 (3)	166 (11)	18,431 (12)	104,615 (23)	49,812 (8)	13,923 (7)
37	Transport equipment and parts	300 (5)	5,514 (15)	7,118 (16)	4,962 (41)	12,631 (5)	110,639 (17)	72,163 (11)	51,825 (22)
38	Other manufacturing industries	897 (65)	16,562 (88)	2,043 (51)	907 (69)	100,901 (83)	1,363,427 (95)	97,026 (56)	51,230 (65)
39	Repair services	11,471 (97)	141,415 (98)	8,672 (84)	6,633 (91)	287,437 (95)	2,538,660 (93)	170,356 (71)	116,078 (79)
	Total	142,369 (61)	552,831 (69)	89,280 (19)	45,236 (42)	3,268,026 (51)	36,785,414 (84)	2,902,179 (23)	1,268,028 (37)

SOURCES: India, Ministry of Planning, CSO (1989); India Ministry of Planning NSSO (1989a).
NOTE: Figures in parentheses are the percentage share of unregistered sector total in that industry.

hectare of cultivated area almost tripled from 1960–61 to 1987/88 (table 3.4). The increases for cotton and sugarcane were also significant. The yield index for all crops (base triennium ending 1969/70 = 100) rose from 74 in 1960/61 to 178 in 1987/88. In addition, the technological breakthrough brought impressive increases in labor productivity in both wheat and paddy, and in the total factor productivity in wheat and rice.

The Solow index of technical change shows highly positive technological changes in both wheat and rice but is negative for cotton. Between 1971/72 and 1983/84, the index value for the three crops together was 2.89, which indicates that technological change for the agricultural sector as a whole was positive and significant.

Changes in Factor Shares

Between 1970/71 and 1983/84, the trend value of value added as a proportion of the value of output was −0.003 for wheat and −0.002 for cotton. In contrast, the trend value for paddy was 0.0102, which was both positive and significant. The time coefficients of the ratio of wages to value added in paddy and wheat production were −0.025 and −0.002, respectively, which showed a declining trend. For paddy, the trend was statistically significant, whereas for wheat, it was not.

Wage rates for all the three crops showed a statistically significant relation with labor productivity over time. The regression coefficients (in double log equations) were 0.62 for wheat, 0.41 for paddy, and 0.64 for cotton. Thus the rate of growth of money wages was only 41 to 64 percent of the rate of growth of labor productivity in these crops.

Real wages for all crops taken together grew only 0.91 percent per year during the period 1970/71 to 1984/85. This slow growth can be attributed to both a large-scale inmigration of laborers from poorer states and the mechanization of agriculture.

Over the period 1970/71 to 1986/87, there was evidence of increasing mechanization in farm production. The trend value of the share of depreciation and interest in value added (0.0049) was both positive and significant for wheat, but the time coefficients for paddy and cotton, though positive, were insignificant. The trend in the share of rent in value added declined for all these crops but was significant for paddy. This trend contradicts the findings of a study on rice cultivation in Southeast Asia (Hyami et al. 1980).

One consequence of the increasing mechanization in Punjab is that the elasticity of employment with respect to agricultural output has begun to decline. The initial period of the green revolution in Punjab was highly labor absorptive. Whereas agricultural output rose at the rate of 8.2 percent per year from 1962–65 to 1970–73, the number of male agricultural workers grew at the rate of 3 percent, which was well above the national rate of 1.8 percent. The growth rate of agricultural output dropped to 5.4 percent per year between

1970–73 and 1980–83, and that of male agricultural workers fell to 1.4 percent. Thus the elasticity of labor absorption was 0.4 during the first period and 0.3 during the second (Bhalla 1987:545; Bhalla and Tyagi 1989). By the same token, labor productivity and wages in agriculture show a rising trend (see also India, Ministry of Finance, 1990).

Sharing the Gains of the Green Revolution

The changes in factor productivities and shares do not indicate how the gains of the new technology were distributed among the various categories of cultivators and landless labor. Unfortunately, there are no up-to-date secondary data or studies on income distributed among the peasantry in Punjab. However, two studies (Bhalla and Chadha 1983; and Singh 1991) provide a basis for some broad generalizations on income distribution.

Gains from the new technology seem to have trickled down to all sections of the rural population. But the distribution was quite inequitable, since these gains were distributed more or less in proportion to the initial landholding position, which was highly skewed. Despite the limited land base, the total crop output and farm business income per unit of area of small and marginal farmers were almost as high as that of the larger farmers. Their technological level was nearly as good, and they made optimum use of surplus family labor. They also supplemented their earnings with wage and other income from nonagricultural occupations. Nevertheless, many were still living below the poverty line. Although there is evidence that landless labor has also obtained higher wages from agriculture and expanded nonagricultural occupations, many of them also remained below the poverty line. Even so, the Punjab experience shows that rapid agricultural growth over a long period makes a significant dent in rural poverty (Ahluwalia 1978). NSS data show that the state has the lowest poverty ratio among the larger states of India (India, Planning Commission, 1986; India, NSSO, 1990b).

According to data on asset distribution for 1971 and 1981, the average value of assets in rural Punjab was 2.68 times that for rural India as a whole, which reflects the general prosperity in the state, but these assets were unequally distributed. In 1981, 60 percent of households with assets of less than Rs 50,000 accounted for only 9 percent of assets. At the other extreme, rich households with assets in excess of Rs 100,000 accounted for 27 percent of households and 81 percent of the total value of assets (RBI 1977, 1987).

Determinants of Agricultural Transformation

The state and the public sector have played a crucial role in the rapid growth of Punjab agriculture since independence and its phenomenal transformation since the mid-1960s. On the eve of independence, Punjab had the most developed canal irrigation network in the country. It also had an enterprising peasantry that had been acquainted with irrigation technology for a long time.

Many of the pioneering families that helped to develop the canal colonies of Lyallpur, Sargodha, and Montgomery came to east Punjab after partition and brought with them their rich experience and enterprise.

Institutional factors also played an important role. Although land reforms during the mid-1950s were limited, they abolished landlordism and thus made it possible for self-cultivation to become the predominant mode of production. By 1982, 81 percent of the net operated area was under self-cultivation, in comparison with only 60 percent during 1953/54. With the removal of inter-mediaries, the self-cultivators had a personal stake in augmenting production through investment in new technology.

Large-scale planned investment in rural infrastructure from the beginning of planning in 1951 laid the basis of the technological breakthrough in Punjab agriculture. Among the states, Punjab had the highest per capita plan expenditure during the first three plans and the second highest in subsequent plans. According to various plan documents, during the First Five Year Plan per capita plan expenditure was Rs 174 in Punjab, compared with Rs 26 in Bihar and Rs 38 for India as a whole. During the Seventh Plan the corresponding figures were Rs 1729 for Punjab, Rs 622 for Bihar, and Rs 980 for India as a whole.

Rural Infrastructural Investment

The plan investment in Punjab gave top priority to rural infrastructure such as irrigation and power, agriculture, community development, credit, markets, and research and extension, which together constituted nearly 70 percent of the total outlay during all the plans.

POWER. During all the plans, the highest expenditures in Punjab were for power and irrigation. The per capita consumption of electricity increased from 6 kilowatt-hours in 1951 to 478 in 1986/87, whereas consumption for India as a whole increased from 18 kilowatt-hours to only 259. By 1981, all Punjab villages were electrified as against only 47 percent in India. By 1986/87, 44 percent of the electricity was being consumed in agriculture in Punjab, as against only 21 percent at the national level. The availability of power in rural Punjab made possible the electrification of thousands of pumpsets and tube-wells and enabled farmers to use power threshers, sugarcane crushers, and chaff cutters on a large scale. This reduced the drudgery associated with traditional operations. Electric lights and electrical appliances helped some farmers improve their quality of life. However, the demand for power exceeded the supply, and an even higher investment was needed.

IRRIGATION. Because of large public investment, the proportion of gross irrigated area to gross cropped area in Punjab rose from 52 percent in 1950/51 to 91 percent by 1985/86, which was far above the 32 percent for India as a whole. Tubewells accounted for 59 percent of gross irrigated area in the state during 1987/88 (Punjab, ESA, various years). Because of this large investment, the irrigation base of the small and middle farmers became as good as that of large farmers (Chadha 1986, 94, table 35).

COOPERATIVE CREDIT. A rapid increase in cooperative credit to cultivators was another important component of infrastructural development. Total loans by primary agricultural cooperative credit societies in Punjab rose from only Rs 22 million in 1950/51 to Rs 3,104 million by 1986/87. Loans per hectare rose from Rs 7 in 1951/52 to Rs 430 in 1986/87 in Punjab, compared with an increase from Rs 2 to Rs 245 for India as a whole. The per hectare disbursement of short-term cooperative loans for the purchase of fertilizers and other inputs was much higher for holdings of less than 2 hectares than for medium and large holdings (Chadha 1986, 81, table 3b). In addition, cultivators were able to obtain long-term loans for the installation of tubewells, the purchase of tractors, land improvement, and allied agricultural activities. These loans were made by the primary cooperatives and the state land development banks, regional rural banks, and commercial banks.

INFRASTRUCTURE. The state's massive program of infrastructural development brought a marked improvement in roads, extension services, agricultural research, and education. By 1985, nearly all villages were linked by metalled roads, and the proportion of surfaced roads per 100 square kilometers of area far exceeded that for India as a whole. Between 1965 and 1988, the number of passenger vehicles increased by nearly 350 times and goods vehicles by more than 75 times. The number of regulated markets and the storage capacity of procurement agencies increased sharply (Punjab, ESA, various years).

The National Extension Program, the Panchayati Raj, and the Community Development Program introduced during the 1950s created a cadre of trained agricultural extension workers. The Punjab Agricultural University at Ludhiana contributed to the development of new seed varieties and has been active in research, extension, and training programs.

Once educationally backward, Punjab has become one of the leading states in education facilities at schools and universities, as well as in engineering and medicine, as a result of the substantial investment in education. The enrollment of rural males and females at the primary, middle, and higher secondary levels has increased quite rapidly. According to most indicators, Punjab is now second only to Kerala in education, health, and social development (Nag 1989, 143–170).

Agricultural Price Policy

A favorable price climate since the establishment of the Agricultural Price Commission in the mid-1960s also contributed to the rapid growth of agriculture in India, particularly in Punjab. Most studies have shown that the minimum support prices fixed by the government on the recommendations of the commission were remunerative. The procurement price of wheat that the Food Corporation of India paid in Punjab from 1967/68 to 1985/86 ranged from 104 to 152

TABLE 3.5 Index of total factor productivity and technology change (Solow Index) in Punjab and India, 1979/1980 to 1985/1986

Code	Industry Name	Punjab				India			
		1979–80	1982–83	1985–86	Solow Index[a]	1979–80	1982–83	1985–86	Solow Index[a]
20–21	Food products	100	112	111	5.63	100	123	139	12.64
22	Beverages, tobacco, and tobacco products	100	163	142	8.36	100	107	88	5.65
23	Cotton textiles	100	60	65	-6.91	100	70	72	-2.64
24	Wool, silk, and synthetic fiber textiles	100	100	113	3.73	100	86	104	1.97
25	Jute, hemp, and mesta textiles					100	99	74	-8.78
26	Textile products	100	111	102	3.45	100	122	108	4.62
27	Wood and wood products, furniture, and fixtures	100	41	15	-15.35	100	75	71	-1.46
28	Paper and paper products	100	32	130	8.57	100	69	71	-4.24
29	Leather and fur products	100	204	31	-10.07	100	119	111	5.49
30	Rubber, plastic, petroleum, and coal products	100	96	158	10.54	100	118	166	5.28
31	Chemicals and chemical products	100	258	249	19.14	100	107	108	4.13
32	Nonmetallic mineral products	100	69	37	-13.75	100	94	78	0.32

Code	Industry							
33	Basic metal and alloys	100	65	75	−5.31	100	104	99	−2.06
34	Metal products and parts	100	77	72	−4.51	100	84	87	−0.47
35	Machinery, machine tools, and parts	100	129	136	0.96	100	106	114	3.23
36	Electrical machinery and apparatuses, appliances	100	110	55	−13.87	100	133	127	6.49
37	Transport equipment and parts	100	99	83	0.62	100	123	121	5.02
38	Other manufacturing industries	100	176	194	8.93	100	144	278	17.45
97	Repair services	100	108	131	5.84	100	110	104	2.16
2–3	Manufacture (20–21 to 38)	100	117	129	4.47	100	105	108	3.91
	All industries	100	96	102	−0.14	100	106	108	3.08

SOURCE: India, Ministry of Planning, CSO (various years).
NOTE: Total factor productivity is the ratio of the index of net value added to weighted input index. Where the weighted input index is the addition of the index of labor and capital, the weights are cost of labor and capital in the base year.
aSolow Index: rate of growth (v/l) − b rate of growth (k/l) where b is the capital share in net value added in base year.

percent of the average cost of production. The procurement price for paddy ranged from 107 to 124 percent of the average cost (India, ESA, various years). The cost of both grains included the imputed value of rent, which constituted between 25 and 33 percent of the cost of production. The Punjab farmers who produced large amounts of wheat, rice, and cotton for the market were the major beneficiaries of the new price policy (Bhalla 1989, 48, 53).

Manufacturing Sector

Before the middle of the twentieth century, industrialization in India was fairly limited. Initially, most of the industries were concentrated around the port towns of Calcutta, Bombay, and Madras. Industrialization in Punjab did not begin until the mid-1920s, when the coming of canal irrigation stimulated agricultural growth. Completion of the railway network contributed to the commercialization of agriculture. Agricultural growth also encouraged the development of agroprocessing and agro-input machinery industries. In response to the increased demands created by the two world wars, Lahore, Amritsar, Dhariwal, Sialkot, Wazirabad, Batala, and a few other towns emerged as important industrial centers.

The partition of India in 1947 disrupted the entire economy of Punjab, and its industrial production came to a near halt. According to the Census of India for 1951, only 7 percent of the total work force in Punjab was engaged in industries, construction, and public utilities compared with 65 percent in agriculture and allied occupations, 10 percent in commerce and transport, and 18 percent in services (India, Ministry of Home Affairs, 1951). A substantial proportion of those in manufacturing were independent workers assisted by family labor and used little or no power. Most of the manufacturing was done in the small-scale sector. There were only about 1,000 registered factories (employing more than 10 workers and using power), which provided employment to not more than 50,000 people. In 1950 Punjab accounted for less than 2 percent of the total value of output by the registered sector in India, compared with 33 percent for Bombay, 27 percent for Bengal, and 12 percent for Madras (Khanna 1983, 119–24, appendix B-I–B-IV).

Manufacturing began to increase in the mid-1950s, as the result of concerted efforts to create a pool of trained workers and provide incentives to entrepreneurs as a part of the rehabilitation program for displaced persons. Planning helped channel resources to priority areas. In all the five-year plans, the state government gave the highest priority to investment in power and other infrastructure.

Increasing agricultural output during the 1950s created a demand for more agroprocessing, agro-input, and machine goods. This was supplemented by an increased demand from the rest of India for such products as machine goods, hosiery, knitwear, textiles, and sporting goods. These factors encouraged industrial development in Punjab, particularly among small-scale industries. By the beginning of the 1960s, Punjab was also producing agricultural implements, bicycles, and foundry products.

A few towns emerged as industrial centers after independence. Most of these towns were on the grand trunk road to Delhi. By the middle of the 1960s, Ludhiana had surpassed Amritsar in manufacturing engineering and consumer products. Gobindgarh's numerous steel rerolling mills produced various iron products. These developments notwithstanding, the state's industrial activity remained rather limited until the green revolution of the mid-1960s, which brought unprecedented growth in agricultural output. Because of close input, output, and consumption linkages, rapid agricultural growth was accompanied by even faster growth in the secondary and tertiary sectors of the Punjab economy. Consequently, between 1967/68 and 1987/88 the income from manufacturing in Punjab grew 7.6 percent per year compared with 4.5 percent for agriculture and 5.2 percent for manufacturing in India as a whole (table 3.1). Net per capita domestic product originating in manufacturing in Punjab rose from a ranking of sixth among the major states of India in 1960/61 to third by 1985/86.

Data Base for Manufacturing

The Annual Survey of Industries (ASI), which is based on a census and sample survey, covers all of India's manufacturing units registered under the Factories Act that employ 10 or more workers and use power, along with all units that employ 20 or more workers and do not use power. Except for statistics on capital invested, the data are fairly reliable. The data on capital employed, which is estimated on the basis of historical costs depreciated on a straight-line method, suffer from serious limitations. The ASI data for states are published regularly by the Central Statistical Organization (CSO). The CSO and the various state statistical organizations also use the ASI data to estimate value added from the registered sector (India, CSO, Annual Survey of Industries, various years).

The data base for the unregistered sectors is very weak. Until recently, estimates of the value of output and value added for some specific unregistered enterprises were obtained through ad hoc surveys by the NSSO. Consequently, it was not possible to build reliable data series for most of these industries. One of the earlier sources for Punjab was the Census of Unorganized Industries conducted in 1975–77. This was a one-time survey that covered only urban units employing more than five workers.

Recently, the CSO introduced economic censuses to remedy this deficiency. Comprehensive data on the unregistered sector both for India and all the states are available for only 1984/85. This sector includes both directory enterprises employing six or more workers, with one hired worker on a fairly regular basis, nondirectory enterprises employing fewer than six persons with at least one hired worker on a regular basis, and own-account enterprises with no hired workers on a regular basis.

Some information is also available on small-scale industries in which fixed investment does not exceed Rs 3.5 million (Rs 4.5 million in the case of ancillary units) in assets, plant, and machinery. These units are registered with the district industries centers for the purpose of receiving various incentives. But not all of these units are registered under the Factories Act, and therefore data on small-scale industries cannot be correlated with other available information. These limitations should be kept in mind in the analysis of unregistered sectors in the state.

Structure of Manufacturing: Significance of the Unregistered Sector

Industrialization in Punjab continues to be dominated by the unregistered enterprises to a much greater extent than in the country as a whole. The unregistered sector accounted for approximately half the value added in manufacturing during 1967/68 and 1987/88 (table 3.1). For India as a whole, the share fell from 41 percent to 39 percent. The 5,344 registered manufacturing units under the factory sector in Punjab in 1984/85 (excluding "electricity") had fixed capital assets worth Rs 8,918 million, employed 236,159 persons, generated Rs 5100 million worth of value added, and produced Rs 39,015 million of output. The 292,843 unregistered enterprises—which included 236,080 own account, 47,814 nondirectory, and 8,949 directory establishments—had assets of Rs 14,237 million, engaged 552,831 employees, but produced only Rs 4,524 million of value added and Rs 8,928 million of output. Thus, with 60 percent more fixed capital, the unregistered sector generated more than twice as much employment as the registered sector.

The highest value of output from the unregistered sector came from food production, textile products, machinery, transport, repairs, wood, and furniture. Repair services provided the largest employment (table 3.4). In 1984/85, the unregistered sector contributed nearly 70 percent of industrial employment in the state. Because of lower productivity, however, its share in the total value of output was only 19 percent and that in value added 42 percent.

In terms of the value of output, the registered sector was dominant in food products, cotton textiles, wood, silk and synthetic fibers, chemicals, basic metals, nonelectrical machinery, and transport equipment. The small-scale sector dominated in textile products, wool and wood products, leather products, nonmetallic mineral products, metal products, and repair services. In terms of employment, it was dominant in many other areas. Output and value added per employee were much lower in the unregistered sector than in the registered sector in both Punjab and in India as a whole. This was true at the aggregated levels and for most individual industry groups. In 1984/85, for example, the value of output per employee for all manufacturing industries (except electricity) in the registered sector in Punjab was nearly 10 times that in the unregistered sector, and value added per employee was 2½ times greater. The only notable exceptions were in rubber, plastic, petroleum and coal products, and transport equipment, where the reverse seemed to be true.

Higher labor productivity in the registered sector ought to reflect higher capital intensity. However, reported data on capital employed do not reflect this difference adequately, since capital per employee in the registered sector was only one and a half times that in the unregistered sector.

Although labor productivity in the unregistered sector was lower than in the registered sector in Punjab, it was much higher than in India. This was also the case for most of the unregistered industries at the two-digit level (a more detailed classification of industry). The only exceptions were in paper and paper products and electrical machinery. The higher per worker productivity in the unregistered sector in Punjab was primarily due to more fixed capital per employee (table 3.4).

Growth of Registered Manufacturing

Registered manufacturing units have also made rapid progress since the mid-1960s. This is evident from an analysis of ASI data on output, employment, and capital invested for the factory sector. While registered factories increased from 3,023 in 1967 to 5,710 by 1985/86, net fixed capital rose from Rs 2,277 million to Rs 37,438 million, and the number of employees from 114,213 to 321,877 (India, ASI, various years). During this period, both capital employed per employee and the value of output per employee nearly doubled. Because of more capital employed per worker, Punjab had much higher labor productivity than India as a whole in food products, beverages, cotton textiles, textile products, chemical products, and basic metals and alloys (India, ASI, various years).

Between 1978–79 and 1985–86 the annual trend growth rates for manufacturing output and employment in the factor sector were 6.9 percent and 4.7 percent for Punjab and 6.2 percent and 0.4 percent for India. Unlike the industries in India, those in Punjab experienced high output growth generally in association with high employment growth. The elasticity of employment for total manufacturing during 1978/79 to 1985/86 was 0.70 percent for Punjab and 0.06 percent for India. For most individual industries, Punjab's employment elasticities were also much higher (derived from India, ASI, various years).

Factor Productivity and Technological Upgrading

Some studies for Punjab based on censuses concluded that during 1966/67 to 1973/74 the growth of the registered factory sector was hampered by the inefficient use of resources. Total factor productivity declined at both the aggregated and disaggregated levels (Dhesi et al. 1983; Singh 1990). Furthermore, the manufacturing sector appeared to be suffering from technological stagnation. The Solow index of technological change was also negative. These results contrast with those obtained for India, which showed total factor productivity increasing and positive. The Solow index was also positive.

These relationships changed radically during the 1980s.[3] For example, in the registered manufacturing sector in Punjab (according to both census and sample data), excluding power, total factor productivity increased from 100 in 1979/80 to 129 in 1985/86 but rose from 100 to only 108 for India. The performance of the "power" sector has been declining at a rapid rate, in part because of the large subsidies being given for power to the agricultural sector. Unlike the power sector, however, most of the important manufacturing subsectors have performed well.

Solow's index shows that most of the industries in the registered sector are undergoing technological upgrading (table 3.5). However, the period under consideration is too short to permit firm conclusions about these trends.

Main Features of the Industrial Sector

Like most developing regions, Punjab has a pyramidical industrial structure. At the bottom are nearly 293,000 own-account household and village industries that use traditional methods of production. They produce traditional goods for local markets and employ a large number of people. The productivity of these industries is low. In the middle are small-scale industries, most of which produce high-quality commodities by modern methods, though some still use traditional methods of production. At the top are a few medium- and large-scale industries that use fairly advanced methods of production and modern forms of organization.

Another feature of Punjab's industries is that they are dominated by small-scale enterprises. Punjab has only 2.5 percent of the population of India but more than 8 percent of the registered small-scale units. In 1984/85, the small-scale sector accounted for nearly 70 percent of total employment and 42 percent of total income generated in manufacturing. Obviously, the state is a land of small-scale enterprises.

Some scholars attribute the continued dominance of small enterprises to historical factors (Khanna 1983, 99). Others think it is due to the influx of entrepreneurs after partition and the incentives and other assistance provided by the state (Singh 1983).

Unlike the small enterprises in many other states, those in Punjab do not rely on traditional methods of production and organization that are largely independent of other units in the economy. Instead, most use power, and many operate as ancillary units of modern enterprises. Their technology improved considerably after they entered the export market.

---

3. For Punjab, the earlier data apply only to the census sector, whereas the latter data (census plus sample) pertain to the factory sector of the ASI.

The fastest-growing small and medium firms in Punjab rely almost entirely on the rest of India or foreign countries for their raw materials and markets. For example, wool is imported from Kashmir and Australia, while coal and pig iron come from the rest of India. Diesel and petroleum fuel is also imported. Only the agroprocessing industries are largely dependent on local raw materials.

In spite of a rapid rise in local demand after the advent of the green revolution, many small-scale industries are highly dependent on sales to the rest of India and abroad. Until recently the main market for hosiery goods, for example, was the former Soviet Union. According to one writer, Ludhiana accounts for nearly 20 percent of the total (noncommunist) world exports of cycle parts (Dasgupta 1989). Similarly, hand tools, sewing machines, cycles, and many engineering goods have their main market outside the state. Thus earlier characterizations that portrayed India's small-scale industries as lower forms of production with independent cycles of reproduction are no longer valid in Punjab (see, e.g., Shirokov 1980, 265–302).

Modern small-scale units in Punjab have flourished despite competition from large units, partly because of government support, but also because of their ability to defray costs through the sharing of risks. Entrepreneurs are able to take advantage of interlinkages among formal and informal, agricultural and nonagricultural, and rural and urban sectors. Many workers engaged in small-scale manufacturing, for example, also do seasonal agricultural and casual industrial work. This practice enables the entrepreneurs to cut costs without losing control of their labor force. Small-scale units are seldom covered by labor legislation as they generally employ, or manage to show that they employ, fewer than the number of workers that would require them to pay minimum wages or social security benefits to workers. They are resilient also because they are able to share production risks. The interpersonal relations enable them to reduce costs through mutual obligations. Another significant advantage enjoyed by small-scale units is that they are family run and have low overhead costs. In many instances family members work long hours, as is typical in self-exploitation. Cheap power is available from hydroelectric plants in the state. Industrial centers like Ludhiana, Gobindgarh, and Batala provide a pool of trained labor, state-run tool rooms, banks, export firms, and credit facilities. A prosperous agriculture has provided a market for many small-scale industries manufacturing agricultural machinery and consumer durables.

The state has played a crucial role in the development of the small-scale sector in Punjab, providing adequate power, land for plant location, research facilities, credit, and subsidized raw material. The state also undertakes active promotional efforts such as education and training and makes available modern decentralized technologies to independent entrepreneurs.

Contribution of Agriculture to Industrialization

Punjab is one of the few states in India in which rapid agricultural growth has induced rapid industrialization. Much of the recent literature on economic development has emphasized the rural-led employment-oriented strategy of growth, especially for developing countries with a labor surplus (Mellor 1976, 181). Some argue that a major constraint to employment growth is the availability of foodgrains. It is claimed that acceleration in the growth rate of foodgrains production from 2.5–3.0 percent to 4.0–5.0 percent would greatly advance the growth of employment. It is generally recognized, however, that the rapid growth of foodgrains production alone will not generate much employment. Consequently, high agricultural growth is sought in combination with accelerated growth in employment in other sectors. Some also point out that increased production of nonfoodgrains would stimulate output in the livestock sector, which would provide increasing employment opportunities because consumption demand would likely shift from cereals to milk and milk products. Since the livestock sector is highly labor intensive, its capital requirements are likely to be much lower than those of many other consumer goods industries. A formal model of this type developed and tested by Mellor and Mudahar (1974) has suggested that the process of integrated rural development from this strategy would have many advantages. First, income would continue to increase in rural areas. Second, a major proportion of increased demand would be for nonfoodgrains. Third, the rapid growth in agriculture would likely necessitate the development of rural infrastructure such as irrigation, roads, and electrification. Fourth, the developed infrastructure would attract trained personnel to the rural areas. Fifth, increased infrastructure would reduce disparities in rural-urban price relationships. Sixth, rural industries would be labor intensive, though new agriculture technology would be likely to widen income inequalities. Seventh, it would be possible to tap rural savings through taxes for infrastructure or for investment in small-scale firms. Eighth, widened rural income disparities would increase the need for a broad range of state-based public health and education facilities. Under this strategy, it would also be necessary to set up institutions in small market-towns as focal points for organization and decisionmaking.

To sum up, the necessary elements suggested for a policy for rural-led strategy were (1) accelerated expansion in foodgrains production; (2) massive public investment in transportation, communication, and electrification in rural areas; and (3) a shift in the structure of industrial production toward small-scale enterprises producing consumer goods in rural or semiurban areas (Mellor 1976).

Many of Mellor's preconditions seem to have been satisfied in Punjab. First, between 1967/68 and 1987/88 Punjab recorded annual growth of 4.9

percent in wheat, 15.6 percent in rice, and 6.6 percent in foodgrains, as against the suggested growth of 4 to 5 percent per year. Second, and particularly important, demand shifted in favor of livestock products, and both rural and urban consumption of milk recorded sharp increases. Between 1967/68 and 1987/88 income originating in animal husbandry grew at a phenomenal annual compound rate of 7.3 percent per year (table 3.1). This subsector accounted for 27 percent of the income generated in agriculture during 1987/88. Finally, large public investment in rural and urban infrastructure, particularly in power, roads, and communications, fostered the growth of small-scale industries in agroprocessing, agro-input, and consumer goods.

Although industrial growth in Punjab was creditable, many scholars believe that it fell far short of expectations, primarily because the state failed to tax the financial surpluses of agriculture and invest in manufacturing. This brings up another point of view concerning appropriate development strategies based on accelerated growth in agriculture.

As pointed out above, the agricultural sector can contribute to industrial growth in many ways: by providing foodgrains, releasing surplus labor for nonagricultural activities, providing raw materials for agroprocessing industries, creating demand for agro-input industries, and above all, creating a market for consumer goods industries through widespread income generation in agriculture. Some scholars give special emphasis to shifting the financial surpluses of agriculture to industry for capital formation, and simultaneously transferring labor from low-productivity agriculture to manufacturing, where labor productivity is significantly higher. This strategy has long been stressed by classical and Marxist writers. The historical development of industrial capitalism has also been explained in these terms by scholars such as Simon Kuznets and Colin Clark. Both emphasized that the success of this strategy depended on the rapid growth of labor productivity in agriculture.

A distorted application of this strategy can be seen in the former Soviet Union, in the form of Stalin's collectivization of agriculture. What Stalin failed to appreciate was that once a goose is killed, it stops laying eggs. Forcibly extracting surplus from stagnating agriculture can be both painful and often counterproductive. In contrast, policy measures that help agricultural growth can provide resources for capital formation in industry. Whatever strategy is adopted will have important political implications.

The recent revival of theoretical approaches stressing resource transfers from agriculture for industrial growth owes a great deal to Japanese and Taiwanese scholars, who have used this conceptual framework to explain rapid industrialization in their economies.

To a great extent this approach complements Mellor's strategy and perhaps helps strengthen it. It also brings out the importance of political processes, the relative strength of rich peasants, their role in initiating and spreading new technology that augments output, and their increasing influence and clout in different political regimes.

Japan and Taiwan started out by investing heavily in rural infrastructure, which buoyed agriculture. In both Japan and Taiwan, public investment in irrigation and other infrastructure was initially supplemented by large private investments. This led to a rapidly growing and prosperous agriculture. These countries then designed specific policies to extract large agricultural surpluses for investment in manufacturing. They were able to do so because of political conditions. However, the balance of political forces is likely to be quite different in a democracy where farming interests that benefit from public and private involvement in agriculture might command a predominant voting strength. Therefore the experience of India (and Punjab) must be explained in the context of its democratic polity and, to use Myrdal's term, of its "soft state." But before critically examining this issue, it is useful to look at some of the evidence.

Unfortunately, not much work has been done on intersectoral resource flows in India, particularly at the state level. Some estimates of net resource flows from agriculture to industry have been contradictory. According to Mundle (1977, A-52), the net inflow into agriculture was nearly Rs 9,000 million in 1951/52, but by 1970/71 about Rs 6,000 million were flowing out of agriculture annually. According to Mody (1981, 425–40), however, there was a substantial resource flow into agriculture during 1950 to 1970.

Unlike Mundle, Mody based his estimates on financial flows (i.e., receipts, tax payments, government expenditure) in agriculture and financial assets and liabilities of the agricultural sector. Like Ishikawa, he appreciates the necessity of resource flows into agriculture during the initial period of development for building rural infrastructure, whether or not these are reversed subsequently. The success of industrialization will depend to a large extent not only on the capability of agriculture to generate surpluses but also on whether and how these surpluses can be channeled into industrial investment.

The estimates of both scholars suffer from two deficiencies. They cover only the period up to the early 1970s, and they are for all of India and do not take into account the country's wide regional disparities.

Ashok Gulati (1989) recently computed aggregate subsidies to agriculture on various inputs at state level. Gulati estimated that for India as a whole during the 1980s annual subsidies to agriculture averaged Rs 90,000 million and constituted 16 percent of NSDP from agriculture. Subsidies for Punjab alone averaged Rs 7,162 million per year and constituted 24 percent of the agricultural NSDP.

Since Gulati did not compute direct and indirect taxes or other financial flows in and out of agriculture, it is not possible to determine conclusively the direction of resource flows. There is, however, indirect evidence that financial resources are now flowing out of agriculture. The first is the large increases in savings, most of which come from rural households. The second is the fact that during 1975–90 the terms of trade moved against agriculture.

In a recent study Bhalla and his associates (1990, table 17) attempted to estimate the net resource flow out of the total Punjab economy. They found that by the end of the 1970s the state had become a highly export-surplus economy. In 1979/80, the net trade surplus for Punjab was Rs 7,739 million, or 17 percent of its gross domestic product. Most of it originated in agriculture, which had an export surplus of Rs 12,217 million. It is obvious that an export surplus of this magnitude must have created assets outside the state.

Another indicator of net financial flows from the state to the rest of the country is the credit-deposit ratio of commercial banks. In 1973, the credit deposit ratio in Punjab was 36 percent compared with 75 percent for Maharashtra and an all-India average of 69 percent. The ratio of Punjab moved up to 60 percent by 1987/88 (RBI, 1982/83, 1987/88).

To sum up, existing literature on flow-of-funds analysis does not permit definite conclusions about intersectoral resource flows in Punjab. Indirect evidence suggests that resources are flowing out of agriculture, but there is virtually no evidence that indicates how much is being used for industrial investment.

Available data make possible some conclusions on the movement of labor from agriculture to industry. In 1961, 56 percent of the male workers in Punjab were engaged in agriculture, which contributed 48 percent of total state income. By 1971, the proportion of male workers had increased to 63 percent. Agriculture's share of state income had marginally declined to 45 percent. The increase in the percentage for male workers reflected rapid growth in agriculture. During 1961/71, agricultural output increased 8 percent in Punjab and only 2.4 percent in all of India. The male agricultural labor force growth rate of 3.1 percent per year was nearly double the national rate. The growth rate started to decelerate during the next two decades and declined sharply to about 1.4 percent both during 1971/81 and during 1981/91. For India as a whole, the annual growth rate of male agriculture labor was 1.74 percent even during 1981/91. In Punjab, the proportion of male agricultural workers to total male workers also declined, from 63.0 percent in 1971 to 57.3 percent in 1991 (India, Registrar General). The NSSO data for 1988 confirm that the percentage of workers engaged in agriculture declined from 61 percent in 1977/78 to 50 percent in 1987/88. The comparative figures for India were 71 percent and 62 percent (India, NSSO, 1990a).

Some scholars have analyzed the influence of agricultural growth on industrial growth by building macroeconometric models. Rangarajan (1982, 87) in his study of India concluded that 1 percent growth in agricultural output increased industrial production by about 0.5 percent and national income by 0.7 percent. Another notable study (Hazell and Roëll 1983) used data on expenditure patterns of farm and nonfarm households to quantify forward and backward linkages. A recent study on Punjab (Bhalla et al. 1990) used the detailed input-output tables for 1969 and 1980 to estimate the contribution of rapid agricultural growth to the development of the agro-input, agroprocessing, and consumption goods industries through backward, forward, and consumption linkages. An attempt was also made to calculate the extent of forward and backward linkages with the nonagricultural sectors.

The increasing use of intermediate modern inputs in the new agricultural technology stimulated the demand for fertilizers, pesticides, power, diesel, and other nonagricultural inputs for current production. With increased capital investment in agriculture, the demand for capital goods such as electric motors, diesel engines, threshers, tractors, and construction materials also rose rapidly. These demands were partly met through imports but also gave a fillip to local industries. As a result, vibrant engineering and hand-tool industries emerged. These industries also started selling large quantities to the rest of the country. The value of production of agricultural implements grew 10 percent annually between 1970/71 and 1982/83. In the meantime, production and employment for hand tools and nuts and bolts was high. Domestic production of fertilizer was up sharply, but large quantities were also imported.

Increases in output and marketed surplus of agricultural commodities also led to the rapid growth of industries processing agricultural products. Many of them catered mostly to local demand, but over time exports also became important. For example, nearly 93 percent of the total paddy production in Punjab is marketed. Since Punjab is a new rice-producing state, it did not have a tradition of hand pounding of rice and was able to directly graduate to modern mechanized rice shelling. All the marketed paddy is now being converted into rice through modern shellers. Higher income per capita of Punjab's large rural population has pushed up the demand for consumption goods. As in most states, consumption is the most important component of final expenditure. Both the direct and indirect income generated by consumption is high. A consumption multiplier of 1.6 during 1979/80 indicates the importance of consumption-based activities in the state. Imports of consumer goods from the rest of India have increased, and the state's consumer goods industries have expanded rapidly.

The composition of consumption has also changed, particularly for income-elastic foods such as livestock products, beverages, cloth, consumer durables, and some other commodities. Among the food items, the highest proportion, that is, 17 percent of the total expenditure, went for milk and milk products; 14.4 percent for sugar, salt, and spices; 10.9 percent for cereals; and 3.8 percent for beverages and refreshments. Among nonfood items, clothing accounted for 9.4 percent, fuel and light for 6.5 percent, and consumer durables for 3.05 percent of total expenditure (India, NSSO, 1990b).

The increased consumption induced rapid expansion in Punjab's manufacture of food products like dairying, grain mill products, edible oils, and breweries and beverages. There was also a big spurt in the domestic production of textiles and durable consumer goods such as sewing machines, bicycles, radios, and television sets.

An IFPRI study (Bhalla et al. 1990) recently examined the development process of agro-input, agroprocessing, and consumer goods industries, along with the intersectoral linkages in the Punjab economy. An attempt was also made to find out the direct and indirect quantum and strength of forward and backward linkages generated by different sectors, and to trace the direct and indirect impact of final expenditures on sectoral output, income, wages, and employment through multiplier analysis, with special attention to the linkage between the agricultural and nonagricultural sectors. The input-output model was modified to take into account import leakages from the Punjab economy. It was found that direct and indirect increases in the demand for intermediate nonagricultural inputs strengthened the linkages between the agricultural and nonagricultural sectors. But many of the modern intermediate inputs, especially fertilizers and petroleum products, were imported from outside the state. The incremental direct and indirect output requirements from the domestic economy were found to be notably smaller in Punjab than in India as a whole, because of the high level of these imports. The inducement effect of consumption on the state economy was also considerably reduced because of imports of consumption goods from the rest of India.

A condensed five-sector input-output table for Punjab and India for 1979/80 was used to bring out the important differences in their linkages. These differences arose, first, because in Punjab agricultural production made much greater use of nonagricultural inputs than agricultural production in India as a whole and, second, because Punjab had much higher import leakages.

When the import leakages in Punjab were taken into account, a Rs 1.00 increase in final demand from agriculture led to a direct and indirect output of only Rs 0.998 in agriculture and Rs 0.10 in manufacturing. When import leakages were neglected, the direct and indirect output levels were Rs 1.11 in agriculture and Rs 0.22 in manufacturing. For India also, the incremental outputs of various sectors were reduced because of imports, although to a much smaller degree (Bhalla et al. 1990).

In the case of Punjab, import leakages were even higher when final demand from manufacturing was increased. Thus, a unit increase in the final demand from manufacturing resulted in a direct and indirect output of only Rs 0.85 in manufacturing, compared with Rs 1.66 when import leakages were not taken into account. In the case of India, direct and indirect output in manufacturing decreased from Rs 1.67 to Rs 1.43, even after accounting for import leakages. Because of a very high degree of interdependence with the rest of the country, many of the gains of rapid development in Punjab were shared with the rest of India. At the same time, Punjab benefited immensely from the existence of an assured market for wheat and rice surpluses and other industrial products and from the easy availability of modern intermediate inputs, such as fertilizers and diesel fuel, at nationally subsidized rates. The modernization of agriculture and the rapid growth of the manufacturing and tertiary sectors tended to strengthen the links between the state economy and the national economy and integrate it with the national market.

A disaggregated analysis of sectoral linkages and changes therein was also conducted for the period 1969/70 to 1979/80 using information from a 36-sector input-output table for 1969/70 and a 39-sector input-output table for 1979/80. It turned out that in 1969/70 only the agricultural sectors (including animal husbandry) and some agroprocessing sectors were generating high forward and backward linkages. In 1979/80, the farm sectors and agroprocessing sectors continued to generate high forward and backward income linkages. When linkages were considered with or without import leakages, however, many more sectors fell into this group, and this change indicated that the economy was functioning at a higher technological level (Bhalla et al. 1990, 5.7).

The multiplier analysis in the study further confirmed that important changes had taken place in the structure of the Punjab economy between 1969/70 and 1979/80. In 1969/70, it was primarily the agrobased industries that demonstrated the highest levels of indirect income and employment in response to changes in their final demand. In 1979/80, other industries—such as basic metals, metal products, "other chemicals," machine goods, electrical and nonelectrical machinery, and drugs and pharmaceuticals—also showed high indirect income and employment levels. The production of consumption goods remained a major economic activity in the state, and very high induced incomes were recorded by agriculture-based industries that had an important place in the consumption basket. Some other basic and heavy industries—such as basic metals, electrical machinery, and basic chemicals—also became important because of direct and indirect effect. In 1979/80, in addition to many manufacturing sectors, construction also emerged as significant in the generation of indirect as well as induced income and employment (Bhalla et al. 1990, 83–84).

Urbanization

The nature and pattern of urbanization in a region can only be understood in terms of the region's economic structure. The distinctive pattern of urbanization in Punjab was due to rapid agricultural growth combined with the dominant position of small-scale industry. Since agriculture is still the largest sector of the economy, the extent of urbanization is limited. In 1991, nearly 30 percent of Punjab's population lived in urban areas compared with 26 percent for India as a whole and 39 percent and 34 percent for Maharashtra and Gujarat, respectively, the two most industrialized states.

Urbanization accelerated during 1961 to 1981, particularly in agricultural marketing cum trading towns. The marketing of large agricultural surpluses stimulated urban marketing and trade. The agroprocessing, agro-input, and consumer goods industries also got a boost as the income of the agricultural population rose. This led to greater occupational diversification. By 1987/88, half of the work force was engaged in nonagricultural occupations compared with 39 percent in 1977/78 and 43 percent in 1983 (India 1988). The rate of urbanization was faster during the 1970s than in the 1950s and 1960s. The urban population grew by 44.5 percent during 1971/81 compared with only 25 percent during the preceding decade. According to data from the latest (1991) census, the growth rate of the urban population in Punjab (as in all other states) fell to 29 percent during 1981/91, and Punjab's proportion of urban population increased to only 30 percent in 1991. In the meantime, the share of urban population in India increased from 23 percent to 26 percent. Punjab now ranks fifth in urbanization among the larger states (India, Ministry of Home Affairs, 1991).

Urbanization and agricultural development are closely linked in Punjab. Although industrialization remains the main force for urbanization, many small and medium firms specialize in the trade, marketing, and processing of agricultural produce, and provide agricultural implements and other inputs. Since agricultural development is fairly evenly distributed over the whole state, the development of agroprocessing and agro-input industries also is spread widely among small and medium market towns. At the same time, numerous large industries and modern small-scale industries have begun to cluster in large cities on the grand trunk road from Delhi to Amritsar. Consequently, the pattern of industrialization now emerging in Punjab exhibits a high level of spatial inequality, with a large proportion of the nonhousehold manufacturing activities concentrated in a few cities of the state with a population in excess of 100,000 (class I cities). This is likely to adversely affect the balance of urbanization in the future.

At present, the distribution of the urban population by city size is somewhat more balanced in Punjab than in India as a whole (table 3.6). There were only 10 cities in Punjab with a population greater than 100,000 (class I) and these held only 54 percent of the urban population compared with 65 percent living in class I cities in India. The 43 small and intermediate towns with a population of 20,000 to 99,000 account for 33 percent of the urban total compared with an urban population of 24 percent that lived in towns of similar size in India. Thirteen percent of the urban population lives in 67 small towns with a population of less than 20,000. The comparative figure for India is 11 percent. The growth rates for all categories of towns in Punjab were higher in 1971/81 than in 1961/71 but were lower in 1981/91 than in 1971/81. While the growth rate of intermediate towns was slightly higher than that of 7 big cities during 1971/81, the reverse was the case during 1981/91 (Bhalla et al. 1982).

Small market villages and towns on main roads connecting larger town-

TABLE **3.6** Distribution and growth of urban population in Punjab and India, by city size

Class	Population	Punjab 1991		Punjab Growth Rate		India 1991		India Growth Rate	
		Number of Towns	Percentage Distribution	1971–81	1981–91	Number of Towns	Percentage Distribution	1971–81	1981–91
I	>100,000	10	54.36	39.40	35.54	296	65.20	41.41	34.49
II	50,000 to 99,999	18	19.79	43.06	29.77	341	10.95	36.15	31.60
III	20,000 to 49,999	25	12.89	33.10	30.33	927	13.19	39.53	29.57
IV	10,000 to 19,999	44	10.46	33.85	21.21	1,135	07.77	35.00	28.41
V	5,000 to 9,999	16	20.30	39.00	25.48	725	02.60	36.99	30.02
VI	<5,000	7	00.47	50.34	12.01	185	00.29	47.74	43.88
	Total	120	100.00	37.96	31.36	3,609	100.00	39.68	32.81

SOURCE: Registrar General, *Census of India*, 1971, 1981, and 1991.

ships have gradually become hubs of economic activity, not only in trading, agroprocessing, and repairs, but also in the provision of social services, health, and recreation. In many cases, these small growth centers serve a network of peripheral villages and provide nonagricultural employment and income to a large number of workers.

Another notable feature of Punjab's pattern of development is that many rural areas have acquired urban functions and amenities owing to their fairly well-developed infrastructure and the good road connections between most villages, but have retained their rural characteristics. Urbanization statistics fail to reflect this important phenomenon. In a sense, rapid rural development has inhibited urbanization by providing increasing employment to the rural population and thereby reducing rural-urban migration.

As is the case for agriculture, industrial development in Punjab owes a great deal to state policies. In particular, the government's decision to invest in infrastructure and provide other basic facilities to entrepreneurs played a vital role in industrial development.

The State and Industrial Development

Policymakers in Punjab have been acutely aware of the need to accelerate industrialization. It is much more difficult, however, to provide comprehensive investment, input, marketing, and infrastructural support to the industrial sector than it was for agriculture. The geographic location of the state puts it at a serious disadvantage. Basic raw materials such as coal, pig iron, and petroleum products have to be brought in from long distances. Similarly, the market for many of its industrial products lies outside the state. And being a border state, Punjab finds its entrepreneurs have to be given special incentives to attract capital. Despite these drawbacks, policymakers have taken several steps to accelerate industrialization in Punjab.

In India, the macroeconomic policy of state governments is part and parcel of national policy. This is particularly true for licenses, controls, tariffs, custom duties, export and import duties and subsidies, and investment policy. Although the state has benefited immensely from national assistance in planned investment in infrastructure, licensing policy has in general curbed the development of sufficient capacity, particularly in agroprocessing industries.

The main objectives of Punjab's industrial policy as enunciated in the Industrial Policy of 1978 and the New Industrial Policy of 1989 were to develop village and small industries, encourage as many industrialists and small entrepreneurs as possible to set up industries in the state with special incentives for nonresident Indians, maximize sales of industrial products outside the state, attract investment in new technology and agrobased sectors, provide technical facilities and financial assistance for upgrading technology and modernization, and encourage young people to enter into business and bring industries to the area known as the "no industry block" (a small administrative unit covering several villages) (Punjab 1978, 1990).

The state government introduced several packages of incentives for setting up and promoting industries. The first were enunciated in 1973 and the New Policy in April 1978. The main promotional packages concentrated on infrastructural facilities, incentives to new industries, incentives for locating industries in backward districts, assistance to small industries, and the establishment of promotional and financial and research institutions.

INFRASTRUCTURAL FACILITIES. An important component of infrastructural support was the move to set up focal points and industrial estates (parks) in different parts of the state. The focal points and industrial estates were provided with power, roads, and communication. In some cases, research and training institutes were also set up in these centers. The main objective was to provide entrepreneurs with all the infrastructural facilities they needed, including sheds in industrial estates. In addition, a substantial land subsidy was made available to prospective entrepreneurs.

INCENTIVES TO NEW INDUSTRIES. A variety of tax incentives are available to entrepreneurs interested in setting up new industries. These include exemption from the municipality border tax (*octroi*) and terminal tax, a depreciation allowance, and a capital investment subsidy. Interest-free loans given to new industries are equivalent to 5 to 6 percent of their annual sales subject to a ceiling of Rs 0.5 million to Rs 0.7 million per year. The loan periods range from 5 to 10 years depending on the degree of backwardness of the location. In addition, interest subsidies are given for small loans up to Rs 25,000 carrying an interest rate of 8 percent or more. Also, new units are not required to pay for electricity duty (*ceso*) for 5 to 10 years.

INCENTIVES FOR LOCATING INDUSTRIES IN BACKWARD DISTRICTS. The central government has introduced numerous incentives to attract industries to backward districts such as Hoshiarpur, Sangrur, Bhatinda, and Faridkot. All industries set up in these districts receive a central subsidy of 15 percent on fixed capital investment (land, buildings, and machinery) of up to Rs 1.5 million. The state gives similar subsidies to all new industries set up in the districts and in submountainous and other backward areas.

According to a study by the Economic Adviser to Government (Punjab 1984), industries that received such subsidies experienced higher growth than industries in the rest of the state. In most cases, however, the disbursement of announced subsidies was delayed, and the amounts were very small in relation to the capital outlay. The supply of raw materials to these units was irregular, particularly for engineering-based units. These industries had difficulty getting raw material from the Steel Authority of India and had to buy it at a higher price in the open market. Other problems included power shortages, a lack of housing, a lack of skilled labor, inadequate credit, poor communication facilities and other social infrastructure, and difficulty in making full use of capacity (Punjab 1984).

ASSISTANCE TO SMALL INDUSTRIES. Several promotional measures, incentives, and training programs have been designed to develop small-scale industries at both the national and state level. Initially, their objective was to protect small industries from competition with large units. Accordingly, the number of items reserved for manufacture in the small-scale sector rose from 47 in 1967 to 838 in 1989; however, the reserve did not apply to large units that export 75 percent of their output (India, NSSO, 1989a, 8–9). Other protective measures included exemption from excise duty up to a certain limit, credit on the modified value added tax, government purchases earmarked for this sector, and controlled prices for scarce raw materials.

The most important promotional programs for small-scale enterprises at present are those that provide refinancing facilities through the Industrial Development Bank of India and the National Bank for Agricultural and Rural Development. Commercial banks provide credit for working capital on a priority basis, and the State Financial Corporations do so for investment capital. Institutions such as the National Small Industries Corporation and the State Small Industries Development Corporation also provide financial help, some of which is in the form of hire-purchase assistance for acquiring machinery.

The central government has made a considerable outlay for direct assistance and for infrastructure. In addition, the state government has provided technical assistance and common service facilities through a network of quality marking centers, industrial development-cum-service centers, testing and toolroom facilities, and research and development facilities for all types of industries. The upgrading of technology is also being promoted by the Hand Tool Design Institute at Jalandhar, Machine Tool Design and Development Center at Batala, Research and Development Center for Bicycles at Ludhiana, and the Sewing Machine Development Center at Ludhiana. These and other facilities are being set up with the assistance of the central government and the United Nations Development Programme and the United Nations Industrial Development Organization.

The state government has established district industrial centers in each district to expedite the implementation of the programs for small-scale industries to reduce delays and to help prospective entrepreneurs. All services are to be made available from a single office.

PROMOTIONAL AND OTHER FINANCIAL AND RESEARCH INSTITUTIONS. The main institutions promoting and financing industrialization in the state are the Punjab State Industrial Development Corporation (PSIDC), the Punjab State Financial Corporation (PSFC), and the Punjab State Small Industries and Export Corporation Limited (PSSIEC). The PSIDC promotes equity among entrepreneurs, and provides term loans (up to Rs 9 million) over and above those from the PSFC. The PSFC distributes term loans up to Rs 3 million to small and medium industries, and the PSSIEC is a multiservice corporation that provides industrial sheds, distributes raw materials to small units, and provides marketing support.

These institutions have played an important role in industrialization in Punjab. The PSIDC has promoted 60 projects since its inception in 1972, and 48 of these have already been commissioned (Punjab 1986). Numerous corporations also have been set up to develop and upgrade technology in areas considered important to industrial development, such as electronics, hosiery and knitwear, handloom materials and textiles, and leather and agroindustries. Some of the public sector promotional corporations have performed creditably, but a few have been corrupt and inefficient. The Vidhan Sabha Committee on Public Undertakings has suggested a number of measures for improving the performance of these enterprises (Singh 1983).

The large number of promotional measures, financial incentives, and other facilities offered by the central and the state governments have played a crucial role in fostering industrialization in Punjab. One drawback to this system is that when raw materials are scarce, the quotas and permits given to small industries fetch a high premium. These often are cornered by politically influential middlemen and sold on the black market, with the result that some end up buying raw material at prices much higher than controlled prices. Those who are able to obtain permits and quotas earn extra profits (see Bhagwati and Desai 1970).

Although some public and private sector enterprises have performed well, many have reached the point at which they ought to be made to stand on their own feet and become cost conscious and efficient. Consequently, government policies—including controls, quotas, and subsidies—require some serious attention.

Summary and Conclusions

Agriculture has been a fast-growing sector in Punjab, thanks to large investments in irrigation both before and after independence in 1947. The introduction of seed-fertilizer technology during the mid-1960s led to unprecedented growth in agricultural output, particularly in wheat and rice among foodgrains and cotton and sugarcane among commercial crops. Animal husbandry also experienced phenomenal growth.

On the eve of independence, Punjab was industrially backward in comparison with the other states of India. It then introduced programs to rehabilitate refugee entrepreneurs and workers and made large investments in infrastructure such as power, industrial estates, transport, and communications. This state intervention created a favorable environment for industrial development, which was accelerated by the increasing demand from Punjab's rapidly growing agriculture and rising export demand. By the beginning of the 1960s, Punjab had become known as the land of small-scale enterprises. Nevertheless, the income from manufacturing was still only 7.3 percent of the state total.

During the mid-1960s industrialization in Punjab received a big boost as a result of the rapid growth in agricultural output spurred by new technology. The rapid growth in agriculture and manufacturing was also accompanied by fast growth in the tertiary sector.

The Punjab experience illustrates that rapid agricultural growth stimulates growth in other sectors through input, output, and consumption linkages and thereby helps transform the economy. As the productivity and per capita income of the agricultural work force rose to much higher levels, the demand for consumption goods also increased. This change not only made a deep dent in rural poverty, but also led to the development of other sectors through forward and backward linkage effects.

Although the growth rate in the secondary and tertiary sectors in Punjab has been creditable, the growth of manufacturing has fallen considerably short of expected levels. This assessment, however, is based on growth calculated for value added rather than on the value of output. An annual growth rate of about 7 percent for value added in manufacturing (as in table 3.1) would imply a growth rate of about 9–10 percent in the value of output. However, even a 9–10 percent rate for manufacturing growth is not consistent with the rapid agricultural growth recorded in the state.

Import leakages may be one reason why manufacturing growth lagged behind expectations. Because Punjab's economy is linked with the rest of the country, it has a comparative advantage through specialization in certain crops and in a few manufacturing lines. For many important agro-inputs such as fertilizers, petroleum products, and agricultural machinery and for numerous consumer goods, however, the state is highly dependent on inputs from the rest of India.

A second, related reason is that, because of the extraordinary increases in the output of many agricultural products, processing capacities in Punjab fell far short of requirements. The problem here is that the regional distribution of manufacturing tends to be historically determined, particularly in agroprocessing and agro-input industries. These industries often do not conform to current patterns of agricultural output, particularly in areas that recently started to produce substantial marketable surpluses. A lack of sufficient investment in agroprocessing seems to have been a major constraint. In 1988/89, for example, Punjab produced 24.4 percent of India's raw cotton but had only 1.9 percent of all installed spindles and 0.6 percent of all looms. The lack of investment in processing facilities for wheat and sugarcane also helps account for the slower-than-expected growth of manufacturing.

The large outflow of financial resources from the state played a role as well. Despite the substantial increase in imports of raw material and consumption goods, Punjab has become an export-surplus economy, primarily because of its large marketed surpluses and exports of wheat, rice, and cotton and some industrial products. A large part of the balance of trade surplus is not being returned to the state for investment in the nonagricultural sectors.

Although the data on intersectoral commodity and resource flows are poor at both the national and state levels, the available evidence suggests that surpluses arising out of prospering agriculture in many parts of India, including Punjab, are not flowing into manufacturing. Agriculture is receiving large subsidies in the form of fertilizers, power, irrigation, and credit, particularly in Punjab, which uses more modern agricultural inputs. As was discussed earlier, developing countries with a labor surplus need to invest large resources from other sectors in rural infrastructure in order to accelerate agricultural growth. Once agricultural incomes start growing rapidly, however, it is important to invest the surplus incomes in the nonagricultural sector. In the case of Punjab, not enough surpluses were transferred from agriculture to industry to achieve an adequate level of growth in manufacturing. Because rich farmers now have considerable economic and political clout, it is more difficult to mobilize the surplus through input prices or by taxation. This is an important constraint at India's present stage of development.

Note, too, that an employment-oriented development strategy requires that the increase in incomes be spent on consumer goods produced through labor-intensive techniques. In Punjab, the large demand for milk and milk products is being satisfied through the rapid development of labor-intensive animal husbandry. In the nonagricultural sector, in contrast, the recent liberalization of capital imports has, in many cases, led to the growth of capital-intensive consumer goods industries, particularly, consumer durables. This difference may in part be due to sociological factors. It generally takes a long time for peasant societies to adjust to the regular rhythm and discipline of an industrial culture. Furthermore, recent tensions in Punjab have driven away prospective entrepreneurs and thus slowed down industrial investments.

Punjab's experience of agriculturally induced growth in a partly "open" economy represents a special case. This framework has many advantages, but may also impose some constraints. On the one hand, a region can benefit from specialization and comparative advantage because for a small region in a large country demand and supply constraints do not operate with the same rigor as in a closed economy. At the same time, a region operates within the national policy framework, which in this case brought large grants from the center that enabled Punjab to invest in irrigation and power infrastructure and to pioneer the green revolution. Punjab exported its entire food surplus to the rest of India at favorable prices. It also found a ready market throughout the country (and sometimes abroad) for many of its industrial products, while easily obtaining raw materials and manufactured goods from the rest of the country. It also benefited from the policy of Indian Railways to equalize freight for bulk commodities.

On the other hand, Punjab has had to share the gains of development with the rest of the economy. Substantial funds from Punjab have evidently been invested in the rest of India since the state began producing an agricultural surplus. In addition, many agricultural laborers have migrated to Punjab from Bihar and other less developed states.

Another important aspect of the national policy of India is that it contributed to the development of Punjab's infrastructure. During the first two economic plans, planned investment in the state was financed largely by the national government. But the national system of licenses and controls discouraged many entrepreneurs from setting up agroprocessing industries there such as sugar mills and cotton textiles. National policy was also restrictive in the sense that it was inward looking and thus has been blamed in some quarters for India's failure to take advantage of the boom in international trade during the 1960s. That would certainly have kept Punjab from participating in the export boom.

The recent liberalization of capital imports has moved the country away from an emphasis on agriculture-based employment. Instead, the government is encouraging the production of various types of consumer durables with the use of highly capital-intensive technologies. Above all, it is important to recognize that in a large country such as India the regional economies are interdependent. As a result, Punjab had to share both prosperity and misfortune with its neighbors. The situation is quite different in the world economy, where countries with varying fortunes coexist.

References

Ahluwalia, M. S. 1978. "Rural Poverty and Agriculture Performance in India." *Journal of Development Studies* 14:298–323.

Bhagwati, J. N., and P. Desai. 1970. *India: Planning for Industrialization.* London: Oxford University Press.

Bhalla, G. S. 1989. *Administration and Implementation of Price Policy in India: A Case Study in Selected Country Studies on Implementation and Administration of Agricultural Price Policy in Asia.* Vol. 1. Rome: Food and Agriculture Organization.

Bhalla, G. S., and G. K. Chadha. 1983. *The Green Revolution and the Small Peasant: A Study of Income Distribution among Punjab Cultivators.* New Delhi: Concept.

Bhalla, G. S., and Amitab Kundu. 1984. "Small and Intermediate Towns in India's Regional Development." In *Small Cities and National Development,* ed. Om Prakash Mathur. Nagoya, Japan: United Nations Center for Regional Development.

Bhalla, G. S. et al. 1990. *Agricultural Growth and Structural Changes in the Punjab*

Economy: An Input-Output Analysis. Research Report 82. Washington, D.C.: International Food Policy Research Institute.

Bhalla, G. S., and D. S. Tyagi. 1989. *Pattern in Indian Agricultural Development: A District Level Study*. New Delhi: Institute for Studies in Industrial Development.

Bhalla, Sheila. 1987. "Trends in Employment in Indian Agriculture, Land and Asset Distribution." *Indian Journal of Agricultural Economics* (October–December).

Bell, C., and T. N. Srinivasan. 1989. "Interlinked Transactions in Rural Markets: An Empirical Study of Andhra Pradesh, Bihar, and Punjab." *Oxford Bulletin of Economics and Statistics* 51 (February).

Chadha, G. K. 1979. *Production Gains of New Agricultural Technology*. Chandigarh: Punjab University Press.

———. 1986. *The State and Rural Economic Transformation: The Case of Punjab, 1950–85*. New Delhi: Sage.

Dasgupta, S. 1989. "The Spirit of Success." *India Today*, October 31.

Darling, M. L. 1938. *The Punjab Peasant in Prosperity and Debt*. Cambridge: Oxford University Press (4th ed., 1947).

Dhesi, A. S., and B. S. Ghuman. 1983. "Productivity Trends and Factor Substitutability in Manufacturing Sector of Punjab Implications for Planning." *PSE Economic Analysis* 3 and 4:27–40.

Gulati, Ashok. 1989. "Input Subsidies in Indian Agriculture: A Statewise Analysis." *Economic and Political Weekly* 24:A57–A66.

Hazell, P. B. R., and A. Röell. 1983. *Rural Growth Linkages: Household Expenditure Patterns in Malaysia and Nigeria*. Research Report 41. Washington, D.C.: International Food Policy Research Institute.

Hirashima, Shigemochi. 1978. *The Structure of Disparity in Developing Agriculture*. Tokyo: Institute of Developing Economies.

Hyami, Y., and M. Kikuchi. 1980. "Changes in Community Institutions and Income Distribution in West and Java Village." Research Paper 50. Philippines: International Rice Research Institute, July:14–16.

India, Cabinet Secretariat. 1955. *NSS Report on Land Holdings: 8th Round 1953–54*. NSS Report 36. New Delhi.

———, Cabinet Secretariat. 1983. *Report on Land Holdings: 37th Round 1982*. NSS Report 331. New Delhi.

———, Ministry of Agriculture. 1976. *Report of National Commission on Agriculture*. New Delhi: Controller of Publication.

———, Ministry of Agriculture and Cooperation, Economic and Statistical Adviser (ESA). Various years. *Comprehensive Scheme for Studying Cost of Cultivation of Principal Crops in India*. New Delhi.

———, Ministry of Finance, Economic Advisory Council. 1990. *Towards Evolving an Employment-Oriented Strategy for Development in the 1990s: Interim Report*. New Delhi.

———, Ministry of Food and Agriculture, Directorate of Economics and Statistics. 1968. *Growth Rates in Agriculture, 1949/50 to 1964/65*. New Delhi.

———, Ministry of Home Affairs, Registrar General of India. 1951. *Census of India, 1951*. New Delhi.

———, Ministry of Home Affairs. 1991. *Census of India, 1991*. Paper 2. New Delhi.

————, Ministry of Industry, Small Industries Development Organization. 1989. *Annual Report, 1988/89.* New Delhi.

————, Ministry of Planning, Central Statistical Organization (CSO). Various years. *Annual Survey of Industries: Summary Results of Factory Sector.* New Delhi.

————, Ministry of Planning, CSO. Various years. *National Accounts Statistics.* Delhi.

————, Ministry of Planning, National Sample Survey Organization (NSSO). 1975. *Tables on Land Holdings at State Level: Punjab.* Vol. 1. New Delhi.

————, Ministry of Planning, NSSO. 1986. *Report on Land Holdings, 37th Round.* New Delhi.

————, Ministry of Planning, NSSO. 1989a. *Directory Manufacturing Establishments Survey, 1984–85.* New Delhi.

————, Ministry of Planning, NSSO. 1989b. *Tables with Notes on Survey of Unregistered Manufacturing: Non-directory Establishments and Own Account Enterprises.* 42d round. New Delhi.

————, Ministry of Planning, NSSO. 1990a. *Key Result of Employment and Unemployment: All India.* Part 1, NSS 43d round. Special Report 1. New Delhi.

————, Ministry of Planning, NSSO. 1990b. *Key Result of Consumer Expenditure.* NSS 44th round, 1988/89. Special Report 2. New Delhi.

————, Planning Commission. 1981. *Technical Note on the Sixth Plan of India.* New Delhi.

————, Planning Commission. 1986. *Technical Note on the Seventh Plan of India (1985–90).* New Delhi.

Johar, R. S. 1983. "Decentralization of Industrial Development with Special Reference to Punjab." In *Studies in Punjab Economy,* ed. R. S. Johar and J. S. Khanna. Amristar: Punjab School of Economics, Guru Nanak Dev University.

Johar, R. S., and J. S. Khanna, eds. 1983. *Studies in Punjab Economy.* Amristar: Punjab School of Economics, Guru Nanak Dev University.

Jose, A. V. 1988. "Agricultural Wages in India." *Asian Employment Programmes Working Papers.* New Delhi: ARTEP, ILO.

Khanna, J. S. 1983. "Lagging Industrial Development in Punjab." In *Studies in Punjab Economy,* ed. R. S. Johar and J. S. Khanna. Amristar: Punjab School of Economics, Guru Nanak Dev University.

Mathur, Om Prakash. 1982. *Small Cities and National Development.* Nagoya, Japan: United Nations, Center for Regional Development.

Mellor, John W. 1976. *The New Economics of Growth: A Strategy for India and the Developing World.* Ithaca, N.Y.: Cornell University Press.

Mellor, J. W., and M. S. Mudahar. 1974. "Modernizing Agriculture, Employment and Economic Growth: A Simulation Model." *Cornell Agricultural Economics Occasional Paper* 75. Ithaca, N.Y.

Mody, Ashok. 1981. "Resource Flows between Agriculture and Nonagriculture in India, 1950–70." *Economic and Political Weekly* 16:425–40.

Mundle, Sundipto. 1977. "Home Market, Capitalization in Agriculture and Drain of Agriculture Surplus." *Economic and Political Weekly* 12:A49–A54.

Nag, Moni. 1989. "Alternative Routes of Fertility and Mortality Decline: A Study of Kerala and Punjab." In *Population Transition in India,* ed. S. N. Singh et al. New Delhi: B. R. Publishing Corporation.

Punjab, 1901. *The Punjab Alienation Act, 1901*. Lahore.

————, Director of Industries. 1978. *Industrial Policy Statement, 1978*. Chandigarh.

————, Department of Planning. 1986. *Seventh Five-Year Plan, 1985–90: Annual Plan, 1985/86*. Chandigarh.

————, Department of Planning. 1990. *Draft Annual Plan, 1990/91*. Chandigarh.

————, Economic Adviser. 1990. *Economic Survey of Punjab, 1989/90*. Chandigarh.

————, Economic and Statistical Adviser. Various years. *The Statistical Abstract of Punjab*. Chandigarh.

————, Economic and Statistical Organization. 1984. *Report on Impact of Incentives to Set-Up Industrial Units in Centrally Backward Districts of the State*. Publication 435. Chandigarh.

Rangarajan, C. 1982. *Agricultural Growth and Industrial Performance in India*. Research Report 33. Washington, D.C.: International Food Policy Research Institute.

Reserve Bank of India (RBI). 1977. *All India Debt and Investment Survey 1971/72: Assets and Liabilities of Rural Households*. Bombay.

————. 1987. *All-India Debt and Investment Survey, 1981/82*. Bombay.

Shirokov, G. K. 1980. *Industrialization of India*. 1st Indian ed. New Delhi: People's Publishing House.

Singh, Harbans. 1991. *Agricultural Development and Rural Labour—A Case Study of Punjab and Haryana*. New Delhi: Concept.

Singh, Iqbal. 1985. "The Changing Tenancy Structure in a Developing Agricultural Region: A Case Study of Punjab." Ph.D. diss., Jawaharlal Nehru University, New Delhi.

Singh, Lakhwinder, 1990. "Industrial Development in Punjab: An Analysis of Growth of Productivity and Structure of Wages." Ph.D. diss., Punjab University, Patiala.

Singh, Pritam. 1983. *Emerging Pattern in Punjab Economy*. New Delhi: Sterling Publishing.

4 Rapid Agricultural Growth Is Not Enough: The Philippines, 1965–80

ROMEO M. BAUTISTA

The Philippine growth experience may be described as a case of agriculture-led development that failed. Rapid agricultural growth during 1965–80 did not translate into sustainable economic growth, and only a small segment of the population benefited to any extent from the observed gains in national income.

Agriculture itself appeared to be doing fairly well: production grew at an average annual rate of 5.6 percent over this period, which was nearly double the 2.9 percent estimated for the preceding 10 years (David, Barker, and Palacpac 1987). Moreover, gross value added in "agriculture" (including also fishery and forestry) increased at a rate of 4.6 percent per year, which is markedly higher than the average 3.0 percent estimated by the World Bank for all developing countries and compares favorably with the corresponding agricultural growth rates for the three neighboring, heavily agricultural economies of Indonesia, Malaysia, and Thailand (table 4.1).

During 1965–80 real GDP in the Philippines grew at a rate of 5.9 percent per year. This is higher than the rate of 5.2 percent achieved in 1955–65 and matches the average growth of all developing countries for 1965–80. The GDP growth rates of its three neighbors, however, were closer to 7.2 percent. Furthermore GDP growth in the Philippines fell to -0.5 percent a year in the period 1980–87. Although adverse external conditions such as the sluggish growth in the industrial countries and their increasing protectionism, not to mention the steep fall in world commodity prices, undoubtedly had a negative effect on economic performance throughout Southeast Asia, GDP growth rates were considerably higher for Indonesia (3.6 percent), Malaysia (4.5 percent), and Thailand (5.6 percent). Interestingly, agricultural and GDP rates are quite similar over 1980–87 in all three of these countries and the Philippines.

The calculated values of the ex post elasticity of GDP with respect to agricultural production (i.e., the ratio of the GDP growth rate to agricultural growth rate) during 1965–80 are as follows: Philippines, 1.28; Indonesia, 1.86; Malaysia, 1.64; and Thailand, 1.56. These values suggest a somewhat weaker

113

TABLE 4.1 Average annual GDP and agricultural and manufacturing growth rates of four Southeast Asian countries, 1965–80 and 1980–87 (percent)

Country	Real GDP		Agricultural Value Added		Manufacturing Value Added	
	1965–80	1980–87	1965–80	1980–87	1965–80	1980–87
Philippines	5.9	−0.5	4.6	1.8	7.5[a]	−1.1
Indonesia	8.0	3.6	4.3	3.0	12.0	7.8
Malaysia	7.4	4.5	4.5[b]	3.4	10.0[b]	6.3
Thailand	7.2	5.6	4.6	3.7	11.2	6.0

SOURCES: World Bank (1989); Asian Development Bank (1983).
[a]Note that this rate is even higher than the 6.9 percent average annual rate from the official (and updated) national income accounts data.
[b]The rate for 1972–80.

link between agricultural growth and economic growth in the Philippines, as is reflected also in the higher manufacturing growth rates achieved by its three neighbors (table 4.1).

Since the Philippine economy depended on imported crude oil for more than 90 percent of its commercial energy requirements in the early 1970s, it is reasonable to suppose that its performance was affected by the oil price shocks of 1974 and 1979–80. Remarkably, the growth rate for 1965–80 was higher than for 1965–73 (5.4 percent) (Bautista 1988a). This growth was made possible by an expansionary macroeconomic policy, financed by sharply expanded foreign borrowing. By 1983, however, the economy was in the midst of a debt-service and foreign exchange crisis, which ushered in the economic recession of 1984–85. Real GDP subsequently declined by about 10 percent, and the country's per capita income fell to its 1975 level.

Another troubling aspect of the country's postwar development record is that the distribution of family income remained heavily skewed (Bautista 1992), in part as a result of the high rates of labor unemployment and under-employment through the late 1970s and the 1980s. Also, poverty increased, particularly among rural families, who in 1985 accounted for nearly three-fourths of the country's total poor.

To add to this problem, economic activity and income growth were concentrated in Manila and the surrounding areas. In the mid-1980s, Metro Manila accounted for about one-third of the country's GDP and more than one-half of total manufacturing value added. Per capita regional GDP in Metro Manila was more than double the next highest GDP and more than five times the lowest GDP of the other twelve regions in the country.

The present study examines these problems up to the year 1980, the point at which the deterioration in Philippine economic performance received added fuel from factors exogenous to agriculture. There were also some major policy developments in the early 1980s that can be considered either transitional or in the nature of emergency measures—which would only complicate the intended analysis of long-run relationships among the macroeconomic environment, agricultural growth, and economic performance.

The Macroeconomic Environment

The macroeconomic conditions that influenced the performance of Philippine agriculture and its interaction with the rest of the economy during 1965–80 can be usefully discussed in terms of the government's foreign trade and payments regime, interest rate and credit policies, pattern of investments, and human resource development.

Trade Policies, Industrial Protection, and the Real Exchange Rate

Trade policy in the early 1950s more or less set the tone for the next three decades. Among its more notable features were comprehensive direct controls on imports and foreign exchange designed to cope with a severe balance-of-payments problem and a massive overvaluation of the domestic currency (which kept the pre-World War II exchange rate in spite of high wartime inflation). This strategy created market distortions and encouraged rent-seeking activities that the government failed to address despite various changes in the policy landscape.

As has been well documented (e.g., Power and Sicat 1971), the "essentiality" rule governing the allocation of import licenses and foreign exchange in the 1950s stimulated the production of import-substituting industrial consumer goods in the early years but penalized backward integration, agricultural production, and exporting. The special tax exemptions to "new and necessary industries" only served to reinforce the trade policy biases of the prevailing incentive structure. The chronic trade deficits in the 1950s, which were particularly severe during the second half of the decade, reflected the government's inability to stimulate new exports and the increasing dependence of domestic industries on imported intermediate and capital goods.

In 1960–62 the government gradually lifted import controls and adjusted the exchange rate from 2.0 to 3.9 pesos per U.S. dollar. These policy changes had little effect on the incentive structure favoring import-substituting industries because the highly protective tariff system that had been introduced in 1957—but was offset for a time by the import and foreign exchange controls—now became applicable. The average effective protection rate (EPR) for industrial consumer goods in 1965 was 70 percent, in marked contrast to the 27 and 16 percent estimated for intermediate products and capital goods, respectively

(Power and Sicat 1971).[1] Nonetheless, the shift from import quotas to tariffs served to reduce the severity of industrial protection. It also enabled small producers to have greater access to imported inputs and the government to collect tariff revenue from importers who previously benefited from the scarcity premiums connected with quantitative import restrictions.

Under the expansionary fiscal and monetary policies adopted by the new Marcos government in the second half of the 1960s, the inflation rate rose significantly and the trade balance deteriorated. In late 1969 the Philippines experienced another foreign exchange crisis, precipitated by the need to service the short-term credit that had financed the trade deficits in the immediately preceding years. A floating exchange rate system was introduced in February 1970 to cope with the balance of payments problem. The 61 percent de facto devaluation over the year served to improve the price competitiveness of export industries, which were given a further boost by the enactment of the Export Incentives Act of 1970. Under this act, manufacturing enterprises registered with the Board of Investments were accorded various kinds of tax exemptions, deductions from taxable income, and tax credits. Selective financial and infrastructural support was also provided to nontraditional export producers, and it compensated in part for the still-pervasive policy bias against exporting. Although certain import controls were lifted, trade restrictions, specifically the protective and distorted tariff system, remained the primary source of this bias. In 1974 the EPR for export-oriented industries averaged only 4 percent, whereas for the entire manufacturing sector it was still 44 percent (compared with 52 percent in 1965). The EPR average for agriculture and other primary industries was 9 percent (Tan 1979).

Restrictions on foreign trade affect relative prices and sectoral production incentives not only through the differential effect on tradable goods prices (as represented in the EPR measure) but also through the effect on the real exchange rate, which affects the domestic currency prices of tradable goods in relation to nontradables. For example, import duties and quotas directly raise the domestic price of import-competing products in relation to exportables and thereby encourage a shift away from export production. The same policy instruments reduce the demand for imports and thus the price of foreign exchange, making the domestic prices of tradable goods fall in relation to nontradables and hence indirectly biasing production incentives against both import-competing and export goods. The restrictive trade regime associated with the industrial protection system therefore doubly penalizes export production.

The overvaluation of the Philippine peso induced by trade policy distortions seemed to weaken during 1950–80 (Bautista 1987). The import and

1. The EPR represents the excess of domestic value added in a production activity over its value added at international prices; it includes the protection of outputs and the penalty from the protection of inputs. A high EPR is presumptive evidence of high excess profits, or a high level of inefficiency, or a combination of the two.

foreign exchange controls of the 1950s caused the real exchange rate to deviate from the free-trade value by about 49 percent on average. After "decontrol," the degree of overvaluation dropped to 35 percent in the 1960s. With the adoption of more outward-looking trade policies in the early 1970s, the overvaluation arising from trade restrictions was further reduced to an average 16 percent through 1980.

In many cases, domestic currency overvaluation is caused by unsustainable deficits in the external account. Macroeconomic policies that lead to such balance of payments disequilibrium help defend an overvalued exchange rate. In the Philippines, the substantial increases in foreign borrowing and accompanying expansionary demand management during 1975–80 accounted for about one-third of the total policy-induced real exchange rate overvaluation, which amounted to 23 percent.

The large current account deficits in the 1970s were, of course, related to the external shocks that buffeted the Philippine economy during the decade. In response to the adverse exogenous developments (chiefly, the sharp oil price increases in 1974 and 1979–80 and the continuous deterioration in the terms of trade during 1974–80), the government decided to accommodate the huge trade deficits through external financing. As a result, annual foreign borrowing increased from less than $60 million in 1972–73 to $800 million in 1974–77 and $2,040 million in 1978–80. To sustain the growth momentum initiated in the early 1970s, the government also implemented what was considered a counter-cyclical strategy by adopting highly expansionary fiscal and monetary policies. Thus, during 1974–80, government spending and the money supply grew at average annual rates of 22 and 18 percent, respectively, which were much higher than their trend rates.

The observed overvaluation of the Philippine peso has had a significant impact on the domestic price structure. In view of the high degree of tradability of agricultural output, it has been estimated that the elasticity of the agricultural terms of trade with respect to the real exchange rate is 0.33 (Bautista 1987, 60). Apart from the induced disparity in effective protection rates between the agricultural and manufacturing sectors already alluded to as a direct effect, trade restrictions designed to protect domestic industry (together with the exchange rate effect of balance of payments disequilibrium) led to a further (indirect) effect: they lowered the domestic terms of trade by 16 percent during 1962–69, by 7 percent during 1970–74, and by 9 percent during 1975–80 in relation to what it would have been without the exchange rate distortion.

Interest Rate and Credit Policies

Before the financial reform of the early 1980s liberalized interest rates and lifted various banking restrictions, the government tightly regulated interest rates on bank loans and deposits. Ceiling rates on secured and unsecured loans—12 and 14 percent, respectively—followed the statutory limits set by the Anti-Usury Law of 1916. These loan rates were much lower than the interest rates the market would bear, at least from the mid-1960s, since the nominal rates of return on industrial investments were typically 25 percent or more. By contrast, the central bank's interest rates on savings and time deposits were set at 6 to 8 percent.[2] In addition, the central bank provided rediscounting privileges at very low rates of interest that also ensured a large profit margin for banks.

The organized financial market was therefore something of a regulated oligopoly: entry was restricted, but there was little room for existing banks to expand given the regulated interest rates. A natural consequence was that financial activity expanded rapidly in the less regulated nonbanking areas, as reflected in the marked increase during 1965–80 in the assets of finance companies and investment houses. These nonbank institutions offered higher "money market" rates to financial savers and thereby captured an increasingly large share of available savings (ILO 1974, 231). But they also charged higher lending rates, catering mostly to commercial banks needing short-term credit to cover their reserve requirements and to large companies with cash flow problems. Because of the high minimum placement, money market instruments were available mainly to institutional investors and wealthy families.

Such organizational structure and "disequilibrium" interest rates had significant effects on the supply of loanable funds and their allocation. The low interest rate for long-term credit reduced the effectiveness of financial intermediation in the economy and inhibited the flow of resources into the organized financial market. The demand for long-term funds became excessive and could only be accommodated by credit rationing. The system of credit allocation therefore came to depend on collateral and personal connections and to favor large urban-based borrowers and capital-intensive industrial enterprises, and in the end served to reinforce the bias of industrial and trade policies. Small farmers were forced to pay much higher interest rates in the unorganized financial market. Agricultural loans from institutional sources went largely to the big landowners; in 1974, for example, farmers owning more than 5 hectares, who represented about 15 percent of total farms and 45 percent of total farm area, received 72 percent of total agricultural credit. Because the loan rates did not reflect the social scarcity of capital, the system encouraged the wasteful use of capital and underutilization of the labor force. Large-scale farming tended to be more mechanized, displacing labor without much effect on yields. Moreover, the overvalued exchange rate and low tariffs on capital goods favored the use of large imported agricultural machinery (e.g., four-wheel tractors) over the locally produced smaller equipment (e.g., power tillers).

Private financial institutions and government policy alike effectively dis-

2. During 1965–80 the consumer price index increased at an average annual rate of 12.8 percent, which implied a negative real return to bank depositors in this period.

criminated against labor use. Less than 10 percent of the loans granted by the government-owned Development Bank of the Philippines, the most important investment lender in the country, went to small farmers and labor-intensive industries. The central bank granted special rediscounting privileges to private development banks that would lend to investors in preferred production activities at concessionary interest rates. Industrial enterprises registered with the Board of Investments under the Investment Priorities Plan were a major beneficiary; not surprisingly, they were found to have large-scale and capital-intensive operations (Bautista, Power, and associates 1979).

The agricultural sector, especially food production, also benefited from government credit rationing. An important element of the Masagana 99 program, which actively promoted the adoption of new rice technology during 1973–77, was the provision of noncollateral low-interest loans. Also, beginning in 1974 all lending institutions were required to allocate at least 25 percent of their loanable funds to agricultural production.[3] Despite such efforts to promote lending to agriculture, agricultural loans as a whole decreased in real terms from the late 1960s to the mid-1970s, and in relation to nonagricultural loans through the end of the 1970s (David 1989, 167). About one-third of total investible resources were directly controlled by government-owned financial institutions, notably the Philippine National Bank and the Development Bank of the Philippines, which were the country's largest commercial and development banks, respectively. Although agricultural loans granted by these two banks increased in real terms during 1966–67 and 1973–75, the share of agriculture in total loans declined significantly in the 1970s.

Public Investment

It is generally accepted, although not widely documented, that "public inputs" in the form of government spending in rural infrastructure, agricultural research, and extension are an important determinant of agricultural output and productivity in developing countries. In nine countries of Latin America, for example, government expenditures contributed an average of about 7 percent of the observed agricultural growth during 1950–80, which represents half of the residual growth not explained by the physical increases in land, labor, and capital (Elias 1985). When applied to the Philippines for the period 1948–84, the "profits function" methodology yields significant elasticity estimates of agricultural output supply with respect to rural road density (0.32) and stocks of regional research (0.18), national research (0.13), and extension (0.03) (Evenson 1986).

Government investment expenditure in the Philippines in the 1960s aver-

---

3. Alternatively, private institutions can deposit the required amount with a government bank that will lend the funds to agricultural borrowers, or they can purchase "loan participation certificates" from other banks with more than 25 percent of their loanable funds in agricultural credits or in government securities.

aged less than 2 percent of GNP, which was very low in comparison with that in other developing countries. In the 1970s, however, there was a marked expansion of public investment, consistent with the policy of counteracting the recessionary conditions in the international economy. Relying on budgetary deficits and public borrowing, the government invested heavily in the energy sector to reduce the country's dependence on imported oil, in industrial import substitution in capital-intensive intermediate products, and in large irrigation projects to promote the rapid diffusion of high-yielding rice varieties. Consequently, the overall public investment rate increased continuously, until it peaked at 8.7 percent of GNP in 1981. Two years later the debt-payment and foreign exchange crisis came to a head and forced a drastic fiscal retrenchment in the 1980s.

From 1960–61 to 1979–80, government expenditures on agriculture expanded nearly sevenfold in real terms, and the agricultural share in total public spending rose from 6.2 percent to 9.5 percent (David 1989, 169). The largest increase was in irrigation investments, whose share in agricultural expenditure climbed from 14 percent in 1960–61 to 52 percent in 1979–80. This increase reflected the need to provide irrigation water to rice farms, many of which had adopted high-yielding varieties during the period, as well as the availability of external financing for large-scale irrigation projects, especially in the 1970s.

Public investment in agricultural research also expanded significantly. Despite its more than eightfold increase (in real terms) from 1960–61 to 1979–80, however, government research expenditure in the Philippines in 1980 was much lower than in Thailand, both absolutely (US\$9.5 versus US\$21.6 million) and as a percentage of agricultural GDP (0.16 versus 0.26) (Pray and Ruttan 1985). Two possible reasons are the greater use of the research output of the International Rice Research Institute (IRRI) on rice and the more active role of the private sector in research on export crops and livestock in the Philippines.

Of the various categories of public agricultural investment, it would appear that the construction of rural roads was given the least attention. The share of rural roads (and bridges) fell from 12.2 percent in 1960–62 to 2.0 percent in 1978–80, in large part because of the massive shift to irrigation investment (Intal and Power 1990, 262). Indeed, the very poor condition of the rural road network was widely considered a major constraint to sustained agricultural growth in the 1980s (e.g., World Bank 1987). Remarkably, even though about 40 percent of total public investment went into roads and road transport during the period, Metro Manila, and to a lesser extent other urban areas, received the bulk of the allocation of infrastructure funds.

The neglect of rural infrastructure mirrored the urban bias in the government's overall infrastructure policy. The combined effect of these policies was a highly uneven regional distribution of infrastructure facilities. Luzon, the country's main island, which is where Manila is located, accounted for 74 percent of the government's expenditure on infrastructure during 1971–81

(Ranis and Stewart 1987, 188) and 86 percent of the installed electricity capacity of the National Power Corporation in 1978–80, 85 percent of which was in Metro Manila (NEDA 1985, 578–9). Also, Metro Manila's road density in the late 1970s was about nine times higher than that of the entire country, 98 percent of its households had access to electricity versus an average 48 percent for the other 12 regions (PIDS 1990, table IV-5), and its share of gross value added in "utilities" from the national income accounts was more than 70 percent.

The underdevelopment of infrastructure outside Metro Manila, especially in rural areas, was no doubt related to the trade and industrial policies adopted, particularly the import restrictions and bureaucratic controls that encouraged centralized industrialization rather than the dispersal of industries away from Metro Manila. As discussed below, this approach had adverse consequences not only on agricultural growth but also on rural nonagricultural growth and on the linkage of agriculture with the rest of the economy.

Human Resource Development

Human resources, as well as physical capital, play a significant role in economic growth. Improvements in the education and health of a country's work force have positive effects on labor productivity, entrepreneurial skills, and technological innovation that are crucial to economic efficiency and competitiveness. Some studies have provided strong evidence of higher productivity among farmers with four years of primary education than among those with no schooling, whether or not the complementary inputs necessary for the adoption of improved farming techniques are available (World Bank 1980, 48). Researchers have also reported relatively high social rates of return to primary, secondary, and higher education (albeit lower returns for the second and third levels) in low- and middle-income developing countries. Both education and health have been found to be positively correlated with economic performance in 15 Asian developing countries (Pernia 1990); interestingly, the Philippines and Sri Lanka are the two outliers whose GNP per capita during 1965–87 grew at a lower rate than would be predicted from their education and health status.

According to the enrollment ratios for the three levels of education (in percentages of relevant age-group populations), the Philippines has had a head start in educational progress in comparison with its three Southeast Asian neighbors (table 4.2). The Philippines apparently attained universal primary education by 1965, at which time only 90 percent of primary school-age children were enrolled in higher-income Malaysia and not even 80 percent were enrolled in Indonesia or Thailand. These disparities were even greater in secondary and tertiary education. Although all three neighbors made substantial progress in raising the secondary enrollment rate in 1965–80, their levels remained lower than that of the Philippines.

Infant mortality and life expectancy in the Philippines in 1965 indicated

Table 4.2 Indicators of human resource development, four Southeast Asian countries, 1965 and 1980

Indicator	Philippines		Indonesia		Thailand		Malaysia	
	1965	1980	1965	1980	1965	1980	1965	1980
Enrollment rates (percentage of age group)								
Primary	113	110	72	98	78	96	90	92
Secondary	41	61	12	28	14	29	28	53
Tertiary	19	25	1	3	2	13	2	5
Infant mortality rate (per	72	55	138	93	88	55	55	31
1,000 live births)[a]		(24)		(33)		(38)		(44)
Life expectancy at birth	55	64	44	53	55	63	60	64
(years)[b]		(36)		(25		(32)		(20)

SOURCES: World Bank (1983, 1984, 1989).
[a]Numbers in parentheses indicate percentage reduction from initial values.
[b]Numbers in parentheses indicate percentage reduction in the shortfall from 80 years.

that its general population was in better health than that in Indonesia or Thailand, while Malaysia was at the top of the list, owing to its higher-income status. Over the next 15 years, however, the Philippines registered the least improvement in infant mortality, although it showed the most significant improvement in life expectancy, calculated as the percentage reduction in the shortfall from the "maximum attainable" age (80 years) (Sen 1981).

On balance, therefore, it would seem that human resources did not deter economic growth in the Philippines, at least in comparison with its three neighbors. If anything, human capital might have offset some of the effects of unfavorable policy and institutional influences on agricultural growth, with the result that agriculture in the Philippines was able to expand as fast as it did in the three other countries during 1965–80, which was a period of rapid technological change.

In the case of economic growth as a whole, as already noted, the Philippine growth rate for that period was significantly lower and also turned out to be unsustainable. This outcome was undoubtedly related to the disparities in education and health among the urban and rural populations and the various income classes. Whereas nearly every adult in Metro Manila was literate by 1980, more than one-third of the adult population in the much poorer regions of Central and Western Mindanao remained illiterate. Moreover, the infant mortality rate in these two regions was more than 2.5 times higher than that in Metro Manila, and the life expectancy was 10 years lower. Not surprisingly, Central Luzon and Southern Tagalog, the two regions closest to Manila, also had fairly high levels of education and health. Because of this skewed distribution of educational and health benefits, the supply of nonagricultural labor responded weakly to the demand arising from the rapid agricultural growth and increased incomes of 1965–80.

Agricultural Growth

Between 1950 and 1980 agricultural output in the Philippines grew at a compound annual rate of 4.9 percent.[4] The most rapid growth (6.8 percent a year) occurred during 1950–55 and was stimulated by the increased demand for agricultural exports at the same time that domestic demand was on the rise because of the rapid growth in population and per capita income. From 1955 to 1965 agricultural growth slowed down to an average of 2.9 percent per year. "During this period tariffs and trade quota on previously favored exports to the United States were gradually imposed, domestic currency became increasingly overvalued, and population growth began to press on limited supply of land" (David, Barker, and Palacpac 1987, 412).

But then the growth rate of agricultural production rose to 4.0 percent a year in 1965–70 and to 6.5 percent in 1970–75. Over these two periods, many farmers adopted high-yielding rice varieties, and the government invested massive amounts in irrigation. Agricultural growth was no doubt also favorably affected by the improved domestic terms of trade related to the trade liberalization of the early 1960s, the floating of the exchange rate in 1970, and the world commodity boom in 1972–74.

Unfortunately, these favorable events were followed by a steep decline in world prices for the country's leading export crops, and "increasing distortions in the exchange rate and agricultural output and fertilizer prices . . . further exacerbated the squeeze on agricultural incentives" (David, Barker, and Palacpac 1987, 412). These circumstances explain in part why the agricultural growth rate dropped to 6.0 percent in 1975–80 and then to 0.3 percent in 1980–82, which was when the external terms of trade worsened.

In view of the significant bias in government price interventions, agricultural growth in the Philippines during 1965–80 might well have been even greater than the observed annual average of 5.6 percent. The problem was that to achieve and sustain overall economic growth, the Philippines actually needed a more broadly based expansion of agricultural income. This is an important argument that will be developed later in the chapter.

Sources of Growth: Supply Factors

Up to the late 1950s, the observed growth of farm output was primarily due to increases in the land area under cultivation. This land-extensive growth subsequently gave way to land-intensive growth, and the expansion of culti-

---

4. In this section, agricultural output is defined to include only crops and livestock. The data come from David, Barker, and Palacpac (1987).

vated land stabilized at an annual rate of 1.3–1.4 percent (David, Barker, and Palacpac 1987).

The growth of agricultural output accelerated in 1965–70, mainly in response to the adoption of improved technologies (especially in rice production), the expansion of irrigated areas, and the increased use of current inputs (fertilizer for crops and imported feeds for livestock). The newly introduced high-yielding varieties of rice raised the productivity of irrigation water and led to the large public investment in irrigation and of fertilizer use, especially after the decline in the ratio of fertilizer to rice price. With this new source of output growth, yield increased dramatically, and the ratio of output land increased by an average 2.7 percent per year (versus 0.5 percent in 1955–65). The annual growth rate of total factor productivity also jumped to 1.4 percent from a negative average value in the preceding ten years.

The momentum of growth picked up in the 1970s, fueled by increasing rates of employment and an improvement in total productivity. The ratio of land to labor fell at an average annual rate of 2.6 percent, but yield increases averaged nearly 5 percent a year, with the result that labor productivity increased significantly over the period. Improved technologies in nonruminant livestock and in nontraditional export crops were also adopted, having been made possible by substantial private investments. The second half of the decade was marked by increased farm mechanization, as reflected in the significant rise in the growth rate of fixed capital services.

Commodity Structure of Growth

A frequently used classification of agricultural crops in the Philippines distinguishes between food and export crops. The food crop category has been dominated by rice and to a lesser extent corn, which in 1965 accounted for 25 and 5 percent, respectively, of total crop production. The two most important export crops have been coconut and sugarcane, which contributed 15 and 12 percent of the total crop, respectively. These four major crops accounted for about 86 percent of the total area harvested in 1965.

As table 4.3 shows, the annual growth rate for rice doubled during 1965–70 in relation to the preceding ten-year period. This increase was a manifestation of the supply responsiveness of Filipino farmers to a new, demonstrably superior technology. Corn output grew at an even higher rate, owing in part to the supplementary demand for feedgrains by the fast-growing livestock industry. In contrast, sugar production in 1965–80 was much the same as in 1955–65, as a result of the termination of the country's access to the restricted U.S. market in 1974, followed by the precipitous decline in world market prices and increase in exchange rate overvaluation in the second half of the 1970s. Coconut, however, expanded at an increasingly rapid rate through the end of the 1970s.

Another notable development during the study period, especially in the

TABLE 4.3 Average annual growth rates of agricultural production by commodity, 1955–1980 (percent)

Commodity	1955–65	1965–80	1965–70	1970–75	1975–80
All crops	3.4	5.2	3.5	6.0	6.1
Rice	2.3	4.3	4.6	4.0	4.6
Corn	5.3	5.6	6.6	5.8	4.4
Sugar	2.9	2.9	4.2	6.3	−1.7
Coconut	3.4	4.2	1.2	3.6	7.7
Other crops	4.4	7.3	2.3	9.8	9.7
Livestock	2.0	6.4	5.3	7.4	6.4

SOURCE: David, Barker, and Palacpac (1987, 413).

1970s, was the rapid expansion of nontraditional agricultural exports. Foreign exchange earnings from exports of fruits and vegetables (especially, bananas, mangoes, and pineapple products) increased continuously, from US$17 million in 1965 to US$35 million in 1970 and US$365 million in 1980 (Bautista 1987, 17). Similarly, exports of coffee, animal feeds, and miscellaneous preparations rose from almost negligible levels in 1970 to US$129 million in 1980. This compensated for the decline in some of the country's traditional exports of abaca and tobacco, and together with the high income elasticity of domestic demand for the newly important horticultural products, enabled farmers to expand the production of "other crops" markedly in the 1970s (table 4.3).

Livestock products, also highly income elastic, accounted for 30 percent of agricultural production in 1965. The accelerated growth of livestock output after 1965, particularly of the nonruminants, was the result not only of the rapid expansion of national income but also of the significant price increases for chicken and pork in relation to the price of feedgrains.

The Narrow Base of Agricultural Income

As mentioned earlier, the income gains from agricultural growth in the Philippines during 1965–80 were not widely shared. Consequently, the demand stimulus to nonagricultural production was weakened, and the national economy grew at a lower rate than would have been otherwise expected.

One of agriculture's problems was that the dramatic productivity improvements associated with the green revolution in rice bypassed a large segment of the farming population that did not have access to irrigation water. The new technology was much less effective in raising yields where water levels could not be strictly regulated. In 1966, only 10.4 percent of total arable land in the Philippines was irrigated in comparison with 33.1 percent in Indonesia, 27.0 percent in Malaysia, and 15.5 percent in Thailand (Vyas 1983, 33). Despite the rapid expansion of irrigated lands in subsequent years (which reached an average of 3.9 percent a year during 1966–80), the ratio of irrigated to arable land increased to only 18.0 percent by 1980. Thus it is not surprising that the average rice yield per hectare in the Philippines remained the lowest among the Southeast Asian countries (James 1982, 66).

The bias against small farmers in the structure of income growth can also be attributed to the greater availability of effective subsidies on credit and fertilizer for large producers as well as their greater access to infrastructure investments (irrigation, electricity, and roads) (David 1983). As in most developing countries, the poorest of the poor in the Philippines, are landless rural families that depend on wage labor as their main source of income (they accounted for about 20 percent of all rural households in 1965). Like the small farmer, they did not benefit much from the accelerated agricultural growth; in fact, their real wage rate fell significantly from the mid-1960s to 1974. Thus it is not surprising that the distribution of rural household income worsened from 1965 to 1971 (the index of quintile inequality increased from 0.38 to 0.41 and the Gini coefficient from 0.42 to 0.46). Although the "legislated" wage rate (in real terms) for nonplantation workers increased, agricultural employers did not fully comply with legislated supplementary payments (cost-of-living and other allowances). According to farm survey data collected by the Bureau of Agricultural Economics, real wages for specific crops, except in sugarcane, increased in 1975 and 1976 but then declined continuously until about 1980, at which point they were back down to the levels of 1974.

Agricultural labor has not been helped by the substantial mechanization of some farm operations, particularly the preparation of land for rice and threshing of the crop. There is ample evidence that the adoption of agricultural machinery over the study period (power tillers, four-wheel tractors, and mechanical threshers) not only displaced labor and depressed wages, but also failed to improve yields (Ahammed and Herdt 1985; Sison, Herdt, and Duff 1985). As pointed out above, labor was effectively subsidized by cheap credit, low tariff rates on imported capital goods, and exchange rate overvaluation.

Another factor bearing on the distribution of income gains from agricultural growth was the unequal distribution of landholdings. Technological change that increases land rent (and the return to agricultural capital) but not the real wage can be expected to worsen the distribution of rural income. In the early 1960s about half of Philippine farms were fully or partly owned by the operator, a third were share-tenanted, and the rest were under other forms of tenancy. Because of the substantial inequity in share-cropping practices, the net income of owner-operators in the rice-growing region of Central Luzon during 1963–70 averaged about 2.3 times that of share tenants (ILO 1974, 475).

Although the government attempted redistributive agrarian reform under Operation Land Transfer, which began in October 1972, this tenancy reform excluded the landless. Moreover, the coverage was limited to rice and corn; the exclusion of land under other crops, which constituted about half of the total crop land area, severely restricted the program's effectiveness in redistributing land ownership and in alleviating rural poverty (Mangahas 1985).

Agricultural income growth was further concentrated by the large presence of foreign firms engaged in plantation farming and large-scale processing of export crops. The effect of such concentration can be seen by comparing the Philippine and Taiwanese experiences in the production and exporting of pineapples and bananas. Taiwan successfully met world demand by relying on dispersed smallholder production and decentralized processing facilities that required low levels of capital and technology and by supplying canned pineapple for the lower-quality segment of the export market. In contrast, the multinational-dominated organizations in the Philippines used sophisticated and expensive equipment and secured supplies mainly from large-scale farmers or plantations (Ranis and Stewart 1987, 159).

Despite rapid agricultural growth, rural household incomes in the Philippines failed to keep up with the general price increases of 1965–75. Since the agricultural terms of trade improved over this period, the slight deterioration in the real income of rural households may be attributed to a decline or stagnation in agricultural wage earnings (as indicated above), and possibly to the nonagricultural component of rural income. The share of nonagricultural income in rural household income certainly stagnated during 1971–75 (at 16–17 percent) (Oshima 1985). Furthermore, it was also much lower than the share in Thailand (about 38 percent for the 1970s) or in Malaysia (28 percent for 1979). Apparently there was little incremental demand for the labor-intensive products of rural nonagricultural industries generated by the rapid agricultural growth in the Philippines. The more affluent rural households that did increase their incomes significantly in all likelihood spent more on capital-intensive goods produced by urban industries or imported from abroad.

Nonagricultural Growth

Manufacturing has been so dominant within the industrial sector that in most discussions of Philippine economic development it is not unreasonable to use the two terms interchangeably. In 1965 the Philippines had already had 15 years of import-substituting industrialization, which, as already mentioned, was promoted in large measure by a heavily protective trade regime, overvalued exchange rate, and low interest rate policy. At first the import-substitution strategy appeared to be succeeding, since manufacturing output increased at an average annual rate of 12.6 percent during 1949–57. During 1957–61, however, manufacturing growth slowed to 5.7 percent, and then to 4.8 percent in 1961–65. This decline reflected the gradual exhaustion of the domestic market for "easy" import substitutes, which in turn was related to the lack of demand among the rural population.

The trade policy reforms adopted in the early 1960s failed to redirect the manufacturing sector away from its import-substitution bias toward a more outward-oriented development. In contrast, some Asian developing countries, most notably Taiwan and South Korea, encouraged the exporting of labor-intensive manufactured goods into world markets through policy changes that reduced industrial protection and introduced more realistic exchange rates (and built up the export infrastructure).

Growth of Manufacturing Production and Productivity

In 1965 Philippine industrialization was pushed into a second phase of import substitution as the government's protection policies were extended beyond light industry into the more capital-intensive upstream industries producing previously imported intermediate products and consumer durables. Again, there was an immediate payoff in increased output, and it contributed to the significant upturn in the growth of manufacturing, which averaged 6.8 percent a year during 1965–70. Between 1965 and 1969 industrial composition shifted away from final consumer goods (footwear and other apparel, wood and cork products, furniture and fixtures, and leather and rubber products) toward producer goods (textiles, chemical and mineral products, transportation equipment, and miscellaneous manufactures). There was also little growth in industrial exports, whose share in total merchandise exports remained at less than 10 percent during 1965–70. By comparison, the export share of manufactures in Taiwan and South Korea reached 79 and 75 percent, respectively, in this period. This increase, particularly in the Taiwanese case, can be traced mainly to small- and medium-scale industries. Philippine industries, in contrast, emphasized high-cost production backed by heavy protection and thus were unable to compete in world markets.

With the adoption of outward-oriented policies in 1970, the country's exports underwent substantial expansion and diversification in the following decade. Until 1970 10 traditional primary products in unprocessed or semi-processed form accounted for more than three-quarters of total export earnings. By 1980 these exports were contributing less than one-half. Total exports (in U.S. dollars) grew at an average annual rate of 23 percent during 1970–80; in terms of volume, the growth rate was 9.4 percent (Tecson 1983, 396). The latter figure is much higher than the export growth registered in the preceding decade (5.0 percent annual average), as is consistent with the more favorable policy climate for exports in the 1970s. The incentive bias toward nontraditional manufactured exports is reflected in the higher annual growth rate of earnings for this export category (34.8 percent). The share of nontraditional manufactured exports to total exports increased from 8.3 percent in 1970 to 22.3 percent in 1976 and 36.4 percent in 1980. Consumer electronics, garments, food products, and handicrafts were among the fastest-growing nontraditional exports.

Given such improved export performance, the 7.0 percent annual growth of manufacturing output during 1970–80 would seem unimpressive since it was

TABLE 4.4 Average annual growth rates of sectoral real value added, 1960–1985 (percent)

Sector	1960–65	1965–70	1970–75	1975–80	1980–85
Agriculture	4.4	4.2	4.3	5.4	2.1
Manufacturing	4.5	6.8	7.0	7.0	−1.3
Services	4.5	4.8	5.3	5.3	−0.3

SOURCE: NEDA, *Philippine Statistical Yearbook,* various issues.
NOTE: Agriculture includes crops, livestock, fishery, and forestry, and therefore these rates differ somewhat from those given earlier for crops and livestock only.

only slightly higher than the 6.8 percent growth for 1965–70 (table 4.4). Economic instability was a worldwide phenomenon in the 1970s, however, and the experience of the Philippines was no exception. That is why manufacturing grew at such an uneven pace: during 1970–73 it reached a peak of 13.9 percent under the influence of domestic policy reforms and the world commodity boom, but plunged to an average 4.7 percent in 1974–76 during the recession in the aftermath of the first oil price shock, experienced a strong recovery in 1977, and then continuously slowed down to 4.2 percent in 1980. Over these years industrial production was unable to resume the rapid growth of the early 1970s, despite the demand stimulus from export expansion. This outcome can be attributed in large part to a weakening domestic demand that was not prevented by the government's countercyclical macroeconomic policy. In the absence of significant, broadly based increases in rural income, exports would have had to expand more vigorously to sustain the growth momentum of manufacturing output.

On the supply side, the productivity of the manufacturing sector is a critical factor in its long-term development. In the Philippine case, total factor productivity (TFP) in manufacturing *decreased* by an average 0.15 percent a year between 1956 and 1980 (Hooley 1985). The growth in TFP related to industrial growth was estimated at 0.49 percent, while that due to an interindustry shift was −0.64 percent. The latter estimate is consistent with the significant loss in TFP in 1956–65 arising from the inefficient allocation of resources among manufacturing industries, which in turn was attributed to import controls and protective tariffs associated with import substitution (Williamson and Sicat 1968). Indeed, a regression analysis at the three-digit ISIC level of interindustry differences in TFP growth rates reveals that effective protection had a negative influence owing to "the dysfunctional impact of tariffs on decisions for combining inputs in the production process and probably a 'disincentive' impact on entrepreneurial behavior as well" (Hooley 1985, 54).

Export orientation is also found to have a significant effect on TFP growth. Other things being equal, the greater the share of an industry's output that is exported, the more rapidly productivity improves, presumably because of the competitive abilities that arise from production for contestable export markets and the constant need to adopt cost-reducing measures. It is surprising, then, that estimated TFP growth rates for the 1970s were negative (-0.55 percent in 1971–75 and -1.90 percent in 1976–80), since this was a period of improved industrial export promotion and performance (especially in the first half of the decade). Such a trend "reflects the national policy bias towards 'heavy' import substitution industries (petroleum, iron and steel, transport equipment, etc.)" (Hooley 1985, 28) prevailing at the time, which must have more than offset the subsidization of priority export industries.

Another explanation for the observed decline in TFP relates to the increasing importance of government corporations, whose share in total nonfinancial corporate assets doubled—from 13.5 to 27.1 percent—between 1965 and 1980. These figures are based on stock ownership of more than 50 percent by the government or government agencies, and they understate the actual magnitude of asset control, particularly during the martial law period of the 1970s, since many corporations are "government-affiliated through control by members of the military or close associates of powerful political/military families" (Hooley 1985, 29). This reversal of the government's declining role in productive activities in the 1950s and 1960s must have had an adverse effect on the provision of public goods. For various reasons (such as employment, rather than profit and weak accountability standards), government corporations tended to be inefficient in the use of capital and especially labor in comparison with private corporations. Total factor productivity during 1960–70 was an estimated 56.2 percent higher in private corporations (Hooley 1985, 29).

The increase in the capital intensity of domestic industry was particularly inappropriate in the second half of the 1970s, when the government financed its expansionary "countercyclical" policies through increased foreign borrowing (Bautista 1988b). Government financial institutions bankrolled many large investment projects of doubtful economic viability whose proponents were politically well connected (Alburo and Shepherd 1986). The high rate of bankruptcy among these projects (which were subsequently taken over by government banks or agencies) reflected the inefficient use of foreign resources, which must have contributed to the further deterioration of manufacturing TFP during 1976–80.

Although difficult to document, the increased centralization of political decisionmaking and politicization of economic activity since the declaration of martial law in 1972 would also have had a negative effect on total factor productivity. Industrial policies were less predictable, as is evident from the frequent complaints, especially by foreign investors, of sudden, arbitrary changes in the rules governing access to fiscal incentives (or in their interpretation). Rent-seeking became more profitable for private producers than trying to reduce costs and improve efficiency.

Industrial Incentives and Relative Factor Use

Public policy in the 1950s and 1960s was obviously biased toward the excessive use of capital in providing incentives for manufacturing investment. In the 1950s the "essentiality" rule governing the allocation of foreign exchange conferred a large windfall on imports of capital equipment, which were obtainable at artificially low prices because of the overvalued exchange rate. Thus, not only were capital-intensive industries favored, but the choice of production techniques was distorted toward the use of capital. This bias was reinforced by preferential access to low-interest loans from government financial institutions. Also, some of the tax exemptions granted to "new and necessary industries" (for a period of four years from the date of organization) were related to the acquisition of capital and hence were also biased against the use of labor.

With the lifting of import and foreign exchange controls and exchange rate adjustment in the early 1960s, the burden of industrial promotion fell on tariff policy and government lending to industries. However, the highly distorted tariff structure served to perpetuate the low effective protection on capital goods (Power and Sicat 1971).

The Investment Incentives Act of 1967 and the Export Incentives Act of 1970 represent two of the country's most important pieces of postwar economic legislation concerning inducements for industrial investments. It has been found that fiscal incentives administered by the Board of Investments (BOI) may reduce the user cost of capital by as much as 49 to 71 percent (depending on whether it is domestic or imported, and whether invested in a pioneer or nonpioneer project, a new or an expansion project, or an exporting or nonexporting project). Furthermore, labor costs may decline by 3.5 percent for nonexporting firms and 22 percent for exporting firms (Gregorio 1979). The estimated effects on the capital-output ratio and employment (based on certain assumptions about a project's economic lifespan, discount rate, and elasticity of factor substitution) are reductions of 35.6 percent and 26,100 workers for the BOI-registered nonexporting firms and 6.9 percent and 8,400 workers for exporting firms.

Two influences on relative factor prices are not reflected in these estimates. One is that BOI-registered firms have preferential access to low-interest credit—which also reduces the cost of capital, by 9 to 35 percent (Mejia 1979). The other is that the required minimum wage and supplementary allowances for workers make the actual wage rate for unskilled workers higher than their social opportunity cost. The BOI subsidy on labor use does not appear to fully match the difference between the market wage rate and the estimated shadow price of labor (Medalla 1979). Significant disemployment effects of minimum wage legislation have been documented at the firm level (in the pineapple industry) and for two-digit ISIC manufacturing industries (Armas 1975).

Changes in the composition of manufacturing output in the 1950s and 1960s are consistent with the hypothesis that the incentive system encouraged the growth of capital-intensive industries more than those using the country's abundant labor resources more intensively. Production in the more labor-using industries—for example, garments, footwear, other leather products, wood products and printed materials—had not grown as rapidly during those two decades as production in the rest of the manufacturing sector, as is evident from the declining relative contribution of these industries to total manufacturing value added (see Bautista, Power, and associates 1979, table 4.2). In the 1970s, the trend was reversed for some labor-intensive industries, largely because of the rapid growth of nontraditional manufactured products that were accorded various benefits under the Export Incentives Act.

Estimates of partial factor productivities in Philippine manufacturing suggest that from 1956 to 1970 labor intensity decreased in relation to either capital or intermediate input, and that the drop was substantial in the years of foreign exchange and import controls (1956–60) (Hooley 1985). By contrast, during 1970–80 (especially in the first half of the decade), when the exchange rate was allowed to float and labor-intensive manufactured exports were being promoted, labor employment increased in relation to the use of intermediate input and (particularly) capital. It is notable that the increasing labor intensity of the manufacturing sector in the 1970s was accompanied by a rising average productivity of capital, which represented a reversal of the downward trend of the preceding decade.

No discussion of postwar industrial promotion policy in the Philippines would be complete without some reference to the government's unusually active support for the so-called eleven major industrial projects (MIPs) from the mid-1970s to late 1983. These were all large-scale and highly capital-intensive projects that included, among others, a copper smelter, diesel engine manufacturing, an integrated steel mill, an aluminum smelter, and a petrochemical complex. The total cost of setting up the eleven projects was close to US$4 billion (at 1981 prices), a substantial part of which was financed through foreign debt. When the external debt-related foreign exchange crisis broke out in late 1983, the government's active pursuit of the MIPs had to be dropped after only a few projects were completed. For the time being, the economy did not have to face the prospect of being presented with numerous "white elephants."

Size Structure and Location Choice

Trade and industrial policies since the early 1950s have contributed significantly to the underdevelopment of small- and medium-scale enterprises and the regional concentration of industries. These two related features of the manufacturing sector have important implications for the supply response to the demand stimulus from agricultural growth.

In the 1950s the system of import and foreign exchange controls favored large firms in and around Manila and in effect discriminated against the relatively small and regionally dispersed manufacturing enterprises. Similarly, the latter did not benefit much from the tax-exemption privileges for "new and necessary industries" and the wider fiscal incentives granted to BOI-registered firms (under the Industrial Incentives Act of 1967 and the Export Incentives Act of 1970). Small and remote firms had difficulty meeting the bureaucratic requirements that would have allowed them to qualify as a priority industry.

The policy bias toward large-scale manufacturing is reflected in the differential incidence of effective protection. From EPR estimates for 1974 (Tan 1979), it has been calculated that about 80 percent of employment in small industries, in contrast to only 45 percent in large industries, can be found in the "underprotected" sectors (defined to include those with EPRs of less than 25 percent); "indeed, 68 percent of those employed in small industries are in sectors with negative EPRs" (Anderson and Khambata 1981, 121). Earlier studies (ILO, 1974; Bautista, 1979) have also documented cases of low effective protection for a small-scale, labor-intensive industry (garments, leather products) that had to rely on a costly and inferior material input (textile, leather) produced locally by a highly protected, large-scale, and capital-intensive industry.

Such an incentive system would have contributed to the dualistic structure of Philippine manufacturing, in which high employment was concentrated in very small and very large establishments. During 1965–80, establishments with 1–4 workers, which constituted the "informal" (or unorganized) sector, accounted for 60–70 percent of total manufacturing employment; those employing 20 or more workers, the "modern" sector, contributed 25–35 percent, about 90 percent of whom would be in the "large" firms with 100 or more workers. This left a very small percentage (less than 10 percent) for the small- and medium-scale enterprises with 5 to 100 workers. The large establishments clearly dominated in terms of value added; in 1969–71, for example, they accounted for 80 percent, whereas at the other end, the informal sector contributed less than 6 percent of manufacturing value added.

In comparison with other developing countries, "large-scale manufacturing appears to be well developed" (ILO 1974, 540) in the Philippines, which is what would be expected in view of the large industry bias of government policies. Also, the informal sector seems "very large" by the standards of developing countries at similar levels of per capita income. Presumably there has been little transformation of informal manufacturing into modern small- and medium-scale industries, which again is to be expected from an industrialization process biased toward the growth of large-scale, regionally concentrated industries. Even with the moderately rapid expansion of large industry, the manufacturing share in total employment remained roughly constant at 11–12 percent, and average capital productivity even decreased in the 1960s (as noted earlier).

The relationship between the number of employees in manufacturing establishments, on the one hand, and labor intensity and capital productivity, on the other, are not necessarily monotonic at a disaggregate level. Estimates of capital per worker and the ratio of value added to capital (based on border prices) for three-digit ISIC manufacturing industries and four employee size groups show wide variations in both capital intensity and capital productivity across and also within industries (ILO 1974, 145). Furthermore, a mixed pattern of efficiency is evident with respect to the size of structure, smaller establishments appearing more labor-intensive and more efficient in capital use in some industries but not in others.

Government efforts to promote small industries in the Philippines took many forms. As of 1974—when the Commission of Small and Medium Industries was created to integrate their activities—at least 12 government agencies were directly involved in the provision of credit, labor training, and technical support to small- and medium-scale enterprises. Even so, less than 25 percent of these industries appeared to be aware of such programs (except for the credit programs of the Development Bank of the Philippines), and of these, less than 10 percent appeared to have sought or received assistance. Furthermore, those that received assistance performed rather poorly in terms of efficiency and growth in comparison with the group as a whole (Hife 1979).

The spatial development of Philippine manufacturing was also strongly influenced by the trade regime and macroeconomic policy. The heavy reliance on imported material inputs and capital equipment that was fostered by the import-substitution policies of the 1950s and 1960s, and to a lesser degree by the export promotion drive of the 1970s, created a strong incentive to locate plants near the source of supply, Manila (the principal port).[5] These policies in turn stimulated the development of nearby areas through agglomeration economies and spillover effects (Sicat 1972; Pernia and Paderanga 1983). Moreover, Metro Manila was the principal market for the import-competing industries that benefited from heavy protection and exchange rate overvaluation. The more geographically scattered, resource-intensive industries were not favored by those policies, and their slow growth contributed little to the regional dispersal of industries. Such regional bias in the choice of location would also have influenced the large-scale and capital-intensive character of Philippine industrialization to the extent that manufacturing establishments were drawn away from the small local markets and low-cost labor in the outlying regions.

Under an infrastructure policy that promoted the idea of Manila as a "metropolis of international stature," this metropolitan area also received a disproportionately larger allocation of public investment funds than other re-

5. Regression analysis of industrial concentration in Metro Manila, using cross-sectional data for 1975 from three-digit industries, indicates that the fraction of material inputs imported, the proportion of output exported, and the effective protection rate all had a significant positive effect (Hermoso 1983).

gions and thus became more attractive to industries and migrants (NEDA 1982). Reinforcing these tendencies was the need to obtain tax and credit favors from the centrally run financial and government institutions in Metro Manila, which became even more centralized in the 1970s; even the mining and lumber companies based in the outlying regions found it necessary to maintain large offices there.

As a result, manufacturing growth was highly uneven among the country's 13 regions. According to census data, Metro Manila and the adjoining Southern Tagalog region accounted for 49.1 percent of total manufacturing value added in 1948; this increased to 64.0 percent in 1961, and to 81.6 percent in 1978 (NEDA 1983, 471). And despite additional fiscal incentives to locate in certain designated (less developed) areas, more than three-fifths of the 590 new enterprises that registered with the Board of Investments during 1968–74 were based in Metro Manila and Southern Tagalog (World Bank 1976, 238). Because the other regions have been unable to expand their manufacturing production to any extent, there are still large disparities in regional per capita incomes (Moran 1978).

Growth of the Service Sector

With commerce and services as its main components, the service sector accounted for about two-fifths of domestic production during 1965–80 and was the second most important source of employment after agriculture. It expanded less rapidly than manufacturing in terms of value added (table 4.4), but more rapidly in terms of employment. Average labor productivity in the service sector therefore declined in relation to that in manufacturing, and indeed the growth rate was negative, particularly during 1960–70.

In the 1960s and 1970s real value added in the service sector grew at a much lower rate in the Philippines than in its three Southeast Asian neighbors, except Indonesia during 1960–70 (Oshima 1982). Furthermore, average labor productivity showed positive growth in Indonesia, Malaysia, and Thailand during both 1960–70 and 1970–80 but declined in the Philippines in each of the two decades.

This poor performance was a result of the highly dualistic character of the service sector in the Philippines and its linkages with the other production sectors. In part, the service sector consists of a large, "informal," labor-intensive subsector (accounting for more than 60 percent of total service employment), but it also contains a small number of "modern," capital-intensive service establishments catering to the needs of large industry and commercial agriculture. The rapid growth in service sector employment and the accompanying decline in labor productivity occurred mainly in the informal subsector. There are two possible sources of such employment growth. On the demand side, it would be a linkage effect of the increased expenditure on informal service output as agricultural and manufacturing incomes grow over time.

Given the inequitable pattern of agricultural growth in the Philippines and the dualistic development of the industrial sector, it is doubtful that this represented a major source of growth of informal service employment. The other, more likely possibility, would be that the stagnation of rural incomes and rapid population growth encouraged migration to the urban areas (see DeVoretz 1972) and that the inability to find manufacturing employment forced migrants to take jobs in the low-paying informal services. Although some branches of modern urban-based services might have expanded together with the rest of the modern economy to which they are linked, their labor-absorptive capacity was quite limited.

In effect, the growth performance of the service sector in the Philippines during 1965–80 reflected the uneven pattern of development in the other leading production sectors of the economy. More broadly based agricultural growth and more labor-intensive industrialization would have brought with it a more rapidly growing, more productive service sector.

Demand Structure and Growth Linkages

The antiemployment and antiequity biases of Philippine economic policies since the early 1950s clearly had a negative effect on the structure and growth of effective demand, since they favored capital-intensive products and imported goods, rather than labor-intensive, locally produced goods. This emphasis in turn would have weakened the intermediate and final demand effects on the domestic economy, making rapid economic growth unsustainable. The sudden slowdown in the growth of the manufacturing sector in the late 1950s and late 1960s—after brief periods of "easy" industrial import substitution in consumer and producer goods, respectively—demonstrates this hypothesis very well.

A similar relationship applies to agricultural growth. Increases in agricultural output arising from, say, technological change and productivity growth stimulate the demand for production-related products (like fertilizer and farm equipment) from the nonagricultural sectors, as well as expand the supply of agricultural products used as intermediate inputs (such as raw materials) to nonagricultural production. These two types of production linkage are referred to as "backward linkage" and "forward linkage," respectively. Agricultural crop and livestock production is generally characterized by a "weak" backward linkage and "medium-strong" forward linkage, which prompted A. O. Hirschman (1958, 110) to remark that "the superiority of manufacturing in this respect is crushing." This viewpoint has empirical support in the Philippine context (ILO 1974, 659–73). Moreover, the results of input-output analysis of the Philippine economy indicate that export-oriented agriculture and livestock have stronger backward linkages than the food crop sector, and that the modern consumer goods and services sectors have weaker backward linkages than their traditional counterparts. It bears emphasizing, however, that the adoption of new technologies in the food crop sector after 1965 would have increased the backward linkage effects in view of the greater use of fertilizer and farm equipment, among other things.

Apart from the linkage effects on the production side, agricultural growth also raises the real income of farmers and hence their demand for food and other agricultural products, as well as industrial consumer goods and services. Such consumption linkages set in motion a sequence of employment and income multiplier effects at the rural, regional, and national levels. On the basis of surveys of several areas of the Philippines (Gibbs 1974; Sander 1979; Wang-wacharakul 1984; Ranis and Stewart 1987), Ranis, Stewart, and Reyes (1989, 60, 62) have concluded that "rural nonagricultural employment is dominated by consumption-linkage activities" and that agricultural growth leads to the "expansion of employment in absolute terms . . . [that is] significantly the highest in consumption-related activities." The employment growth accounted for by consumption linkages ranged from 63 percent to more than 80 percent of the total increase in nonagricultural employment. The dominance of the consumption linkages over the production linkages has been attributed in part to the greater intensity of labor in consumption-related rural industries.

The employment expansion in production-related activities appeared to be more closely related to forward than to backward linkages, which is consistent with the comparative results of sectoral input-output analysis. Note, too that a greater stimulus to local production was associated with income growth among the lower-income rural households (Wangwacharakul 1984).

Agricultural growth obviously has some further ramifications beyond the local economy. Even in the first round of effects, there will be goods produced outside the local economy that will be demanded by farmers and rural households in production and in consumption. In the second round of effects, the main forces at play will be the forward and backward linkages of the increased nonagricultural production outside the rural economy, as well as the final demand effects of the increased income.

In view of the linkages between agricultural growth and the rest of the economy, it is reasonable to assume, at the aggregate level, that nonagricultural production is in part a function of agricultural production. If it is further assumed that consumption linkages are dominant, an additional explanatory variable on the demand side is the volume of exports (representing foreign demand). When that factor is taken into account, regression analysis suggests that the "growth linkage elasticity" is 1.27 (Bautista 1990), which means that a 1 percent increase in agricultural production results in more than 1 percent growth in nonagricultural production.[6] This conclusion is consistent with re-

---

6. The estimates were based on five-year moving averages of annual growth rates of nonagricultural value added, agricultural value added, and exports of goods and services (each expressed at constant prices) during 1961–84.

sults based on microeconomic evidence indicating that "even where conditions are not especially conducive to higher linkages, growth in agricultural output leads to substantial growth in nonagricultural opportunities" (Ranis and Stewart 1987, 164). The significant point, however, is that the linkage elasticity could have been higher. Not surprisingly, higher estimates were obtained for Indonesia (1.35) and Malaysia (1.60).

Another quantitative investigation of the economywide repercussions of increasing agricultural production (generated by an exogenous improvement in agricultural productivity) employed a multisectoral, general equilibrium model of the Philippine economy (Bautista 1986). In this case, it was assumed that equilibrium was initially static, as approximated by the observed condition in 1978, and then was disturbed by a 10 percent increase in total factor productivity in each of the four food and agricultural sectors distinguished in the model. The simulation results, reflecting the adjustment of the economy to a new equilibrium position, indicate significant macroeconomic effects, including those on government income (3.7 percent), total investment (2.6 percent), and national income (2.2 percent). The model does not distinguish between small and large agricultural producers and between low- and high-income rural households. It is reasonable to suppose, however, that the resulting benefits to the national economy would be greater if a larger share of the increases in productivity and income went to the smaller farms and lower-income households. Conversely, to the extent that the productivity and income improvements favored the large and the prosperous, the simulation results would have tended to overstate the positive macroeconomic effects.

This observation leads to the central thesis of this study. Despite the rapid adoption of improved technologies and expansion of agricultural output during 1965–80, income growth was not broadly based and employment generation was limited. The resulting increases in consumption demand for the products of rural-based, labor-intensive industries were therefore much less than they would have been otherwise. Because the growth of agricultural income was concentrated on the more affluent rural households, the pattern of effective demand that evolved was biased toward the products of urban-based, capital-intensive industries and imported goods.

Similarly, supply conditions in the nonagricultural sector were not conducive to the expansion of regionally dispersed, small- and medium-scale industries. Large industry and the supporting modern, urban-based service sector in the Philippines became overdeveloped by the standards of developing countries (at comparable income levels), but their growth was bound to be unsustainable because domestic demand was limited and they were unable to compete in world markets. Informal nonagricultural production, which was crowded out in capital allocation and productivity improvement, prevented their rapid transformation into modern small- and medium-scale enterprises.

As a final point, the physical and social infrastructure in the rural areas and outlying regions remained underdeveloped in relation to the urban centers, especially Metro Manila, as mentioned earlier. This, too, would have significantly impeded the transmission of growth impulses from agriculture to non-agriculture within the rural and regional economies and weakened the further growth linkages to the rest of the national economy.

Urbanization

The spatial distribution of a country's population is affected, among other things, by the location and labor-absorptive capacity of its industries and by the growth and structure of the agricultural sector.[7] The population factors of policy interest in the Philippines are the concentration in urban areas, that is, the level and rate of urbanization; the concentration of urban population in the primate city, Manila; and the regional imbalance in urbanization.

Since urbanization is perhaps an inevitable concomitant of economic development, there is nothing inherently wrong about a general shift in the distribution of population over time from rural to urban areas. It is the pattern of urbanization that may present some problems concerning the social costs of agglomeration, the differential access of people to information, resources and markets, disparities in income opportunities, and the resultant political alienation.

Comparative data on some indicators of urbanization and urban concentration during 1960–80 show that the level of urbanization was higher in the Philippines than in any of its three Southeast Asian neighbors throughout the period (World Bank 1983). In terms of the rate of urbanization, however, it was second, after Indonesia. Urban concentration in the primary city, as commonly measured, was much higher in the Philippines than in Indonesia and Malaysia. Indeed, the index of primacy for the Philippines was highest among thirteen Asian countries (Pernia and Paderanga 1983).

In developing countries, the level of urbanization (or urban-rural ratio) is usually positively associated with the manufacturing share in GDP, as exemplified by the rapid urbanization in the industrializing East Asian economies during 1950–80 (Pernia and Paderanga 1983, 11). This relationship is only partly borne out in the Southeast Asian countries. Although the Philippines did have the largest share of manufacturing in GDP throughout the period, Indonesia's smaller share in relation to Malaysia and Thailand did not match its higher level of urbanization in 1980.

When the differences in degree of industrialization among the four countries are taken into account, the comparative values of the urbanization ratio

---

7. Demographic factors are also important. For example, rural-urban differences in fertility and mortality rates can outweigh the effects of rural-urban migration. The rate of urbanization can also be influenced indirectly by population growth through the latter's effects on industrialization and agricultural development.

suggest that Malaysia was the "most urbanized" in 1960; by 1980, however, the Philippines and Indonesia jointly occupied the top position, and Thailand was consistently far below them. As Ranis, Stewart, and Reyes (1989) have argued, a higher urbanization ratio is associated with more concentrated industrialization and weaker intersectoral linkage effects.

With respect to urban primacy, even after one adjusts for the greater share of Philippine manufacturing in GDP, urban concentration was higher in the premier city of the Philippines than of either Indonesia or Malaysia. It is noteworthy that between 1960 and 1980 both urbanization and primacy ratios declined most markedly in Malaysia, which, among the four Southeast Asian countries, was the least protective of domestic industry (Ariff and Hill 1985).

The urban primacy of Metro Manila was already established by 1960. This region was close to being wholly urban; in sharp contrast, the next highly urbanized area held only about a quarter of the population and the remaining two regions less than a fifth (table 4.5). In the following two decades, the rate ("tempo") of urbanization in Manila was significantly higher than in any of the three regions. This implies that the latter became even less urbanized in relation to Metro Manila, and thus that the regional imbalance in the urbanization process had grown even worse.

This imbalance was due in part to the heavy concentration of manufacturing industries and supporting service establishments in the Metro Manila area. The trade and macroeconomic policies of the 1950s and 1960s had encouraged import-dependent firms to set up their operations in the national capital region where import licenses, foreign exchange allocations, tax incentives, and low-interest loans were granted to "preferred" industries. Despite the low labor-absorptive capacity of large industries and modern services, many workers

TABLE 4.5 Regional urbanization, 1960, 1970, and 1980 (percent)

| | Level[a] | Tempo[b] | |
Region	1960	1960–70	1970–80
Metro Manila	98.1	4.9	4.0
More urbanized: Central Luzon, Southern Tagalog, Western Visayas, Central Visayas	26.1	1.9	2.8
Less urbanized: Ilocos, Bicol, Eastern Visayas	19.8	0.4	1.7
Rural: Cagayan, Western Mindanao, Northern Mindanao, Southern Mindanao	18.6	−0.2	2.6

SOURCES: Pernia and Paderanga (1980) for 1960–70; 1970–80 figures calcuated from basic data in NEDA (1985).
[a]"Level" is the percentage of population in urban areas.
[b]"Tempo" represents the difference between urban and rural growth, expressed as the compound annual rate.

from the outlying regions migrated to Manila expecting high wages. Instead, the only employment most of them could find was in low-paying informal service activities.

In the early 1970s the government took some steps to disperse industrial activity away from the Metro Manila area. For example, new industries were not allowed to become established within a 50-kilometer radius of Manila. The impact of this ban was greatly weakened, however, by the numerous exceptions permitted by the Human Settlements Commission. These exceptions were based on such criteria as conformity with the development plan of the Metro Manila municipality or city, location within the identified growth centers, and need for the firm to be near an international airport.

Under the regional dispersal policy, export enterprises locating in designated areas outside Metro Manila were eligible to receive a tax deduction equal to the sum of the cost of local raw materials and double the direct labor cost, but with a maximum allowable deduction of 25 percent of export revenue. Also, firms were offered a tax credit covering the entire amount of infrastructure expenses they incurred by setting up operations outside Manila. Neither of these two fiscal incentives proved effective, however (Moran 1979). On one hand, a large number of sample firms were not even aware of those incentives, or of the available technical, financial, and management assistance, and on the other hand, many firms considered the economic benefits insignificant. The location decision of most firms appeared to be dictated by market factors relating to input supply and product markets. New firms seemed to have the same concerns as old firms, whether local or foreign, and direct government intervention seemed to have no influence on the location decision at all (Herrin and Pernia 1987, 126).

Urbanization is also affected by developments in the rural-agricultural sector. Agricultural growth that raises rural household incomes also reduces the economic incentive to migrate to urban or industrial regions. If significant rural nonagricultural employment is also induced through the various linkage mechanisms, the supplementary earnings from that source will provide an additional incentive for rural workers and their families not to leave. Because Philippine agricultural growth during 1965–80 was not accompanied by a significant increase in the average rural income and was not strongly linked to rural industries, its negative influence on the rate of urbanization was presumably weaker than it would have been otherwise. To the extent that the limited employment generation in agriculture and in rural nonagricultural production was responsible for the considerable migration of workers to Metro Manila—either directly or indirectly, via second-stage migration from smaller cities and towns—government policies that fostered such an outcome in rural labor absorption would also have contributed to the observed high level of urban concentration (primacy) in the Philippines.

The role of institutions and infrastructure in promoting urban primacy also bears emphasizing. All the government and financial institutions from which private investors obtain tax and credit favors are concentrated in Metro Manila. From its colonial past it also inherited a heavy concentration of the country's institutions of learning, culture, and recreation—amenities that help influence the location decision of business executives, employees, and their families. All these factors continued to draw industries and migrants to the national capital region.

Poverty

In view of the fact that income distribution in the Philippines was stable between 1965 and 1980 (Bautista 1992) and that per capita income increased appreciably (at an annual rate of nearly 3 percent), a rising incidence of poverty would seem unlikely. However, existing estimates indicate that poverty did increase, at least from 1965 to 1975 (Mangahas 1976; Tan and Holazo 1978; NEDA 1986).

Measuring the level and trend of poverty is, of course, fraught with conceptual and statistical difficulties (see Foster 1984). In the absence of adequate data, poverty in the Philippines must be measured by a headcount index representing the proportion of the population that falls below (but ignoring how far below) a given poverty line. The choice of poverty line itself is a source of considerable disagreement. In view of the well-known underestimation of income in the Family Income and Expenditure Survey (FIES) series, survey data on expenditures are sometimes used. These data yield lower values of poverty (i.e., they underestimate "true" poverty to the extent that low-income families actually dissaved in the years under consideration), but they still show that poverty increased from 1965 to 1971.

Owing to the many problems in estimating poverty trends in the Philippines, one study (World Bank 1980, 17) concluded that poverty "increased to some extent in the first half of the 1970s, partly due to some transitory factors," but decreased in the second half, as indicated by a significant increase in nutritional intake. What is perhaps indisputable is that the incidence of poverty in the Philippines was at its highest in 1985, according to government estimates; this is presumably related to the 15 percent decline in per capita GNP that accompanied the adoption of IMF-prescribed macroeconomic stabilization measures during 1984–85.

If poverty did increase, or remained at about the same level, during 1965–80—which would have been unusual, indeed, given Fields's (1989) empirical generalization that economic growth and poverty reduction in developing countries go together—the nature of the growth process can provide at least part of the explanation. The majority of the poor in the Philippines consist of landless rural workers, small landowners, farmer-tenants, and unskilled urban laborers, all of whom were bypassed in a pattern of development that was both inefficient and inequitable. The rapid growth of the labor force (about 3 percent a year) and the antiemployment bias of government policies (which favored the large farms and firms over the small, and the capital intensive over the labor intensive) helped perpetuate the dualistic structure and labor-surplus character of the economy and prevented real wage rates from improving over time. Direct government interventions to increase the endowment of income-generating assets for the poor—either by redistributing existing assets (e.g., through land reform) or by concentrating asset increments (e.g., human capital investments) on the poor—had also been ineffective.

In the 1970s about three-fourths of the poor families were in rural areas (World Bank 1980). Poverty was more widespread among rural households than urban households (79.1 versus 48.5 percent); and great disparities existed in the quality of life in these areas, as assessed by access to electric energy, safe water, and strong shelter (Alburo and Roberto 1980, 139). It may also be recalled that indicators of human resource development (adult literacy, infant mortality, and life expectancy) had been much more favorable to Metro Manila than other regions of the country (table 4.2).

There appears to be a negative correlation between poverty incidence in rural areas and various indicators of agricultural productivity at the regional level (World Bank 1980). Central Luzon, which had the lowest incidence of poverty in 1971, ranked either first or second in each of the productivity measures, presumably because the region had the highest proportion of crop area irrigated. At the other end, three regions of "high incidence"—Central Visayas, Eastern Visayas, and Bicol—were consistently among those with the lowest productivity. A possible reason for the high level of poverty in Cagayan Valley, despite its relatively high agricultural productivity, is that its access to markets outside the region was severely restricted because of its remote location and undeveloped infrastructure. High agricultural productivity apparently did not translate into a low incidence of poverty in Northern Mindanao or Western Visayas, either. The high productivity of the former region was related to forestry activities and pineapple-growing in plantations operated by multinational firms; and in the latter region it was connected primarily with sugar plantations. As is well known, the income gains from these sectors were not widely shared. At any rate, it seems clear that the incidence of poverty was significantly influenced by factors other than agricultural productivity.

Conclusions

Rapid agricultural growth in the Philippines during 1965–80 did not provide a strong impetus to overall economic growth in large part because income gains were concentrated in the already more affluent segment of the rural population. As a result, rural consumption favored capital-intensive products and imported goods rather than labor-intensive, locally produced goods. From the demand side, this response reinforced the antiemployment bias of the concurrent industrial development, which favored large industries and firms based in Metro Manila. Thus there was also no stimulus to the growth of broadly based nonagricultural income, which could have generated significant employment multiplier effects on the local, regional, and national economies. Accordingly, the rate of labor absorption in both agriculture and industry was very low, and given the rapid expansion of the labor force, it prevented real wage rates from moving upward. As a result, income inequality persisted and the incidence of poverty increased over the period.

The benefits from the green revolution in rice were not shared equitably because large producers had greater access to the infrastructure investments and effective subsidies on irrigation water and credit. Small-scale and rainfed agriculture that produced food crops were to a large extent bypassed. At the same time, income growth in the export crop sector was also concentrated in plantation production and large-scale processing by multinational companies. In addition, the large inequality in land ownership and high tenancy rates that prevailed during 1965–80 meant that the agricultural income gains were not likely to be widely shared.

In the industrial sector, the continued emphasis on import substitution behind heavy protection, first in final consumption goods and then in intermediate products and consumer durables, encouraged the growth of large-scale, capital-intensive manufacturing to the detriment of smaller, labor-intensive enterprises. It also accentuated existing biases toward industrial concentration in Manila and the surrounding areas, which in turn led to increasing urban concentration in the primate city. Furthermore, the highly restrictive foreign trade regime imposed by the industrial protection system gave rise to a substantial overvaluation of the Philippine peso, which in effect penalized export production, both agricultural and nonagricultural. Although various incentives to manufactured exports were granted selectively in the 1970s, the induced export expansion was not sufficient to compensate for the declining effective demand in the domestic market. The slow growth (perhaps, even stagnation) of rural incomes during the period became a constraining influence that limited the further growth of nonagricultural production. In like manner, the marked expansion of foreign borrowing to finance the "countercyclical" growth policies in the second half of the 1970s, which had little effect on the real income of the rural population, did not lead to self-sustaining economic growth.

In view of the country's labor surplus, it would have been impossible to achieve rapid, sustainable, and equitable economic growth without adequate productive employment. The employment objective was severely compromised, however, by government policies that promoted the excessive use of capital—through low tariffs on equipment and machinery (tariff-free importation for BOI-registered firms), exchange rate overvaluation, a low interest rate, and in the second half of the 1970s the BOI's strong encouragement of large-scale, capital-intensive industrial projects. By discriminating against the de-velopment of small industries in its allocation of capital and technological improvements, government policy also hindered the modernization of low-productivity, "informal" manufacturing, and service activities and helped per-petuate the dualistic structure and regional concentration of the nonagricultural sector.

Had an effective land reform program been implemented and access to rural infrastructure been more equal, the rapid growth of productivity in Philip-pine agriculture during 1965–80 would have led to more broadly based income growth among rural households. This growth would have generated a greater incremental demand for labor-intensive products in which small rural enter-prises have a comparative advantage over large-scale, urban-based industries. On the supply side, a more favorable incentive climate for the development of small industries, including a more uniform protection system and more rational credit allocation, would have induced more labor-intensive, regionally dis-persed nonagricultural growth. The employment and income multiplier effects of the increased rural incomes would therefore have been greater and would have improved the prospects for rapid and equitable growth of the national economy.

Another point that should not be overlooked is the supply pressure in the labor market that arose from the rapid expansion of the Philippine labor force during 1965–80. Although not easily amenable to policy influence in the short run, a slowdown in the growth of labor supply would perhaps have been needed, in addition to a more labor-intensive growth of agricultural and non-agricultural production, if the real wage rates were to rise significantly. Such a slowdown ultimately might have been the key to translating the rapid agri-cultural growth of this period into rapid, self-sustaining, and equitable econom-ic growth.

References

Ahammed, C. S., and R. W. Herdt. 1985. "A General Equilibrium Analysis of the Effects of Rice Mechanization in the Philippines." In *Modelling the Impact of Small Farm Mechanization*. Philippine Institute for Development Studies Monograph Series 5. Manila.

Alburo, F. A., and E. L. Roberto. 1980. "An Analysis and Synthesis of Poverty Research in the Philippines." In *Survey of Philippine Development Research 1.* Manila: Philippine Institute for Development Studies.

Alburo, F. A., and G. Shepherd. 1986. "Trade Liberalization: The Philippine Experi-ence." Paper prepared for the World Bank research project, "Timing and Sequenc-ing of a Trade Liberalization Policy." Washington, D.C.

Anderson, D., and F. Khambata. 1981. "Small Enterprises and Development Policy in the Philippines: A Case Study." World Bank Staff Working Paper 468. Washington, D.C.

Ariff, M., and H. Hill. 1985. *Export-oriented Industrialization: The ASEAN Experience.* Sydney: Allen and Unwin.

Armas, A. 1975. "The Constraint of Minimum Wage Legislation on the Long-run Choice of Technology in the Canned Pineapple Industry." *Philippine Review of Business and Economics* 12.

Asian Development Bank. 1983. *Key Indications of Developing Countries of ADB.* Manila.

Bautista, R. M. 1979. "Domestic Resource Costs in the Leather and Leather Goods Industries." In *Industrial Promotion Policies in the Philippines,* R. M. Bautista, J. H. Power, and associates. Manila: Philippine Institute for Development Studies.

———. 1986. "Effects of Increasing Agricultural Productivity in the Philippines." *Agricultural Economics* 1:67–85.

———. 1987. "Multisectoral Analysis of Trade Liberalization: The Philippines, 1978." *Philippine Economic Journal* 26.

———. 1988a. "Agricultural Growth as a Development Strategy for the Philippines." *Philippine Economic Journal* 27:9–19.

———. 1988b. "Foreign Borrowing as Dutch Disease: A Quantitative Analysis for the Philippines." *International Economic Journal* 2:35–49.

———. 1990. "Agricultural Growth and Food Imports in Developing Countries: A Reexamination." In *Economic Development in East and Southeast Asia: Essays in Honor of Professor Shinichi Ichimura,* ed. S. Naya and A. Takayama. Honolulu: Institute of Southeast Asian Studies, Singapore and East-West Center.

———. 1992. *Development Policy in East Asia: Economic Growth and Poverty Alleviation.* Singapore: Institute of Southeast Asian Studies.

Bautista, R. M., J. H. Power, and associates. 1979. *Industrial Promotion Policies in the Philippines.* Manila: Philippine Institute for Development Studies.

David, C. C. 1983. "Economic Policies and Agricultural Incentives." *Philippine Economic Journal* 11:154–82.

———. 1989. "Philippines: Price Policy in Transition." In *Food Price Policy in Asia,* ed. T. Sicular. Ithaca, N.Y.: Cornell University Press.

David, C. C., R. Barker, and A. Palacpac. 1987. "Philippines." In *Productivity Measurement and Analysis: Asian Agriculture.* Tokyo: Asian Productivity Organization.

DeVoretz, D. J. 1972. "Migration in a Labor Surplus Economy." *Philippine Economic Journal* 11:58–80.

Elias, V. J. 1985. *Government Expenditures on Agriculture and Agricultural Growth in Latin America.* Research Report 50. Washington, D.C.: International Food Policy Research Institute.

Emerson, C., and P. G. Warr. 1981. "Economic Evaluation of Mineral Processing Projects: A Case Study of Copper Smelting in the Philippines." *Philippine Economic Journal* 20:175–97.

Evenson, R. E. 1986. "Infrastructure, Output Supply and Input Demand in Philippine Agriculture: Provisional Estimates." *Journal of Philippine Development* 23: 62–76.

Fields, G. S. 1989. "Changes in Poverty and Inequality in Developing Countries." Paper presented at the IFPRI–World Bank Poverty Research Conference, Airlie, Va.

Foster, J. E. 1984. "On Economic Poverty: A Survey of Aggregate Measures." *Advances in Econometrics* 3:215–51.

Gibbs, A. 1974. "Agricultural Modernization, Non-Farm Employment and Low Level Urbanization: A Case Study of a Central Luzon Subregion of the Philippines." Ph.D. diss. University of Michigan.

Gregorio, R. G. 1979. "An Economic Analysis of the Effects of the Philippine Fiscal Incentives for Industrial Promotion." Ph.D. diss. University of the Philippines.

Hermoso, V. P. 1983. "The Development of the Philippine Space Economy, 1900–75." In *The Spatial and Urban Dimensions of Development in the Philippines,* E. M. Pernia et al. Manila: Philippine Institute for Development Studies.

Herrin, A., and E. M. Pernia. 1987. "Factors Affecting the Choice of Location: A Survey of Foreign and Local Firms in the Philippines." *Journal of Philippine Development* 24:89–140.

Hife, E. A. 1979. "Survey Results on the Impact of Industrial Policies on Small Industry Development." In *Industrial Promotion Policies in the Philippines,* R. M. Bautista, J. H. Power, and associates. Manila: Philippine Institute for Development Studies.

Hirschman, A. O. 1958. *The Strategy of Economic Development.* New Haven: Yale University Press.

Hooley, R. 1985. *Productivity Growth in Philippine Manufacturing: Retrospect and Future Prospects.* Philippine Institute for Development Studies Monograph Series 9. Manila.

Intal, P. S., and J. H. Power. 1990. *Trade, Exchange Rate and Agricultural Pricing Policies in the Philippines.* World Bank Comparative Studies on the Political Economy of Agricultural Pricing Policy. Washington, D.C.

International Labour Office (ILO). 1974. *Sharing in Development in the Philippines.* Geneva: International Labour Office.

James, W. E. 1982. "Asian Agriculture and Economic Development." Asian Development Bank Economic Staff Paper 5. Manila.

Mangahas, M., ed. 1976. *Measuring Philippine Development.* Manila: Development Academy of the Philippines.

———. 1985. "Rural Poverty and Operation Land Transfer." In *Strategy for Alleviating Poverty in Rural Asia,* ed. R. Islam. Bangkok: International Labour Office, Asian Employment Programme.

Medalla, E. M. 1979. "Estimating the Shadow Price of Labor." In *Industrial Promotion Policies in the Philippines,* R. M. Bautista, J. H. Power, and associates. Manila: Philippine Institute for Development Studies.

Mejia, W. V. 1979. "Financial Policies and Industrial Promotion." In *Industrial Promotion Policies in the Philippines,* R. M. Bautista, J. H. Power, and associates. Manila: Philippine Institute for Development Studies.

Moran, P. B. 1978. "Regional Structure of Philippine Manufacturing, 1948–1974." *Philippine Review of Business and Economics* 15:117–42.

———. 1979. "The Impact of Regional Dispersal Policies on the Location Choices of Some Manufacturing Firms." In *Industrial Promotion Policies in the Philippines,*

R. M. Bautista, J. H. Power, and associates. Manila: Philippine Institute for Development Studies.

National Economic and Development Authority (NEDA). 1982. "Regional Development: Issues and Strategies on Urbanization and Urban Development." In *Philippine Development Planning Studies*. Regional Planning Studies Series 8. Manila.

―――. 1983. *Philippine Yearbook 1983*. Manila.

―――. 1985. *Philippine Statistical Yearbook 1985*. Manila.

―――. 1986. *Medium-Term Philippine Development Plan 1987–1992*. Manila.

Oshima, H. T. 1982. "Postwar Philippine Economic Growth in Comparative Perspective: An Overview." Paper presented at the Second General Meeting of the Philippine Society for International Development, NEDA, Makati, Metro Manila.

―――. 1985. "Levels and Trend of Farm Families' Non-Agricultural Incomes and Different Stages of Development." *Philippine Review of Economics and Business* 12:123–54.

Pernia, E. M. 1990. "Economic Growth Performance of Indonesia, the Philippines and Thailand: The Human Resource Dimension." Asian Development Bank Report Series 48. Manila.

Pernia, E. M., and C. W. Paderanga. 1980. "Urbanization and Spatial Development in the Philippines: A Survey." In *Survey of Philippine Development Research 1*. Manila: Philippine Institute for Development Studies.

―――. 1983. "The Spatial and Urban Dimensions of Development." In *The Spatial and Urban Dimensions of Development in the Philippines*, E. M. Pernia, et al. Manila: Philippine Institute for Development Studies.

Philippine Institute for Development Studies (PIDS). 1990. *Balanced Regional Development Study*. Final Report to the Asian Development Bank. Manila.

Power, J. H., and G. P. Sicat. 1971. *The Philippines: Industrialization and Trade Policies*. London: Oxford University Press.

Pray, C. E., and V. W. Ruttan. 1985. "Completion Report of the Asian Agricultural Project." Economic Development Center Bulletin 85-2. St. Paul: University of Minnesota.

Ranis, G., and F. Stewart. 1987. "Rural Linkages in the Philippines and Taiwan." In *Macro-Policies for Appropriate Technology in Developing Countries*, ed. F. Stewart. Boulder, Colo.: Westview Press.

Ranis, G., F. Stewart, and E. A. Reyes. 1989. "Linkages in Development: A Philippine Case Study." Philippine Institute for Development Studies. Working Paper Series 89-02. Manila.

Sander, W. 1979. "The Upper Pampanga River Project's Impact on Non-farm Employment and Regional Growth." School of Economics Discussion Paper 7918. Manila: University of the Philippines.

Sen, A. K. 1981. "Public Action and the Quality of Life in Developing Countries." *Oxford Bulletin of Economics and Statistics* 43:287–319.

Sicat, G. P. 1972. "Regional Development: Interaction of National and Regional Policies." In *Economic Policy and Philippine Development*, G. P. Sicat. Quezon City: University of the Philippines Press.

Sison, J. F., R. W. Herdt, and B. Duff. 1985. "The Effect of Small Farm Mechanization on Employment and Output." *Journal of Philippine Development* 12:29–82.

Tan, N. A. 1979. "The Structure of Protection and Resource Flows in the Philippines." In *Industrial Promotion Policies in the Philippines,* R. M. Bautista, J. H. Power, and associates. Manila: Philippines Institute for International Studies.

Tan, E., and V. Holazo. 1978. "Measuring Poverty Incidence in a Segmented Market." School of Economics Discussion Paper 78-14. Quezon City, Metro Manila: University of the Philippines.

Tecson, G. R. 1983. "Trade and Promotion Policy in Philippine Industrial Development." *Developing Economies* 21:386–414.

Vyas, V. S. 1983. "Asian Agriculture: Achievements and Challenges." *Asian Development Review* 1:27–44.

Williamson, J., and G. P. Sicat. 1968. "Technical Change and Resource Allocation in Philippine Manufacturing, 1957–1965." School of Economics Discussion Paper 68-21. Quezon City, Metro Manila: University of the Philippines.

Wangwacharakul, V. 1984. "Direct and Indirect Impact of the New Cropping Systems Technology and Irrigation in a Community Economy: The Case of Oton and Tigbauan Municipalities, Iloilo Province, Philippines." Ph.D. diss., University of the Philippines, Manila.

World Bank. 1976. *The Philippines: Priorities and Prospects for Development.* World Bank Country Economic Report. Washington, D.C.

———. 1980. *Aspects of Poverty in the Philippines: A Review and Assessment.* East Asia and Pacific Regional Office. Report 2984-P17. Washington, D.C.

———. 1983. *World Development Report 1983.* New York: Oxford University Press.

———. 1984. *World Development Report 1984.* New York: Oxford University Press.

———. 1987. *Philippines: A Framework for Economic Recovery.* World Bank Country Study. Washington, D.C.

———. 1989. *World Development Report 1989.* New York: Oxford University Press.

5 Land-Abundant Agricultural Growth and Some of Its Consequences: The Case of Thailand

AMMAR SIAMWALLA

Agricultural growth in Thailand from the Second World War until about 1980 was dominated by a massive expansion in the land area under cultivation. During this period Thailand was probably the only country in Asia that saw an expansion in cultivated land per agricultural worker (figure 5.1). The availability of land allowed agriculture to continue to absorb large amounts of labor, with the consequence that Thailand still has a larger proportion of its labor force in agriculture than other Asian countries at similar income levels (figure 5.2).[1]

The plentiful availability of new land allowed Thailand to have a strong comparative advantage in agriculture. During the 1960s and the 1970s, the foreign exchange earnings brought in by agricultural exports enabled the Thai government to follow a relatively liberal trade and foreign exchange regime. As a result, the strong hand of the government (which is usually associated with credit and foreign exchange rationing) never made itself felt. To be sure, the Thai economy was never run on strictly laissez-faire principles: the Board of Investment actively encouraged new investments in what it deemed to be sunrise industries; and the tariff rates were also quite high, ranging from 30 to 90 percent. Except for the implicit restraint caused by the expansion of promoted industries and the occasional ban on new entry that ensued, the government seldom imposed direct controls on the growth of any industry through licensings and bans.

This growth pattern shifted after about 1980. Land was no longer in plentiful supply. Since then, the land area per agricultural worker has been declining at the rate of about 1 percent per year (see figure 5.1). Agricultural output, which grew at 4.2 percent per year between 1970 and 1980, thereafter grew at 3.4 percent (table 5.1). Compounding the problem was the worldwide agricultural depression of the early 1980s, which led to a decline in domestic prices. The consequences of these developments for the standard of living of

---

1. As explained later, there are certain problems with the data in figure 5.2, but they will do for now as a crude indicator of the concentration of the labor force in agricultural activities.

FIGURE 5.1 Cultivated area per agricultural worker, 1961–1987

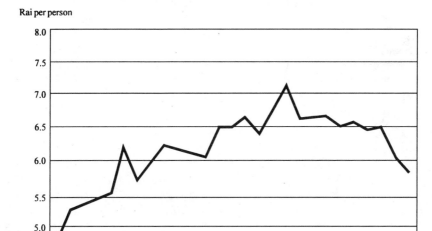

Rai per person

Sources: Cultivated area figures for the 22 most important crops are from the Office of Agricultural Economics, compiled by the Thailand Development Research Institute; unpublished data from Thailand Agricultural Workers Population Census and interpolations for intervening years.
Note: One rai is approximately 0.16 hectare.

the rural population was immediate and palpable. The poverty level—and Thai poverty is almost entirely a rural phenomenon—increased between 1981 and 1986 for the first time since income and expenditure statistics were kept, although between 1986 and 1988 the farm price recovery again led to a decline in the poverty rate, back to what it was in the early 1980s. The net result was an unchanging absolute poverty level in the 1980s after two decades of continuous and substantial decline.

As the comparative advantage of agriculture declined with the closing of the land frontier, manufactured exports became a source of foreign exchange. Between 1980 and 1988 manufacturing's share in the exports of goods jumped from 53 to 74 percent. Another nonagricultural source of foreign exchange earnings was income from tourism, which contributed an additional 19.8 percent to the earnings from goods exported in 1988, up from 13.5 percent in 1980. This restructuring of the country's export revenues was not entirely painless, for it was followed by a sharp slackening of economic growth in the period 1982–86.

Thailand's growth experience has thus been closely connected to its two

FIGURE 5.2 Relationship between share of agricultural labor force and GDP per capita, selected Asian countries, 1965–1983

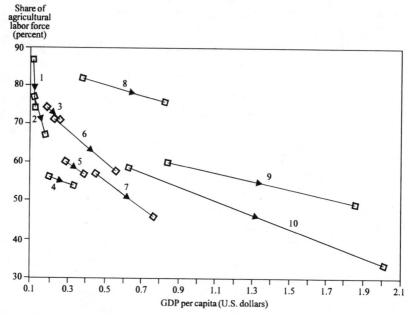

Source: World Bank (1985).

Note: 1=Bangladesh, 2=Burma, 3=India, 4=Sri Lanka, 5=Pakistan, 6=Indonesia, 7=Philippines, 8=Thailand, 9=Malaysia, and 10=Republic of Korea. Initial point, 1965; end point, 1983.

tradable sectors: agriculture and manufacturing. The large and amorphous remainder of the economy (which accounts for about half of the total GDP) produces largely nontradable goods, although income from tourism does contribute a significant amount to the value added in this sector.

On the surface, Thailand's shifting comparative advantage is reflected in

TABLE 5.1 Growth rates of real GNP and various sectors, 1970–1988 (percent)

Sector	1970–80	1980–86	1986–88
Agriculture	4.2	3.7	1.9
Mining	6.0	4.9	7.9
Manufacturing	9.7	4.1	13.7
Others	7.1	6.4	8.7
GNP	6.9	5.3	8.5

SOURCE: National Accounts Division, National Economic and Social Development Board, new series.

NOTE: Growth rates are obtained by regression analysis.

competitive rather than complementary growth of agriculture and manufacturing. It seems that expansion of the one can take place only if it takes away resources from the other. This notion, of course, presupposes a fully employed economy. But if the economy is less than fully employed, then the expansion of one may induce expansion in the other through demand linkages, and the familiar multiplier process. Regardless of whether the economy is fully employed, the expansion of either tradable sector or both would raise the demand for the nontradable sector, and perhaps its prices in relation to the tradable sectors.

The main task of the chapter is therefore to determine whether this description is indeed borne out by the data at hand, both at the aggregate and microeconomic levels.

A Brief Macroeconomic History, 1970–1988

The first task in assessing the role of comparative advantage in the growth of Thailand's agricultural and manufacturing sectors is to determine whether policies allow comparative advantage to play its proper role. Recent literature has stressed that macroeconomic policies greatly influence the degree to which international relative prices are reflected in domestic relative prices (Krueger, Schiff, and Valdes 1988). It is, therefore, important to start the discussion with the country's macroeconomic history.

Traditionally, Thailand's monetary and fiscal policies have been disciplined by two overriding objectives: the reluctance to change the nominal exchange rate and a very strong central bank desire to avoid quantitative foreign exchange controls. For 26 years (1955 to 1981), the baht/dollar exchange rate remained at 20–21 baht. This ability to maintain the nominal rate without extensive foreign exchange control requires conservative monetary and fiscal policies. This approach has been, with one exception, the normal policy stance of the Thai government.

The combination of fixed exchange rates and conservative monetary and fiscal policies appears to have been very successful during the 1960s, when the world as a whole was under a fixed exchange rate system. With the increasing instability in the international exchange rates during the 1970s and the 1980s, Thailand's fixed nominal exchange rate began to create problems for macroeconomic management, inasmuch as policymakers believed their task was not so much to maintain the value of the baht in some general sense, but specifically to maintain the baht/dollar exchange rate. As the dollar began to soar against other currencies (particularly the yen) in the world exchanges between 1979 and 1985, Thailand's policy of maintaining the baht/dollar parity caused the baht to become seriously overvalued, with the result that export performance suffered a setback while the flow of imports increased.

Despite these pressures on the balance of payments, the government was able to maintain the nominal exchange rate in part because of its willingness (perceived as necessity) to borrow overseas as the current account deficits began to widen. This borrowing, in conflict with the traditional reluctance of the Thais to borrow excessively overseas, began in 1977 independently of the problems with the baht. The borrowing gathered momentum after the second oil shock and the accompanying upward movement of the baht in 1979 (figure 5.3). It was accompanied by large fiscal deficits, amounting at times to about 10 percent of GNP. This borrowing of the late 1970s and the early 1980s was an uncharacteristically loose policy stance.

Eventually in 1983, after discussions with the International Monetary Fund, the government embarked on a long and painful reversal of these policies. The fiscal deficits were gradually tightened by introducing a zero-growth (in real terms) budget, by terminating open-ended subsidies to various public enterprises, and by placing a cap on the aggregate foreign borrowing by the public sector; all these measures were in addition to the 15 percent devaluation in November 1984. This devaluation was actually the second one in the 1980s. The baht had already been devalued once (by 10 percent against the dollar in July 1981), as a consequence of a speculative run on the currency.

At the time of the second devaluation, the baht was to be pegged to a

FIGURE 5.3 Current account deficit as a percentage of GNP, 1970–1988

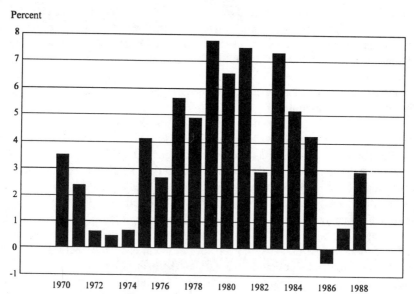

Sources: Current account deficit is from Bank of Thailand; GNP is from National Accounts Division, National Economic and Social Development Board.

basket of currencies. But as the dollar began to drift downward in the second quarter of 1985, the share of the dollar in the basket was apparently lifted from about a half to close to 90 percent, marking the first time since 1955 that Thai policymakers had made deliberate, if cautious, use of the nominal exchange rate as a policy instrument.

Altogether, there were three devaluations of the baht in the 1980s: two apparent ones in the baht/dollar rate in 1981 and 1984, which merely corrected the earlier involuntary revaluation, and a deliberate one beginning in mid-1985, which lowered the effective exchange rate against the trade-weighted basket of other currencies and therefore increased the competitiveness of Thai manufactured goods exports.

These manipulations of the exchange rate, and the concomitant discipline in macroeconomic policies, meant that in 1986 the exchange rate was overvalued in relation to a free-trade exchange rate by about 10 percent, which is a low degree of overvaluation by historical standards (Siamwalla and Setboonsarng 1989). The economy was therefore well poised for the strong performance of the ensuing three years.

Sectoral Linkages: The Macroeconomic Picture

The movement in the relative prices of agriculture and mining, on the one hand, and manufacturing, on the other, as against the "other" (i.e., nontradable) sectors, presents a rather interesting picture (figure 5.4). For most of the 1970s relative agricultural prices were high but then experienced a sharp fall during the 1980s (the price indices used here are the sectoral GDP deflators). These movements reflect more or less faithfully worldwide trends in commodity prices. The only deviation would arise from domestic policy changes, particularly policies at the border. Note that Thai agricultural export policies were completely liberalized during the 1980s, after three decades of heavy taxation of agriculture (particularly rice) (Siamwalla and Setboonsarng 1989), but it was insufficient to offset the downward trend in world prices. As the next section makes clear, this downward trend in prices had a strong impact on the level of poverty in the country.

A different logic altogether drove the movement in the relative prices of manufacturing (figure 5.4). This movement lagged behind the movements in the real exchange rate by about two years.[2] The apparent reason for this lag was that the nominal price for manufactured goods was somewhat sticky, while that for nontradables was more flexible.

In Thailand, price formation in agriculture differs from that in manufactur-

---

2. The real exchange rate displayed in figure 5.3 is defined as the nominal exchange rate divided by the ratio of the weighted average of the inflation rates of Thailand's trading partners and the domestic inflation rate.

FIGURE 5.4 Relative price of tradables to nontradables, 1970–1988

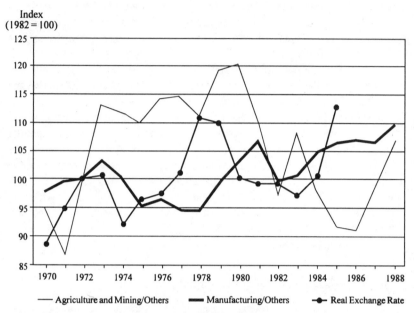

Sources: Sectoral value-added deflators (which provide the prices for agriculture and mining, for manufacturing, and for the other sectors) are from the National Accounts Division, National Economic and Social Development Board; real exchange rates from Siamwalla and Setboonsarng (1989).

ing. Essentially, agriculture (mining) is in a flexprice world, in which its nominal price level moves quite freely over a wide range, usually in response to world market conditions and to government border measures. Manufacturing, in contrast, is in a fixprice world; hence its price in relation to nontradables is a better indicator of the domestic macroeconomic environments than are agricultural prices.

Agricultural output is by and large supply determined; in the long run, it is subject to changes in the overall comparative advantage of the Thai economy, and in the short run, to weather conditions. Agriculture does respond to price (through which demand makes itself felt), but the response in the short to medium run is quite small. In any case, the price to which agriculture does respond is essentially exogenous to the domestic economy. Manufacturing output, on the other hand, can be strongly influenced in the short run by shifts in demand, both domestic and foreign. Its output flexibility makes up for its lack of price flexibility.

A simple regression test of the hypothesis of the linkage between agriculture and manufacturing can be performed using the following equation:

$(1 - cL)$.ln (Real Manufacturing Output) = Constant
+ a.ln (Real Agricultural Income)
+ b.ln (Industrial Countries' GNP)

where L is the lag operator, and a and b measure the responsiveness of the manufacturing output to the two autonomous demand shifters, while c is the lag coefficient.

The real output of the manufacturing sector (i.e., the output from the manufacturing sector at constant prices) is taken to be the dependent variable. The first independent variable, real agricultural income, is defined as the nominal value of agricultural and mining output deflated by the price deflator for the nontradables (i.e., sectors other than agriculture, mining, and manufacturing). This variable can also be expressed as the product of real agricultural and mining *output* and the real price of agriculture and mining (deflated by the nontradable goods prices), which in this instance is the measure of real agricultural and mining *income*.

The problem in estimating this equation is that the variables are subject to strong time-trends, so that although apparently good results can be obtained (with high R^2 and good t-statistics), as indicated in the first column of table 5.2, one cannot be sure that the correlation is not spurious. The results reported are

TABLE 5.2 Estimates of regression explaining the logarithm of real manufacturing output, 1971–1988

Variable Used	Actual	Detrended
Lag coefficient	0.460	0.000
Constant	−1.790	0.000
Logarithm of real agricultural and mining income		
Coefficient	0.236	0.633
T-statistic	2.884	9.591
Implied long-run coefficient	0.438	0.633
Logarithm of industrial countries' GNP		
Coefficient	1.148	—
T-statistic	9.033	—
Implied long-run coefficient	2.125	—
Durbin-Watson statistic	1.539	1.863
Adjusted R^2	0.980	0.836

SOURCE: Real manufacturing output and real agricultural and mining income from the National Accounts Division, National Economic and Social Development Board. Industrial countries' GNP from OECD.
NOTE: All logarithms are to the base e.

obtained by experimenting with different value of c, the lag coefficient, and choosing a value that yields the best fit, subject to the constraint that the Durbin-Watson statistic does not indicate a significant serial correlation in the error term. Table 5.3 presents the results of this experiment. A lag coefficient of 0.46 (see table 5.2) gives the best result, according to which the long-run values of the responsiveness of manufacturing output to the two autonomous demand shifters (i.e., the values of $a/(1-c)$ and $b/(1-c)$) are robust and do not vary significantly whatever the value of c. This seems to be a safe conclusion, although nothing can be said about the short-run responsiveness of manufacturing output to the two independent variables.

To be sure that the results were not entirely the outcome of a spurious correlation between strongly trended variables, all the three variables were detrended by taking the residuals from their log-linear regression trend lines and then regressing them. In this case, real agricultural income remains significant as a determinant of manufacturing output (table 5.2, second column), whereas the GNP of industrial countries is no longer significant. These results indicate that the correlation between real manufacturing output and real agricultural income is most certainly not spurious. However, the correlation between detrended variables does not indicate a long-term relationship, since the long-term characteristic of the variable, namely its trend, has been removed.

Although agricultural and mining income does indeed appear to have a significant impact on manufacturing output, the policy implications of this finding are as yet unclear. It is well known that in most Asian countries any real expansion of agricultural output in the long run cannot stray much from the range 1 to 5 percent. An effort to boost agricultural growth in Thailand permanently by, say, two percentage points—in itself a striking performance—would accelerate the growth of manufacturing output by only about one percentage point. Such acceleration should be set against the normal long-run growth rate in manufacturing, which runs at 8 to 12 percent.

TABLE 5.3 Robustness of estimated parameters in table 5.2

Assumed Value of Lag Coefficient	Estimate of a (short run)	Estimate of $a/(1-c)$ (long run)	Estimate of b (short run)	Estimate of $b/(1-c)$ (long run)	D-W Statistic	Adjusted R^2
0.00	0.477	0.477	2.131	2.131	1.184	0.98795
0.20	0.372	0.465	1.704	2.130	1.298	0.98756
0.40	0.268	0.446	1.276	2.127	1.484	0.98355
0.46	0.236	0.438	1.148	2.125	1.539	0.98038
0.60	0.163	0.408	0.848	2.121	1.621	0.96235
0.80	0.059	0.294	0.421	2.103	1.597	0.79977

SOURCE: Author's computations.

Demand Linkages: The Microeconomic Data

A more direct approach to estimating the size of demand linkages is to examine the response of consumers in different sectors to an increase in income. Data from the socioeconomic surveys of 1975 and 1988 were used to estimate the Engel curves for different groups of the population in Thailand. The population was divided into three geographical groups: rural, urban outside Bangkok, and Bangkok. Since the difference between the two sets of urban areas turned out to be small (there is a slight tendency for urban people outside Bangkok to consume more food), the discussion below refers collectively to all urban areas. Owing to the lack of space, only the figures on rural consumption are presented here (table 5.4).

The population was also divided into three income classes: the bottom three deciles (labeled "poor"), the top three deciles (labeled "rich"), and the middle four deciles (labeled "medium"). The division lines are based on ranking in the national population and are not regional ones. Thus in these calculations the poor in Bangkok have roughly the same nominal incomes as the poor in rural areas.

The specification follows closely that of Hazell and Röell (1983). Table 5.4 shows the absolute and marginal budget shares for the various categories of goods and services for the rural areas of Thailand. Consumption categories have been used to describe the various goods and services, which were grouped somewhat arbitrarily according to their production characteristics, in the absence of an input-output table. "Meals and beverages away from home," for example, includes both a service component and a goods component. "Shelter" includes embodied manufactured goods in the form of brick and mortar. Similarly, "transportation" includes expenditures on vehicles of all sorts. Nevertheless, the grouping provides a convenient peg on which to hang the discussion that follows.

The rural consumption pattern (in comparison with its urban counterpart) exhibits some surprising features: a distinctly smaller share of the marginal budget goes to food, compensated by a larger (and increasing) share going to services. Notable among the food items are the values of both the average and the marginal shares of cereals and what may be called the second tier of food (the category termed "meat, poultry, etc."). Cereals and grain products in Thailand are now in effect inferior goods, and the income elasticity of the second tier (measured by the ratio of the average and the marginal budget shares) is also rapidly dwindling. The rural population in particular spends little extra money on this group of commodities. Indeed, when the figures in table 5.4 are compared with similar data in Hazell and Röell, the marginal budget share for food, beverages, and tobacco appear to be uniformly below that in the Muda scheme in Malaysia in 1972/73 (Hazell and Röell 1983, 45). Because linkages through food consumption, both in the rural and urban areas, are fairly small,

TABLE 5.4 Average and marginal budget shares of rural households (percent)

Commodity Group	Year	Poor		Medium		Rich	
		Average	Marginal	Average	Marginal	Average	Marginal
Food, beverages, and tobacco							
Grains and cereal products	1975	29.5	-3.9	24.1	-9.3	14.2	-15.8
	1981	23.9	-0.3	18.3	-3.1	10.7	-6.7
	1988	20.1	-0.5	14.4	-3.4	7.6	-7.6
Meat, poultry, fish, seafood, dairy products, oils, fats, fruits, and vegetables	1975	29.0	12.8	29.7	7.3	24.4	0.4
	1981	27.7	12.0	26.0	7.2	21.0	0.9
	1988	23.0	9.1	21.8	4.1	16.8	-2.6
Sugar, spices, coffee, etc.	1975	2.6	1.6	3.1	1.1	2.6	0.5
	1981	2.1	1.6	2.3	1.2	1.9	0.7
	1988	3.1	1.9	2.9	1.3	2.6	0.6
Meal and beverages away from home	1975	0.8	5.9	1.7	7.4	3.3	9.2
	1981	3.6	9.4	5.5	10.2	8.8	11.4
	1988	5.0	10.1	6.3	10.8	9.7	11.8
Beverages, alcoholic and nonalcoholic	1975	0.9	2.9	1.3	3.3	1.8	3.8
	1981	1.1	2.6	1.4	2.9	1.7	3.2
	1988	1.3	2.2	1.4	2.1	1.9	2.0
Tobacco products	1975	3.1	1.4	3.1	1.0	2.7	0.6
	1981	2.6	1.5	2.5	1.4	2.5	1.2
	1988	2.0	1.4	1.9	1.4	2.0	1.3
Subtotal	1975	65.9	20.7	63.0	10.9	49.0	-1.3
	1981	60.9	26.8	55.9	19.8	46.5	10.7
	1988	54.5	24.2	48.8	16.3	40.6	5.5

Manufactured goods							
Clothing and footwear	1975	10.4	21.0	12.8	21.7	14.0	22.7
	1981	8.6	9.5	9.1	8.7	8.1	7.6
	1988	7.5	8.0	6.9	7.1	7.1	5.7
Fuel and light	1975	4.2	2.2	4.1	2.2	3.7	2.2
	1981	4.8	2.6	4.5	2.3	3.9	1.8
	1988	5.1	2.4	4.7	1.7	4.1	0.7
Consumer durables	1975	4.7	9.4	5.6	9.8	6.7	10.3
	1981	4.7	7.4	5.3	7.5	6.1	7.6
	1988	5.2	5.0	5.2	4.6	5.3	4.0
Pharmaceutical and medical services	1975	4.3	8.6	4.7	9.3	4.8	10.0
	1981	4.2	5.3	3.8	5.5	3.4	5.7
	1988	4.2	6.2	3.7	6.5	4.2	7.1
Subtotal	1975	23.6	41.2	27.2	43.0	29.3	45.3
	1981	22.4	24.8	22.6	23.9	21.5	22.7
	1988	21.9	21.6	20.5	19.9	20.8	17.6
Services							
Personal services, recreation, and education	1975	2.9	11.3	4.0	13.2	7.1	15.6
	1981	2.9	11.4	4.3	13.5	6.5	16.1
	1988	3.9	9.5	5.0	10.8	6.5	12.3
Transportation	1975	7.3	23.2	5.0	28.4	12.9	34.8
	1981	4.3	15.2	5.6	17.4	9.6	20.4
	1988	4.8	21.6	7.2	25.5	14.3	30.9
Shelter	1975	0.3	3.6	0.8	4.5	1.7	5.6
	1981	9.5	21.7	11.5	25.3	15.9	30.2
	1988	15.0	23.1	18.5	27.5	17.8	33.6
Subtotal	1975	10.4	38.1	9.8	46.1	21.7	56.0
	1981	16.7	48.3	21.4	56.3	32.0	66.7
	1988	23.6	54.2	30.7	63.8	38.6	76.9

SOURCE: National Statistical Office, *Socioeconomic Surveys*, data tapes.

NOTE: Poor households refer to the lowest three deciles, using the national population as the basis to mark the deciles; rich households refer to the top three deciles; and medium households the remaining four deciles.

there is little impact on the agricultural production of these items. The growth statistics on agricultural production by crops, both for the entire period and for the more depressed early 1980s, suggest that the rapid expansion of some of the commodities during this decade is primarily a result of the export market environments (i.e., the prices were particularly good). This was the case, for example, for rubber, and for commodities favored by the government's protective policies (oil crops).

Among the nonfood items, the main surprise is the relatively small share of the manufactured goods and the large and increasing share of services in both the average and the marginal budgets. The categories of clothing and footwear, shelter, and transport are particularly noteworthy. The figures for shelter in 1975 appear unusually low. Because these figures are for the most part imputed, there is a strong possibility of error, particularly in those in 1975.[3] Nevertheless, the average and marginal budget shares for shelter were in all likelihood significantly lower in the 1970s than in the 1980s, at least in the rural areas, because the deforestation associated with the expansion of land under cultivation peaked in the mid-1970s. Poor households in rural areas and in urban areas outside Bangkok benefited from having access to cheap (almost free) timber for their housing. In the 1980s, the almost free timber was replaced by industrial materials, such as cement blocks, and those who were better off began to embellish their houses with glass. The roofing used shifted from corrugated iron to fiber cement. Thus by the 1980s, rural households were spending a larger share of their marginal incomes on shelter than were their urban counterparts.

An independent confirmation of the importance of the expenditures on shelter comes from a study of migrants from northeastern Thailand who were employed overseas (mainly in the Middle East). Migrating households were found to spend about one-third of the inflow, net of the costs of migration and the interest payments, on housing (Sangthanapurk 1988, 96–97, 103). This, of course, represents a cash outflow toward investments in housing, in contrast to the figures from the socioeconomic surveys presented in table 5.4. Even so, the expenditure on housing is clearly important.

This heavy expenditure on shelter (even if much of it is imputed rather than "real") points to the linkages that one would expect to occur. Indeed, most villages in Thailand can now boast a gang of construction workers whose job it is to build houses for their fellow villagers. Villagers in the north, with more experience in woodworking, are beginning to specialize in furniture production, not only for their home villages but for other villages as well, and many

3. Varai Woramontree, acting chief of the Socioeconomic Surveys Division of the National Statistics Office, indicates that 1975 was the first time the survey attempted to impute the rent on owner-occupied dwellings. Therefore, enumerators were quite inexperienced in the methods to be used. Most of these mistakes were corrected by the 1981 surveys (personal communication, February 5, 1991).

have become itinerant producers traveling throughout the country.

Ironically, the heavy expenditure on shelter seems to indicate that most rural households want to stay put, despite the rapid industrialization of the economy and the lure of urban areas.

Expenditures on transport service also account for a large share of marginal income. The rural labor market in Thailand is a highly active one, and workers regularly (or seasonally) commute long distances. About 200,000 sugarcane harvesters come down every year from the northeast to the sugarcane-growing areas in the Central Region. Within this region itself, labor moves across districts and sometimes across provinces during the peak demand periods of transplanting and harvesting. These workers are sometimes transported by their employers, and sometimes by labor contractors, whose main asset is their pickup truck or van.

In contrast, the marginal budget shares for housing of the top decile in two rural areas in Malaysia are below that of the poor in Thailand (see Hazell and Röell 1983). The difference in the expenditure on transportation is even greater. It should be added, however, that income distribution in the rural areas of Muda (even in 1972/73, the date of the Hazell-Röell data set) is unlikely to be lower than that in rural Thailand in 1988.

Note, too, the relatively small share (about a fifth) spent by all households on manufactured goods as a group (other than those embodied in "shelter" and "transportation"). This share is noticeably constant both across urban and rural areas and across income classes.

Within the manufactured goods category, the expenditures on clothing and footwear claim a large share of income in the 1970s but have since declined sharply. Of course, the large average and marginal figures for 1975 may be an overestimate, corresponding to the underestimation in the figures for shelter (all average and marginal budget shares have to sum to one), but one would not expect this category to pick up the entire error. Thus there appears to have been a real shift in the expenditures for clothing and footwear between the 1970s and the 1980s.

Interestingly, a good deal of the demand linkages arising from an increase in rural incomes accrues to suppliers in the local area. Of the major items, that is, those items for which the marginal budget shares are high, transport services are provided within the local areas. Admittedly, a large proportion of the cost would accrue to the producers of the vehicles used for the service. Nevertheless, transport services are employing increasing numbers of rural people, albeit people with the capital to invest in the necessary equipment, and therefore not necessarily the poorest among them.

Last but not least, the majority of villages in all regions of Thailand boast at least a village retail shop, and some villages have three or more shops vying for customers. Only two decades ago, such a statement would have been true only for the Central Plains.

During Thailand's rapid agricultural growth in the 1970s and in the latter half of the 1980s, there was no doubt that a linkage effect had occurred, but it was felt mainly in the nontradable sectors, especially in the rural areas. Little of the increased purchasing power spilled over into the manufacturing sector, except perhaps in the construction materials and the vehicle assembly sectors in the 1980s and the textile and garment sectors in the 1970s.

Yet the success of Thai manufacturing industries in the 1980s was not entirely based on rural income increases. The star performers in the industrial sector at this time were textiles and garments, gems and jewelry, canned tuna fish, and toys. None of these owe their success to the domestic market, least of all to the rural market, perhaps with the exception of textiles and garments, which experienced their boom in demand in the 1970s. When rural incomes again rose substantially in the late 1980s, after a long hiatus, rural demand did add somewhat to the boom in the industrial sector. And it is noteworthy that the sectors that felt the supply constraint the strongest during the boom are the two just mentioned, namely, vehicles and construction materials. Of all the commodities in the manufacturing sector, they were the closest to being nontraded goods—by virtue of policy in the case of transport equipment, and bulkiness in the case of construction materials.

Interindustrial Linkages

The Thai economy has an overwhelming concentration of nonagricultural activities in the Bangkok Metropolitan Area, where 78 percent of the manufacturing value added takes place (Chintayarangsan 1990, 1). As the main port of the country, Bangkok draws all the industries that depend on imported raw materials. As the capital city, it is the seat of government. And as a cultural center, it keeps business managers from moving to outlying provinces. Many industries that have located there for these and other reasons have helped raise income levels in the capital, and its regional product to 49.0 percent of the national product, even though it has only 15.8 percent of the population. (Chintayarangsan 1990, 22).

According to shift-share data for 1981–87, the growth of the manufacturing sector in most of Thailand has kept pace with the growth of the overall economy, whereas in the south manufacturing lags behind (Tamboonlertchai 1990, 12–15, 30). Studies of the tiny proportion of the manufacturing sector outside Bangkok indicate that they concentrate largely on processing raw materials originating in local areas (Chintayarangsan 1990; Tamboonlertchai 1990, 31). Apart from the obvious reason that most of these industries are weight-losing, many of them are located outside of Bangkok because of the seasonality of their production. Their labor demand dovetails nicely with that in the agricultural sector, although the rapid growth of the agricultural sector in the 1970s led to greater seasonality in employment. Outside Bangkok, where agriculture leads in importance, manufacturing has to accommodate itself to this characteristic of the labor market.

Given this peculiarity of the Thai industry, agriculture and manufacturing are trivially linked. Many of the processing industries do not generate a great deal of value added per worker, because seasonality in production and labor availability preclude a high degree of capital intensity. High value added per baht of agricultural output is also precluded by the crops Thai farmers have chosen to grow. They have concentrated on basic carbohydrate crops such as rice, maize, cassava, and sugarcane, all of which need little processing in order to become tradable. Once a crop becomes tradable (i.e., the weight-loss advantage no longer applies), then comparative advantage (plus cascading tariff protection) govern the location of further processing. Thailand certainly does not possess comparative advantage in corn-milling, or in feeding the cassava to its livestock. In the case of the tire industry, which prima facie would have appeared attractive in view of the country's large natural rubber production, the main raw material used is carbon black, which has to be imported. More significantly, local tire industries find it more profitable to use imported synthetic rubber than the locally available natural rubber—despite the implicit protection given to the tire industry by a high tax on natural rubber exports.

Because the market forces in favor of a Bangkok location have been so powerful, industrialists have resisted government efforts to encourage factories to move to the provinces. It is only in the last three years that Bangkok has become extremely congested and the government has pushed forward with the idea of developing a new deep-water port on the eastern seaboard, that new industrial centers are being developed outside Bangkok and its immediate environment.

This failure of industry to develop in the provinces (particularly in the 1970s) thus indicates that the interindustrial linkages have not led industries (other than agroprocessing) to locate in the provinces in response to the rapidly growing agricultural sector.

Supply Linkages: The Labor Market

The changes in agriculture and manufacturing have had considerable impact on the labor markets, although census data tend to exaggerate the share of the labor force in agriculture (see figure 5.2). This problem arose because enumerators would ask respondents their primary occupation in the previous year, and farmers would identify themselves as such, even though a substantial portion of their income may have originated outside agriculture. Data from the labor force surveys, which the National Statistical Office has conducted three times a year since 1985, give a more detailed and truer picture of the industrial distribution of labor, as respondents are asked what they were doing in the previous week. Unfortunately, the great drawback of survey results is that

FIGURE 5.5 Dry season employment as a percentage of previous wet season employment

Percent

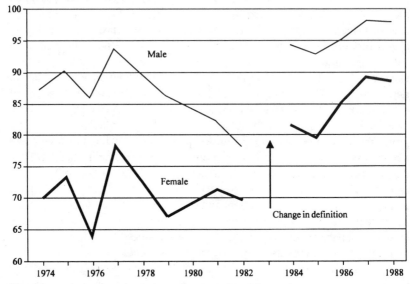

Source: Unpublished data from Thailand Agricultural Workers Population Census and interpolations.

definitions constantly change. The figures reported below represent periods in which they were consistently defined.

The seasonality of the employed labor force (see figure 5.5) has been argued at length by Bertrand and Squire (1980). It has been found, in addition, that female labor adjusts more strongly to the varying demand in the agricultural cycle. This should be borne in mind in interpreting the industrial distribution of the labor force below.

Table 5.5 shows changes in the industrial distribution of the labor force for the period 1974 to 1979. During that time agricultural prices were high, and land was still available. Remarkably, agriculture was able to absorb almost the entire increment of the labor force during the wet season. The share of labor in agriculture during the wet season actually increased. Equally striking is the fact that the share of the labor force going into agriculture during the dry season was proportionately less, despite the rapid increase in dry-season cropping following on the completion of the Chao Phraya irrigation system and the introduction of the new photoperiod-insensitive varieties of rice. The rapid expansion of area under cultivation during the 1970s was actually making Thai agriculture more seasonal than before, because much of the expansion was into rainfed areas. The graph for the male labor force in figure 5.5 seems to bear this out.

TABLE 5.5 Structure and changes in the Thai labor force, 1974–1979 (thousands)

Industry and Location	Wet Season						Dry Season					
	Level 1974		Increments 1974–79		Level 1979		Level 1974		Increments 1974–79		Level 1979	
	Male	Female	Male	Female	Male	Female	Male	Female	Male	Female	Male	Female
Employment by industry												
Agriculture	6,015.3	5,210.9	1,821.0	1,971.5	7,836.3	7,182.4	4,411.8	2,643.8	1,345.1	1,282.0	5,756.9	3,925.8
Mining	41.6	8.0	−9.8	−1.2	31.8	6.8	34.0	15.4	30.3	6.2	64.3	21.6
Manufacturing	939.4	754.2	24.5	6.7	963.9	760.9	1,157.1	968.3	104.2	−52.4	1,261.3	915.9
Construction	243.6	33.2	109.6	23.4	353.2	56.6	291.8	33.5	204.1	49.4	495.9	82.9
Utilities	49.2	12.4	−2.4	−5.4	46.8	7.0	50.6	10.7	−6.3	−3.7	44.3	7.0
Commerce	748.2	880.4	43.2	69.8	791.4	950.2	780.4	898.0	81.4	117.5	861.8	1,015.5
Transport	437.7	27.4	−43.2	3.4	394.5	30.8	493.2	31.8	−48.0	−0.4	445.2	31.4
Services	1,016.5	740.2	−45.6	104.1	970.9	844.3	1,032.2	791.0	−19.4	78.3	1,012.8	869.3
Others	0.8	0.1	−0.8	−0.1	0.0	0.0	0.1	0.1	−0.1	−0.1	0.0	0.0
Total	9,492.3	7,666.8	1,896.5	2,172.2	11,388.8	9,839.0	8,251.3	5,392.5	1,691.2	1,476.9	9,942.5	6,869.4
Employment by location												
Rural	8,249.2	6,863.2	1,493.1	1,751.4	9,742.3	8,614.6	7,037.1	4,598.1	1,286.2	1,090.6	8,323.3	5,688.7
Urban	1,243.1	803.7	403.4	420.7	1,646.5	1,224.4	1,214.2	794.5	405.0	386.2	1,619.2	1,180.7

SOURCE: National Statistical Office, *Labor Force Surveys*, data tapes.

167

Although almost the entire increment of the labor force was going into agriculture during the wet season, it implies that growth in other sectors would at best be constrained by the need to accommodate to the rhythm of the agricultural cycle. Clearly, such a labor market would make it difficult for Thailand to have a comparative advantage in capital-intensive activities (such as manufacturing), which also require large numbers of year-round workers.

Within a decade, all this changed. Agriculture was no longer taking up most of the incremental increase in the labor force (table 5.6). Indeed, the number of women working in agriculture during the wet seasons declined absolutely. A phenomenon of the labor market during the 1980s was that the nonagricultural sectors were absorbing more women than men. Since proportionately more females than males were shed from the labor force during the slack dry season of the 1970s (i.e., the female labor force was more "in surplus"), it was not surprising that industries employing these females had a comparative advantage in the 1980s, and these sectors therefore grew rapidly during the last decade.

While the increment of the labor force in the wet season went mostly out of agriculture, the dry-season increments were still going into agriculture. This suggests that the labor force in both agriculture and nonagriculture was becoming more specialized and that both activities are now beginning to take place year round.

Rural Incomes and Poverty

It is extremely difficult to arrive at an occupational classification of Thai workers. Aggregate rural incomes increased sharply between 1976 and 1981 (by about 23 percent), but then wobbled during the 1980s—incomes in 1986 being 11 percent lower than in 1981, because of poor agricultural prices, but then they recovered back to the 1981 levels in 1988.

Also noteworthy are the changes in the structure of rural incomes. The share of farm income in the entire rural population has declined, whereas the share of wage incomes (some of which may be earned from the agricultural sector) has continued to increase, as did the share of all other incomes.

The picture is repeated in each occupational group, although not as dramatically. Thus, although the rural population's share of farm income declined from 53 percent in 1975 to 40 percent in 1988, that of middle and large farmers only declined from 77 to 72 percent. Small farmers experienced roughly the same decline. These two farmer categories account for the bulk of farm income. This suggests that there has also been a shift among the occupational groups, away from those who are primarily farmers (69.3 percent of the entire rural population in 1976) to nonfarmer categories (58.2 percent in 1988). The expansion has been in the category of workers, from 10.3 percent of the entire rural population in 1976 to 12.2 percent in 1988, and among "others," whose share rose from 20.3 to 29.1 percent.

TABLE 5.6 Structure and changes in the Thai labor force, 1983–1988 (thousands)

| | Wet Season | | | | | | Dry Season | | | | | |
| | Level 1983 | | Increments 1983–87 | | Level 1987 | | Level 1983 | | Increments 1983–87 | | Level 1987 | |
	Male	Female	Male	Female	Male	Female	Male	Female	Male	Female	Male	Female
Employment by sector												
Agriculture	9,055.4	8,345.9	483.8	−96.0	9,539.2	8,249.9	6,730.7	4,797.8	1,890.8	1,762.5	8,621.5	6,560.3
Mining	44.4	6.2	−2.3	6.7	42.1	12.9	48.3	17.7	27.9	−10.6	76.2	7.1
Manufacturing	1,013.2	829.2	259.3	336.1	1,272.5	1,165.3	1,402.7	1,133.8	47.0	177.8	1,449.7	1,311.6
Construction	426.9	84.6	116.2	10.8	543.1	95.4	639.7	105.7	169.4	−0.2	809.1	105.5
Utilities	90.0	16.3	7.7	5.1	97.7	21.4	89.7	16.9	7.1	3.5	96.8	20.4
Commerce	990.1	1,203.7	383.1	418.9	1,373.2	1,622.6	1,109.6	1,303.8	411.9	338.8	1,521.5	1,642.6
Transport	488.6	46.1	82.6	15.5	571.2	61.6	568.2	51.0	62.2	5.0	630.4	56.0
Services	1,329.9	1,206.5	115.3	294.9	1,445.2	1,501.4	1,403.2	1,214.0	47.7	405.9	1,450.9	1,619.0
Others	2.4	2.3	17.4	0.8	19.8	3.1	2.3	0.4	2.1	3.1	4.4	3.5
Total employment	13,440.9	11,740.8	1,463.1	992.8	14,904.0	12,733.6	11,994.4	8,641.1	2,666.1	2,685.8	14,660.5	11,326.9
Employment by location												
Rural	11,615.0	10,324.7	870.6	399.2	12,485.6	10,723.9	10,205.4	7,267.3	1,983.9	2,009.9	12,189.3	9,277.2
Urban	1,825.9	1,416.1	592.5	593.6	2,418.4	2,009.7	1,789.0	1,373.8	682.2	675.9	2,471.2	2,049.7

SOURCE: National Statistical Office, *Labor Force Surveys*, data tapes.

Poverty in Thailand is almost entirely a rural phenomenon, with 85–90 percent of those characterized as "poor" residing in villages. "Poverty," as defined by acceptable minimum standards of caloric intake (plus some adjustments for nonfood expenses), has steadily declined in Thailand since 1962/63, except in the period from 1980/81 to 1986. The most recent figures are shown in table 5.7.

This decline is largely a result of agricultural growth. Not only are most of the poor rural, but most are farmers. Even though the share who are farmers has been steadily declining, they still accounted for more than three-quarters of all the poor in 1988, which was more than their share in the total population. Before the 1980s, new land was continuously being brought into cultivation, and if farmers had access to this land, this in itself would have helped reduce the incidence of poverty. With land becoming more of a constraint, poverty will not decline as readily. To add to their problems, farmers—the poor among them included many who supplied surpluses to the market—were also hard hit by falling prices in the 1980s. This was a key factor behind the increase in poverty in 1986. With the rise in agricultural prices, it is now estimated that the incidence of poverty has fallen to roughly the same level as in 1980/81. In short, progress on poverty reduction ground to a halt in the 1980s.

Has the locus of poverty shifted? How has the availability of land and the agricultural growth that accompanied it affected the poverty levels in the different regions of the country? Answers to these questions will provide clues to the contribution of agriculture to the growth of the rest of the economy.

In general, the rural poor may be classified into two categories: those who have land in poorly endowed areas, for example in the northeast, and those who have no land or very little land and therefore have to rely almost exclusively on selling their labor time. Because land was abundant in the past, most of Thailand's poor fall in the first category, although the landless appear to have been increasing. The percentage of landless (officially classified as farm workers and general workers) nationwide has increased from 10.4 in 1975 to 12.8 in 1988, while the percentage among the poor has increased from 8.4 to 18.7.

Despite this large increase in the proportion of the landless among the

TABLE 5.7 Incidence of poverty, selected years (as percentage of total population)

Year	Rural	National
1975	36.5	30.0
1981	27.3	23.0
1986	35.7	29.5
1988	26.8	23.5

SOURCES: 1975, 1981, and 1986 (national) from Hutaserani and Jitsuchon (1988); the remainder from *Socioeconomic Surveys* data tapes.

poor, farmers still accounted for about three-quarters of the poor in 1988. Among these, the proportion of small farmers (defined as holders of less than 4 rais or 0.64 hectares if an owner-cultivator, and 5 rais or 0.8 hectares if a tenant—average farm size in Thailand is about 3 hectares) remains small at 10–15 percent of all farmers. Most of the poor farmers have land that places them above the category of small farmers.

If poverty is associated with landlessness, and if it is assumed that landlessness increases the mobility of individuals, then poverty should be distributed more or less uniformly across the country. If anything, there may be a concentration of landless laborers in the more prosperous regions, because that is where the jobs are. For the same reasons, one would expect also a considerable amount of urban poverty.

If, on the other hand, poverty is associated with holdings of poor land, then it would be distributed according to the resource endowment of the particular locality. In the northeast, a resource-poor area overall, the proportion of the poor fluctuated between 55 and 62 percent from 1975 to 1988, which is much larger than the one-third share in the northeast. In other words, the incidence of poverty (the probability that a person will be poor) in the northeast in 1988 was about 36 percent, while the overall incidence in the country was 27 percent.

A more detailed picture can be constructed from the sample villages in the socioeconomic surveys and the per capita income of the sampled individuals in the village. The national median is then used to divide all the villages in the sample into rich (above median) and poor (below median) villages. According to that exercise, three-quarters of the poor live in poor villages, whereas the null hypothesis would predict that half the poor would live in poor villages. There has been little change in this share for more than a decade, even though the constraints facing rural people have changed tremendously, and the number of landless households has increased significantly.

To summarize, agricultural growth during the 1970s contributed to the decline in poverty, but with the slowdown in the rate of land expansion in the 1980s, the easy route to agricultural growth and rural poverty reduction disappeared. Furthermore, the agricultural sector was hard hit by the sharp fall in worldwide agricultural prices up to the mid-1980s. This then caused the level of poverty to increase.

The Path of Economic Growth

In view of the land abundance of the 1960s and the early 1970s, and then its disappearance in the 1980s, the story of economic growth in Thailand holds few surprises. Abundance meant that agricultural growth could be easily achieved, and it gave agriculture a comparative advantage. Before the comparative advantage could be turned to good account, a liberal trade and exchange rate regime was essential. This has by and large been Thailand's approach. Admittedly, Thai agricultural export policies have at times been highly restrictive. However, it is significant that the most restrictive policies were applied to rice and to some extent rubber (Siamwalla and Setboonsarng 1989). The upland crops that are grown on most of the new lands have gotten off relatively lightly.

Comparative advantage also depends on a good infrastructural base, particularly for transport. It must be remembered that where there are new lands, there are by definition relatively few people. There must be a willingness to invest ahead of the traffic. Motivated primarily by security considerations, the Thai government invested heavily in roads throughout the 1960s and the 1970s.

Because increasing land is an easy way to increase labor productivity, the seed-fertilizer technology that has been such an important factor in the agricultural growth of the rest of Asia has played a much smaller role in Thailand. Yields in Thailand, particularly for rice (1.9 tons of paddy per hectare), are among the lowest in Asia. The public research system has not felt the intense pressure to perform that was exerted in most Asian food-importing countries. New crops were brought in by market forces, largely by the middlemen, and it was not until rice cultivation expanded that a research program was initiated.

Mechanization, on the other hand, has been an essential part of the story. Not only does land abundance lead to a higher ratio of land to man, which itself favors mechanization, but the tractor emboldens farmers to claim much larger land than they would otherwise have had they relied on animal power. Note that farmers preferred to grow crops with relatively low labor intensity on much of the new land, notably maize and cassava. The only exception to this rule was sugarcane, which is a heavily protected crop.

The income increases that the new lands gave to Thai farmers appeared to have been expended mainly on things other than manufactured goods. The major beneficiary of the Thai agricultural growth seems to have been the services sector, particularly in rural areas, rather than manufacturing. Thai farmers appear to spend much of their income increases on construction materials and vehicles. The construction material industry produces mostly nontradable products, and therefore no judgment needs to be made as to Thailand's comparative advantage in it. The vehicle industry, particularly cars and trucks, is extremely inefficient, despite, or perhaps because of, two decades of protection.

Unlike intensification, the extensification of agriculture is, almost by definition, not conducive to the growth of towns, as it means greater dispersal of the population. It is important to stress that the problem does not lie with the low use of purchased inputs, as would be the case if the seed-fertilizer technology was more widely applied. If Thailand has lagged behind in this respect (see the section "Demand Linkages"), it has made up for this lapse by using more machinery. Although this tends to generate its own support industry, the industry has to follow its clientele into the countryside.

Before 1980, Thailand had a comparative disadvantage in manufacturing. Growth in manufacturing was limited, import intensive, and therefore concentrated in Bangkok; and it was highly protected, in part through the low price of rice, which had been made possible by export taxation. Even more limited was the growth in exports of manufactured goods. Related to this phenomenon was the limited urbanization in Thailand.

In the 1980s the comparative advantage in agriculture began to disappear, hastened in part by the fall in world commodity prices, and Thailand switched to exporting manufactured goods. This had a number of consequences.

To begin with, the range of products for which Thailand had found a niche in the world market had nothing to do with what the agricultural sector had been demanding in the previous period of strong agricultural growth. Most of the products took full advantage, however, of the cheap labor that the agricultural depression of the 1980s made available to Thailand.

Because of their agriculture-based economy, most of the population did not see much need for extensive schooling, even though increased primary schooling had had a demonstrable effect on labor productivity in agriculture. Since rural households do not see any need for higher education, Thailand has one of the lowest secondary enrollment ratios in Asia. The problem seems to be a lack of demand by the parents rather than a shortage of space, although rural parents may still be quite rational as the quality of rural schools is poor. The schooling problem implies that Thailand will face constraints in moving up the industrial ladder, in competing with other Asian countries.

A shift to a manufacturing base will ease the pressure on the forest cover after four decades of continual land expansion. The absolute size of the (permanent) agricultural labor force is expected to shrink sometime during the 1990s. This will lower the demand for land.

With the continued expansion of land becoming unprofitable and the expected downward trend in agricultural prices after the boom of the late 1980s, it can no longer be assumed that rural poverty will be automatically reduced through agricultural growth, as in the 1960s and 1970s. The only way to induce a further decline in rural poverty is to bring in new technology or to provide agricultural protection.

New technology will be available mainly in the better irrigated areas. As this chapter has shown, a great deal of the poverty in Thailand occurs in areas with an unfavorable production environment. Therefore, as far as the poor are concerned, new technology is not the solution—unless by some miracle, the new technology turns out to be suitable for rainfed areas.

Agricultural protection has been increasing, although currently the political economy of the protectionist policies is having little effect on the poverty problem.

References

Chintayarangsan, Rachain. 1990. "Industrial Structures and Inter-Industry Linkages." Rural Industries and Employment Project. Bangkok: Thailand Development Research Institute.

Hazell, Peter B. R., and Ailsa Röell. 1983. *Rural Growth Linkages: Household Expenditure Patterns in Malaysia and Nigeria.* Research Report 41. Washington, D.C.: International Food Policy Research Institute.

Hutaserani, Suganya, and Somchai Jitsuchon. 1988. "Thailand's Income Distribution and Poverty Profile and Their Current Situations." 1988 TDRI Year-end Conference on Income Distribution and Long-term Development. Bangkok: Thailand Development Research Institute.

Krueger, Anne O., Maurice Schiff, and Alberto Valdes. 1988. "Agricultural Incentives in Developing Countries: Measuring the Effect of Sectoral and Economywide Policies." *World Bank Economic Review* 2 (3):255–71.

Sangthanapurk, Hongpha. 1988. *The Consequences of Overseas Migration on Rural Labour Market: Udonthani.* M.Econ. thesis, Faculty of Economics, Thammasat University, India.

Siamwalla, Ammar, and Suthad Setboonsarng. 1989. *Trade, Exchange Rate, and Agricultural Pricing Policies in Thailand.* World Bank Comparative Studies on the Political Economy of Agricultural Pricing Policy. Washington, D.C.

Tamboonlertchai, Somsak. 1990. "A Profile of Provincial Industries." Rural Industries and Employment Project. Bangkok: Thailand Development Research Institute.

World Bank. 1985a. *World Development Report 1985.* New York: Oxford University Press.

———. 1985b. *World Tables.* Baltimore, Md.: Johns Hopkins University Press.

6 Agricultural Growth in Argentina

YAIR MUNDLAK AND ROBERTO DOMENECH

The most striking characteristic of Argentina's economic history in the twentieth century is the sharp decline in its growth performance. Between 1900 and 1930 Argentina outperformed countries with similar resource endowments such as Australia, Brazil, Canada, and the United States. It lost its lead in the 1930s, and since then it has fallen further and further behind these countries. Not only was the average growth rate low, but the performance was also subject to wide fluctuations. The deterioration reached its peak in the 1980s, when per capita output declined at an annual rate of 2.7 percent, inflation hit 100 percent a year with a hyperinflationary explosion in 1989, and foreign debt ballooned almost beyond control. This unfortunate record yields some valuable lessons about how to pursue economic growth.

Argentina is well endowed with land and a climate suitable for agricultural production, and consequently agriculture played an important role in the development of the Argentine economy. Early in this century, Argentina attracted immigration, and population increased at fairly high rates, reaching an average annual rate of 3 percent in the 1920s. Thus, the initial conditions were very favorable. What then went wrong? The answer, given by Mundlak, Cavallo, and Domenech (1989a), is clear: wrong economic policies. In this chapter we take a closer look at the evolution of these policies.

Linking growth paths to policies is not an immediate or obvious procedure and therefore an explanation is needed before the conclusions can be evaluated. It is provided in the second part of the chapter. First, however, some questions should be raised about the policies themselves, regarding their origin and evolution. If these policies were so harmful, as it is claimed, why were they initially installed and why were they maintained for such a long period? It is difficult to give an explicit answer to these questions. What can be said is that these policies were based on inappropriate economic analysis and in part were motivated by political forces that were rationalized by misguided economics, but that might have emerged even in the absence of such ideological support. The first part of the discussion is devoted to this subject.

175

The most interesting finding of this study is that if Argentina had relied more on trade and had restricted its macroeconomic policies to stabilizing short-term fluctuations, it probably could have had the same growth trajectory as Australia, which means that its income level in 1984 would have been 63 percent higher.

The Evolution of the Growth Strategy

An important feature of the Argentine development strategy is that it gradually closed the economy and thereby precipitated a drastic decline in the relative importance of trade. Exports had accounted for about 40 percent of GDP before 1930 and fell to about 10 to 13 percent during 1950–75 (Walkie 1980). Subsequently, the trend was reversed somewhat, and this share reached a range of 15 to 25 percent. During this period there was an expansion in world trade in general and in agricultural products in particular and consequently the share of Argentine exports in world trade decreased. This policy also restricted imports, with the result that their share in GDP declined, except in the short-lived episode of 1978–80, when imports increased considerably thanks to trade liberalization and a strong overvaluation of the peso.

The closing of the economy stood in sharp contrast to the wide integration into world trade and capital markets that had prevailed since the late nineteenth century. This policy shift can be traced to two events: the external shocks of the Great Depression, and the fact that the limit of expansion had been reached in the Pampas.

The depression disrupted world trade and international capital flows, and most countries restricted imports and adopted exchange controls to deal with the imbalance created in the external sector. Argentina was no exception to these policy changes. Tariffs on imports doubled from an average of 7.5 percent in 1925–29 to an average of 15 percent in 1930–34 (Mundlak, Cavallo, and Domenech 1989b, tables 4, 19). Exchange controls were legislated in 1934 after the creation of the central bank and other regulatory agencies. A gap then developed between the exchange rates for imports and exports, and a black market appeared. The share of the fiscal deficit in GDP increased, on average, from 1.5 to 2.3 percent for the same periods (Mundlak et al. 1989b, table 20). In addition, expansionary fiscal policies were applied in an attempt to preserve the standard of living and to avoid high unemployment.

Coincidentally, agriculture reached the frontiers of the Pampas by 1930. This expansion had led the growth process during the preceding five decades. From then on, agricultural growth could only come from higher productivity or expansion to less fertile, non-Pampas land.

These two events, one external and the other internal, brought to an end a long period of growth in which per capita income had grown at an average annual rate of 1.8 percent, except for a slowdown during the First World War.

This rate was higher than that of Australia (0.8 percent), Brazil (1.2 percent), Canada (1.2 percent), and the United States (1.3 percent) (Mundlak et al. 1989a). This rapid growth had enabled Argentina to rise to a respectable position in the world, making it second only to the United States in the Americas in terms of total and per capita income, and above Italy and Spain, the countries from which most of its immigrants originated.

The domestic policy response to these events implied a drastic change in the structure of incentives. As a result, the composition of demand shifted from foreign to domestic goods, and a spontaneous rise of import substitutions gave birth to light industries, oriented mainly to the production of nondurable consumption goods.

By the end of the 1930s, the economy had recovered from the ravages of the Great Depression, and during 1935–39 it achieved per capita output growth of 0.4 percent, compared with a decline of 2.5 percent during 1930–34 (Mundlak et al. 1989b, tables 3, 23). The recovery and expansion originated in nonagriculture, particularly in light manufacturing, where imports enjoyed high protection, which increased to an average tariff of 20 percent in that period (Mundlak et al. 1989b, tables 4, 19). At the same time, Argentina was faced with adverse prices and stagnation.

Although the 1930s marked the beginning of interventionism in Argentine economic life, as in most other economies it was very tenuous in comparison with its future course. In particular, the import substitution process that encouraged manufacturing was not the result of a deliberate policy of industrial promotion but rather the outcome of policy actions designed to cope with external imbalances and domestic unemployment.

Import Substitution Deepening

World War II caused another interruption in Argentine trade flows at a time when the economy was vacillating between world trade expansion, on the one hand, and timid industrialization under moderate protection, on the other. Argentina chose the latter course and pursued it with vigor. Higher protection and government aid were given to domestic activities with the explicit aim of promoting industries that were intensive in domestic inputs or as essential as defense.

The idea was to promote industrialization by means of sectoral incentives, which included protection to final output, but without impediments to the importation of necessary inputs, subsidized credits, technical assistance, and tax exemptions. This program offered no incentives for export. Instead, its policies relied on import duties and quotas and the benefits to be awarded on the basis of national interests. This legislation marked the beginning of a series of similar policies throughout the postwar period that initiated the inward looking growth strategy.

After the war ended, world trade expanded vigorously, reaching unprecedented levels. However, Argentina only took advantage of the exceptional recovery in foreign prices and high demand for its exports by selling the enormous grain stocks it had accumulated during the war and did not seek greater integration into world markets. On the contrary, as just mentioned, it turned drastically inward: the government increased protection to domestic industry, stimulated domestic demand through expansionary macroeconomic policies, and redistributed income to favor urban wage earners.

Quantitative restrictions on imports were used indiscriminately whenever necessary to insulate domestic industries from foreign competition. There is no quantitative measure that summarizes the degree of the import quota in the form of a time series. When exchange controls were introduced, however, a premium in the black market for foreign exchange was created, reflecting the demand for illegal imports. Thus, the importance of the quantitative restrictions can be approximated by the premium in the black market. This premium was negligible in 1944–45, but it rose to an average of 126 percent during 1946–50, and then to a peak of 314 percent in 1951 (Mundlak et al. 1989b, table 9).

The exchange controls imposed in 1946 also caused a strong overvaluation of the peso in response to the faster growth in domestic prices compared with nominal devaluation. The resulting misalignment of the real exchange rate inflicted a negative effect on exports and exacted high rents from the licensed imports.

Although no explicit taxes were imposed on exports, the government monopolized agricultural exports and set producer prices below market prices. This implicit tax created a large distortion between the border and the effective prices to producers and had a negative effect on agriculture. An indicator of this wedge is provided by the 270 percent difference between the foreign and domestic terms of trade during the period 1947–51.

This increasing intervention was also reflected in macroeconomic policy. The share of government consumption in GDP increased from an average of 9 percent in 1940–45 to an average of 14 percent in 1946–50, hitting a maximum of 17 percent in 1949 (Mundlak et al. 1989a, table 4). This was also reflected in the fiscal deficit which more than doubled as a share of GDP over the same periods, from 4.3 to 9.8 percent (Mundlak 1989a, table 20).

Another salient feature of the policy changes was the significant sectoral reallocation of credit that took place during 1946–50 by means of the central bank monopoly on financial deposits. Thus, the share of agriculture in total loans fell from 19 percent in 1944–45 to 10 percent in 1948–50, while that of the industrial sector doubled, from 27 to 55 percent (Gerchunoff 1989).

The combined effects of policy changes allowed larger profit margins in domestic activities, particularly industry. This, in turn, permitted substantial increases in real wages. Thus between 1944–45 and 1949–50 real wages increased by 16 percent in agriculture, 48 percent in nonagriculture, and 43 percent economy-wide. This significant income redistribution to wage earners was also supported by minimum wage and other regulatory legislation aimed at protecting workers.

This combination of policies set the stage for a series of measures that would affect Argentina's economic growth for decades to come. In all, they prompted the expansion of import-substituting activities, mainly manufacturing, and thereby discriminated against traded activities, particularly agriculture. The resulting antitrade bias is clearly reflected in the sharp decline in the economy's degree of openness. The average share of imports plus exports in GDP fell from 43 percent in 1930–39 to 10 percent in 1945–55 and oscillated around this level thereafter (Mundlak et al. 1989b, table 4).

The decline in foreign trade after the Great Depression, although precipitated by external circumstances, was further fueled by the fact that exports were concentrated in a few countries and were not very diversified. Argentine foreign trade no doubt constituted an important restriction to the rapid recomposition of commercial flows toward new markets, although the main reason Argentina lost its share in world exports after the war was that its internal policies did not respond appropriately to the external shocks. Other countries that continued to participate in world markets and thus avoided excessive discrimination against agriculture, were able to maintain and even increase their participation in world trade.

The extent of these lost opportunities can be seen in some international comparisons. Argentine exports of feedgrains (corn, sorghum, barley) declined from 48 percent of the world total during 1934–38 to less than 10 percent during 1971–75. The case of corn is the most extreme: its share fell from two-thirds of the world market in the 1930s to only 8 percent in 1976–80. In contrast, the United States increased its participation from 8 to 74 percent, and world trade increased by 300 percent in the same period (Sturzenegger 1989). In the case of beef, Australian exports, which were equal to only 23 percent of Argentine exports in 1938–43, rose threefold by 1975–77. This result is a consequence of the persistent stagnation of Argentine beef exports and sustained growth of Australia's exports.

It is important to note that the output of the growing sectors, especially manufacturing, did not offset the fall in agricultural exports. It was not until the 1970s, as a result of the subsidies, that manufacturing increased its share to about 30 percent of GDP by the 1980s (Ministry of Economy, various years).

The Conceptual Foundations of the New Growth Strategy

Argentina's inward-looking growth strategy was based on three premises. First, the long-term deterioration in the foreign terms of trade for primary producing countries dictated a pessimistic outlook for such economies unless they rapidly transformed their sectoral structure to give significant weight to industries. At the same time, manufacturing was identified as the most dynamic sector in the diffusion of growth and the idea of backward and forward linkages to the rest of the economy was introduced to emphasize this property.

Second, Argentina's isolation from world markets during World War II led to the belief that, from a geopolitical and strategic point of view, domestic markets offered a safer and more promising alternative for sustained growth than did unpredictable world markets. Furthermore, the widespread belief that a Third World War was imminent led the government to take an extreme nationalistic position that served to consolidate a political alliance among the nationalistic wing of the military, unionized labor, and a segment of business linked to the newly established protected industries.

It was also argued that agricultural supply was price-inelastic. Therefore, taxing agriculture would be costless since there would be no reduction in output. By distorting prices in favor of industry, however, the policy would stimulate industrial expansion. Other factors, such as Argentina's uneven land distribution and an absentee system of production in the Pampas, helped further distort market incentives against agriculture.

The Consolidation of Industrialization by Import Substitution

Under the import-substitution strategy, the government was able to consolidate industrialization through taxes on agricultural exports, quantitative restrictions, duties to imports, and expansionary macroeconomic policies (monetary and fiscal). In addition, selective credit and direct subsidies tilted relative prices in favor of industrialization. At times these policies produced a substantial overvaluation of the domestic currency and a price structure that preserved the closed structure of the economy.

These policies gave rise to a trade imbalance and a recession in 1949, accompanied by inflation. In response, the government granted a larger share of credit to agriculture, but these measures proved inadequate because of the steep fall in the external terms of trade. A new setback took place in 1952 when a crop failure related to a drought triggered an episode of inflation, which ushered in a second year of negative trade balance. Although the government was well aware of the misalignment of the exchange rate, it feared an inflationary outburst and chose to postpone corrective measures. Instead, it endeavored to alleviate the extremely adverse profitability conditions in agriculture to some extent by redirecting credit to this sector. As might be expected, the economic policies had a cumulative effect on trade and the inflow of capital. Although it did not abandon its nationalistic rhetoric against foreign capital, the government began taking a more friendly attitude toward foreign investment and promulgated the first legislation (Law No. 14222, 1952) intended to promote foreign investment, especially in the petroleum and automobile industries. However, the much-desired capital inflow needed to strengthen the external sector was not achieved because of the highly distorted economic environment.

Following the overthrow of the Peronist government in 1955, the new regime promised a so-called liberating revolution (Gerchunoff 1989), but the economic changes introduced were very mild, with the exception of a drastic devaluation of the peso. Instead, the transition military government concentrated on overcoming the external imbalances, which nevertheless persisted until 1958.

The external crises proved to be the Achilles' heel of the growth strategy. The new authorities installed in 1958 recognized that import restrictions were to blame for the lack of sustained growth in domestic industries, particularly manufacturing, which relied on imports of intermediate and capital goods. Therefore, the import substitution that had been promoted since the 1930s was to be consolidated, by focusing on the so-called basic industries such as petroleum, natural gas, chemistry, petrochemistry, steel, coal, and iron. Capital goods and automobiles were also included. But to achieve this goal, Argentina needed the unrestricted participation of foreign investment to supplement domestic saving. It was thought that once the accumulation process was well under way, the saving gap would disappear.

Unfortunately, the policy and institutional changes that followed were not deep enough to eliminate the distortions (Petrecolla 1989). As a first step, Argentina joined the International Monetary Fund and signed a stand-by agreement, which included a stabilization plan that outlined some conventional measures of monetary and fiscal restraint, as well as measures of trade liberalization and deregulation in domestic markets. The drastic devaluation and quantitative restrictions on foreign trade were both eliminated. Nevertheless, import duties ranging from zero to 300 percent were imposed in order to protect existing industries. In practice these duties gave rise to a spectrum of multiple exchange rates for imports. Advance deposits to imports also served to restrict trade. Moreover, explicit taxes were levied on the export side, although they were revoked in due course. Most price controls were eliminated, with two noticeable exceptions: urban rents and interest rates remained in place. Wage indexation was eliminated and collective negotiations were agreed, but a ceiling was set on wage increases that turned out to be less than inflation.

The decision to permit freer market conditions was supplemented by strong incentives to foreign direct investment. New legislation (Law No. 14780 of 1958) was therefore enacted to promote industrialization in specific sectors and geographic areas. Equal rights were granted to foreign and national capital, along with tax exemptions and guaranteed repatriations. Although the share of foreign capital in industry during 1958–62 was only about 10 percent, which was far less than the level before the 1930s, it helped spur industrialization because the investment was directed to a few strategic activities that brought about profound technological changes and spearheaded the accumulation process throughout the 1960s and mid-1970s.

This successful period of growth was supported by the relatively stable macroeconomic environment, which kept the annual rate of inflation in the range of 10 to 30 percent. This stability was achieved by avoiding a misalignment of the exchange rate, ensuring that macroeconomic policy did not discriminate against agricultural exports, and making an effort, though insufficient, to introduce a more open trade regime. Despite some oscillations, the foreign terms of trade were, in addition, becoming more favorable, and world trade had entered a period of sustained expansion.

Nonetheless, these policy changes failed to take into account the negative effect of industrial protection on the performance of agriculture, particularly in the form of high tariffs on the importation of agricultural inputs such as tractors, machinery, and chemicals. Consequently, the share of agriculture in imports was negligible. This policy accounts for the considerable lag in technological advancement in this sector, which was still well below world levels. Crop yields in the late 1970s were about three times higher in the United States than in Argentina (Mundlak et al. 1989a). One of the problems was that hybrid seeds were not fully introduced to corn and sorghum areas until the end of the 1960s. The high-yielding (Mexican) varieties of wheat were also introduced slowly, and even at the end of the 1970s they accounted for only 60 percent of the wheat area. Furthermore, mechanization in agriculture proceeded at a snail's pace until the second half of the 1960s since the supply of materials came from the domestic-protected industries, although some machinery was imported at the end of the 1970s as a consequence of the short-lived attempt at trade liberalization.

Although nutrient consumption did increase from 0.6 kilogram per hectare in 1960 to 4.3 kilograms by 1986, these quantities are negligible by international standards (see Reca and Cirio 1983): world nutrient consumption increased from 27 kilograms per hectare in 1961–65 to 77 kilograms in 1979. Argentina's poor performance can be attributed to the high price of fertilizers, which was set by a monopoly that protected nitrogen fertilizers. The domestic price was 58 percent above the CIF price (Zarate 1978). Needless to say, the low prices paid for agricultural produce augmented the negative effect of the high price of fertilizer.

Unfortunately, the government's efforts to support extension and research efforts (through the creation of the Instituto Nacional de Tecnologia Agropecuaria, INTA, in 1959) did little to improve productivity. The problem here was that the restrictions on imports and product prices had discouraged farmers from incorporating the more advanced technologies available for agriculture (Cirio, Canosa, and White 1980).

During 1950–78 the incidence of government expenditures (extension and research) on agricultural value added fluctuated roughly between 2.5 and 4.5 percent of the sector's value added and showed no significant trend (Elias 1981). In contrast, Mexico and Chile increased these shares from roughly 6 percent of the sector's value added in the early 1950s to more than 20 percent in the 1970s. Private efforts in this direction have been launched recently by regional groups for agricultural extension, but the adverse profitability conditions have made it difficult to take full advantage of the green revolution and the substantial increases in productivity that it has made possible elsewhere.

From Unbalanced Growth to Absolute Decline

Except for a few interruptions in 1952, 1959, and 1962–63, Argentina's industrial sector grew rapidly in the postwar period, particularly during 1960–74. Toward the end of the 1960s, however, the economic environment began to change. Direct foreign investment was on the decline, and a rebirth of a nationalistic spirit halted the trend, albeit a weak one, toward a more open economy. This spirit was already in evidence in 1969, in the Ley de Compre Nacional, or buy-domestic program. Under this program, domestic firms had the exclusive right to supply inputs to the public sector (to federal, state, and city governments, as well as government-owned enterprises).

When, during the early 1970s, fiscal policy became more expansionary, the share of public consumption in GDP increased markedly, from an average of about 14 percent during 1955–69 to 20 percent during 1970–74. The share of fiscal deficit in GDP also increased, from 3 percent during 1960–69 to 4.6 percent during 1970–74. This expansion of domestic demand was reinforced by increased exports in response to the favorable terms of trade during the commodity boom of 1970–73. With the expansion of total demand, imports increased. Because Argentina's petroleum imports were fairly small, energy prices did not jump too high in the early 1970s. Consequently, the augmented imports could be financed by the expanded value of exports without causing a trade imbalance.

With the return of a Peronist government in 1973, expansionary macroeconomic policies and market intervention came into full force. By 1975 Argentina was struggling with an unsustainable trade deficit and was on the verge of hyperinflation, whereupon the democratic government was overthrown by the military.

From then on, the macroeconomic environment became highly unstable. Several attempts were made to implement a stabilization program, but they failed to address the fundamental problems and thus were short-lived. The share of public consumption in GDP rose to an average of 22 percent during 1975–89 (Mundlak 1989b, table 4). This increase was associated with an unprecedented increase in the fiscal deficit, which rose to 11 percent of GDP during 1975–79, 14 percent during 1980–84, and 12 percent during 1984–89 (Mundlak 1989b, table 20).

In the midst of this macroeconomic disequilibrium, which was made all the worse by the excess liquidity in international markets, Argentina attempted to liberalize trade during 1977–80 and introduced some structural reforms aimed at recreating a free-market environment. Price controls and capital market regulations were also phased out. Because of the inconsistent and untimely combination of trade and macroeconomic policies, however, this episode ended in a dramatic failure and a return to a more repressed economy, not to mention an enormous foreign debt.

The increase in import demand revealed that despite protection, Argentina's industries could not compete in world markets. Instead of addressing this problem, the government promulgated new legislation in the late 1970s promoting industrial development. This program was carried out in part by the provincial governments. It consisted of overlapping and loosely structured (and frequently incompatible) incentives. Moreover, it established two centers of economic decisionmaking: the national and provincial governments. A number of plants took advantage of the incentives and relocated, but in retrospect the program produced little genuine capital accumulation or technical change and had little effect on the size or competitive position of industry.

The market distortions introduced by these industrialization policies severely repressed agriculture and had an adverse effect on import-intensive industries. The severe discrimination against agriculture created an antiexport bias that prevented industry from meeting its export potentials. Consequently, the growth strategy lacked a sustainable capacity to import the goods necessary for the development of industry.

To conclude, Argentina's industrialization policy relied heavily on government intervention rather than on market forces. Not surprisingly, the raison d'être of all the legislation on industrial promotion failed to pay attention to the role of market forces in industrialization. Instead, it relied entirely on government aid and intervention.

The Structure of Foreign Trade

The unbalanced growth strategy followed by Argentina in the postwar period greatly affected the structure of exports and imports.[1] The share of consumption goods in imports declined from more than 35 percent before 1930 to less than 5 percent for most of the 1960 period. In a way, this was a mark of the success of Argentina's import-substitution policy. Since the share was higher in the years of short-lived trade liberalization, however, it was evident that this change depended on massive protection. The reduction in the share of consumption goods was accompanied by an increase in the share of capital and intermediate goods, from 57 percent in 1930 to 88 percent in 1960 and thereafter. The share of oils and fuels increased only moderately.

In contrast, there was little change in export structure before the 1960s, with agriculture constituting 90 percent. The picture then started to change as the share of the agricultural component declined to 60 percent and that of the industrial component increased to about 30 percent. These changes were a

1. The data used in this section are from Secretaria de Comercio del Ministerio de Economia (various years).

result of the specific incentives to industrial exports, such as subsidies, credit facilities, and drawbacks, which were supposed to compensate for the government's general antiexport bias. Also, the transition was facilitated by the substantial progress in intra-Latin American trade agreements.

Even though the industrialization promoted by import substitutions succeeded in reducing the import share in GDP, the program fell short of achieving the much-desired self-sufficiency and, more important, failed to improve the competitiveness of industrial output. In fact, it had the opposite effect. That is to say, industry remained essentially nontraded and heavily dependent on agricultural exports to finance its inputs. This was the direct result of the foreign exchange restriction embodied in the postwar growth strategy discussed in the preceding section.

Moreover, this inward-looking strategy of industrialization by import substitution could not be sustained without expanding domestic demand. Such an expansion turned out to be feasible only in relatively short periods, when the foreign exchange restriction was overcome by either favorable terms of trade (1946–49 and 1970–73) or fiscal discipline in the absence of excessive real exchange rate misalignment (1960–69), or when the excess liquidity in international capital caused an inflow of foreign savings (1977–80). Paradoxically, the strategy of import substitutions that sought to achieve economic self-sufficiency led to the opposite outcome, as well as a weak economic performance and a production structure dominated by price distortions and inferior technology.

Sectoral Development

Data on sectoral growth in the period under consideration indicate that the share of agriculture in GDP declined from about 30 percent in 1913 and 1940 to approximately 11–12 percent throughout the 1970s and the 1980s. The sharpest fall, from 29 percent to 18 percent, occurred during the 1940s. The shares of crops and livestock fluctuated over the period, averaging about 50 percent each (Mundlak et al. 1989b; Reca 1980). Other products and fish account for only a small proportion of the total output.

The share of the nonagriculture grew accordingly, from 63 percent in 1913 to 88 percent in the 1980s. The sectoral composition of nonagriculture varied somewhat over the period, but the most striking change was the growth in the share of government services, from 4.5 to 12.5 percent, whereas private nonagriculture only grew from 59 to 75 percent over the same period. Within private nonagriculture, the share of manufacturing increased from 13.6 percent in 1913 to 21.3 percent in 1940, 27.9 percent in 1950, and reached its highest value of 31.6 percent in the 1960s. It then declined to 24.4 percent in the 1980s, and in this respect shows the same pattern as that of agriculture. Private services, in contrast, show an upward trend from 36.6 percent at the beginning of the period to 46.6 percent at the end of the period.

Analysis

Economic growth is widely perceived as a process that increases the consumption possibilities of the individuals in a society, or simply, the per capita consumption. Growth is generated by the accumulation of physical and human capital, by technical change and by the efficiency of resource utilization. Technical change itself is related to the pace of capital accumulation. The reason for the widespread interest in economic growth is that all societies desire to increase their standard of living. Although this notion is clear and obvious, sometimes its direct implications are overlooked. It is sometimes perceived as an abstract concept formulated by some economists and policymakers that is unrelated to what individuals actually do. The fact is, however, that society consists of individuals who want to improve their welfare. Thus there is no other way to approach the subject but to postulate that their action is motivated by the same simple desire. A discussion of the subject must therefore begin by asking how the decisions of individuals, producers, or consumers affect growth and how their decisions are related to policies. The remainder of the chapter is devoted to showing how sectoral incentives are affected by trade and macro-economic policies, and how these incentives in turn affect resource allocation and productivity.

Characteristics of the Economic Sectors

In view of its structural characteristics, the Argentine economy can be disaggregated into three sectors: agriculture, the sector that generates the bulk of exports; nonagriculture (industry, mining, and private services), the sector that basically produces import substitutes and demands the bulk of imports; and government, the sector that produces only nontraded services. Such disaggregation makes it possible to analyze the differential effects of economy-wide government policies. A government's policies have different effects on agriculture and nonagriculture because of two basic characteristics of these sectors: their degree of tradability and capital intensity.

Both agriculture and nonagriculture produce tradable as well as nontradable products. However, the share of the tradable component is higher in agriculture. Thus agriculture is said to be more tradable than nonagriculture. In practice, it is conceptually difficult to measure directly the share of the tradable component in total output, and therefore we propose to measure it indirectly, through the dual cost function, explained below. On average, for the period 1913–84, 67 percent of agricultural output in Argentina was traded as compared with 47 percent of nonagricultural output. The degree of tradability was higher for both sectors before 1930, at which time the traded components accounted for 75 and 55 percent of sectoral outputs, respectively. These values decreased to a minimum (55 and 43 percent, respectively) during 1950–54. From 1955 on, agricultural output increased its tradability to reach a share similar to that prevailing before 1930, whereas nonagriculture kept working under a closed regime, as indicated by an average traded output of 45 percent (Mundlak et al. 1989a).

Changes in factor prices affect relative product prices differentially, depending on the factor shares. We refer to agriculture as the capital-intensive sector because it has a higher factor share for capital than nonagriculture. During the period 1913–84, on average, the capital shares of the two sectors were 60 and 42 percent, respectively. This difference was greater at the beginning of the period, 70 and 40 percent, respectively (Mundlak et al. 1989a).

Characteristics of Economic Policies

Government actions or economic policies are classified here into three main groups: macroeconomic, income, and trade policies.

Macroeconomic policy includes the size of government expenditures in relation to total national income, the way in which they are financed, and the rate of growth of the money supply. Three relevant macroeconomic policy indicators were constructed for the period analyzed. The first is the share of government consumption in total national income. This provides a measure of the size of government expenditures. This measure shows a clear, upward, long-term trend. After the mid-1940s, several significant ups and downs are observed. This suggests that government expenditures drastically increased but reached levels that were unsustainable at the time. Therefore, the high levels dropped after a few years.

Another indicator of macroeconomic policies is the fiscal deficit. It is measured as a proportion of national income. As already mentioned, Argentina's fiscal deficit increased until to a point in excess of 10 percent of total income during some subperiods in the 1970s and thereafter. The sources of fiscal deficit financing changed frequently during the study period. The money supply over and above the rate of growth of output valued at foreign prices was very unstable after 1930. Some years showed large expansions followed by large contractions.

Incomes policy includes measures designed to manage some crucial prices and wages. It is usually used to implement income distribution goals. In the Argentine economy, the two prices most commonly managed, at least in the short run, were the official price of foreign exchange and wages. A good indicator of incomes policy is the government wage corrected by average labor productivity. Whenever it moves upward, the government is attempting to redistribute income in favor of labor. This attempt is usually accompanied by an expansionary monetary policy.

Trade policy includes taxes on exports and tariffs on imports, as well as quantitative restrictions on both sides of foreign trade. The wedge between domestic and foreign prices caused by Argentina's taxation on foreign trade increased significantly after the Great Depression. In addition to taxes on imports and exports, there were periods when the exchange rate was not the same for import and export. This implies an implicit tax in addition to the direct tax on the two traded commodities. These two types of taxation were not determined independently. In practice, whenever the official exchange rate for imports is set at a lower level than the exchange rate for exports, there is an implicit subsidy for imports that offsets the effect of taxes. This effect came into play during 1975–76, when the rate for imports was considerably lower than the rate for exports.

Although taxes have been the most important trade restriction on the export side, imports were governed by quantitative restrictions especially after the 1940s. There is no direct measure of quantitative restrictions in Argentina, but they usually became more stringent whenever the black market exchange rate departed from the official rate.

Sectoral Prices and the Real Exchange Rate

In an open economy, the prices of tradable products are determined by their world prices, nominal exchange rates, and taxes. Some products are not tradable, however, and therefore their prices are determined domestically by domestic supply and demand. Inasmuch as the behavior of agents depends on relative prices, some important decisions depend on the ratio of the price of tradables to that of nontradables, or simply, the real exchange rate. Clearly, the real exchange rate is determined domestically within a framework that has the important features of a closed economy. As such, it depends on local determinants of supply and demand, including actions by the public sector.

The discussion of the real exchange rate is generally conducted at a high level of aggregation for an economy that is divided into tradable and nontradable sectors, although it should be added that no sectors of the economy can be classified as purely tradable or nontradable. To illustrate, a television set is a tradable product, but the price of a television set quoted in a department store at the Ginza district of Tokyo reflects inputs such as location, which is nontradable. Thus, if the purpose of an analysis is to understand price differentials over time, or across sectors or countries, a measure of the degree of tradability is required.

The degree of tradability reflects the share of the tradable component in the price of a product. Hence, policies or shocks that affect the prices of tradables also affect product prices, depending on their degree of tradability. Similarly, policies or shocks that affect the prices of domestic resources affect the product prices, depending on their degree of nontradability. This conceptual framework is useful in evaluating the response of sectoral prices to policies that are not sector specific. This concept is applied empirically. It is done by first analyzing the determinants of the real exchange rate and then relating the real exchange rate to sectoral prices. The analysis of the real exchange rate includes the effects of macroeconomic variables that are often ignored. The structural relationships depend on the degree of openness of the economy. This variable is determined jointly with the other variables in the system. The empirical analysis consists of simultaneous estimation of four equations: real exchange rate, two sectoral prices deflated by the price of government services, and the degree of openness of the economy.

The effect of commercial policy, as indicated by taxes on exports and imports, is unambiguously negative. The intensity of these effects factors depends on the economy's openness. Before 1930, when Argentina's economy was very open, the price of domestic goods was more closely related to the price of imported goods than to that of exported goods. This reflected a high degree of substitution in production and demand between domestic and imported goods. As the economy became more closed, in response to import restrictions designed to protect industry, the price of domestic goods became more closely related to the domestic price of exports, because of a high degree of substitution in production and demand between exported and domestic goods.

This has often been mentioned as a structural characteristic of the postwar Argentine economy: namely, that the domestic prices of exports affect the cost of living because exports are mainly wage goods. As such, they strongly influence wages and domestic prices.

When the economy is closed on the import side, the low degree of substitution in production and demand between imported and domestic goods found in the empirical results have important consequences for commercial policy. In this case, a reduction in the taxes on exports only results in an increase in the real exchange rate for exports of 25 percent of the tax cut. This is because the incentive to increase the production of exportables generates a trade surplus, and the money supply increases. As a consequence, domestic prices increase and the real exchange rate decreases. Clearly, the outcome would be different if imports were not restricted.

The empirical analysis conducted in this study shows that macroeconomic policies have a marked effect on the real exchange rate. First, because the government has a larger component of nontraded goods than private expenditures taxed away, the increase in its expenditures depresses the real exchange rate. This effect, however, is only significant when the economy is closed on the import side. In this case, a 10 percent increase in the share of government consumption decreases the real exchange rate by 7.5 percent.

Second, the increase in government borrowing to finance the fiscal deficit also depresses the real exchange rate. This is related to the financial openness of the economy. Thus, in periods of unrestricted capital movements, increased borrowing raises the interest rate and produces capital inflows. This, in turn, produces either a decline in the nominal exchange rate or an increase in domestic prices, or both. When capital movements are restricted, the effect is milder because government borrowing crowds out private expenditures.

Third, monetary expansion in excess of nominal devaluation, foreign inflation, and money demand growth affects the real exchange rate negatively. In this case, the effect is stronger when the economy is more closed to financial transactions with the rest of the world.

The real exchange rate influences the prices of agriculture and nonagriculture in relation to the price of domestic goods, depending on the sectoral degree of tradability. It therefore follows that, in Argentina, changes in the real exchange rate had a stronger effect on agriculture, which is the more tradable sector. The intensity of the differential effect of economy-wide policies on sectoral prices depends on the difference in the sectoral degree of tradability. The same effect exists for price ratios of different outputs within each sector. This point is important to note, in view of the fact that some industrial activities, particularly during the past two decades, have increased their traded component in final output.

Productivity, Resource Growth and Allocation

The discussion now turns to the link between sectoral prices and factor supply, intersectoral resource allocation, and productivity, and thereby sectoral outputs.

Resource Growth

Labor supply showed a positive response to real wages in the private sector. It was negatively affected when wages paid by the government increased above the economy's average productivity. Real wages fluctuated widely around an upward trend. These swings reflect the short-run cycles in the economy.

Cultivated land, a resource specific to agriculture, responded positively to sectoral profitability and negatively to credit restrictions to agriculture. Until the expansion of agriculture reached the frontier of the Pampas in 1930, the cultivated area grew steadily. The cultivated area grew at a rate of 1.3 percent annually during the period 1913–30 and reached about 27 million hectares in 1930. Thereafter, profitability in agriculture started to deteriorate and the cultivated area remained unchanged until the late 1950s. It increased again, reaching nearly 30 million hectares during the 1960s, but, by the end of the 1980s this figure declined to about 27 million hectares (Mundlak et al. 1989a). These figures do not include pasture, which serves as a substitute to crops. As such, the annual variations are also affected by the relative price of crops to livestock.

Another important factor to consider is the changes in the cultivated land, adjusted for quality. The index used in this study weights the cultivated areas by the crop's value of production. In the Argentina case, the index increased at an average annual rate of about 1 percent during the period 1913–89. This growth was faster during 1913–39 (1.6 percent) and 1970–89 (1.8 percent) in comparison with the period 1940–69 (0.8 percent). During this last period nonagriculture, particularly industry, experienced rapid expansion (Mundlak et al. 1989a).

Capital accumulation in the private sector is determined by net private investment. The empirical results show that private investment responded positively to the expected rate of return to capital and to the acceleration in output growth. In an open economy, investment is financed by domestic and (net) foreign savings. Thus, domestic investment is competing for resources with the rest of the world and it gains ground as domestic profitability improves.

The empirical analysis shows that private investment in Argentina responded positively to public investment. This is consistent with the view that public investment provides the infrastructure necessary to host private investment. However, an increase in fiscal deficits had a negative effect on private investment. Thus, when public investment is financed through borrowing, the crowding-out effect causes interest rates to rise and investment to fall. In our model, there is also an indirect effect on the real exchange rate and therefore on the profitability of production, which affects the rate of return. Thus the net effect of public investment depends on the strength of these two opposing effects.

Moderate levels of borrowing to finance fiscal deficits and well-planned government investment in infrastructure during the period 1958–72 encouraged private investment, which grew at a cumulative rate of 5.6 percent. As noted earlier, this was a period of rapid industrialization, which also affected the incentives. However, fiscal deficits and government debts increased significantly in the early 1970s, and private investment started to slow down.

Resource Allocation

The empirical analysis shows that the sectoral allocation of labor and capital respond to differential returns. First, off-farm labor migration depends on income in agriculture in relation to that in nonagriculture. After 1947, wage differentials in Argentina began to favor urban activities because of the expansion of industries and services. This upward shift in urban labor demand was met by the steady migrations that took place throughout the postwar period. As a result, the agricultural labor force declined from a historical maximum of 1.63 million persons in 1948 to about 1.24 million persons during the 1980s.

Although it was found that urban unemployment had a negative effect on migration, the incentive provided by relative incomes was stronger until the end of the 1980s. Since then, higher unemployment in urban activities has put a stop to migration and has stabilized the agricultural labor force.

The sectoral allocation of net investment was also affected by the differential rate of return to capital between agriculture and nonagriculture. During the period 1930–89, the incentives to invest began to favor nonagriculture. Thus, before 1930, the agricultural share in investment averaged 31 percent, it declined to about 14 percent during the 1940s and 1950s, and fell to less than 4 percent during the 1980s. The share of private nonagriculture increased until the end of the 1960s, but the trend was reversed in favor of public investment during the 1970s and 1980s. It should be noted that this reversal is the combined result of a sharp decline in private investment and a moderate increase in public investment.

These dynamic trends in the sectoral allocation of investment led to a capital deepening in nonagriculture, particularly manufactures. Thus, during 1913–40, agriculture and nonagriculture had approximately equal shares in the total capital stock, whereas, by the 1980s the shares were about 20 and 80 percent, respectively.

Resource Productivity

Technology is a key concept for evaluating the changes that an economy is undergoing in the short and the long run. Ordinarily, in most economic analyses, it is assumed that at any time the economy has a single production function. Technical change is perceived as a change of this function. This reflects a rather simple-minded view of the world. Clearly, looking at any sector of the economy, one can find numerous ways of producing a given product. Neglecting this fact leads to a distorted view of the world. This distortion arises mainly from the fact that when there is a choice of techniques, economic considerations dictate the choice. Consequently, the set of the techniques that are implemented at any time reflects the conditions at that time. How does it differ from the standard approach? The standard approach assumes that the economic conditions determine only the location of the agents on a given production function, whereas in the present analysis, this is extended to allow for a choice of the implemented technique. This way, the market conditions have a much stronger influence on the economy. This concept is relevant not only for explaining the past but also for explaining how a change in economic environment is likely to affect the future development of the economy.

By way of generalization, new, more advanced techniques are capital intensive and therefore the pace of their implementation depends on the availability of capital, as well as on their profitability. As noted above, profitability also affects the investment, and thereby the rate of capital accumulation. These are the channels through which market incentives affect factor productivity.

The implementation of these concepts in empirical analysis calls for a measure for expected profitability. Such a measure depends on the nature of demand facing the sector. In the case of agriculture, which is by and large a traded sector, the price or a measure of the real rate of exchange can be used to represent demand. In the case of industry, however, the tradable component is smaller and the price itself is insufficient to represent demand. The demand for nonagricultural activities is affected by government expenditures and by macroeconomic shocks. The empirical findings show a positive effect of relative prices on sectoral outputs and a strong direct influence of government consumption on nonagricultural activities.

Another important source of demand that influences production is intermediate inputs. The empirical results show that the sectoral cross-effects on the productivity of a given sector, measured by the other sector's output, are positive. The influence of agriculture on nonagriculture is much stronger, which reveals the existence of the "external restriction" on foreign exchange described above. Such cross-effects also represent technology.

The closing of Argentina's economy restricted imports of agricultural inputs. Such a move becomes particularly restrictive when expansion is based on productivity increases. The observed high protection to agricultural inputs, such as nutrients and machinery, has restricted productivity improvements in this sector. The empirical results show that the economy's openness has a positive effect on agriculture. As might be expected, this is also true for non-agriculture.

The large fluctuations experienced by an economy over its entire history generate uncertainty about future conditions, which affects the cost and the accuracy of forecasting. Furthermore, since investment is made for a long period of time, its efficiency tends to decline with fluctuations in the economy because more versatile techniques are required to cope with extreme market conditions. In this case, the actual fluctuations in prices are introduced by a measure of sectoral price volatility. The empirical findings are consistent with this view in that they show a negative effect of these variables on productivity (for international comparisons, see Cavallo, Cottani, and Kahn 1990).

Policy Implications

Policy changes that affect economic incentives cause changes in the pace of resource growth and allocation. A model of sectoral growth in the Argentine economy has been constructed to evaluate the cost, in terms of long-term growth, of the economic policies that were applied to cope with external shocks or short-term economic goals for three important periods in the country's economic history (Mundlak et al. 1989a). This was done by comparing the trajectories that the economy could have attained under alternative economic policies.

The first episode begins in 1929 and goes through the end of the 1930s. Here, economic policy reacted to the drastic disruption in world trade that was caused by the Great Depression. The second episode goes from 1946 to the mid-1950s. The focus of attention in this period was the income distribution program implemented by President Juan Peron during his first and second administrations. The third episode goes from 1970 to the mid-1980s, which was a period of contradictory policies that were first aimed at deepening the import-substitution process and redistributing income in favor of labor but later were reversed because of extreme macroeconomic instability and excess liquidity in world financial markets.

As indicated above, the single most striking characteristic of Argentine economic history is the long-lasting reversal in its once large share in world trade and finance. Before the Great Depression and for several decades, Argentina's growth had been tightly integrated with that of the world economy. Since 1929, however, a combination of external shocks and internal decisions has forced the economy to turn inward and to become less integrated into world trade and capital markets.

The costs in terms of long-term growth of the inward-looking strategy followed after 1929 have been the subject of heated debates and discussions among students of Argentine economy (such as Diaz-Alejandro, Ferrer, Mallon and Sourrouille, Cavallo, De Pablo, Llach, Diamand, Frigerio). Two opposing viewpoints emerged. Some argue that the strategy followed had merit, whereas others claim that it was detrimental. To address this controversial issue, the model is used to simulate the trajectory of the economy under a set of policies designed to preserve the outward-looking strategy that prevailed before 1930. The results are then compared with the actual trends.

In this exercise, public expenditures were adjusted so as to avoid the sharp increases that were not sustainable in the longer run. Therefore, reducing public expenditures reduced the need for borrowing in this simulation, and the fiscal deficit financed by borrowing was adjusted accordingly. The monetary exchange policy was designed to stabilize the ratio of money to income, evaluated in terms of foreign prices, at the average level actually observed during the period 1930–84. The structural scenario of an open economy was simulated by imposing a uniform and constant tariff of 10 percent on imports and no taxes on exports, and by eliminating quantitative restrictions and exchange controls, which amounted to no premium in the black market for foreign exchange.

The results of this exercise show that relative prices strongly responded to the policy changes. On average, during the 55-year period, real agricultural prices would have been 45 percent higher and real prices of private nonagriculture 20 percent higher.[2] By the end of the period, agricultural output would have more than doubled its historical level as a consequence of both input expansion and productivity growth. Employment in agriculture would have increased by 64 percent, physical capital by 59 percent, and cultivated land by 37 percent. In private nonagriculture, output would have increased by 65 percent, with a small decline in employment and a 50 percent increase in the stock of capital.

To allow for such resource growth and reallocation in the private sectors of the economy, employment in the government sector would have had to be 35 percent lower. This decline in government employment does not affect the level of government services, under the assumption that labor productivity in this sector increases at the same rate as in the rest of the economy.

The figures for the overall economy are quite impressive. Total output would have been 63 percent higher, investment would have doubled, and exports almost tripled.

---

2. Real prices are the ratio of sectoral prices to the price of government services, which serve as a measure of the domestic good.

These results have all the limitations that econometricians are well aware of when working with simulations involving large policy changes. With this caveat, the results can be put in a perspective that will allow readers to judge their relevance for themselves. The outcome of the more appropriate policies is that Argentina's performance could have been similar to that of the countries that are similarly endowed and that continued to take advantage of opportunities offered by the world markets.

References

Cavallo, Domingo. 1982. *Volver a Crecer.* Buenos Aires: Sudamericana-Planeta.

Cavallo, D., J. Cottani, and S. Khan. 1990. "Real Exchange Rate Behavior and Economic Performance in Less Developing Countries." *Economic Development and Cultural Change* 39(1).

Cirio, Felix, Rafael Canosa, and Diego White. 1980. "Aspectos Economicos del Empleo de Fertilizantes en el Agro." *Convenio* 2:1–57.

Elias, Victor. 1981. "Government Expenditures on Agriculture in Latin America." Research Report 23. Washington, D.C.: International Food Policy Research Institute.

Gerchunoff, Pablo. 1989. "Peronist Economic Policies, 1946–55." In *The Political Economy of Argentina, 1946–83,* ed. Guido Di Tella and Rudiger Dornbusch. Hong Kong: Macmillan.

Mundlak, Yair, Domingo Cavallo, and Roberto Domenech. 1989a. "Agriculture and Economic Growth in Argentina, 1913–84." Research Report 76. Washington, D.C.: International Food Policy Research Institute.

——. 1989b. "Data Supplement to Research Report No. 76." Washington, D.C.: International Food Policy Research Institute.

Petrecolla, Alberto. 1989. "Unbalanced Development, 1958–62." In *The Political Economy of Argentina, 1946–83,* ed. Guido Di Tella and Rudiger Dornbusch. Hong Kong: Macmillan.

Reca, Lucio. 1980. "Argentina: Country Case Study of Agricultural Prices and Subsidies," World Bank Staff Working Paper 386. Washington, D.C.

Reca, Lucio, and Felix Cirio. 1983. "Fertilizantes Quimicos: Fuente de Crecimiento Subutilizada en la Agricultura Pampeana." Buenos Aires: Fundacion de Estudios Cooperativos. Mimeo.

Secretaria de Comercio del Ministerio de Economia (Argentina). Various years. Boletín de Comercio Exterior Argentino. Buenos Aires.

Sturzenegger, Adolfo. 1989. "The Political Economy of Price Discrimination in the Argentine Pampas." Background paper. Washington, D.C.: World Bank. Mimeo.

Walkie, W. ed. 1980. "Statistical Abstracts of Latin America." UCLA Latin America Center Publication.

Zarate, Carlos. 1978. "Fertilizantes: Panorama en la Argentina." II Congreso Latin.

7 Linkages from Agricultural Growth in Kenya

ARNE BIGSTEN AND PAUL COLLIER

Kenya is an exciting case for those who suspect that agriculture has powerful linkages with the rest of the economy. Over the period 1965–87 Kenya's agricultural production consistently surpassed the average for Sub-Saharan Africa. The same was true of its manufacturing and services (see World Bank 1989, table 7.1). One possible explanation for this performance is that agricultural growth stimulated growth in the other sectors of the economy. Such a hypothesis is a priori plausible because Kenya's government policy, in contrast to that of other African governments, was not heavily biased against agriculture. Thus, it makes more sense to attribute the country's good agricultural performance to pro-agricultural policy than to attribute its good industrial performance to pro-industrial policy. It appears that Kenya's policy had an exogenous influence that tended to favor agriculture, and this partiality generated indirect benefits for the rest of the economy. Elsewhere in Africa, policy heavily favored industry and services, but any indirect benefits from these sectors to agriculture were evidently negligible. The situation in Kenya suggests that a pro-agriculture policy not only promotes agricultural growth but also helps industry and services achieve faster growth than they would if those sectors were favored.

Kenya's economy has always been heavily dependent on agriculture. As of 1987, almost 30 percent of GDP and more than 60 percent of exports were agricultural. For the past two decades, no long-term trends have been discernible owing to a series of large, short-term shocks—both positive and negative, agricultural and nonagricultural—originating at times in exogenous price changes and at others in exogenous quantity changes. In some instances these primary shocks triggered inappropriate policy reactions that had their own repercussions. The economy barely emerged from the policy aftermath of one shock before it was hit by a new one. Much of the macroeconomic regulatory environment, that is, the "control regime," is best understood as an accretion of crisis responses that account for the disjointed nature of that performance.

The key changes in agricultural policy took place nearly a decade before

Kenya gained independence in 1963. Under the Swynnerton plan of 1954, peasants were allowed to grow cash crops, the White Highlands were opened, and supporting services were organized. These changes led to a rapid expansion of peasant production, which marked the transition to a more commercially oriented agriculture. After independence, agricultural marketing monopolies were extended and some land redistributed. Industrial development was supported through an import substitution policy. The 1960s were a period of successful economic development, with an economic growth rate of over 6 percent per year, fiscal balance, low inflation, and a stable exchange rate.

In the early 1970s the balance of payments deteriorated because of falling terms of trade and a Keynesian experiment with expansionary budgets. In response, the government adopted a contractionary policy and introduced price and import controls, which it by and large retained in the years to follow. In 1973 oil prices quadrupled and export volumes fell. In 1974 agriculture was hit by a severe drought. This conjunction of negative shocks gave rise to a serious balance of payments crisis. The required adjustment in living standards was deferred during the next two years by a combination of short-term foreign borrowing and sharply reduced investment. This reaction was unsustainable and would have had to be reversed in the late 1970s, except for another exogenous event. Just as Kenya was starting its adjustment, a severe frost occurred in Brazil, and the real price of coffee more than doubled between 1975 and 1976. Kenya's trade balance and investment then recovered dramatically and its ideas for restructuring the economy were abandoned.

Against all domestic and world professional advice, Kenya's president decided that the increase in coffee prices should be passed on to the peasants. Initially, the increased revenue accrued to the private sector, but after a time, government revenues increased, and eventually public expenditure did so as well. This trend continued after the boom itself had ended. By that time the government had started to lose control over its expenditures, and this weakening set the stage for what was to follow. Many expenditure plans that were conceived during the boom had their major impact after it had passed. Most of the new investments in production went into import-substituting industries, such as nonfood manufacturing.

Between 1978 and 1980, coffee prices fell to more normal levels, but import prices rose sharply in the wake of the second oil shock. As a result, the terms of trade fell drastically. Moreover, the government had now built up a foreign debt that had to be serviced. The budget and balance of payments deficits soared, and inflation accelerated. Once again, the government chose to rely on foreign borrowing rather than real adjustments.

In spite of the large deficits on the current account in 1979 and 1980, the government refused to devalue. Instead, it attempted an uncoordinated trade liberalization in 1980, which merely exacerbated the deficit. In reaction, imports were reduced drastically. The deteriorating economic position perhaps contributed to the coup attempt of August 1982. Although the coup failed, it led to capital flight, which prompted a number of policy changes. The government reintroduced an export compensation scheme, curtailed its investment in projects and enterprises, increased support to private industry and to the development of agriculture, and committed itself to bringing the macroeconomy into balance.

As part of the new strategy, the government moved from a fixed exchange rate against the U.S. dollar to a more flexible rate with the shilling pegged to the special drawing rights (SDR). In practice the policy has been one of crawling-peg depreciation. Interest rates were raised to a positive level in real terms in 1983, and subsequent monetary policy was aimed at keeping real interest rates positive.

In 1984 Kenya was hit by one of the worst droughts on record. It led to a decline in the production of products like maize, wheat, tea, and livestock, and a fall in total agricultural production of 3.9 percent. Later in the year, the economy was helped by a mini-boom in tea, which approximately offset the drought. However, the aftereffects of the drought persisted into 1985 in the form of a substantial drop in coffee output that year. There was also a decline in livestock production owing to a decline in the herds the previous year.

A new drought in Brazil in 1985 caused coffee prices to rise by about 40 percent between 1985 and 1986. This, together with falling oil prices, enabled Kenya to improve its balance of payments, and allowed real incomes to rise. The boom, however, was short-lived and its consequences were not as dramatic as those of the earlier boom. During the second coffee boom the government embarked on new fiscal initiatives and there was now a built-in stabilizer in the form of a progressive coffee tax.

In 1986 Kenya had a record maize harvest, but in 1987 the yield declined because of poor rainfall in some parts of the country. At the same time, real coffee and tea prices fell to very low levels. With the drop in coffee prices, the foreign exchange situation began to deteriorate. As in previous negative external shocks, the government's initial reaction was to become more restrictive in the administration of the import schedules. After 1988, there was some liberalization again, since the rains were good and several crops had a record year.

In the aftermath of these various shocks, Kenya made some important changes to macroeconomic policy during the 1980s. The fixed exchange rate regime gave way to a flexible system with frequent adjustments. Low interest rates were replaced by rates above the rate of inflation. The budget deficit was reduced. In agriculture, producer prices of a range of crops were raised and fertilizer supply improved. Marketing arrangements were also changed. The new system is somewhat more efficient, since there are fewer delays in payment, although some parastatals are still highly inefficient. The industrial program concentrated on import liberalization and tariff rationalization, price decontrol, improved export and investment incentives, a restructuring of financial institutions and the development of financial and capital markets (Kenya, 1986a). Despite these efforts and a substantial real devaluation exports continued to perform poorly. The bright spot was that Kenya's tourism expanded rapidly after 1983, and in 1987 tourism overtook coffee as the main foreign exchange earner.

The fortunes of the agricultural sector seem to have played an important part in the macroeconomy of Kenya. The rest of the chapter probes deeper into this issue and analyzes the linkages between agriculture and the rest of the economy from different angles. The analysis focuses on the period from 1972 onward, which is when all the shocks described occurred. It is also the period for which a consistent data set is available. For the econometric analysis, however, the sample goes back to 1964, to obtain a longer time series.

Agricultural Performance and Its Causes

Ecological conditions vary greatly throughout Kenya, as does agricultural potential. These differences are reflected in the settlement pattern. Since most of the country can only be used for stock-raising of varying intensity, population density on the average is less than 50 persons per square kilometer. However, the areas inhabited by smallholders tend to be densely populated.

With the arrival of the British, agriculture developed a dual character (see Bevan, et al. 1989). On the one hand, the agriculture of white settlers concentrated on producing for export, and this sector received substantial support. In the 1930s, for example, boards were established to control production and to protect the interests of settler producers. Local farmers, on the other hand, received little support. The only African farmers who were able to sell some of their produce for cash were those within reach of the newly developed commercial links and centers. Since the only way for those in peripheral districts to get cash was to move to these centers, labor migration became extensive.

The situation improved in 1954, however, when the Swynnerton plan proposed the development of extension services in the African areas, access to credit, permission to grow cash crops, and land consolidation and registration to encourage African agricultural production. With restrictions on coffee growing lifted and with the establishment of the Kenya Tea Development Authority, coffee production among Africans and smallholder tea production expanded rapidly. Cash crop production was also facilitated by the research and experimentation already undertaken by the settlers. As a result, the rate of growth of marketed output from smallholders increased from 7.3 percent a year in 1954–63 to 12.6 percent in 1964–70. By 1967, half of the marketed output came from smallholdings. This percentage has since remained fairly constant.

After independence, the European farms in the mixed farm areas gradually changed hands. Some 40 percent of this land was devoted to settlement schemes, while the remaining 60 percent was sold intact to individuals or companies. To a large extent, ranches and plantations remained in foreign hands, and most of the highlands are still dominated by large-scale agriculture. Thus, by and large, Kenyan agriculture retained its dual structure after independence.

Agricultural Growth since 1972

Between 1965 and 1972 agricultural growth accelerated at a pace of 5.2 percent a year because of the increase in smallholder cash crop production. After 1972, growth fluctuated, but on the average remained at about 3.7 percent per year up to 1989. Agriculture therefore grew at about the same rate as the population over the entire period, but more slowly than most other sectors. GDP grew by 4.6 percent per year. Manufacturing was the most rapidly growing sector, with an average rate of 7.1 percent, while private and public services expanded at 5.5 and 5.6 percent, respectively. The construction sector grew by only 1 percent per year on average. In other words, since independence the emphasis has shifted somewhat from agriculture to manufacturing and services, while construction has grown surprisingly slowly.

Of course, fluctuations in agricultural growth have a great deal to do with the vagaries of the weather. Three severe droughts occurred in this period, in 1974, 1979, and 1984, the last of which was particularly harsh. There have also been substantial positive deviations from the trend growth of output. After the price increase of the coffee boom, output increased substantially, and there was an incentive to apply more fertilizer and increase labor input.

Consider now the growth of the constituent parts of agriculture. Because of data limitations, once we disaggregate we are confined to components of gross marketed production, but we may note that the total increase of this is the same as that of agricultural value added, including subsistence (see table 7.1). Although it is at times difficult to separate smallholder from large-scale agricultural production, the share of output marketed by smallholders appears to have been about 50 percent throughout the period, although it was slightly lower in the last few years. Once subsistence production is included, the share of the large farm sector shrinks to about 40 percent.

In aggregate, marketed production has increased at an average rate of about 3.7 percent per year since 1972. The production of cereals, mainly maize, was gravely affected by the droughts, but otherwise did fairly well during the 1980s. The production of permanent crops, such as the major foreign exchange earners coffee and tea, has grown throughout the period, with a temporary peak during the coffee boom. Livestock production has not shown any marked trend, until the sharp upswing in the past few years. And temporary industrial crops show a mixed pattern: pineapple and tobacco production has grown, sugar has stagnated, the once-important crop pyrethrum declined substantially during the 1980s, and cotton production has collapsed, in part because of long delays in payments.

TABLE 7.1 Indices of gross marketed production, 1972–1989

Year	Cereals	Annual Crops	Perennial Crops	Livestock	Total	Share of Smallholders in Total (percent)
1972	100.0	100.0	100.0	100.0	100.0	52.5
1973	108.2	107.9	111.5	94.2	103.6	51.3
1974	103.5	123.5	111.9	85.7	102.6	50.6
1975	119.9	132.7	106.0	86.3	104.5	55.6
1976	145.0	125.1	121.2	81.4	111.1	50.7
1977	115.1	129.5	150.7	94.3	122.5	50.3
1978	89.3	157.3	138.9	107.7	119.8	55.8
1979	99.9	191.8	131.9	92.3	114.3	52.7
1980	99.6	240.4	146.7	85.1	126.0	52.2
1981	133.7	243.7	146.9	89.1	131.2	53.8
1982	154.9	224.6	148.0	85.2	131.7	51.7
1983	161.4	183.8	170.2	92.3	142.4	51.2
1984	121.4	167.0	191.4	88.1	144.8	51.0
1985	144.9	185.6	188.1	101.3	151.8	54.2
1986	161.9	189.0	202.2	110.7	163.4	45.1
1987	143.2	200.2	201.4	118.2	164.5	47.2
1988	134.0	204.2	237.1	141.8	177.3	47.1
1989	150.3	224.9	219.0	143.7	184.5	49.3

SOURCE: Kenya, *Statistical Abstract*, various years.

The relative shift out of cereals production is not due to changes in relative prices. For the period 1972–89 as a whole, the price indices (set to 100 in 1972) were, by 1989, 596 for cereals, 591 for temporary industrial crops, and 503 for permanent crops. The prices of major cash crops such as coffee, pyrethrum, and cotton have thus increased at a slower rate than the price of maize, and one would expect this relative price shift within agriculture to benefit the poorer farmers or those in the less fertile regions, who are less able to grow nonfood crops.

Factor Accumulation

Because Kenya had large expanses of unused agricultural land at independence, the impressive performance of agriculture since then has been based largely on an increase in acreage. The large farm area has increased somewhat over the period, but it is primarily smallholders who have plowed new land. There has also been considerable migration into semiarid areas.

Between 1972 and 1984 agriculture on average grew by 3.1 percent per year, in large part because of land expansion, which accounted for an increase of 2.4 percent (Cleaver and Westlake 1987). Now there is scarcely any new land available, and future increases in production must come mainly from increases in the output of existing land.

Labor's contribution to agriculture has followed a pattern similar to that for land. Wage employment in large-scale agriculture has expanded only slowly, while smallholder labor almost doubled between 1972 and 1989. However, not all of these workers are employed in agriculture. Some smallholder households sell their labor in the labor market. In particular, males in the smallholder labor force migrate to other areas to look for jobs. Although nonresident household members constitute perhaps only 5–6 percent of the extended household, they are considerably more important economically than this indicates. Participation in the labor market tends to be highest for the categories with the least land. In spite of labor sales, households operate their holdings with vastly different endowment ratios. These differences may be offset in part by changes in the cropping pattern, but such changes have only a limited effect on the endowment ratios.

The land market, it should be added, is very restricted. Smallholder households sell land only when there is a pressing need for cash. Hardly anybody sells land to adjust the endowment ratio or to finance investments in agriculture, for example, and the resulting suboptimal allocation of resources has no doubt had an adverse effect on efficiency. Another important endowment is human capital. The educational levels of the younger cohorts are dramatically higher than those of the older ones. To the extent that better education means higher productivity, there should be scope for increased production inside and outside agriculture.

Agricultural Policies

Whatever its other biases, policymaking in Kenya has exhibited less urban bias than is evident in some other countries in the region. The critical variables are said to be land policy and the tolerance for, or encouragement of, private investment in agriculture by the members of the political elite; the elite's investment in agriculture has contributed greatly to the evolution of a policy environment favoring agricultural producers (Lofchie 1989). In Tanzania, in contrast, the elite has cut itself off from land ownership, and the welfare of agricultural producers has come to be a more peripheral goal (in spite of the officially proclaimed ideology). Kenya's government has been more cautious than many others in Sub-Saharan Africa about intervening directly in agricultural production. It has seen its role mainly as a facilitating one (Johnston 1989, 231).

Agricultural policies have dealt with new technologies, marketing, pricing, and infrastructure. The major breakthrough in cereals technology in Kenya was the development of high-yielding varieties (HYV) of maize. HYV maize has been adopted extensively in Kenya, but many farmers have been unable to extract its full potential because they have neglected to apply the full package of fertilizers that is needed (Ongaro 1988). They have not done so because they have not received the necessary information from extension workers or have no access to credit. The latter has proved to be a major constraint on the application of the appropriate husbandry practices, particularly among smaller farmers. Nevertheless, the new maize varieties have undoubtedly been an important factor behind the growth in cereals production.

Great strides have also been made in coffee research. Since the early 1970s the Coffee Research Foundation has developed a high-yielding variety that is resistant to coffee berry disease and rust. This is a major improvement since farmers tend to spend about a third of their gross revenue on spraying.

Since the colonial period, Kenya's agricultural marketing system has been characterized by a high degree of regulation and control. Intervention increased after independence, and there are now more than a dozen parastatals involved in the marketing of output. Some cooperatives also engage in marketing. The marketing system of the large-scale producers is fairly simple. They sell most of their produce through the established, formal channels. The situation among smallholders is more complex. Their sales go through not only the formal channels but also a thriving informal system of local rural markets. The typical pattern of trade in the formal system is that the board receives deliveries from traders, cooperatives, or large farms, which it then delivers to processors and wholesalers. In the case of export crops, the board usually sells the processed products to overseas firms in Nairobi. Marketing boards have at times adversely affected output because of their illiquidity.

Kenya has two types of farm cooperatives: the older large cooperatives, which now are large national organizations, and the newer small cooperatives, which operate in the major smallholder regions. The cooperative movement has grown rapidly since independence. The most important union is the coffee union, which has a high turnover and a large membership. The cooperatives market, process, collect taxes, distribute inputs, and handle credit. The cooperative movement has been fairly successful in the most developed smallholder regions, but in the less advanced areas it has made only limited progress.

The government has also intervened in the marketing of fertilizers. As a result, smallholders have difficulty gaining access to fertilizer, whereas large-scale farmers are usually well supplied. Seeds distribution, however, is less problematic. Here, private traders supply small packages that are appropriate for smallholders. Fertilizer distribution has been hampered by price control, which has reduced margins to the point where it is not viable to provide dispersed smallholders with small quantities of fertilizers. The application of fertilizers has been profitable for maize, however (Ongaro 1988). Since 1987, the government has increased the availability of fertilizers and brought prices more in line with world market prices.

Indeed, price regulation has been an important part of government agricultural policy. In the 1970s the government sometimes maintained a gap between domestic and world market prices, but in the 1980s, as just mentioned, reversed this policy. The producer prices for major food crops have been maintained at the level of import parity since the mid-1980s. There is still a desire to smooth out some fluctuations.

In 1980 the weighted average of producer prices (except for sugar) was 24 percent below import parity prices, and farm incomes were 7 percent below what they would have been with import parity prices (Cleaver and Westlake 1987, 26). This income transfer accrued to the consumer in the form of lower prices and to the government in the form of reductions in the subsidies to the parastatals. By 1986, however, the weighted producer prices (with the exception of sugar) were only 7 percent below import parity prices. This substantial shift in policy was of benefit to the farmers: whereas distorted prices in 1980 reduced the share of agriculture in GDP by 2.4 percent, the loss was down to 0.5 percent by 1986. In other words the price distortions were almost eliminated.

Over the past twenty years Kenya has initiated a number of development schemes, including the Special Rural Development Program, the Kenya Livestock Development Program, the Nordic Cooperative Project, and the Integrated Agricultural Development Program (IADP). The emphasis in these programs has tended to be on credit. Their results have been mixed (see Lele and Meyers 1989).

Since the late 1960s loans to smallholders have to a large extent come from the cooperatives, which can recover the funds from crop deliveries. The recovery rate is very good. It is more difficult to obtain loans from the Agricultural Finance Corporation (AFC), although it also provides some support to agriculture. Banks are only a minor source of credit. Normally, bank loans can only be obtained by a household member who gets his salary directly through the bank. Informal credit is only given between relatives. There is no system of private moneylenders, although a small consumption credit can sometimes be obtained from a local shopkeeper.

In the 1970s various kinds of different credit schemes were pushed by, among others, the World Bank (Raikes 1989). The IAPD program attempted to concentrate on the inexperienced, poorly trained, or corrupt unions. Since management was weak, the loans were obviously risky and the repayment rate was low. Instead of improving efficiency in agriculture, this credit program led to a misappropriation of funds and increased marketing costs. There is anecdotal but convincing evidence that credit was a "hard sell," and that extension officers went so far as to say that the money was essentially a grant if farmers were reluctant to accept it. It is therefore not surprising that the repayment rate on some of these schemes has only been about 30 percent.

One credit scheme that has been functioning well with a repayment rate of about 90 percent was organized and administered by the cooperative movement itself. It consists of loans of members' savings to other members. This scheme was built up more gradually, and concentrated on more developed areas where there was an economic basis for the program.

In the AFC, only the large-farm component seems to be functioning, and the system is having difficulty delivering credit to the smallholders and achieving sustainable recovery levels. Most of the land in Kenya is located in sparsely populated areas of low potential, but the government is searching for methods of tapping even this potential, since it has been argued that "there is considerable scope for substantial increases in productivity in utilizing the resource potential of Kenya's arid and, especially, its semi-arid lands" (Johnston 1989). It remains to be seen whether any substantial progress can be made in this direction.

Although extension services expanded rapidly during the 1960s, the initial optimism about their potential faded in the 1970s. The government of independent Kenya was not much more successful than the colonial government had been in developing a viable strategy for developing agriculture in the poorer areas.

Linkages—An Analytic Framework for Kenya

The hypothesis explored in this chapter is that agricultural growth has positive repercussions throughout the economy. Such a linkage is not inevitable, but it can arise through several distinct mechanisms. This section investigates those mechanisms that may be pertinent in Kenya. The growth of per capita agricultural income can occur for three reasons: the relative price of agricultural output can rise, output might increase as a result of investment, or technical progress can raise the productivity of existing factors. At various stages, Kenyan agriculture has experienced each of these types of growth.

When the world price of agricultural output increases, there are three possible consequences for the rest of the economy. If the economy is small (in the sense of being a price taker on world markets), is fully open (in that all goods are internationally tradable), and has perfect factor markets, there can be no beneficial effects for the rest of the economy. Any expansion of agriculture is at the expense of the rest of the economy. Once nontradable goods are introduced, there are pecuniary but not real effects. That is, agricultural growth can benefit other sectors only to the extent that such growth causes relative prices to turn against agriculture, thereby transferring income to those engaged in other activities. With pecuniary effects, other sectors can indeed benefit from agricultural growth, but since these benefits are only transfers, in aggregate this is not a real gain for the economy. When market imperfections are introduced, agricultural growth can give rise to income gains in other sectors over and above those arising from transfers. Transfers induced by agricultural growth may be referred to as a pecuniary multiplier, and growth in nonagricultural output induced by agricultural growth may be considered a real multiplier. Under certain circumstances, an improvement in the agricultural terms of trade can give rise to either of these types of multiplier.

An Economy without Multiplier Effects

In a small, fully open economy with perfect factor markets, an improvement in the agricultural terms of trade generates no multiplier effects. Kenya is not a fully open economy: there are government restrictions on trade, and many goods and services are intrinsically not tradable in world markets. Nor are its factor markets "perfect": labor and capital are to varying degrees immobile between sectors and there are some price rigidities. Nevertheless, a useful benchmark case is provided by the linkages that might be expected were this the case. The essential feature of such an economy is that the relative price of goods would be determined on world markets over which Kenya has virtually no influence. In turn, factor prices would be determined by technology and the relative price of goods. As a result, linkages from agriculture would work only through factor markets. There could be no pecuniary multiplier, let alone any real multiplier, via price changes that would generate income transfers. If the world prices of agricultural produce rose, then agriculture would expand at the expense of other sectors. It would bid factors away from other sectors and drive up the relative price of labor (the factor used most intensively in agriculture). Agricultural and nonagricultural growth would be negatively correlated and causally connected.

Pecuniary Multiplier Effects

Once it is no longer assumed that the prices of all goods are set on world markets, agricultural growth due to an improvement in the terms of trade will give rise to pecuniary multiplier effects. Growth leads to changes in relative prices, which transfer income to other sectors. In Kenya, pecuniary multiplier effects are generated by three distinct mechanisms. First, a change in consumer demand caused by higher agricultural incomes tends to bid up the price of nontradable goods and services. Second, some of the obstacles to tradability are government-imposed trade restrictions, and these are altered by agricultural performance. And Third, agricultural shocks affect investment, which in turn causes powerful repercussions on nontradable capital goods. Agricultural shocks may thus cause the kinds of construction booms and slumps that have been a striking feature of the Kenyan economy.

Since many goods and services in Kenya are nontradable, their prices are divorced from world markets. This distinction between tradables and nontradables cuts across that between agriculture and the rest of the economy. Most of the nonfood crops are fully traded (notably, coffee and tea). In an average year, however, Kenya is self-sufficient in food. In the period under consideration, this was probably the case because of the high costs of transporting grain. Because of the unpredictability of food production, trade depends in part on the variance in production (part being accommodated by variations in stocks and in consumption). Food may therefore be characterized as nontraded save for the variance in production: an increase in mean production would lower domestic prices. This distinction between tradable and nontradable agriculture is important because of the different transmission mechanisms on the rest of the economy. During the study period, the tradable component of agriculture in Kenya was subject to positive price shocks, notably coffee booms, whereas the nontradable sector was subject to negative quantity shocks, notably droughts. A favorable price shock in the tradable sector has Dutch disease effects. As income is spent, the price of nontradables is bid up, and resources are attracted there away from the nonboom tradable sector. An unfavorable quantity shock in the nontradable sector drives up the price of these nontradables so that resources may even flow into the activity. Since incomes are lower, however, the demand for other nontradables falls, and there is a contraction in the nonslump nontradable sector.

In Kenya, the nonagricultural tradable sector is primarily import-substitute manufacturing. This activity is subject to quantitative restrictions (QRs) on imports. Were the QRs fixed, manufacturing would therefore be a nontradable activity at the margin. The coffee booms would therefore have raised prices in this sector, whereas the drought would have lowered them. During the study period, however, QRs were adjusted as the primary macroeconomic policy instrument by which the balance of payments was equilibrated. In other words, trade policy was endogenous to the macroeconomic environment. When the agricultural shock took the form of a coffee boom, there was a direct increase in foreign exchange earnings, which made it possible to liberalize trade. Whenever Kenya suffered a drought, food had to be imported, the balance of payments deteriorated, and QRs had to be tightened. These variations in trade policy tended to reverse the price effects on manufacturing, which would have taken place had QRs been constant. Recall that were QRs constant, the qualitative behavior of manufacturing would have resembled that of the nontradable sector, benefiting from agricultural growth through higher relative prices, which is a pecuniary multiplier. Because trade policy was endogenous to foreign exchange availability, however, agricultural growth triggered trade liberalization, which inflicted a negative transfer on manufacturing. Hence, the pecuniary multiplier was negative.

The remaining mechanism behind a pecuniary multiplier affects the construction sector. An agricultural shock changes current income in relation to permanent income and thus leads to a change in savings. In Kenya, the main coffee boom led to a massive increase in savings, the main drought to dissavings. Because the economy is not well integrated into world capital markets (largely because of exchange controls), these changes in savings cause corresponding changes in investment. Since tradable capital (such as machinery) and nontradable capital (such as buildings) tend to be complementary, large changes in the demand for investment in the aggregate tend to be spread over both tradable and nontradable capital. The sector that produces nontradable capital goods, namely construction, is therefore subject to large swings in demand resulting from agricultural shocks.

Pecuniary multiplier effects of agricultural growth are good news for nonagricultural sectors but bad news for agriculture. If they are powerful, they indicate that the changes in primary income in agriculture will be transferred to other sectors. However, these transfers, by their nature, leave aggregate income unaffected. The mechanisms discussed next enabled agricultural growth to provide the economy with a free lunch.

Real Multiplier Effects

As mentioned earlier, there would be no multiplier effects in a fully open economy with perfect factor markets, but if the assumption of a fully open economy is relaxed, three mechanisms can be found for a pecuniary but not a real multiplier. Now suppose the assumption of perfect factor markets is relaxed. In this case market imperfections can give rise to a real multiplier via three mechanisms as well. The first is labor market rigidity. Such rigidity leads to either unemployment or underemployment, which can, depending on the further specification of the economy, be reduced by agricultural growth. The second is a rigidity in the market for foreign exchange and, in consequence, for intermediate inputs. Agricultural growth related to a terms-of-trade improvement can increase the supply of foreign exchange and thereby reverse import compression. The third mechanism is the credit market. A savings boom resulting from a favorable agricultural shock can release the economy from financial repression and thereby improve the allocation of capital.

Many observers of Kenya's labor market (Harris and Todaro 1970; Stiglitz 1974; Fields 1975) have argued that real nonagricultural wages are fixed above the supply price of labor. The wage premium might induce open unemployment along the lines of Harris and Todaro, or underemployment in the sense that people are employed in the agricultural sector (or some third sector) at a marginal product much below what they would have in the fixed-wage sector. Now suppose that the nonagricultural sector is (in whole or part) producing nontradable goods. An increase in agricultural income would raise expenditure on nontradables and thereby drive up the marginal revenue product of labor in the sector. As a result, more labor could be employed. Either open unemployment would fall or underemployment be reduced. In either case, output in the aggregate would expand because the waste associated with the initial labor misallocation was reduced.

Figure 7.1 illustrates the analysis. There are two sectors, agriculture and industry, in which the marginal revenue product of labor schedules are given by MPL_A and MPL_I, respectively. There is a fixed wage of W_I in the industrial sector, limiting employment to E_I. A Harris-Todaro process generates unem-

FIGURE 7.1 A real multiplier from a labor market distortion

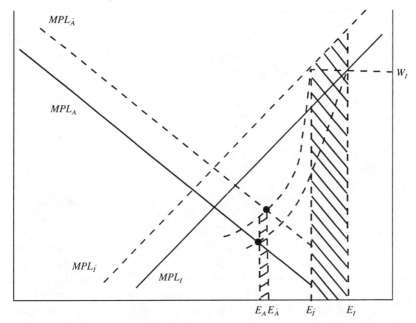

Note: MPL$_A$ = marginal revenue product of labor schedules in agriculture; *MPL$_I$* = marginal revenue product of labor schedules in industry; *W$_I$* = a fixed wage in the industrial sector; E = employment.

ployment of E_A–E_I. Exogenous growth in agricultural income raises the marginal product of labor in the sector to MPL$_{\hat{A}}$. Endogenous growth of income in industry, through a pecuniary multiplier, raises the marginal product in that sector to MPL$_{\hat{I}}$. As a result, industrial employment increases to $E_{\hat{I}}$ and agricultural employment to $E_{\hat{A}}$. The real multiplier stems from the improvement in labor allocation, shown as the two shaded areas. In contrast to the previous cases, here agricultural expansion has a multiplier effect on aggregate output.

The above multiplier effect depended on misallocation in the labor market: too little labor was employed in the nonagricultural sector. Agriculture may also have a multiplier effect if foreign exchange is misallocated. If the exchange rate is overvalued and foreign exchange rationed, the manufacturing sector may be constrained by the lack of imported inputs. As a result, sector-specific capital in the manufacturing sector may be underused (in effect, unemployed). Firms would be prepared to pay more for foreign exchange generated by the agricultural sector, but the fixed exchange rate policy would prevent them from doing so. In such circumstances, an autonomous expansion of the tradable component of agricultural income (either through higher world prices or greater output) can again give rise to a multiplier effect on aggregate output, as idle capital is brought into use in the manufacturing sector.

A third multiplier effect might occur if the economy were financially repressed, as was the case in Kenya for much of the study period. Interest rate ceilings would give rise to a gap between what borrowers are willing to pay at the margin and what savers receive. They would also induce banks to lend to projects that are safe but that have a low return, rather than to more risky projects with higher expected returns. In these circumstances, an expansion in savings could float the economy off financial repression by driving down the market-clearing interest rate below the ceiling. Financial intermediation would then reap the benefits previously missed through intertemporal resource mis-allocation. The scale of investment would cease to be suboptimal and the allocation of savings between firms would cease to be biased against projects with a higher return. A boom in agricultural incomes with consequent high savings rates, such as the one in Kenya during the late 1970s, can therefore generate an expansion in aggregate output.

All three of these mechanisms can operate together. For example, some firms in the manufacturing sector might be rationed in the capital market, others might be rationed in the foreign exchange market, and both groups might have wage rates above the supply price of labor. An increase in agricultural income might expand the sector through extra demand for its output, which would increase the marginal revenue product of labor; extra foreign exchange, which would lead to the utilization of previously idle capital; and extra savings, which would enable capital-starved firms to borrow. The extra output might have little opportunity cost if the capital is sector-specific and labor has a much lower marginal product in the activities from which it is drawn.

Technical Progress Introduced

So far, the discussion has focused on growth in agricultural income brought about by an improvement in the agricultural terms of trade. This has made it possible to distinguish between real and pecuniary multipliers, but it has abstracted from growth induced by technical progress and investment. Consider now the effects of technical progress in the agricultural sector.

Since technical progress in the agricultural sector increases incomes, it can give rise to the pecuniary and real multiplier effects just discussed. However, such progress usually has additional real effects on the rest of the economy, although these need not be positive. There are two offsetting effects. First, because technical progress raises factor productivity, the return on factors used in agriculture increases. This induces factors to shift into agriculture from the rest of the economy. At the same time, technical progress increases the supply of factors available to the economy measured in efficiency units. Two forces can prompt some of these extra factors to locate outside the agricultural sector. The first is if agricultural technical progress happens to be biased toward saving the factor used intensively in the nonagricultural sector. The second is if, as discussed above, a pecuniary multiplier raises the return to factors in the nontradable part of the nonagricultural sector. In either of these cases, it is possible for technical progress in agriculture to induce a shift in factors out of agriculture into the rest of the economy. Since the remaining factors in agriculture are more productive, agricultural output will have increased, but this will have induced expansion elsewhere in the economy. Hence, agricultural technical progress can give rise to a real multiplier. However, a priori it is also possible for there to be a net shift of factors into agriculture, in which case the real multiplier would be negative.

Agricultural Investment Introduced

Investment in agriculture may or may not be at the expense of investment in other sectors, depending on the degree of integration of the capital market. At one extreme, if the national economy is fully integrated into the world capital market, investment decisions will be completely separated from domestic savings decisions. Extra agricultural investment will not be at the expense of investment elsewhere in the economy since at the margin it is financed externally. At the other extreme, capital markets may be so segmented that savings in the agricultural sector are channeled exclusively into agricultural investment. Again, increased agricultural investment will not be at the expense of investment elsewhere in the economy. Only in the intermediate case—in which there is a well-functioning domestic capital market that is isolated from the world market—will agricultural investment be at the expense of investment elsewhere, since it is using savings that would otherwise have been harnessed in some other sector. If agricultural investment has no opportunity cost in terms of investment in other sectors (i.e., either the fully integrated or the fully segmented capital market), then its consequences are closely akin to those of agricultural technical progress. The extra capital can induce labor to shift into or out of the sector and hence it can have either positive or negative effects on real output in the rest of the economy. In addition, the income growth resulting from the investment can cause pecuniary or real multiplier effects, as would a terms-of-trade improvement. If, however, agricultural investment is at the expense of nonagricultural investment, there will be a loss of output in the rest of the economy in relation to what would have happened otherwise.

A Preliminary Conclusion

From the foregoing discussion of the possible links between an increase in agricultural incomes and those in the rest of the economy, it is clear that income can be transferred (the pecuniary multiplier) if there are nontradable goods. More important, income can be augmented in real terms in the aggregate (the real multiplier) if there are distortions in the economy or if the growth is due to technical progress or investment. The first of these effects constitutes a shift toward the production frontier of the economy, the other two constitute an outward shift of the frontier. However, an outward shift in the frontier does not guarantee a positive real multiplier. Rather, it is dependent on the type of technical progress and the state of the capital market. It is therefore an empirical matter whether agricultural growth moves the economy to its frontier, shifts the frontier, or merely moves around the frontier. The next question to consider is how these links function in Kenya.

Links to Nonagricultural Sectors

The links from agriculture to other sectors of the economy took three main forms: macroeconomic shocks, agricultural supply shocks, and a spatial concentration of activities.

TRANSMISSION FROM MACROECONOMIC SHOCKS: THE COFFEE BOOM AND THE DROUGHT. During the study period, agriculture in Kenya experienced two shocks large enough to have discernible macroeconomic consequences. The first of these was the coffee boom of 1976–79 and the second was the drought of 1983/84. As explained earlier, Kenya experienced other agricultural shocks as well, but the coffee boom and the drought were the largest shocks of each type: positive price shocks in the tradable sector and negative quantity shocks in the nontradable sector.

The coffee boom was the result of a frost in Brazil that damaged but did not destroy the Brazilian tree stock. During the boom Kenya's barter terms of trade improved by 54 percent, but this was recognizably a temporary event until Brazilian output recovered. By 1980 the terms of trade had reverted to their 1975 level. In the intervening four years, the improvement in the terms of trade raised real income by about 5.4 percent. Unlike other coffee growing countries, Kenya decided (against the advice of the World Bank and received academic opinion) to pass the entire price increase on to coffee growers. About half of the coffee grown in Kenya was produced by small farmers who were relatively recent entrants into the activity. Hence, the boom accrued in the first instance to many thousands of small farmers who had no previous experience of such a remarkable event (it was the largest price increase for coffee in the entire century).

Coffee farmers appear to have recognized that the windfall would be short-lived since they saved about 70 percent of the income; their normal saving rate was less than 5 percent (Bevan et al. 1989). In the short term, most of these savings took the form of deposits in rural financial institutions. Fieldwork in Muranga (where about 15 percent of coffee farmers lived) showed that by the end of the first year of the boom savings deposits measured in relation to their long-term trend had increased by about half of the windfall coffee income. In the longer term, farmers converted these financial savings into real assets: farm investments and housing improvements. By the early 1980s, savings deposits in Muranga were back to their long-term trend value.

The boom in farm incomes thus led to a large increase in savings and a smaller, but still significant, increase in expenditure on consumption. Both of these responses had repercussions throughout the economy. First, the financial savings forced down the market-clearing interest rate well below the legal ceiling on interest rates. The best guide to market interest rates is the rediscount rate on treasury bills, which in this instance dropped below 1 percent during the course of 1977. Real interest rates were therefore heavily negative. Even so, banks had difficulty finding sufficient borrowers, and their liquidity ratios rose to a peak that was double the legal minimum requirement. The private sector of the economy had a very high investment rate out of the windfall, which in the aggregate amounted to about 90 percent of its windfall income (Bevan et al. 1990). However, this very high rate was in part a consequence of large pecuniary multiplier effects. Income was transferred from all farmers (including non-coffee farmers) to urban firms as coffee boom expenditure enabled firms to increase prices. This was a transfer from those who had a low savings rate out of their normal income to those with a high rate. The high aggregate savings rate was therefore a compound of a high savings rate on the part of the primary windfall recipients (coffee farmers) and a transfer from low savers (other farmers) to high savers (firms).

Consider, first, the pecuniary multiplier effects of the boom. The high savings and investment rate in the private sector implied a fairly modest increase in consumer expenditure but a large increase in the demand for nontradable capital goods. The main pecuniary multiplier effect was therefore likely to be a construction boom rather than Dutch disease. This indeed appears to have been the case, according to estimates of the effects of the boom on consumption and relative prices arrived at through two methods: by positing a simple counterfactual based on the assumption that the economy in the preboom years was in equilibrium; and by constructing a computable general equilibrium model of the economy (Bevan, et al. 1990). Both approaches have their limitations, but they have the virtue of being independent measures of how the economy would have evolved in the absence of the boom. As far as consumption is concerned, both approaches lead to the conclusion that the effect of the boom was quite modest. The simple counterfactual suggests that at the peak of the boom consumption in real terms was 4.6 percent higher because of the boom, while the CGE model generates the slightly lower figure of 3 percent. The relative price of consumer nontradables rose slightly between 1975 and 1977–78 (the peak of the boom). The CGE model predicts a larger increase with the boom (partly because it suggests that in the absence of the boom the relative price of consumer nontradables would have fallen), but there seems no compelling reason to give this prediction much credence. However, even a modest increase in relative prices can produce a sizable transfer of income from the agricultural sector.

The construction boom, by contrast, was substantial. Approved urban building plans rose by about 80 percent between 1975 and 1978. Rural construction, on which there is no comparable evidence, probably increased even more substantially. According to survey evidence, coffee farmers invested heavily in housing improvements. The construction sector expanded substantially in relation to GDP, and the relative price of its output rose sharply. (On this point the simple counterfactual and the CGE model are in broad agreement.) The price rise constituted a large pecuniary multiplier whereby a primary boom in the agricultural sector was transferred to the construction sector.

As explained earlier, a pecuniary multiplier may also come into effect as a result of an endogenous trade liberalization that squeezes the import-competing manufacturing sector. Between 1975 and 1978 ex-factory prices of manufactures fell by about 30 percent in relation to the CIF cost of manufactured imports, which is consistent with the view that trade policy was driven by the availability of foreign exchange. This decline suggests that there was a substantial transfer from the manufacturing sector. Nevertheless, manufacturing output grew rapidly. Whereas in the three years preceding the boom, value added had increased by 26 percent, in 1975–78 it increased by 49 percent, the highest three-year growth rate in the study period.

There are three potential explanations for this growth. First, despite the overall decline in relative prices brought about by the trade liberalization, some firms undoubtedly managed to maintain quota protection, since the liberalization took the form of a piecemeal relaxation of quotas, and thereby benefited from higher prices, as in the case of nontradable goods. Second, there may have been a real multiplier effect through the increased availability of imported inputs, a possibility discussed further below. Third, the savings boom gave rise to an investment boom in the sector. Not only was overall investment greatly increased, but it was skewed toward manufacturing. Thus, the increase in output reflected a shifting of the supply curve to the right rather than a movement up it.

The induced trade liberalization gave rise to a further and ultimately central pecuniary multiplier. Because the government relied on import duties for its revenue, the relaxation of import quotas generated a large increase in revenue. Thus, although the government chose not to tax the primary windfall, it nevertheless gained around half of it in extra revenue through the taxation of second-round expenditures. Initially, the government budget moved into surplus, but the spending departments responded by massively inflating their bids for expenditure. As the terms of trade reverted to their preboom level during 1977–80, government expenditure jumped five percentage points of GDP, and the budget moved into heavy deficit. It took until the mid-1980s to bring the budget back under control. Indirectly, the coffee boom thus led to a public expenditure boom, which itself had powerful repercussions on the rest of the economy. However, these indirect consequences are not considered here.

As for real multipliers, recall that they may come into effect in three ways: through distortions in labor, credit, or foreign exchange markets. Distortions in the labor market are incorporated into the CGE model. The modern sector is assumed to pay a wage above the supply price of labor so that the expansion of employment in the sector generates output well in excess of the opportunity cost of that labor elsewhere in the economy. Furthermore, as the returns to labor rise in agriculture, the supply of household labor is increased. The opportunity cost in terms of foregone leisure is not treated as an offsetting cost (just as unemployment is not valued as a supply of leisure in national accounts). When the effects of the boom on real income are measured for the period 1976–79 and then discounted back at 10 percent to 1975, the CGE model yields an increase of 6.7 percent in the present value of real income. The pure gain in terms of trade is only 5.4 percent, so the residual 1.3 percent is attributable to either the returns on boom-induced investment or to real multiplier effects. The returns to boom-induced investment during the period to 1979 are estimated by calculating windfall investment (as the difference between actual investment and a counterfactual) and assuming a 10 percent rate of return and a one-year gestation period. Since the bulk of windfall income accrued in 1977, the yield on windfall investment was negligible until 1978 and 1979. Again discounted back to 1975, the present value of the returns from this investment raised real income by only 0.2 percent over the whole period 1976–79. This estimate implies, residually, that the labor market effects, which can be regarded as a component of the real multiplier through the labor market, amounted to 1.1 percent extra real income. Since the primary windfall was 5.4 percent, the value of the real multiplier from the agricultural windfall onto the rest of the economy was 0.20.

To reiterate, other than the gain arising from the unwinding of labor market distortions, the potential sources for a real multiplier effect were from credit market and foreign exchange market distortions. The coffee boom led to a temporary financial liberalization as interest rates fell well below the official ceiling. Since foreign exchange therefore became easier to acquire, there was a substantial trade liberalization. Both of these events can be presumed to have enhanced allocative efficiency. Between them they probably account for the bulk of the unusually rapid growth in manufacturing output during the boom. Although the fall in interest rates and the reduction in trade restrictions can be quantified, it is not possible to move from this to the gain in GDP and hence to a value of the real multiplier.

In the decade before the second agricultural shock, the drought of 1983/84, value added had grown at an average rate of 4.5 percent. In 1984, agricultural output fell absolutely and was 10.7 percent lower than it would have been had it maintained the growth of the previous decade. At 1982 prices, this amounted to a shortfall of K£ 112 million, or 3.6 percent of 1984 GDP. Recall that the coffee boom constituted a direct gain of 5.4 percent in real income over a four-year period. Hence, the drought was followed by both a shorter and smaller, but not negligible, deviation in income. Farmers had reacted to the coffee boom by building up assets. They might have been expected to react to a drought in a symmetrical fashion. However, a possible asymmetry is that whereas it is always feasible to accumulate assets, it is not always feasible to accumulate debts, since there may be no willing lender. Whereas for the coffee boom period, savings behavior can be estimated through a purpose-designed survey, there is no survey source for the drought. At the aggregate level, the national accounts identify two private agricultural assets, cattle and land improvement. In the years from 1972 to 1987, except 1984, annual investment in cattle averaged K£ 0.65 million, with no clear trend. In 1984 investment was −K£ 3.44 million, the largest destocking in the period. Hence, there was a turnaround of K£ 4.1 million. Similarly, investment in land improvement averaged K£ 8.4 million (again with no clear trend), whereas in 1984 it was only K£ 5.8 million (the lowest since 1973); a turnaround of K£ 2.6 million. The changes in discernible assets are therefore consistent with the hypothesis that agricultural households responded to the drought by reducing their assets, but they do not make it possible to estimate how powerful these changes were. During the coffee boom, the predominant pecuniary multiplier effect had been transmitted from the savings changes onto investment and thereby to a construction boom. The drought might have triggered the same transmission mechanism: reduced savings leading to a construction slump. There is, indeed, some evidence for such an effect. Output of the construction sector in 1984 was lower than at any other time during 1978–87. The extent of the decline in construction due to the drought is difficult to estimate because there is no "normal" year for the sector. In the late 1970s and early 1980s, the sector was booming in response to the coffee boom and thereafter it was in relative or even absolute decline because of the oil shock and public expenditure reductions. Thus, although there was some growth in GDP, which presumably provided some impetus for expansion, the construction output after 1978 showed no clear trend: output in 1987 was virtually identical to that in 1978. As an approximation, construction output in 1984 can be compared to the average for the rest of the period 1978–87 (all at 1982 prices). On this basis, output during the drought was reduced by 11.7 percent, or by K£ 13.6 million.

Potentially, the other transmission mechanisms from agricultural income that appeared to be operating during the coffee boom also applied during the drought. Although there might be some theoretical reasons to expect differences, as already explained, it is not possible to discern them in the data because the aggregate effects of the drought were small in relation to GDP. In 1984, the terms of trade improved modestly, adding about K£ 90 million (at 1982 prices) when compared with the level that would have been generated by the 1982 terms of trade. Hence, although the drought caused the government to import food and thereby reduced foreign exchange availability in relation to the non-drought counterfactual, this was broadly offset by the changes in the terms of trade. As a result, one should not expect to find any deterioration in foreign exchange availability in relation to its previous level, and hence a comparison of predrought and drought performance cannot be used as a guide to the counterfactual.

The advantage of studying linkages by means of shocks is that there is a greater likelihood of identifying consequences by examining large events. However, it is possible that relationships that hold for short-term fluctuations in agricultural income do not carry over to changes in agricultural growth over long term.

This analysis of the two major agricultural shocks provides evidence for both pecuniary and real multipliers. The pecuniary multiplier operated through the impact of changes in savings on the construction sector, through endogenous changes in trade policy, and through Dutch disease effects on the price of consumer nontradables. Of these, the first was probably the most important and was discernible in both the coffee boom and the drought. This suggests that one of the key transmission mechanisms from agriculture to the rest of the economy is asset markets. Care should be exercised, however, in extrapolating this evidence from agricultural shocks to long-term agricultural growth. It is quite possible, indeed likely, that whereas the propensity of farmers to save (or dissave) out of windfall gains (or losses) is very high, the propensity to save out of normal income is very low. A higher trend rate of agricultural growth might therefore have had little impact on the construction sector, even though variations in agricultural income appear to have been highly important. The same criticism could be leveled at the transmission mechanism operating through trade policy. Although imports were liberalized during an export boom, it does not necessarily follow that had Kenyan agricultural exports been growing at a faster rate there would have been a stronger trend toward liberalization. An alternative would be for the government to have had a faster rate of monetary growth or a slower rate of exchange rate depreciation. Even in the short run, Dutch disease effects (a change in the price of nontradable consumer goods) were modest. Had agriculture grown faster, the Dutch disease effects might have been only negligible, since the long-term supply elasticity of nontradable goods might have been high once factors were able to move into the sector.

Since the real multiplier operated through effects in the labor, credit, and foreign exchange markets, the same critique can be applied: relationships that hold in the short term in response to shocks may not extrapolate well to changes in the trend growth rate. The credit effect is manifestly a short-term phenomenon: a positive shock leads to a savings boom, which lowers the interest rate below the official ceiling and thereby achieves a temporary financial liberalization. Just as with the pecuniary multiplier onto the construction sector, it is unlikely that this would apply to a higher trend growth of agricultural income. The foreign exchange liberalization is closely related to trade liberalization. As just mentioned, it does not necessarily follow that a higher growth rate of agricultural exports would have reduced the intensity of foreign exchange rationing. However, it seems likely that even if some of the benefits of higher growth had been dissipated in faster monetary growth and slower exchange rate depreciation, there would have been some easing of foreign exchange rationing. The most likely of the short-term real multiplier effects to have carried over into the long term is that generated in the labor market. Owing to exceptional historical circumstances, the real wage level in the modern urban sector during the 1950s and early 1960s was both above the supply price of labor and unsustainable (Collier and Lal 1986). It seems that during the 1970s this wage premium was gradually eroded as agricultural incomes rose and urban real wages fell. Faster agricultural growth would, on this analysis, have eroded the premium more rapidly and in the meantime have generated urban jobs that used labor with an opportunity cost below its productivity.

TRANSMISSION FROM AGRICULTURAL SUPPLY SHOCKS OVER THE ENTIRE PERIOD. The effects on real output can now be examined for the entire study period. Only the real multiplier is considered here. The dependent variables are therefore real output in construction, consumer services, and manufacturing. According to the theoretical analysis, those are the sectors that may be subject to a real multiplier. The main explanatory variable is real output in agriculture. As the coffee boom episode demonstrated, however, income changes may not only be due to changes in agricultural output but also to changes in world prices. Changes in real income brought about by changes in the terms of trade are measured in relation to their 1982 level (all at 1982 prices) and are treated as an additional explanatory variable. Since the remaining source of exogenous changes in demand is the government, a series on the real output of government services must also be included (this is measured in the national accounts by the quantity of its inputs, as is customary for government services). This explanatory variable can be used to investigate whether government expenditures crowd in or crowd out other sectoral outputs.

To properly assess the indirect effects of the linkages from agriculture to the rest of the economy, it would be necessary to use a CGE model. For the purpose of this discussion, however, reduced-form econometric techniques are used to establish any linkage effects from agriculture to other sectors of the economy. Nevertheless, this analysis is tentative, and the results must be interpreted with caution. The analysis is confined to the effects of agricultural output (A) on manufacturing (M), construction (C), and nontradable private services (S).[1] The effects from two exogenous variables are taken into account: namely, provision of government services (G) and changes in real income arising from changes in the external terms of trade (T).

Simple correlation tests show that there is a positive correlation between all sectors contemporaneously, but mere correlation cannot, of course, be taken

---

1. We include trade, restaurants, hotels, transport and communications, finance, private household services, and other services.

to prove that there is a significant relationship, or to indicate the direction of causality.

Slightly more advanced tests can be used to try to get more robust conclusions. The purpose of these tests is to see if there is a long-run relationship between the variables. The first is the augmented Dickey-Fuller test. The t values show that the hypothesis of a unit root cannot be rejected in any of the cases of agricultural (A), manufacturing (M), construction (C), or services (S) output with one or two lags or for agricultural output with three lags. The variables concerned are thus not stationary: all of them have a tendency to grow over time. This creates a potential problem: when variables are nonstationary, time-series regressions specified in levels of variables often lead to erroneous inferences. The obtained relationship may be entirely spurious. When variables are nonstationary, the next step in the analysis is to investigate whether they are co-integrated. If two variables are co-integrated, there is a sustained relationship between them. In that case, it is possible to run regressions with the level estimates of the variables.

In the co-integration test, one takes the first differences on the residuals obtained from an OLS regression of, for example, A on M, and then applies the augmented Dickey-Fuller unit root test again. The results from the co-integration test in this study are mixed. For agriculture and industry, t values are not significant, and there is strong serial correlation without the lag. Agriculture and construction are significantly co-integrated, however, so for this relationship (which the analysis of shock episodes suggested might be central) the analysis can proceed by using levels of variables. It should be noted, however, that the co-integration test is weak and that the number of observations is rather small, so the results are uncertain.

In order to investigate relationships between variables that are not co-integrated, one must transform the variables by differencing, since this makes these series stationary, yielding consistent coefficient estimates. The approach used here is to first log all sectoral variables and then take the first differences. This means the analysis is conducted in terms of growth rates for all variables except T, for which the level estimate is used (since T is sometimes negative, one cannot take its logarithm).

The objective here is to determine how agricultural growth affects the growth of manufacturing, construction, and private services, controlling for government expenditures and income shocks arising from changes in the external terms of trade. Different variations of the following formulation can be tried with different numbers of lags (see table 7.2).

$$DLX_i = h(DLA, DLG, DT). \tag{7.1}$$

Note that the F-form value in the first regression (table 7.2, A) is a little high, which indicates some serial correlation. However, neither in this formulation nor in any other similar formulations did agriculture appear to have a

TABLE 7.2 Impacts on manufacturing growth with dependent variable DLM

A			B		
Dependent Variable	Coefficient	Standard Error	Dependent Variable	Coefficient	Standard Error
DLM1	0.405	0.187	DLM1	0.432	0.166
DLA	−0.026	0.156	DT	0.00010	0.00005
DLA1	0.083	0.141	DT1	0.00013	0.00006
DLG	0.030	0.400	Constant	0.036	0.024
DLG1	0.127	0.894			
DT	0.00010	0.00005			
DT1	0.00012	0.00006			
Constant	0.036	0.024			
$r^2 = 0.493$,	$F = 2.22$,	f-form = 5.29	$r^2 = 0.457$,	$F = 5.61$,	F-form = 4.38

SOURCE: Authors' computations.
NOTE: The critical F-form value at the 5 percent level about 4.4.

significant effect on manufacturing. But there was a consistently significant effect of changes in the terms of trade variable, which suggests that income shocks arising from the terms of trade (many of which are agricultural) are an important driving force behind manufacturing growth (see also table 7.2, B). This force may operate through its effect on the balance of payments constraint, changing the ability of industry to import essential inputs.

In table 7.3, A, the dependent variable is construction output. Recall that the co-integration test makes it possible to investigate the relationship between

TABLE 7.3 Impacts on construction and the growth of private services

A			B		
Dependent Variable	Coefficient	Standard Error	Dependent Variable	Coefficient	Standard Error
LC11	0.689	0.145	DLS1	−1.44	0.248
LA	0.805	0.402	DLA	0.292	0.166
LA1	−0.475	0.397	DLA1	0.145	0.154
LG	−1.254	0.183	DLG	0.710	0.417
LG1	1.084	0.351	DLG1	−0.628	0.395
T	−0.00010	0.00013	DT	−0.00004	0.00005
T1	0.00020	0.00012	DT1	0.00004	0.00005
Constant	−0.275	1.933	Constant	0.042	0.022
$r^2 = 0.93$,	$F = 31.16$,	F-form = 5.29	$r^2 = 0.315$,	$F = 1.05$,	F-form = 0.15

SOURCE: Authors' computations.

this output and agricultural output using levels of variables (instead of changes in levels). The regression reveals a powerful, statistically significant and contemporaneous relationship between agricultural output and construction output. A 1 percent change in the former is associated with a 0.8 percent change in the latter. This supports the inferences drawn earlier about the consequences of the coffee boom and the drought. In table 7.3, B, the dependent variable is the output of marketed consumer nontradables (i.e., various types of services). This forces the investigation back onto changes in levels and reveals no significant relationship between agricultural output and the output of these services.

The objective of the final test performed in this study was to determine whether agricultural growth causes growth in the other three sectors in the sense of Granger. This was done by means of two regressions, A and B. In regression A, X is a function of lagged values of itself. In regression B, X is a function of lagged values of X plus lagged values of another variable Y. Then, Y causes X if, compared to A, the information in B significantly improves one's ability to predict X. This can be formulated as follows:

$$\text{A: } X = X_0 + \Sigma_i \beta_i X_{t-1} + \epsilon_i \tag{7.2}$$

$$\text{B: } X = X_0 + \Sigma_i \beta_i X_{t-i} + \Sigma_i \gamma_i Y_{t-i} + \epsilon_i. \tag{7.3}$$

We say that Y causes X if B has significantly smaller residuals than A. Given the small number of observations in the present sample, caution must be exercised in drawing any conclusions from them. A problem with annual data is that the impact may well happen within the year, in which case the causality will not be picked up with this test. Some of the results are reported in table 7.4. Different variations were tried, but they did not significantly change the results.

Recall that the only significant relationship found between agriculture and the other sectors of the economy is the relationship with construction. The

TABLE 7.4 Granger causality tests

Test	F-Value
LM on LA	$F(2,19) = 0.94$
LA on LM	$F(2,19) = 4.72**$
LC on LA	$F(2,19) = 8.31***$
LA on LC	$F(2,19) = 2.10$
LS on LA	$F(2,19) = 0.61$
LA on LS	$F(2,19) = 2.96*$

SOURCE: Authors' computations.
NOTE: In all the reported cases, 1 to 2 lags are used for both variables.
* = significant at the 10 percent level.
** = significant at the 5 percent level.
*** = significant at the 1 percent level.

Granger test supports the interpretation that causality runs from agricultural output to construction (Granger causality being satisfied at the 1 percent level). According to the Granger test, any relationship between agriculture and manufacturing and services, insignificant on the previous analysis, run from these other sectors to agriculture.

Thus there is again no evidence that agricultural growth stimulates either manufacturing industry or consumer services. In an economy where industry is highly dependent on inputs from agriculture, one might expect a causal relationship, but it may be that Kenya's import-substituting industry is not very dependent on inputs from agriculture. To the extent that imported inputs determine its growth rate, as explained earlier, improved terms of trade did have a significant and positive effect on manufacturing output.

LOCATIONAL ASPECTS OF GROWTH AND LINKAGES. So far, the analysis has been confined to linkages at the national aggregate level between agriculture and other activities. A striking feature of Kenya's economy, however, is the spatial concentration of activity. The manufacturing and service sectors are located in large part in Kenya's main city, which is in turn located in the most prosperous agricultural region.[2] Nonagricultural activities that are geographically dispersed tend not to be integrated into a national market. Thus there are two rather distinct spatial linkages. One is that national agricultural income to some extent affects activities that are concentrated in a few urban areas. In turn, urban activity feeds back selectively on rural areas through migration and remittances. The other linkage is that within small rural localities the performance of locally based nonagricultural activities appears to be quite closely linked to agriculture because they are nontradable outside the locality.

The question of interest here is to what extent is agriculture the basis for the development of small-scale enterprises in the rural areas? Official survey data on such enterprises covered all activities carried out in the open air, in market stalls, and in temporary structures (Kenya 1986b). According to this series of surveys, the growth of value added by small-scale enterprises in rural Kenya averaged 17 percent per year during the period 1973 to 1982, and the number of establishments grew by 39 percent per year. These figures may represent an overestimate of the growth, since it is possible that the coverage of the survey has increased over time. In any case, there is considerable additional evidence that the growth has been substantial. For rural Kenya, the consumption linkage is somewhat more powerful than the production linkages in generating nonfarm rural production (Herr 1989). Much of the activity is directly related to farm output, with about 38 percent of total employment in the rural trading centers in food retailing and another few percent in food milling activities. These links could be described as forward linkages from agriculture. Backward linkages, such as the retailing of fertilizers, were not significant.

2. To some extent, this may be biased upward by the underrecording of rural manufacturing.

Together, the forward- and backward-linked activities probably represented 45 percent of the total activities, while the remaining 55 percent could be classified as being linked to consumer demand.

Another study of the rural informal sector in four districts concluded that the type of activities found in the rural areas are similar to those found in the major urban centers (Ngethe, Wahome, and Ndua 1989). The manufacturing sector only made up about 15 percent of the sample, while trade and services made up the remaining 85 percent.

Small-scale rural manufacturing appears to be locally oriented for the most part, with few links beyond this area (Williams and Kabagambe 1982). If this is correct, the present rural nonagricultural sector can only benefit from local expansion. It seems, for example, that the secondary impact of the coffee boom was concentrated in the major coffee growing regions and the urban economy, whereas other rural areas benefited little from this apparently national economic expansion.

Early growth in Kenya was concentrated in large-scale agriculture, plus modern secondary and tertiary activities, and it was located in those regions or urban centers with a favorable infrastructural position. In recent decades, smallholder agriculture has expanded rapidly, but this has been primarily in the regions close to the core areas. Strong cumulative or agglomerative forces favoring continued growth in the centrally located regions therefore persisted. It seems that agricultural development is more easily achieved in densely populated areas.

Apart from infrastructure, which is the result of policy decisions, several endogenous economic forces explain the spatial pattern of growth. In this analysis it is useful to distinguish between economies of scale that are internal to firms and external agglomeration economies. The latter category contains input-output linkages and interactions between final demand and producers. There are three kinds of industries, as defined by locational determinants. First, there are the resource-oriented industries such as agriculture. They have to locate where the resource (e.g., agricultural land) is located. Agriculture is thus by its nature a widely dispersed activity. Second, in some industries economies of scale are small or distance causes considerable friction in the delivery of the final product (e.g., construction and services). The location of these industries therefore tends to reflect the distribution of the demand for their products. Finally, some industries are characterized by indivisibilities and a low distance elasticity of deliveries, such as is part of manufacturing. Their location choices are less obvious. However, the latter firms may chose a central location because of input-output linkages. Firms that exhibit a great deal of interdependence may therefore choose to locate together and thereby support each other's growth.

The supply of agricultural products as inputs to the processing industry may go either to local firms or to firms in the major urban centers. Some processing can be done locally on a small scale. It is the character of agricultural output that determines whether agriculture can stimulate decentralized growth via output linkages.

The second factor that determines how growth impulses are transmitted is the interaction between final demand and production. In Kenya, industrial growth has been based on import substitution, that is, on the production of Western consumer goods. For industries producing consumer goods above a certain level of sophistication and for some industries producing investment goods, a very large share of the market is to be found in the urban centers. Agricultural demand for many of these goods is of secondary importance, so that the power of attraction of rural demand may not be sufficient to make manufacturing industry decentralize. As far as recorded manufacturing is concerned, industry has not been dependent on agriculture, either as a supplier of inputs or as a purchaser of output.

As a result of the forces just described, the structure of regional production in Kenya is highly skewed. In 1976 Nairobi, with about 5 percent of the population then, accounted for 32 percent of production (Bigsten 1980). The other regions that did fairly well were Central, Rift Valley, and Coast with a per capita production between 12 and 18 percent of that of Nairobi. These all have important urban agglomerations, particularly the Coast province, which is the location of Mombasa. In Central and Rift Valley, agriculture also contributes to the favorable position. These are areas with fertile land, and they also include large-scale farms.

Modern manufacturing industry is located in the central areas (more than half in Nairobi), while Nyanza, Eastern, Western, and Northeastern regions have a very small manufacturing base. These regions all lack communication linkages and supporting services and lie outside the pull of the endogenous economic forces discussed above.

Since these regions contain both urban and rural areas (except Nairobi), some attention must also be given to the growth of the urban network. Although the rate of urbanization there has been high, it has emanated from a low base. In 1969 only 10 percent of the population were living in urban areas, half of them in Nairobi. In 1988 18 percent were living in urban centers with more than 2,000 people (there were 172 urban centers), with a third of those living in Nairobi. Nairobi has thus become less dominant in terms of urban population. Although the share of the four largest cities in the national population increased from 5.9 percent in 1962 to 9.6 percent in 1988, their share in the urban population fell significantly. At the same time, the relative importance of secondary centers increased. This growth of the smaller centers has probably increased the local integration of agricultural and nonagricultural activities.

The urban-rural distinction is blurred in Kenya (see, among others, Collier and Lal 1986; Bigsten 1988) because intrahousehold migration is extensive. The main reason for male migration is that the individual is looking for a job or taking up a job offer, and the more educated the migrant, the stronger these reasons become. For female migrants, marriage is the dominating reason, although job search is important for those who are well educated.

According to an analysis of National Social Security Fund data (Bigsten and Collier 1980), the average period of employment in the wage sector is short. A large group of workers seem to enter employment around the age of 25 and quit after five years to return to the nonwage, presumably mainly smallholder, economy. The labor market appears to consist of two distinct behavior groups, a low-wage, high-turnover, probably manual group, and a high-wage, low-turnover, probably white-collar group. An analysis of the household budget survey (Herr 1989) tends to support this conclusion. Temporary migrants remit more than permanent migrants, which is hardly surprising since the former have retained their ties with the household and expect to return home. In 1982 temporary migrants from Central and Nyanza provinces remitted 21 percent and 17 percent of their income, respectively.

Partly as a result of migration, smallholder families are becoming dependent on off-farm sources of income. Income from own-farm production made up 57 percent of the total family income of smallholders in 1974/75 (Integrated Rural Survey), while own business accounted for 9.7 percent, wages 22.4 percent, and remittances 10.9 percent of incomes. According to the regional household budget survey of 1981/82, the share of farm-operating surplus in total smallholder incomes had declined to 48 percent, and about half of households had some wage-employment income. About 1.2 million people in the rural areas were engaged in wage employment, some in the formal sector as teachers and civil servants, and some in the informal sector or wage employment within agriculture. All these are not covered in official estimates of employment, which means that the share of labor in nonfarm employment is underestimated and the share in agriculture overestimated. There were 670,000 households engaged in self-employment. Off-farm activities among smallholder families made up about 40 percent of total working time in Central and Nyanza provinces in 1982 (Bigsten and Julin 1990).

Smallholders with very small holdings were more likely to seek off-farm work. In 1982 up to 74 percent of farmers with less than 1 acre of land worked in wage employment. They worked long hours at a low wage rate. Largeholders may exercise some selectivity in types of wage employment, while smallholders cannot. The same pattern emerges in the results from the 1982 survey in Central and Nyanza. It has been found that a high level of education leads to diversification into urban activities and thus reduces the time devoted to agriculture, but not to rural off-shamba work (Bigsten and Julin 1990). The highly educated tend to specialize more (Herr 1989, 64). Education is a differentiating factor in rural Kenya. It is noteworthy, though, that the regional household budget survey shows no correlation between the education of the head of the household and the returns to farming (Herr 1989, 161).

In conclusion, smallholder families in Kenya are now multiactivity businesses. Smallholder families diversify into other activities while retaining their base in agriculture. Migration to the urban areas is extensive, but typically the migrants return after a longer or shorter period of time. In such an economy the welfare of smallholders is also dependent on what is happening outside agriculture. They benefit from new employment and business opportunities within the rural areas, but through migration to the urban areas they may also benefit from expansion there.

Poverty

Poverty in Kenya is predominantly a rural phenomenon concentrated among the landless, pastoralists, and smallholders (table 7.5). Poverty may be measured through incomes, consumption or a food poverty line calculated in terms of the household's economic ability to achieve an adequate nutrition standard (see table 7.6). Rural poverty is most extensive in the western parts of the country. Smallholders in Central province seem to be best provided, with the lowest share of households below the poverty line.

Because of the country's high population growth, land pressure has increased, but the cities have not yet become a refuge for the rural poor to the same extent as in many other developing countries. Although there is a wide gap between mean incomes in rural and urban areas, the differentials within the areas are even wider, with those in the rural sector accounting for the largest share of income inequality in Kenya (Vandemoortele 1982). The rural household budget survey of 1981/82 showed that the share of the richest 20 percent in rural areas was 53 percent of the total incomes, that the share of the middle 40 percent was 34 percent, and that the poorest 40 percent received about 13 percent of total income.

Landownership is highly concentrated. In 1979, the 115 largest farms in

TABLE 7.5 Rural subgroups below the poverty line, 1982

Subgroup	Percentage of All within the Group
Large farmers	0
Smallholders	29
Migrants to drylands	55
Squatters	33
Migratory pastoralists	85
Sedentary pastoralists	33
Landless with good occupation	0
Landless with poor occupation	50

SOURCE: World Bank (1982).

TABLE 7.6 Estimates of smallholder poverty

	Percentage of Households below Poverty Line			
	Income Based	Consumption Based	Food Poverty Line	
Province	1	2	3	4
Coast	31	44	47	47
Eastern	35	29	20	29
Central	22	18	19	33
Rift Valley	19	39	17	51
Nyanza	38	55	20	48
Western	50	52	39	52
Total	34	39	24	41

SOURCES: Collier and Lal (1980); Livingstone (1986); ILO (1983); Greer and Thorbecke (1983).
NOTE: Poor households are defined as follows: (1) Households with an annual income of less than KSh 2,000 in 1974. (2) Households with consumption expenditures of less than KSh 2,200 in 1974. (3) Households that lack resources necessary to acquire a nutritionally adequate food diet based on 70 percent maize and 30 percent beans. (4) The same as in (3) but based on observed regional diets.

Kenya had an average size of 11,630 hectares and covered 19.3 percent of arable land, while 21 percent of rural households had no land, and 25 percent had holdings smaller than 0.4 hectare (World Bank 1988). However, the connection between landownership and poverty is not as strong as might be imagined. The incidence of poverty, although somewhat higher among those with little land, does not differ markedly by holding size (ILO 1983).

One problem in evaluating the incidence of poverty is that it is difficult to measure change over time. One such attempt based on Sen's poverty index suggests that poverty in Kenya probably decreased up to the 1960s, then increased slightly up to 1969, and thereafter remained unchanged up to 1976 (Bigsten 1986). In addition, a decomposition analysis of growth up to 1976 showed that whenever the growth of smallholder agriculture per capita was positive, poverty decreased.

Beyond 1976, it appears that real wages in both private and public employment fell between the first oil shock and 1985 (World Bank 1988). Incomes in the informal sector increased up to 1979, but they also fell during the period of domestic deflation. But this assessment does not take into account the impact of changes in the distribution of labor force among activities; it just considers changes over time in real income within categories. A comparison of the rural surveys of 1974/75 and 1981/82 suggests that smallholder family incomes increased over this period. The latter conclusion is supported when the budget share of food is used as an indicator of welfare, on the assumption that this will fall as households grow more prosperous (Herr 1989). A comparison of the integrated rural survey of 1974/75 and the 1981/82 rural household budget survey indicates that between these two periods there was a reduction in the overall budget share for food (Herr 1989, 23, 51). This suggests that the welfare of smallholder families improved over this period.

If these estimates are accepted, it seems that both the urban-rural gap and the formal-informal sector gap declined somewhat from the mid-1970s to the mid-1980s. Thus the income distribution within the group of workers and smallholders may have become more even. Whether poverty decreased is not easy to say.

As for income distribution between wage earners, various farmers, and profit receivers, the owners of large farms probably fared better than small-holders between 1979 and 1986 (Bigsten and Ndungu 1992). During the 1980s, the cash crop producers had smaller price increases than food crop producers. Since most of these producers are better off, it is possible that the poorest farmers benefited from this situation. As already pointed out, however, Kenya's smallholder families also live on income other than that from their own farms, and the poorest tend to be net purchasers of food. The level of wage employ-ment has increased substantially since 1979, while wages have fallen. Modern sector agricultural employment, which is particularly important to smallholder families, actually fell up to 1983. Since then it has increased again to a level above that in 1979. The income gain from formal employment must therefore have been limited. The rapid expansion of informal rural activities may have been the factor that helped rural families protect their income levels. The evidence on this is as yet fragmentary, however.

To summarize, there have been offsetting influences on income distribu-tion. On one hand, narrowing gaps between urban and rural areas and between formal and informal employment are likely to have reduced inequality. On the other hand, capital and landowners (other than smallholders) seem to have done better than employees and smallholders. At present, it is not possible to say in what direction inequality may have changed.

A Reassessment of Linkages

The sustained growth experienced by Kenya has clearly been above the African average in both agriculture and other sectors. What the country's pro-agricultural policies contributed to this growth through linkages is not quite as clear.

An examination of the two major agricultural shocks reveals powerful pecuniary multiplier effects, but only a weak real multiplier. The origin of the identified real multiplier effect was a labor market distortion: during the 1960s and 1970s urban wages tended to be well above the supply price of labor from rural areas, although the gap was narrowing. As of the mid-1970s, this gave rise to a multiplier of 1.2, according to CGE results: that is, an increase in agri-cultural income of K£ 1 would raise output elsewhere in the economy by K£

0.2. However, the rural-urban gap probably continued to narrow through the 1980s, and in response to this restoration of allocative efficiency the real multiplier must have diminished.

The pecuniary multiplier traveled along three distinct paths, the predominant one being the impact on the construction sector. During the coffee boom, there was a construction boom; during the drought, there was a construction slump. This hypothesis is supported by the time-series econometric approach adopted in this study. Although no evidence was found to substantiate a link from agricultural growth to manufacturing or consumer nontradable services, there was a large and statistically significant link between agriculture and the construction sector. A further test established that causality ran from agriculture to construction. This link has perhaps received little attention in the literature in comparison with the more glamorous hypothesized link between agriculture and manufacturing. As an intrinsically nontradable sector, however, construction is more likely to experience a powerful pecuniary multiplier than manufacturing (which is either fully tradable or subject to endogenous trade restrictions). Furthermore, if the major real multiplier works through the labor market distortion (as suggested in this chapter), then it is likely to generate a larger real multiplier than an equivalent expansion in manufacturing output, for although subject to the same wage rate restrictions, it is usually more labor intensive.

The locational aspects of linkages in Kenya throw some further light on the agriculture-industry relationship. Although much of industry needs to be in a centrally located agglomeration, some is located in rural areas. A good many of these rural industries were producing output that was nontradable outside the locality and hence, a fortiori, nontradable internationally. Thus these rural industries have economic characteristics which would indeed make them more analogous to construction than to large-scale urban manufacturing (the activity that dominates manufacturing in the national accounts).

The general proposition that tentatively emerges from this analysis is that agricultural performance is likely to give rise to powerful transfers (i.e., pecuniary multipliers) to those nontradable activities in which demand is particularly sensitive to agricultural incomes. Rural industries qualify as such activities if they produce for the local market. Construction is such an activity because agricultural income fluctuates more than other components of national income and so is decisive in savings fluctuations, which are in turn transmitted to nontradable capital goods. In Kenya, as well as much of Africa, large-scale manufacturing is not such an activity because, although protected, that protection varies pro-cyclically with agriculture (since the function of protection is primarily to respond to macroeconomic considerations rather than to act as an instrument of industrial policy). In India, where manufacturing receives virtually blanket protection as a matter of industrial policy, it might be expected to be more sensitive to agricultural performance, but such a speculation is beyond the scope of this discussion.

Pecuniary multipliers are good news for the sectors that benefit from them, but, being transfers, they net out in aggregate growth. The central issue is whether agricultural growth generates a real multiplier. Although there is some evidence for such a multiplier in Kenya, all such effects have originated in either a distortion or failure in some other market such as those for labor and credit, or in agricultural technical progress. Kenya's labor and credit markets have been sufficiently distorted for a substantial multiplier to have been credible. Although they persist, a pro-agriculture policy can be supported on efficiency as well as equity grounds. But a case can also be made for directing policy toward improving the functioning of markets. As such policies succeed, the real multiplier will wither, unless technical progress accelerates, and leave the pecuniary multiplier: in other words, a "trickle down" will replace a "free lunch."

References

Bevan, D. L., P. Collier, and J. W. Gunning, with A. Bigsten and P. H. Horsnell. 1989. *Peasants and Governments: An Economic Analysis.* Oxford: Oxford University Press.
———. 1990. *Controlled Open Economies: A Neoclassical Approach to Structuralism.* Oxford: Oxford University Press.
Bigsten, A. 1980. *Regional Inequality and Development: A Case Study of Kenya.* Gower: Farnborough.
———. 1986. "Welfare and Economic Growth in Kenya." *World Development* 14.
———. 1988. *Smallholder Circular Migration in East Africa.* Memorandum 112. Sweden: Department of Economics, Göteborgs University.
Bigsten, A., and P. Collier. 1980. "Economic Consequences of Labour Turnover in Kenya: A Pilot Application of the National Social Security Fund Data." Oxford.
Bigsten, A., and E. Julin. 1990. *Allocation of Work among Kenyan Smallholders.* Memorandum 138. Sweden: Department of Economics, Göteborgs University.
Bigsten, A., and N. S. Ndungu. 1992. "Kenya." In *Structural Adjustment and the African Farmer,* ed. A. Duncan and J. Howell. London: James Currey.
Cleaver, W., and M. Westlake. 1987. "Pricing, Marketing and Agricultural Performance in Kenya." Draft for MADIA study. World Bank, Washington, D.C.
Collier, P., and D. Lal. 1980. *Poverty and Growth in Kenya.* World Bank Staff Working Paper 389. Washington, D.C.
———. 1986. *Labour and Poverty in Kenya.* Oxford: Oxford University Press.
Fields, G. S. 1975. "Rural-Urban Migration, Urban Unemployment and Underemployment and Job-Search Activity in LDC's." *Journal of Development Economics,* 2.
Greer, J., and E. Thorbecke. 1983. "Pattern of Food Consumption and Poverty in Kenya and Effects of Food Prices." Ithaca, N.Y.: Cornell University.
Harris, J. R., and M. P. Todaro. 1970. "Migration, Unemployment and Development: A Two-sector Analysis." *American Economic Review* 60.

Herr, H. 1989. "Aspects of Agricultural Development and Consumer Demand in Rural Kenya: 1974–82." Nairobi: U.S. Agency for International Development.

International Labour Organization. 1983. *Increasing the Efficiency of Planning in Kenya: Concepts, Methods and Guidelines for Reviewing Performance and Assessing Impact.* Geneva.

Johnston, B. F. 1989. "The Political Economy of Agricultural Development in Kenya and Tanzania." *Food Research Institute Studies* 21.

Kenya. 1984–1988. *Development Plan.*

———. *Economic Survey.* Annual.

———. *Statistical Abstract.* Annual.

———. *Integrated Rural Survey:* 1974–75. Nairobi.

———. 1986a. *On Economic Management for Renewed Growth.* Nairobi: The Government Printer.

———. 1986b. *Report on Small-Scale Enterprises (Formerly Informal Sector) in Rural and Urban Kenya, 1973–1982.* Nairobi.

Lele, U., and L. R. Meyers. 1989. *Growth and Structural Change in East Africa, Domestic Policies, Agricultural Performance and World Bank Assistance 1963–86, Parts I–II.* MADIA Discussion Paper 3. Washington: World Bank.

Livingstone, I. 1986. *Rural Development, Employment and Incomes in Kenya.* Aldershot: Gower.

Lofchie, M. F. 1989. *The Policy Factor, Agricultural Performance in Kenya and Tanzania.* Boulder, Colo.: Lynne Rienner.

Ngethe, N., J. G. Wahome, and G. Ndua. 1989. *The Rural Informal Sector in Kenya: A Study of Micro-Enterprises in Nyeri Meru, using Gishu and Siava Districts.* IDA Occasional Paper 54. Nairobi: IDS.

Ongaro, W. 1988. *Adoption of New Farming Technology: A Case Study of Maize Production in Western Kenya.* Ekonomiska Studier 22. Sweden: Department of Economics, Göteborgs University.

Raikes, P. 1989. *Credit Savings in Rural Kenya: An Example from Kisii.* Working Paper 466. Nairobi: IDS.

Stiglitz, J. E. 1974. "Alternative Theories of Wage Determination and Unemployment in LDC's: The Labor Turnover Model." *Quarterly Journal of Economics* 88.

Vandemoortele, J. 1982. *Income Distribution and Poverty in Kenya: A Statistical Analysis.* Discussion Paper 275. Nairobi: IDS, University of Nairobi.

Williams, K. G., and D. Kabagambe. 1982. "The Impact of the Coffee Boom in Meru District, Ucuya, Ucuya Research Project." Institute of Planning Studies Working Paper No. 2. University of Nottingham.

World Bank. 1982. *Growth and Structural Changes in Kenya—Basic Economic Report 1982, with Annex I: Poverty and Growth in Kenya, and Annex II: Issues in Agricultural Development.* Washington, D.C.

———. 1988. "Employment and Growth in Kenya." Washington, D.C.

———. 1989. *Sub-Saharan Africa: From Crisis to Sustainable Growth.* Washington, D.C.

8 Dynamic Externalities and Structural Change in Kenya

BRUCE F. JOHNSTON AND ALBERT PARK

Economic development and structural transformation are *dynamic* processes in which sectoral interactions are numerous and multidirectional. Recent growth literature has noted that many of these effects occur in the form of externalities not captured in a neoclassical accounting of intersectoral resource flows and price adjustments. This work has emphasized, for example, that increasing returns phenomena such as demand externalities (Murphy, Shleifer, and Vishny 1989a) and human capital spillovers (Romer 1986) can play an important role in leading the growth process. The assessment just presented by Bigsten and Collier in chapter 7 takes a primarily static view of agricultural linkages in Kenya. This chapter points out ways in which such a perspective may overlook important aspects of linkage effects and structural transformation in Kenya. The discussion draws heavily on the successful agricultural and rural development experience in Taiwan to illustrate the potential importance of intersectoral linkages and certain dynamic externalities.

While not claiming to disprove the existence of strong growth linkages between agriculture and other sectors, Bigsten and Collier argue that the only significant connection between agriculture and other sectors is through construction. By way of evidence in support of their view they document the effects of two important agricultural shocks, a coffee boom in 1976–79 and a drought in 1983–84. However, their examination of the short-term macroeconomic transmission of temporary shocks to other sectors of the economy provides little insight into the importance of agricultural development to long-run structural transformation, a question of central and pressing concern. It is not surprising that the results of reduced-form empirical specifications and Granger tests that attempt to encompass complicated and simultaneous underlying structural relationships are not robust. For one thing, the time series is too short and considerable noise is created by a sequence of well-documented macroeconomic shocks during the time period analyzed (1965–87). The perception that gains are transitory, which is especially likely to be true of price shocks, will result in far different behavior than a steady improvement in underlying productivity and employment opportunities.

Increasing Returns and the Importance of Agricultural Growth

Bigsten and Collier fail to address issues of structural and demographic transition because of the analytic framework they have used. In a static context, it may make sense to think that transfers and the composition of aggregate income do not matter and that pecuniary multipliers therefore have no real effects. In a dynamic setting with externalities, however, the transfer of labor and other resources from agriculture to industry may be important, since the potential gains from economies of scale, learning-by-doing, and technological spillovers are significantly higher in the industrial sector than in agriculture. More generally, employment, investment, and output decisions that have small effects on aggregate output in an Arrow-Debreu model can have large effects when prices already diverge from marginal costs (Shleifer 1990).

What are the causes of such divergence? In an economy in which efforts to expand trade (especially of nontraditional export products) is initially problematic and there are increasing returns to scale in manufacturing, the stimulus of agricultural growth for the rest of the economy may be significant. When a country's manufacturing sector is still extremely small, many kinds of products are not being produced because markets are too small to permit technology with increasing returns to break even. And poor-quality product can exclude producers from export markets. Thus, rising agricultural incomes can produce demand externalities for nonagricultural goods and services that allow real gains in growth from increasing returns technologies to be realized (Murphy, Shleifer, and Vishny 1989b; Matsuyama 1992).

Increasing returns to production can stem from economies of scale (Fleming 1955), perhaps as a consequence of large, fixed, start-up costs, or from the effects of learning by doing (Arrow 1962) or learning by using (Rosenberg 1982). These latter effects refer to the improvements in production quality and efficiency over time that result from accumulated experience in producing and using manufactured and other products. In the early stages of development in Taiwan, for example, textiles and other export-leading sectors first went through a period in which product quality was low and most sales were to the domestic market.

These theoretical insights mesh quite nicely with the evidence presented by Bigsten and Collier documenting the strong link between agricultural development and the growth of rural-based small and medium-scale industry. Significantly, the discussion of "locational aspects of growth and linkages" is the only part of their chapter that takes a careful look at microeconomic phenomena and so provides a glimpse of the rich dynamic interactions at work.

Research has shown that the highest expenditure elasticity for rural households is for local nonfood goods and services, which are typically provided by the small-scale industrial sector (Hazell and Röell 1983; Liedholm and Mead 1987). Small- and medium-scale enterprises (SMEs) also tend to be highly adaptable to new technologies and changing market conditions. Moreover, they have steep, upward-sloping learning curves and introduce new products at a rapid rate, itself an important source of sustained growth (Stokey 1988). In Taiwan, for example, rising agricultural productivity and broadly distributed rural income growth provided an important stimulus to rural SMEs, which still dominate Taiwan's industrial sector (Park and Johnston, in press). Such complementarities between sectors that work through market size effects are ignored in a static neoclassical framework. Fleming (1955) emphasizes that a sector producing good A will have large effects of this type if the income elasticity of demand for good A is low, the elasticity of substitution between A and non-A goods is low, and the elasticity of supply in non-A goods is high—all of which are arguably true for agriculture (A) and small-scale industry (non-A).

There are analogous externalities from technological innovations and investment that are not mediated through market externalities but that reflect more direct interactions between agriculture and industry. New machines or techniques related to agriculture, for example, are often imitated with modifications in other industrial sectors. For instance, the small-scale production of agricultural tools in Taiwan led later to the production of spare parts, more complicated equipment such as power tillers and fans, and even electronic products (Johnston and Kilby 1975). Such technological spillovers represent an externality because the returns are never fully captured by earlier innovators.

As is well known, investment in transport and other infrastructure can generate important public goods externalities. By making it possible for goods to be transported at a low cost over a greater area, investments in such infrastructure represent another way in which production based on increasing returns technologies is brought close to feasibility. Transport infrastructure also facilitates intersectoral labor mobility and benefits firms and producers in many different sectors at once.

These ideas are, of course, akin to the Big Push theory of industrialization associated with Rosenstein-Rodan; but that view of industrialization has often been interpreted as justifying the adoption of plans for very big and coordinated investment projects. But such an interpretation can be misleading. Although this logic definitely argues for government provision of essential public goods, reaching a more advanced stage of industrial development is also constrained by learning requirements and limited markets. This dynamic view of industrialization once again suggests an important role for increasing demand for domestic manufactures by fostering increases in farm productivity and incomes and an expanding export sector.

Because of certain factors in the Kenya case, the dynamic externalities there are much smaller than in Taiwan. In parts of Kenya, the distribution of land is highly inequitable and so agricultural income gains are not well-dispersed among the population. Consequently, effective demand externalities are greatly reduced (Murphy, Shleifer, and Vishny 1989b). Also, in many areas, rural infrastructure is too inadequate to permit industrialization and commercialization, with the result that industry has become highly concentrated in Nairobi.

Probably most important, Kenya and other developing countries in tropical Africa face an especially difficult challenge in that they are being pressed to come up with a sequence of technological innovations that small-scale farmers could adopt on a wide scale. Agriculture has performed fairly well in Kenya, especially in comparison with other countries in Sub-Saharan Africa.[1] Its rapid expansion of smallholder production of coffee and tea has been particularly significant, and Kenya was one of a few African countries in which maize production attained rapid growth through smallholder production of hybrid maize and increased application of chemical fertilizers. Those achievements were made possible by the establishment of a fairly strong agricultural research system during the colonial period, trial-and-error learning by the European farmers who pioneered coffee and tea production under Kenya's conditions, and more recent research involving international cooperation, which was especially important for hybrid maize. Institutional innovations such as the Farmers' Training Centers (FTCs) and the Kenya Tea Development Authority (KTDA) played crucial roles in supporting the rapid expansion among African smallholders of coffee and tea and dairy production with "grade cattle" (i.e., crosses between high-yielding European breeds and indigenous Zebu cattle) (Anthony et al. 1979).

Kenya's agricultural progress has, however, been largely confined to areas of high and medium potential. These areas have adequate and reliable rainfall, a relatively good road network, and other types of infrastructure, in addition to ready access to profitable technologies. But they account for only about 20 percent of the total land area. In the past, some 80 percent of the country's rural population lived in these areas.

In recent decades Kenya's semiarid farming areas have faced extraordinarily difficult challenges. Population growth resulting from very high rates of natural increase has been augmented by a rapid in-migration from areas of high potential in which the population density increased to such an extent in the past half century that they can no longer absorb a rapidly growing population. Moreover, ecological conditions in the semiarid areas are extremely diverse, with the result that the constraints and opportunities for various crops and types

---

1. This discussion of Kenya's agricultural performance and of the special difficulties of accelerating technological change in the countries of Sub-Saharan Africa draws heavily on chapter 11 in Tomich, Kilby, and Johnston (1995).

of livestock and for improving the conservation or provision of water vary enormously from one locality to another.

Kenya's experience makes it clear why past exhortations to bring the green revolution to Africa have not been an adequate response to the widespread failure of food production to keep pace with rapid population growth in the countries of Sub-Saharan Africa. Many failed to appreciate that the green revolution that got under way in the mid-1960s (and much earlier in Japan and Taiwan) had its principal impact in countries that had already acquired considerable indigenous research capability. These countries were therefore able to make good use of imported "prototypes" of genetic material, a growing body of scientific knowledge, and effective methodologies for experimental work to develop crop varieties and agronomic practices suited to the conditions in their specific localities. Moreover, much of Asia already had the basic irrigation facilities and other infrastructure required to take full advantage of the yield potential of the improved seed-fertilizer combinations. These facilities only needed to be improved and enlarged.

Sub-Saharan Africa has even more intractable problems arising from the diverse ecological and socioeconomic conditions of the region. Policymakers and researchers have been slow to recognize that the yield-increasing technologies that were immediately profitable to most farmers in Asian countries were often not profitable under African conditions. Farming areas in Africa differ greatly, for example, in the extent to which rural population growth (and other factors) have enhanced the profitability of shifting from extensive to intensive farming. Matlon (1990, 18) puts the point concisely: "Net benefits to yield-increasing technologies are directly related to the cost of land saved, and inversely related to the opportunity cost of the additional capital or labor employed." Although costs can be expected to change in predictable directions with population growth and enlarged commercial demand, it is likely that irrigation, which can greatly reduce the heterogeneity of rainfed agriculture, will continue to be of extremely limited importance in most of tropical Africa. Even if population growth and other socioeconomic factors increase the attractiveness of investing in irrigation, the physical environment in much of Sub-Saharan Africa severely limits the scope for cost-effective investments in irrigation (Moris and Thom 1987).

Experience in Australia, the United States, and a few other developed countries demonstrates that there is considerable potential for increasing the productivity of rainfed agriculture in semiarid regions by soil- and water-conserving technologies. But there is little scope for a direct transfer of those technologies because they are implemented with large-scale equipment that is too capital intensive to be appropriate for African countries, given their need for capital-saving, labor-using technologies.

Animal-powered and other simple, inexpensive items of farm equipment have been neglected in Sub-Saharan Africa, partly because of the erroneous expectation that African farmers could shift directly from the hand hoe and machete to tractors. In fact, wider use of simple but well-designed farm equipment can make two notable contributions. By easing seasonal labor bottlenecks and making it feasible to implement practices such as terracing or tie-ridging, which are usually uneconomic when carried out with hand hoes, an appropriate sequence of mechanical innovations can accelerate the increase in agricultural productivity and output. Moreover, and particularly relevant to this chapter, the local manufacture of such equipment can have a highly beneficial impact on the growth of rural-based manufacturing firms through its effects on dynamic externalities, as well as changes in the composition of income and demand resulting from widespread increases in farm productivity.

In chapter 7 Bigsten and Collier report that the value added of small-scale enterprises in rural Kenya grew at an impressive average rate of 17 percent from 1973 to 1982. The number of such firms grew even faster. It is less meaningful to try to establish whether agricultural growth "caused" that expansion than to note that there were undoubtedly reciprocal and positive interactions between the two processes. Given the extent to which industrial investment has been concentrated in Nairobi and a few other urban enclaves, it is somewhat surprising that the relative importance of secondary centers has increased.

Also, just as in Taiwan, the nonagricultural sources of rural household income in Kenya have become increasingly important over time as a result of sectoral and labor market integration and gradual structural transformation. Here, it is crucial to understand the country's demographic transition.

The Demographic Transition, Labor Slack, and Structural Adjustment

Taiwan's experience demonstrates the importance of taking a *dynamic* view of the development process and of paying due attention to vital factors that tend to be ignored in the comparative statistics of neoclassical economics. A low-income, late-developing country with the structural and demographic characteristics of the Taiwan of 50 or even 30 years ago will be suffering fundamental disequilibria that can only be overcome by the time-consuming process of structural transformation and by completing the half-completed demographic transition. In 1960, Taiwan was still an economy with an abundant agricultural labor force—56 percent of the total labor force depended mainly on agriculture for income and employment, the country's total labor force was increasing rapidly, and the farm labor force was still increasing.

At the present time, Kenya and most of the other countries of Sub-Saharan Africa are still "late-late" developing countries. Table 8.1 summarizes the demographic characteristics of Kenya and Tanzania, along with average figures for 38 Sub-Saharan countries. Note particularly the rates of growth of their agricultural labor force. The rates of growth of their total labor force are, of course, even higher. The rate of growth of their population of working age is

TABLE 8.1 Structural and demographic characteristics of Kenya, Tanzania, and Sub-Saharan Africa

Characteristic	Period	Kenya	Tanzania	Sub-Saharan Africa
Agriculture's share in GDP (%)	1965	35.0	45.0	43.0
	1987	31.0	61.0	34.0
Agricultural labor force (percentage of labor force)	1970	85.0	90.0	76.0
	1985	79.0	83.0	74.0
	2000	72.0	75.0	66.0
Agricultural labor force growth rates (% per year)	1970–80	3.2	2.3	1.9
	1980–85	3.0	2.2	1.7
	1985–2000	3.1	2.3	1.8
Population growth rate (% per year)	1970–80	4.0	3.4	3.0
	1980–85	4.2	3.6	3.1
	1985–2000	4.3	3.8	3.3
Agricultural exports' growth rates (% per year)	1961–70	4.4	4.3	2.3
	1970–80	3.6	−4.4	−2.2
	1980–85	4.0	−4.9	0.4
Agriculture's share in total exports (%)	1983–85	68.0	79.0	26.0
Fertilizers (kg/ha)	1982–84	27.0	5.0	9.0

SOURCE: Alexandratos (1988), tables A.1, A.3, and A.7.
NOTE: Figures for Sub-Saharan Africa are averages for 38 countries.

determined essentially by the population growth rate (although there will obviously be a lag of some 15 years before a reduction in birth rates will begin to be reflected in a slowing of the rates of growth of their populations of working age).

In an earlier version of their chapter, Bigsten and Collier asserted that "in a small fully open economy with perfect factor markets, there are no multiplier effects" because "expansion of agriculture is at the expense of the rest of the economy as the sector bids away labor and capital from other uses." The summary data in table 8.2 point to the importance of "slack" in the agricultural sector of a late-developing country and the large potential that exists for expanding farm output through the interacting effects of technological change, investments in infrastructure, and fuller utilization of the existing stock of farm labor.

The threefold increase in Taiwan's farm output between 1911–15 and 1956–60 cannot be explained simply by increases in conventional inputs of land, labor, and capital. According to various estimates (Lee 1971), more than half of the growth of farm output is to be attributed to increases in *total factor productivity* (TFP). Table 8.2 directs attention to one significant component of that increase in TFP. Substantial "labor slack" existed in Taiwan's farm econ-

TABLE 8.2 Changes in farm output and various inputs in Taiwan, 1911–1915 to 1956–1960 (index numbers except as otherwise indicated)

Period	Total Farm Output	Cultivated Land Areas	Cropped Area	Farm Labor Force	Labor Inputs in Working Days
1911–15	100	100	100	100	100
1956–60	337	127	196	149	198

	Working Days			Fertilizer Consumption (1,000 metric tons)	Total Current Inputs[a]
Period	Per Cultivated Hectare	Per Cropped Hectare	Per Worker		
1911–15	195	167	117	50.8	100
1956–60	305	170	155	663.5	512

SOURCE: Lee (1971).
[a] In contrast with Japan, feed for livestock has long been an important component of current inputs in Taiwan. It accounted for 57 percent of current inputs in 1911–15 and 41 percent in 1956–60, when fertilizer represented 45 percent of the total.

omy because agriculture as the "self-employment" sector par excellence still provided income and employment for the bulk of the country's labor force. As a result of the structural and demographic characteristics that prevailed during that period, the *stock* of farm labor increased by 50 percent over that 45-year period. But the *flow* of labor inputs into agricultural production, measured in working days, virtually doubled. Thus, an important source of the increased farm output was *fuller*, as well as more efficient, utilization of the available stock of farm labor. It is evident from table 8.2 that this fuller utilization of the farm work force was associated with a large increase in working days per cultivated hectare but only a trivial increase in working days per cropped hectare. The explanation, of course, is that expanded irrigation had permitted a large increase in multiple cropping, which in turn explains the increase from 117 to 155 days per year of farm work per worker. The large increase in farm output associated with fuller utilization of the available stock of farm labor was also facilitated by a sequence of technological and economic innovations, such as the introduction of labor-intensive enterprises (e.g., raising mushrooms) that required very little land.

The discussion of "labor market distortion" by Bigsten and Collier, based on their figure 7.1, is particularly misleading. Given Kenya's structural and demographic conditions, increases in nonfarm employment will coexist for many years with a continuing increase in the absolute size of the farm labor force. Because of the agroclimatic conditions in Kenya and elsewhere in tropical Africa, it seems unlikely that the increase in the flow of labor inputs into agricultural production will exceed the growth in the stock of farm labor, as it did in Taiwan between 1910 and 1960. Hence, policies that foster the dynamic externalities between agriculture and industry and that lead to the rapid growth of nonfarm job opportunities are needed to prevent diminishing returns to agricultural labor from making it excessively difficult to increase per capita GNP. According to recent evidence, Kenya has finally entered the declining fertility phase of the demographic transition. This circumstance will, of course, facilitate the transformation of the country's overwhelmingly agrarian structure. But given the extraordinarily high rates of natural increase in recent decades, Kenya will continue to confront a severe labor absorption problem for many years.

Conclusion

In a country such as Kenya with an economy that it still predominantly agrarian, it is essential to consider dynamic externalities associated with linkages between agricultural and nonagricultural growth. As the preceding discussion suggests, those externalities are likely to be very significant because the transfer of labor and other resources from agriculture to industry can lead to important gains from economies of scale, learning by doing, and technological spillovers that are larger in the industrial sector.

Taiwan's well-documented development experience makes it clear that such linkages and dynamic externalities were an important source of that country's rapid growth, especially in the 1950s and 1960s when the country's economic structure was still predominantly agrarian and the growth rates of the population and the labor force were high. Furthermore, Taiwan's experience and the recent growth literature calling attention to the potential importance of externalities not captured in the comparative statics perspective of a neoclassical view of resource flows and price adjustments suggest that a country's success in realizing those potential gains will be influenced strongly by strategic decisions that shape the pattern of its agricultural and rural development.

As noted earlier, emphasis on intersectoral growth linkages has in the past been commonly associated with Rosenstein-Rodan's Big Push theory of industrialization, which supposedly justified very large and coordinated investment projects. In fact, Taiwan's experience points up the advantages of policies and programs that foster a broadly based pattern of agricultural development and geographically dispersed industrialization carried out mainly through the rapid growth of small- and medium-enterprises. Many of those policies and programs are described in detail in chapter 2. But certain elements of Taiwan's strategies for agricultural and rural development merit special attention because they seem to have made notable contributions to growth through their positive impact on dynamic externalities, including increases in total factor productivity.

A short list of key elements in Taiwan's development strategy would certainly include sustained investments in agricultural research, which generated a sequence of labor-using, capital-saving innovations that could be used efficiently by small farmers with limited cash income; investments in rural infrastructure, including the transport and communications network and electricity, in addition to irrigation and drainage facilities; the creation of effective farmers' organizations; investments in education; and investments in public health programs that reached the rural as well as urban population and had a particularly pronounced effect in reducing infant and child mortality, thereby contributing to the subsequent success of family planning programs. Throughout, careful attention was given to sequencing and a "phased approach" and to institutional and organizational factors. Indeed, it has been said that "the main secret of Taiwan's development" was its "ability to meet the organizational requirements" (Hsieh and Lee 1966, 103, 105).[2] Taiwan avoided the common problem of failing to achieve a balance between public sector responsibilities and the resources available for fulfilling those responsibilities because its interventions were *selective*. The knowledge, capabilities, and learning capacity of small farmers were recognized and appreciated. And government action was concentrated in areas where direct intervention is indispensable, notably public goods such as research, extension, infrastructure, and support for local institutions such as the farmers' associations and irrigation associations.

In addition, Taiwan created a policy environment that permitted price and market mechanisms to play a key role in guiding the development process. Thus individual farmers and the entrepreneurs who created and guided the SMEs that played such a crucial role in rural industrialization exercised their initiative by responding to price signals that reflected the social opportunity cost of resources. In part, this was a result of the government's commitment to control inflation and its adoption in the 1950s of monetary and exchange-rate policies that promoted exports. In addition, the government encouraged the use of technologies that required a minimum of capital and took full advantage of indigenous resources, notably Taiwan's abundant supply of increasingly high-quality labor.

References

Alexandratos, N. 1988. *World Agriculture toward 2000: An FAO Study*. Rome: Food and Agriculture Organization.

Anthony, Kenneth R. M., B. F. Johnston, W. O. Jones, and V. C. Uchendu. 1979. *Agricultural Change in Tropical Africa*. Ithaca, N.Y.: Cornell University Press.

2. In a 1990 paper, S. C. Hsieh, currently governor of the Central Bank of China, Taipei, and formerly chief economist and secretary general of Taiwan's Joint Commission on Rural Reconstruction, points out the importance for development of sequencing, a phased approach, and an integrated perspective. In his view, it is vital not only to take into account the linkages between the agricultural, industrial, and social sectors but also the importance of institutional factors and a proper balance between the role of government and the private sector.

Arrow, Kenneth J. 1962. "The Economic Implications of Learning by Doing." *Review of Economic Studies* 29:155–73.

Fleming, M. 1955. "External Economies and the Doctrine of Balanced Growth." *Economic Journal* 65(258):241–56.

Hazell, P., and A. Röell. 1983. "Rural Growth Linkages: Household Expenditure Patterns in Malaysia and Nigeria," International Food Policy Research Report 41. Washington, D.C.

Hsieh, S. C. 1990. "JCRR/ADB Experience and Approaches to Economic Development in LDCs." Paper presented at a seminar held at the Department of Agricultural and Applied Economics, University of Minnesota, St. Paul, September 26.

Hsieh, S. C., and T. H. Lee. 1966. *Agricultural Development and Its Contributions to Economic Growth in Taiwan: Joint Commission on Rural Reconstruction (JCRR).* Economic Digest Series 17. Taipei, Taiwan.

Johnston, B. F., and Peter Kilby. 1975. *Agriculture and Structural Transformation: Economic Strategies in Late-Developing Countries.* New York: Oxford University Press.

Lee, T. H. 1971. *Intersectoral Capital Flows in the Economic Development of Taiwan, 1895–1960.* Ithaca, N.Y.: Cornell University Press.

Liedholm, Carl, and Donald Mead. 1987. *Small Scale Industries in Developing Countries: Empirical Evidence and Policy Implications.* International Development Paper 9. Michigan State University, Lansing, Mich.

Matlon, Peter J. 1990. "Improving Productivity in Sorghum and Pearl Millet in Semi-Arid Africa." *Food Research Institute Studies* 22(1):1–43.

Matsuyama, K. 1992. "Agricultural Productivity, Comparative Advantage, and Economic Growth." *Working Papers in Economics* E-92-3. Hoover Institution, Stanford University.

Moris, Jon R., and D. J. Thom. 1987. *African Irrigation Overview: Main Report.* Africa/USAID Water Management Synthesis II Project. WMS Report 371. Utah State University, Logan.

Murphy, K. M., A. Shleifer, and R. W. Vishny. 1989a. "Industrialization and the Big Push." *Journal of Political Economy* 97(5):1003–26.

———. 1989b. "Income Distribution, Market Size, and Industrialization." *Quarterly Journal of Economics* 104(3):537–64.

Park, Albert, and Bruce F. Johnston. In press. "Rural Development and Dynamic Externalities in Taiwan's Structural Transformation." *Economic Development and Cultural Change.*

Romer, Paul M. 1986. "Increasing Returns and Long-Run Growth." *Journal of Political Economy* 94(5):1002–37.

Rosenberg, N. 1982. *Inside the Black Box: Technologies and Economics.* Cambridge: Cambridge University Press.

Shleifer, Andrei. 1990. "Externalities as an Engine of Growth." Chicago: Graduate School of Business, University of Chicago.

Stokey, Nancy L. 1988. "Learning by Doing and the Introduction of New Goods." *Journal of Political Economy* 96(4):701–17.

Tomich, Thomas P., Peter Kilby, and Bruce F. Johnston. 1995. *Transforming Agrarian Economies: Opportunities Seized, Opportunities Missed.* Ithaca, N.Y.: Cornell University Press.

9   Development in Costa Rica:
The Key Role of Agriculture

RAFAEL CELIS AND EDUARDO LIZANO

Costa Rica is a relatively small country (50,000 square kilometers) with a population of only 2.7 million inhabitants. Its economy is small (GDP $4.7 billion), relatively open (annual imports account for 35 percent of GDP), and relatively poor (per capita yearly income is $1,600). Demographic and economic growth during the period after World War II was extremely rapid: between the periods 1950–52 and 1975–77 its population doubled, as did real per capita income. The 1980s, however, might well be labeled a lost decade. After the second oil-price shock at the end of the 1970s, the economy fell into its worst crisis in more than half a century. The effort to resolve the crisis consumed most of the available resources for several years. It has only been in the past few years that the pace of economic growth has more or less returned to a satisfactory level. Still, economic growth, real per capita income, and affluence indicators remain below precrisis levels.

Economic growth in Costa Rica can be attributed to three principal factors: First, it took advantage of the opportunities offered by external markets, both the global ones (in coffee, bananas, and later sugar and beef), and the regional ones (in manufactured products for the Central American Common Market, CACM). Second, the government's economic policy has by and large maintained economic stability. Thus Costa Rica has avoided the tremendous instability, particularly inflation, that has troubled the economies of many other Latin American countries and created a serious obstacle to higher savings rates and internal investment, as well as foreign investment. Third, the country's long-term social policy has channeled a significant proportion of public expenditure into education and health, as well as into a wealth and income distribution scheme that has addressed inequalities. These policies have enabled Costa Rica to create a framework of social and political stability that has facilitated economic development.

Agriculture has played a vital role in this growth. It has contributed to every aspect of economic activity: GDP, exports, food supply, the production of raw materials for the industrial sector, and employment opportunities. As ex-

TABLE 9.1 Relative importance of agriculture, selected years

Description	1957	1965	1980	1987
Share of agriculture in real GDP[a]	24.4	22.9	18.0	19.0
Share of agriculture in employment	54.7[b]	49.7	27.4	28.1
Share of rural population	66.5[b]	65.5[c]	53.7	56.2
Share of agricultural exports	85.9	74.1	63.6	71.1

SOURCES: Banco Central de Costa Rica (1986, 1987, 1989a, 1989b); and Dirección General de Estadística y Censos (1957, 1965, 1974, 1987).
[a]Base year: 1966.
[b]Figures for 1950.
[c]Figure from 1963 population census.

pected, however, the relative importance of agriculture has declined in the wake of economic development (table 9.1). This structural change has been closely related to the growth of other sectors (industry, services, the public sector), whose activities are by and large concentrated in urban rather than rural areas.

Nevertheless, the agricultural sector is still of primary importance. It accounts for a high proportion of nontraditional exports, which form the foundation of the export-led model of development. According to figures from the Central Bank of Costa Rica, nontraditional agricultural exports account for about 15 percent of total exports and continue to grow steadily. Between 1982 and 1990 nontraditional agricultural production grew at an average annual rate of 17 percent, while exports of these commodities to markets outside the Central American common market grew at an unprecedented rate of 31 percent (Corrales and Monge 1990).

This study covers the years 1962 through 1979. This period begins with the incorporation of Costa Rica into the CACM and ends on the eve of the severe crisis following the second oil-price shock. These were years of rapid growth for both the agricultural sector and the economy as a whole. It is a period long enough for medium- and long-term trends to emerge and recent enough for its lessons to be relevant today.

Growth of Agricultural Production

In the period covered by this study, agriculture expanded at an average real rate of 4.3 percent per year. Its performance reflected the dynamism of agricultural production during this period. As economic growth accelerated, agriculture's importance as a proportion of GDP decreased from approximately one-fourth to slightly less than one-fifth of the total (Banco Central 1986). This trend—namely, rapid diversification of secondary and tertiary sectors—is not untypical of the process of economic development.

Not unexpectedly, the pace of growth was uneven. It was rapid in the periods 1962–68 and 1967–73, but slowed down in 1973–79. The sluggish behavior of this last period can be attributed to a number of factors. For one thing, the external petroleum-price shocks caused a drastic increase in oil prices, the impact of which can be seen in the overall price of imports. For another, banana planting in the Atlantic zone did not expand at the same rate as in the years 1967–72. Furthermore, the lands held by the state for agricultural production had been exhausted. Unused state-held property suitable for agriculture became scarce and growth could not continue by means of incorporating new lands, but rather required more intensive production on lands already in private hands. The "agricultural frontier" had reached its legal limit, though technically and economically speaking such a frontier is still far off. With vacant lands disappearing, some began illegally invading the property of many plotholders. The Instituto de Desarrollo Agrario (IDA), which is in charge of land reforms, reported an increase from 36 cases in 1963–66 to 343 cases in 1983–86. In addition, emphasis was placed on growth in other sectors of the economy, especially industry, in order to take advantage of opportunities in the CACM. This process of industrialization absorbed capital, labor, and entrepreneurial energy, which otherwise would have been partially channeled into the agricultural sector.

The relative growth rates of the principal agricultural products also varied. The leading agricultural exports, such as coffee and especially bananas, grew rapidly in relation to GDP (table 9.2), as did products that sold locally as well as internationally, such as beef and sugar. All of these rates fell substantially in the third subperiod, 1973–79.

Products to be sold in local markets, such as milk and basic grains, show significant expansion in the last years of the period under analysis. This was a result of policies designed to achieve self-sufficiency in basic foodstuffs. Their effect was felt mainly in the national production of basic grains (corn, beans, rice, sorghum) in the years 1974–78. The only other products to show considerable growth were in the fish sector, but they did not play a significant role in total agricultural production.

Crops account for about two-thirds of total production in the sector, livestock about one-fourth, and other activities slightly less than 10 percent. Bananas increased in relation to coffee production in terms of their share in total output of the sector. But these two products, both at the beginning of the period of analysis and toward its end, account for slightly more than 40 percent of total agricultural production in Costa Rica, and in some years exceeded 50 percent of the total. These figures indicate that the behavior of coffee and bananas is the determining factor in the growth of agriculture.

Agricultural production consists overwhelmingly (almost 95 percent) of food products, and far less of nonfood products such as tobacco, cotton, and wood. Part of the production of foodstuffs is used as raw material in the food

TABLE 9.2 Growth rates of real agricultural value added, by products, 1962–1979 (percent per year)

Product	1962–68	1967–73	1973–79
Coffee	3.8	3.1	1.0
Banana	10.8	20.6	−2.1
Sugarcane	7.9	6.0	1.9
Basic grains	1.0	2.6	7.2
Other products	2.3	0.7	2.9
Crops	5.1	7.9	0.8
Beef	4.6	4.9	2.8
Dairy	7.9	3.8	4.7
Other products	1.5	4.3	4.7
Livestock	5.0	4.4	3.7
Wood	9.0	2.4	3.4
Fisheries	13.6	24.5	16.5
Other products	6.6	−10.6	1.6
Others	8.2	0.2	6.3
Total	5.3	6.5	1.8

SOURCE: Banco Central de Costa Rica (1986).
NOTE: Growth rates are compounded. Base year: 1966.

industry. This is the case with sugar, milk, corn, and beef. As a result, the production of goods to be sold in local markets basically depends on population growth, per capita income, and the elasticity of demand for these products. Fluctuation in the industrial sector per se (in textiles, for example), and in other sectors such as construction, do not influence agricultural production *directly* in any large measure (i.e., with regard to the demand for raw materials), but do influence production *indirectly,* through the demand for labor and the resulting derived demand for food. In the period of analysis, the production of food per capita grew approximately 30 percent. This increase is in keeping with the available information concerning general nutritional conditions, which indicate that food availability in terms of calories, proteins, and vitamins, was satisfactory according to the minimum nutritional requirements established by the World Health Organization.

Agricultural production is destined primarily for external markets, not internal ones. Agricultural exports at the beginning of the period of analysis represented almost two-thirds of total agricultural production (see table 9.3). The proportion of products for export continues to grow, in part because the size of the local market is very small, and in part because the medium-term profitability of imported products has been greater than that of local products, even when subsidies have been granted to local producers. But the most relevant factor has been that the size of the local market is too small to serve as a base for

TABLE 9.3 Distribution of agricultural production (percent), various years, 1962–1979

Year	Domestic Consumption	Exports	Total
1962	39.6	60.4	100.0
1967	34.9	65.1	100.0
1973	12.1	87.9	100.0
1979	18.9	81.1	100.0

SOURCE: Banco Central de Costa Rica (1986).
NOTE: Estimated from nominal value-added figures.

rapid and sustained growth in the agricultural sector. Future expansion, as in the past, therefore depends on the sector's capacity to take advantage of opportunities offered by the international economy, both as a result of growth in markets or a reduction in trade barriers. This trend is part of the process of agricultural diversification, which has been manifested more recently in the structural adjustment of the second half of the 1980s, as a result of which nearly all new products are destined for export.

Despite the decline in its relative importance in the economy, agriculture in Costa Rica still plays a central role in development. Over the study period, agricultural products accounted for almost 70 percent of all exports, even toward the end of the 1970s. Moreover, agriculture absorbs more labor than any other sector in the national economy. Of course, the relative importance of agricultural employment has diminished (see table 9.1). At the beginning of the period in 1962, employment in this sector accounted for more than one-half of all national employment, and by the end of the period it had decreased to less than one-third.

Population density is approximately 56 inhabitants per square kilometer. The utilization of territory, however, has intensified substantially—perhaps more than is desirable—as can be seen in the marked expansion of areas dedicated to cattle grazing and an alarming reduction of forests and wooded areas (table 9.4). This trend has brought with it the well-known problems of soil erosion and water shortages. The destructive transformation of woodlands to cow pastures can be traced to several factors: technology is not advanced enough to make intensive cattle raising more profitable than extensive cattle raising (for example, it is conjectured that the present national level of beef production could be achieved with only half the area being used for pasture); land is cheap, because Costa Rica does not have an appropriate system of taxes to encourage a better, more productive use of land and thereby force landowners to pay for inefficient or harmful utilization; and the government's easy-credit policies in the past favored cattle production, such that for each unit of value added received by the activity, it generated three or four times more credit than the rest of the agricultural sector.

TABLE 9.4 Pattern of land use (percent), 1963–1984

Use	1963	1973	1984
Annual crops	15.3	9.1	12.6
Perennial crops	7.5	6.6	7.7
Pastures	35.1	49.9	53.8
Forestland	30.7	22.9	16.0
Other	11.4	11.4	10.0
Total	100.0	100.0	100.0

SOURCE: Dirección General de Estadística y Censos, *Censo Agropecuario* (1965, 1974, 1987).

Coffee and bananas account for at least 40 percent, and at times half of all agricultural production. At the beginning of the study period, these products had an 80 percent share of total exports, but with agricultural diversification and the growth of other sectors such as industry in subsequent years, the relative importance of coffee and banana exports declined. Nevertheless, even in 1979, at the end of the period under analysis, they accounted for more than half of all national exports. At present, their production continues to increase.

Both experienced a large increase in yields per hectare during 1963–73 (table 9.5). It is not difficult to understand why this happened in the banana industry, given the relatively large size of the plantations and the fact that the property is largely in the hands of multinational corporations in which the processes of research and extension are highly integrated to production. In contrast, coffee is produced on a large number of small farms of less than 20 hectares, which find it more difficult to adopt new technologies because financing is a problem for small farmers and they are reluctant to take risks.

Because of the importance of coffee and banana, the present analysis concentrates on these two crops. Basic grains, for example, are excluded because they represent only a modest proportion of Costa Rican farmers' incomes, particularly among smallholders (Celis 1988). Furthermore, it has been shown that variations in the prices of basic grains had a negligible effect on the

TABLE 9.5 Coffee and banana yields, 1955–1984 (metric tons per hectare)

Year	Coffee	Banana
1963	2.7	23.1
1973	4.7	34.6
1979	4.9	38.2
1984	7.1	36.1

SOURCE: Dirección General de Estadística y Censos (1965, 1974, 1987).

total variability of farmers' incomes, as well as on the expenditures of most urban and rural consumers (Hazell 1991). Interestingly enough, these products were granted high levels of protection (Celis et al. 1987; Stewart 1991). In addition, and perhaps for the same reasons, research on these products has declined. As a result, other products are probably less relevant as sources of past and future growth, especially since an effort is under way to remove the heavy protection granted to them.

Determining Factors in the Evolution of Banana and Coffee Production

A number of factors have played a significant role in banana and coffee production in Costa Rica: the natural conditions, human resources, macroeconomic policies, protection of the local market, public expenditure policy, institutional support, research, technical assistance, access to credit, the nature of the market, and the relationship between producers, processors, and exporters.

Natural Conditions

Banana production on a large scale requires very special natural conditions. First, growing areas must be extensive and have high-quality soil. They should also be flat in order to permit the application of specific agricultural techniques such as aerial spraying. Transportation to packing plants must be easy. Second, because the banana belongs to the musaceous family, a regular regimen of intense, almost daily, rainfall is indispensable; at the same time, a large amount of sunlight is also needed every day. This combination ensures rapid growth and maturation of the fruit. Third, since banana is easily damaged by strong winds, the area of production must be free from hurricanes.

Coffee requires fertile soils located between 900 and 1,300 meters above sea level. Seasons with significant differences in rainfall are also needed to allow the plant to rest during part of the year; and sufficient sunlight in conjunction with rainfall promotes flowering, growth, and maturation of the plant.

Certain zones within Costa Rica satisfy these conditions fully—the tropical regions of the Atlantic Coast are ideal for bananas and the valley of the Central Plateau for coffee. Natural conditions in Costa Rica have been exceptionally favorable for the production of both products.

Human Resources

The availability of labor has been favorable for the expansion of coffee and banana production, thanks to rapid population growth (2.5–3.0 percent yearly) and the immigration of laborers from Nicaragua. Wages in these two sectors are among the highest in all areas of agricultural production in the country. There has been a mild upward pressure on real wages, but the relatively stable labor situation has stimulated development and the application of new production techniques. Owners have had to accept a modest, but continual increase in salaries, which has driven them to seek new technologies and production techniques in order to hold down the proportional growth of per unit costs of production.

Macroeconomic Policies

During the period from 1962 to 1979 the Costa Rican economy was very stable. Inflation was not a serious problem during this period; in most years it fluctuated between 3 percent and 5 percent. The only destabilizing factor was of external origin, namely the first oil-price shock. During 1974, 1975, and 1976 prices grew more rapidly than the average for the entire period. The impact, however, was absorbed rapidly, and price stability returned. Furthermore, because prices were stable, there were few serious fluctuations in the exchange rate. Because of this stability, adjustments in the rate of exchange were only minor and sporadic modifications (they occurred three times). This stability was achieved in part because national inflation was maintained at a level very close to the levels maintained by Costa Rica's main trading partners. Finally, the general employment situation evolved satisfactorily in this period owing to rapid increases in both demographic growth and national production. The creation of new employment opportunities thus kept unemployment levels below 5 percent of the labor force.

The stability in prices, exchange rates, and employment was due in large part to a strict monetary and fiscal policy. Costa Rica adopted a monetary policy that closely followed the course of its traditional exports in international markets, as well as the conditions affecting its foreign exchange reserves. Monetary expansion and contraction are basically a function of the behavior of international reserves. In general terms, it could be said that a classic "gold standard" policy was implemented. At the same time, there was a large expansion of international commerce, which kept fluctuations in exports (principally coffee, banana, sugar, and beef) to a minimum. Equally important, Costa Rica was able to avoid significant negative impacts originating in international markets. When fluctuations in external sectors did occur, they could be absorbed without great difficulty through temporary reductions in international monetary reserves, the level of employment, imports, and the pace of economic growth. In few cases did the country resort to temporary external financing by way of standby agreements with the International Monetary Fund.

In this way the government exercised fairly strict control over the balance of payments and maintained public finances within acceptable limits. During this period the public sector experienced a significant expansion through its participation in multiple financial, social, and productive activities. Public finances continued to be more or less in equilibrium year after year, such that public debt (internal and external) did not increase significantly as a proportion of GDP, nor did interest and debt-service costs increase greatly as a proportion of public expenditure. Also, it was unnecessary to increase taxes considerably since tax revenues as a proportion of GDP did not increase sharply. The ratio of tax revenues to GDP grew moderately, from 9.9 percent in 1960 to 11.2 percent in 1980 (OFIPLAN 1982).

During the period under study Costa Rica, like many other Latin American countries, adopted a model of development based on import substitution. Under this model national markets had to be protected so that local producers could produce what before was only imported. This policy promoted industrialization but had a negative impact on the agricultural sector.

One reason for this adverse effect was that industrialization increased the demand for labor, and thereby put upward pressure on wages. Another reason was that local production, sheltered by protectionist tariffs, raised the price and lowered the quality of important agricultural materials in comparison with the imported product; this was the case, for example, with fertilizers, tires, tubes, sacks, barbed wire, and veterinary products. These factors affected the cost of production in the agricultural sector, which in the case of products sold in international markets such as coffee and bananas, could not be passed on to the consumer. A third reason for the negative impact was that part of the subsidies granted to the industrial sector were financed with agricultural export taxes, such as those on coffee and bananas. These two products not only had to compete openly in international markets, with high production costs as a result of the industrialization process, but also had to pay comparatively higher taxes. In spite of these circumstances, both products achieved highly satisfactory results. This progress was due primarily to the excellent natural conditions of the country and an accelerated pace of technological change, which allowed these products to maintain a satisfactory competitive position.

Industrialization did, indeed, produce an antiexport environment, but not inordinately so, since protectionist tariffs were applied not only in Costa Rica, but also to the countries of the CACM. This meant that although national businesses were protected from the international community, they were forced to compete within the CACM. As a result, producers were not able to take full advantage of the protection offered by tariffs. Furthermore, Costa Rican and Central American industrialization did not "take flight" on its own because of the small size of the region's economies. The most dynamic factor in the process of regional integration was the behavior of agricultural exports toward the rest of the world. When exports achieved sufficient growth, demand within the CACM increased, thereby creating new opportunities for production and investment. Thus the government was less inclined to erect export barriers in the agricultural sector, which would have "killed the goose that laid the golden eggs."

Protection of the Local Market

An important characteristic of the political-economy during the period under study was the high degree of protection afforded to the agricultural sector. Protection enabled national producers to take advantage of local markets without much interference from external competition. The barriers erected were not so much tariffs as procedures requiring potential importers to obtain permission from the administration or other nontariff barriers, such as health and safety requirements. For all practical purposes, the nontariff barriers that were used were equivalent to an infinite tariff barrier.

The protected market favored primarily the production of basic grains (rice, corn, beans, sorghum), sugar, and milk. The outcome of protection, however, was unsatisfactory for both producers and consumers. External competition did not force producers to improve the price and quality of their products, which would have benefited consumers, and the producers did not benefit significantly from the situation either. Production increased and became more efficient principally for exports that faced stiff competition. The income levels of producers of products for export increased, whereas those of producers of basic grains did not. Since productivity did not increase, despite subsidized markets—which ended up hurting consumers—the producers of basic grains (especially corn and beans) did not significantly improve their economic well-being.

Public Expenditure Policy

Agriculture also received considerable attention in public expenditure policy, which benefited coffee and banana production in particular. In the Central Valley, the principal zone for coffee production, public investment over several decades gave the region a system of highways for transporting harvests from farms to processing plants and from there to ocean ports. Likewise, railroads were constructed to connect the zones of production with ports on both the Atlantic and Pacific coasts. The railroad has played an indispensable role in the banana industry. Equally important, investments in Costa Rica's ports made it possible to increase load capacities and expedite loading and unloading operations. Support for coffee-producing zones has come mainly from public outlays, whereas banana production has been heavily backed by the producing and exporting companies, which have invested in railroads, ports, irrigation, and drainage.

Traditionally, more than one-third of the national budget has been channeled toward education and health. These expenditures have had an important impact from at least two points of view. First, following the control of certain diseases, such as malaria, the productivity of labor increased. Second, the higher level of education has enabled Costa Ricans to adopt new technologies, without which they would not have expanded banana and coffee production into profitable operations.

Institutional Aspects

Institutional organization has also contributed greatly to the success of both banana and coffee production. The following aspects of Costa Rica's institutions have been particularly important: research, technical assistance, credit, the market, and the system of relations among producers, processors, and exporters.

RESEARCH. A striking feature of the coffee and the banana industries is their continual effort to generate new and improved technologies. Significant progress has been made in developing new varieties that are more resistant to disease. New agricultural practices have been implemented, and new imports (fertilizers, herbicides, and pesticides) have become available. As a result, the volume of production per unit of land has been steadily increasing, and Costa Rica has become one of the leading producers of coffee and bananas.

Technological advances have not been limited just to agricultural activity but have occurred in related areas as well. These advances have considerably improved the packing of fruit (banana boxes), the transportation (containers), and the processing (electronic selection of coffee beans). All of these changes have increased yields by reducing after-harvest losses while improving the quality of the product. As a result of this technological revolution, the unit costs of production have been kept under control, despite continual increases in total costs.

TECHNICAL ASSISTANCE. The new technological knowledge is applied quickly and efficiently, thanks to a high degree of integration between research and technical assistance in the banana companies and the Coffee Institute. This integration ensures that research results will not remain on bookshelves or hidden away in technical journals, but rather, will be applied efficiently to production, and that the problems confronted by producers will quickly be communicated to researchers. A large proportion of the costs of coffee research and technical assistance are borne directly by producers through fees paid to the Coffee Institute. Researchers are therefore motivated to search for new technologies that will boost the financial returns of the producers. Together research and technical assistance have helped increase coffee production from 2.7 tons per hectare in 1962 to 4.9 tons in 1979 and banana production from 22.5 tons to 38.2 tons per hectare.

CREDIT. Credit plays a relatively minor role in the banana industry since banana production can be carried out all year long and bananas can be harvested every two weeks. Also, bananas are highly perishable and therefore must be sold almost immediately. As a result, there is a constant cash flow throughout the year and banana producers rarely have to turn to the financial sector for capital. In contrast, credit plays an important role in coffee production since the harvest period for coffee lasts only several weeks of the year. In addition, coffee is not a perishable product and can be sold throughout the year. Thus producers must obtain financial assistance to run the plantations while waiting to harvest and then sell the crop. The application of new technologies, land acquisitions, or increased production all depend to a large degree on the availability of credit.

Credit for coffee production can be obtained from both internal and external sources. Coffee processing plants play an important role in the credit system. The plants obtain financial backing from local and international banks as well as from exporters and then lend these funds to large medium and small producers. Acting as an intermediary or a rural credit agency, the plants endeavor to guarantee that the producers financed by the processor will deliver the harvest so that it can be processed and subsequently sold.

This system of financing ensures that credit can be obtained quickly, at rates in the financial markets, in order to keep operations going, and it allows producers to dedicate their profits not to the financing of recurrent costs, but instead to the investments needed to improve and expand plantations.

THE MARKET. The boom in coffee and banana production has also been due in part to the organization of markets for both products. In the case of bananas, commercialization in international markets has been largely in the hands of multinational corporations. These companies own plantations but in addition buy from independent producers. Since the product is highly perishable and must be refrigerated while it is being transported over many kilometers, a high degree of coordination is essential between the harvesting of the fruit, its packing, its transport from plantations to ports, overseas transport to foreign ports, and finally transport to the centers of consumption. Meanwhile, coffee is marketed by export companies, which buy coffee beans already prepared by the processing plants. Because coffee is not perishable, trade can be carried out at a slower pace throughout the year.

It should be mentioned that in both coffee and banana production the producer is not directly responsible for commercialization of the product. The producer delivers the fruit to the coffee processor and does not participate in the subsequent processing, storage, transport, or selling of the product. All these activities are carried out by the processors and the exporters. The banana producer also delivers the fruit, already packed to the ports, and from that point on, does not participate in the commercialization of the product. The country has had no major problems in marketing its exportable coffee production in international markets. The International Coffee Agreement, which was in effect during much of the period under analysis, did not prevent exports from increasing: The accord could to a large degree be circumvented by means of various loopholes such as sales to "new" markets, which nullified the system of export quotas.

THE RELATIONSHIP BETWEEN PRODUCERS, PROCESSORS, AND EXPORTERS. Costa Rica has a complicated system for ensuring that producers receive a relatively high proportion of the export price of coffee. Producers cannot sell their harvest on their own but must deliver it to the processor of their choice. This entity processes the coffee and sells it to exporters. Every sale made by a processor to an exporter must be registered in the Coffee Institute, which has the power to abrogate the contract if the stated price does not reflect prices on the international market at any given moment. Meanwhile, the processors make loans or cash advances to each of their clients. Later, when the coffee is exported, the Coffee Institute establishes an average price that the processor must pay to the producer. The institute estimates the amount to be paid to the producer by deducting the exporter's commission, the cost of processing (income of the processing plant), and government taxes. In this way, the relationship among producers, processors, and exporters is regulated to ensure that producers receive a large proportion of the export price and that they (the producers) are responsive to prices on the international market.

The Role of Agriculture in Overall Growth

The direct and indirect role of agricultural growth in fostering growth in the rest of the economy has been widely documented (e.g., Mellor 1976; Bell, Hazell, and Slade 1982; Hazell and Röell 1983; Hossain 1988; Celis and Bliven 1991; Celis and Holleman 1991). This section examines agricultural growth in terms of its conceptual framework, its relationship to nonagricultural growth, the process by which its effects are transmitted, and its social and environmental effects.

Conceptual Framework

Agricultural growth not only has production linkages but also substantial indirect effects on growth in nonfarm incomes and employment. This outcome is due in part to increases in the use of farm inputs and increases in the processing, marketing, and transport services used to handle the larger output. More important, indirect effects originate from increases in household expenditures on consumer goods and services as a result of increased farm incomes.

In developing countries, export-led agricultural growth also has an impact on public finances. How government responds to substantial increases in revenues largely determines the effect on relative prices and the final outcome on overall growth. Colombia's coffee boom of the mid-1970s, for example, showed that an improvement in the terms of trade from an increase in the international price of coffee is not necessarily good for the rest of the traded sectors of the economy if this gain is not adequately offset by other policies that reduce the expenditure effect arising from the gains in terms of trade (García and Montes 1988). This does not necessarily mean cutting government expenditures, but rather redirecting expenditures in a way that will minimize the distorting effect on prices and takes advantage of the extra revenues to invest in the infrastructure and human capital needed to sustain development.

Nonagricultural Growth

Although the connection between agricultural and nonagricultural growth is difficult to establish, in Costa Rica the indirect effects of impressive growth in agriculture can be argued forcefully. Because most of the growth in the agricultural sector relied almost entirely on coffee and bananas and their output expansion went into exports, the increase in agricultural incomes led to an increase in the effective demand for nonagricultural output. This increased demand added substantial support for the expansion of nonagricultural production, which was simultaneously stimulated within the context of the CACM.

The figures in table 9.6 show robust growth in the manufacturing and the services sectors over the study period. This growth was more than double the growth in agriculture, and it undoubtedly benefited from the latter, as can be shown with examples from the food industry. Between 1963 and 1985 the food and tobacco industry grew at an average annual rate of 20 percent, which represents almost five times that of agriculture (Ramírez and Maldonado 1988). Coinciding with this output performance was a rise in employment. More important, during the period 1962–79 the average productivity of labor in manufacturing grew at a rate of 3.6 percent, whereas average labor productivity in agriculture grew 3.9 percent per year (OFIPLAN 1982).

The Process of Transmission

Some of the policies that supported technological change in coffee and bananas—and consequently induced rapid growth in agriculture—also facilitated the transmission of direct and indirect effects to the nonagricultural sectors. For instance, monetary and foreign exchange policies kept inflation down and thus helped maintain the purchasing power of the incomes in the agricultural sector. The effective demand for nonagricultural output therefore increased.

Government investment policies before and during the period of rapid economic expansion were also important. Private investment already ac-

TABLE 9.6 Shares of real GDP and growth rates (percent), 1962 and 1979

Sector	1962	1979	Growth Rate
Agriculture	25.9	18.2	4.3
Industry	13.2	22.0	9.6
Electricity, gas, water	1.2	2.1	10.3
Construction	5.3	6.4	7.4
Commerce	20.0	18.7	6.4
Communications[a]	4.3	6.7	8.9
Financial services	3.6	5.1	8.8
Real estate	10.2	6.8	4.0
General government	10.8	9.7	5.8
Other services	5.5	4.3	5.5
Total	100.0	100.0	6.2

SOURCE: Banco Central de Costa Rica (1986, 1989c).
[a]Includes transport, storage, and telecommunications services.

counted for more than three-quarters of total investment during the period 1957–62, despite the fact that its growth had been negative during the same period (OFIPLAN 1982). A stable political climate plus a generous system of incentives granted during the import-substitution industrialization period (i.e., after 1962) attracted masses of foreign and domestic private investment. As illustrated by the change in the internal terms of trade, relative profitability in agriculture went down, in great part because of the protectionist policies that favored the industrial sector. Consequently, capital that had accumulated in the agricultural sector quickly flowed into the manufacturing and commerce sectors. During the good years of the CACM (i.e., 1962–73) private investment grew at an average annual rate of 9 percent. At the same time, government investments expanded more rapidly, at 11 percent per year. The government had continued its impressive record of investment in health and other supporting services and augmented the rate of investment in education, transport, storage and telecommunications. The final result was a mere 5 percent shift in relative importance from private to public investment during the period 1962–73. After the first oil crisis, private investment grew at a robust rate, but public investment grew almost twice as much.

During this period the government also adopted a policy of starting large, state-owned, manufacturing, processing, and transport companies. These investments account for an unprecedented growth rate of 148 percent in public investment in the industrial sector during the period from 1973 to 1979. Public investment also increased in agriculture, public utilities, financial services, and education.

The state-owned enterprises proved to be a failure. Many went bankrupt owing to the financial hardships imposed by the second oil crisis, plus the domestic and international pressure to stimulate privatization. By contrast, public investments in infrastructure, health, and education played an important role in the postcrisis economic recovery experienced during the 1980s.

Public investment brought many benefits: all-weather roads and gravel roads grew an average 4 percent per year between 1969 and 1979; the use of roads also intensified as the cargo transported by road grew 9 percent per year and passengers transported by road grew 7 percent per year; private telephone lines grew 12 percent and public telephones grew 25 percent per year; coverage of clean water supply went up from 74 percent to 82 for the country as a whole, and from 35 percent to 62 percent in rural areas; the coverage of sewerage systems went up from 38 to 91 percent for the country as a whole, and from 30 percent to 87 percent in the rural areas; electricity users quadrupled; and between 1960 and 1979 the number of primary school teachers rose 3 percent per year and the number of secondary school teachers and school buildings rose 7 percent per year.

In conclusion, the role of government has been fundamental to the strengthening of key institutions and to providing infrastructure for a healthy expansion of the private sector. These factors, complemented by monetary and foreign exchange policies, contributed to the effective transmission of agricultural growth into overall economic growth.

Social and Environmental Effects

The impact of rapid agricultural growth and the subsequent growth in nonagricultural activities has been of special concern in the areas of urbanization, poverty alleviation, and environmental degradation.

URBANIZATION. As in many developing countries, development in Costa Rica has been accompanied by urbanization characterized by high spatial concentration. According to census data, the urban population in Costa Rica increased from one-third in 1950 to 45 percent in 1984. The troublesome feature of this expansion is that about 70 percent of the urban population was concentrated in the Great Metropolitan Area of the capital, San José. This means that roughly one-third of the entire country's population lives there!

The Great Metropolitan Area of San José is located in the Valley of the Central Plateau and includes the cities of San José, Cartago, Alajuela, Heredia, which were founded during colonial times, and their respective suburbs. These cities are separated by distances of less than 20 kilometers. Most of the country's industrial, commercial, and financial activity occurs within their boundaries.

Costa Rican authorities have taken steps to change this pattern of urbanization. For example, they have increased infrastructure and health and education services in rural areas to discourage migration to the metropolitan area. This move seems to be having some effect. Census data indicate that the growth in the proportion of urban population has slowed down somewhat. Between 1950 and 1963, the proportion of urban population increased from 33.5 percent to 34.5 percent; between 1963 and 1973 it increased from 34.5 percent to 40.6 percent; and between 1973 and 1984 it increased from 40.6 percent to 44.5 percent. The 1970s witnessed a concerted effort to establish large state-owned companies in rural areas. Unfortunately, as indicated earlier, they failed because most of them were oversized and fell into liquidity problems.

POVERTY ALLEVIATION. Although many of Costa Rica's workers increased their share of total income substantially over the study period (table 9.7), in 1971 there was a redistribution from the highest income deciles to the middle ones, and in 1977 from the lowest to the highest income deciles. In other words, development in Costa Rica has produced a wealthier middle class. At the same time, the crises in the world economy have severely affected the poorest people.

There is some anecdotal evidence to suggest that the growth in banana and coffee production has fostered growth and improved welfare in rural areas. For instance, banana plantations have attracted large numbers of migrants, who settled there permanently. The majority of these people come from Guanacaste

TABLE 9.7 Income distribution, 1961, 1971, and 1977

	Percentage of Income		
Deciles	1961	1971	1977
1–4	13.8	14.7	11.0
5–8	26.2	34.7	34.0
9–10	60.0	50.6	55.0
Total	100.0	100.0	100.0

SOURCE: OFIPLAN (1982).

Province, where the main activity is cattle ranching. During times of hardship on the banana plantations, laborers do not migrate back to their original towns; rather, they start producing maize and beans in their plots. According to a well-known story in the Atlantic region, in bad times for bananas, the Cousejo Nacionalde Produccion's processing plant, a quasi-abandoned drying and storage facility of the price stabilization and marketing institute, opens its doors to absorb the increased supply of these two grains.

Coffee also attracts masses of seasonal migrants, including children, from both rural and urban areas during harvesting. The revenues accrued to laborers have important multiplier effects because they are generally spent locally to purchase locally produced clothing, food, utensils, furniture, and entertainment. It is also well known that revenues obtained during this period are spent in educational fees and sent as remittances to relatives. Thus, the coffee and banana industry has contributed greatly to the alleviation of poverty.

ENVIRONMENTAL IMPACT. With environmental concerns high on policy agendas around the world, people in Costa Rica have started to reevaluate the effects of both agricultural and industrial growth. As pointed out earlier, land expansion has occurred at the expense of large tracks of forests, which are fast disappearing. Also, the improved technologies for coffee and bananas make use of large quantities of chemical fertilizers with pesticides, which in some areas of Costa Rica have produced a noticeable impact on the quality of freshwater and seawater and have reduced biodiversity. Coffee varieties that in the past required shade trees have been replaced by new high-yielding varieties that do not. This is simply another form of deforestation, which in addition has deprived households of firewood and building materials, now obtained from trees outside the coffee plantations. Deforestation on coffee plantations has also caused soil erosion and the loss of fertility, since the tree species used before were legumes that fixed nitrogen in the soil. Unless measures are taken to compensate for these losses, future improvements in productivity might prove extremely costly.

Conclusions and Policy Recommendations

The period 1962–79 was one of accelerated agricultural growth in Costa Rica. The main engines of growth were coffee and bananas. Both crops experienced substantial improvements in yields per hectare thanks to natural conditions and unique schemes of research and extension that brought together government, universities, and farmers. Equilibrium in the labor market was another contributing factor. Output increases were exported in both cases; hence, agricultural growth relied on external, not domestic markets.

Although the expansion in nonagricultural output was stimulated by protectionist industrial policies, agricultural growth appears to have had a sizable direct and indirect impact on overall growth. The transmission of direct and indirect effects from agriculture into nonagriculture was vastly enhanced by government monetary, exchange rate, and investment policies. Investments in infrastructure, health, education, telecommunications, and financial services grew faster than agriculture and total output.

Although poverty appeared to decline somewhat during the period of rapid agricultural growth, there were no protective measures to prevent further impoverishment of the poorest people. In addition, agricultural development and the industrial growth it engendered had a strong negative impact on the quality of the environment.

Future agricultural and nonagricultural growth in Costa Rica will have to rely on external markets, given the small size of the domestic markets. Care must be taken to pursue a course of policy reform that takes full advantage of external market opportunities. Investment in education, health, housing, telecommunications, and other supporting infrastructure must keep pace with output expansion and the need to improve productivity and competitiveness.

References

Asociación Demográfica Costarricense. Several years. *Encuesta de Fecundidad y Salud.*

Banco Central de Costa Rica. 1986. *Estadística 1950–1985.* División Económica. October.

———. 1987. *Balanza de Pagos de Costa Rica 1987.* Departamento de Contabilidad Social. Sección de Balanza de Pagos.

———. 1989a. *Cuentas Nacionales de Costa Rica 1978–1987.* Departamento de Contabilidad Social. Sección de Cuentas Nacionales. April.

———. 1989b. *Cifras sobre Producción Agropecuaria 1978–1987.* Departamento de Contabilidad Social. Sección de Economía Agropecuaria. April.

———. 1989c. *Estadísticas del Sector Industrial Manufacturero 1978–1987.* Departamento de Contabilidad Social. Sección de Economía Industrial. April.

Bell, Clive, Peter Hazell, and Roger Slade. 1982. *Project Evaluation in Regional Perspective*. Baltimore, Md.: Johns Hopkins University Press.

Celis, Rafael. 1988. "Costa Rica Country Economic Memorandum." Washington, D.C.: World Bank.

Celis, Rafael, and Neal Bliven. 1991. "Household Expenditure Behavior and Household Revenue Determinants." In *Adopting Improved Farm Technology: A Study of Smallholder Farmers in Eastern Province, Zambia*, ed. R. Celis, J. T. Milimo, and S. Wanmali. Washington, D.C.: International Food Policy Research Institute.

Celis, Rafael, and Cindy Holleman. 1991. "The Effects of Adopting Technology on the Household Use of Labor." In *Adopting Improved Farm Technology: A Study of Smallholder Farmers in Eastern Province, Zambia*, ed. R. Celis, J. T. Milimo, and S. Wanmali. Washington, D.C.: International Food Policy Research Institute.

Celis, Rafael et al. 1987. "Protectionism in Basic Grains in Costa Rica (1979–1985): Introductory Analysis and Policy Issues." Washington, D.C.: International Food Policy Research Institute.

Céspedes, S., H. Víctor, and Ronulfo R. Jiménez. 1989. *Evolución de la Pobreza en Costa Rica*. Academia de Centroamérica.

Contraloría General de la República de Costa Rica. Various years. *Memoria Anual*. Departamento de Estudios Económicos.

Corrales, Jorge, and Ricardo Monge. 1990. *Exportaciones No Tradicionales en Costa Rica*. San José: ECONOFIN.

Dirección General de Estadística y Censos. Various years. *Anuarios de Comercio Exterior*. Ministerio de Economía, Industria y Comercio.

———. 1957. *Censo Agropecuario de 1955*. Ministerio de Economía y Hacienda.

———. 1965. *Censo Agropecuario de 1963*. Ministerio de Economía y Hacienda. November.

———. 1974. *Censo Agropecuario de 1973*. Ministerio de Economía, Industria y Comercio. July.

———. 1987. *Censo Agropecuario de 1984*. Ministerio de Economía Industria y Comercio.

———. 1965. *Censo de Población 1963*. Ministerio de Economía y Hacienda.

———. 1974. *Censo de Población 1973*. Ministerio de Economía, Industria y Comercio.

———. 1987. *Censo de Población 1984*. Ministerio de Economía, Industria y Comercio.

———. Various years. *Encuesta de Hogares, Empleo y Desempleo*. Ministerio de Economía, Industria y Comercio.

García, Jorge García, and Gabriel Montes-Llamas. 1988. *Coffee Boom, Government Expenditure, and Agricultural Prices: The Colombian Experience*. Research Report 68. Washington, D.C.: International Food Policy Research Institute.

Gindling, T. H. 1990. "Women's Earnings and Economic Crisis in Costa Rica." Baltimore, Md.: University of Maryland, Department of Economics.

Hazell, Peter. 1991. "Análisis Económico de la Estabilización de Precios de los Granos Básicos en Costa Rica." Seminario sobre Perspectivas para la Liberalización de los Mercados de Granos Básicos en Costa Rica. Costa Rica: Ministerio de Agricultura y Ganadería (MAG) RUTA-UTN, February. Mimeo.

Hazell, Peter, and Ailsa Röell. 1983. *Rural Growth Linkages: Household Expenditure Patterns in Malaysia and Nigeria.* Washington, D.C.: International Food Policy Research Institute.

Hossain, M. 1988. *Nature and Impact of the Green Revolution in Bangladesh.* Washington, D.C.: International Food Policy Research Institute.

Instituto de Investigaciones en Ciencias Económicas. 1990. Evaluación de la Crisis y su Impacto en el Nivel de Pobreza, ed. J. D. Trejos.

International Monetary Fund. Various years. *International Financial Statistics.*

Mellor, John W. 1976. *The New Economics of Growth: A Strategy for India and the Developing World. A Twentieth-Century Fund Study.* Ithaca, N.Y.: Cornell University Press.

Ministerio de Obras Públicas y Transportes. Various years. *Estadísticas del Sector Transporte.* Departamento de Estudios Económicos. Dirección General de Planificación.

Ministerio de Salud. 1969, 1978, 1982. *Encuesta Nacional de Nutrición.*

Oficina de Planificación Nacional y Política Económicas (OFIPLAN). 1982. "Evolución Socioeconómica de Costa Rica 1950–1980." San José, Costa Rica.

Ramírez, Alonso, and Tirso Maldonado. 1988. "Desarrollo Socioeconómico y el Ambiente Natural de Costa Rica: Situación, Actual y Perspectivas." San José, Costa Rica: Fundación Neotrópica.

Stewart, Rigoberto. 1991. "Transferencias de Ingresos Producidos por las Distorsiones de Precios y Consecuencias Económicas de la Liberalización de los Mercados de Granos Básicos en Costa Rica." Seminario sobre las Perspectivas para la Liberalización de los Mercados de Granos Básicos en Costa Rica. San José, Costa Rica: Ministerio de Agricultura y Ganadería (MAG) RUTA-UTN.

10 The Contribution of Agriculture to Growth: Colombia

ALBERT BERRY

As a perusal of Colombia's economic history makes clear, agriculture has been central to the economy's generally satisfactory performance. Agriculture's postwar growth rate (3.7 percent over 1950–80) was well above the average for developing countries and was unusually high in relation to the growth rate of GDP (5.1 percent over 1950–80). During the years of fastest GDP growth (5.9 percent in 1965–80), agriculture grew at 4.5 percent, which was somewhat higher than its longer-period average. This chapter therefore gives special attention to the latter period.

Despite this record, the relatively low ratio of nonagricultural growth to that of agriculture might suggest a smaller positive spinoff from agriculture than might have been hoped for; the nonagricultural sector as a whole grew a little less than 6 percent annually over this period. Why the ratio was low is a complicated matter to explain, since there is no "correct" ratio between the growth of agriculture and nonagriculture, given that countries vary greatly in their resource endowments and policy options. That Colombia achieved its creditable growth rate with a rather low gross investment ratio in comparison with that of other countries of Latin America suggests that its growth process has been relatively efficient.

Of interest from a longer-term perspective, Colombia took off on a path of fairly sustained growth following the rapid expansion of coffee production and exports during the late nineteenth and early twentieth centuries. During much of the nineteenth century, the country had a variety of agricultural and extractive exports, but the quantum per capita remained low. That ratio increased substantially once coffee became the leading export (Ocampo 1984, 1991). Coffee has been the main commodity export ever since, accounting for 60–80 percent of legal exports during most of that period, falling to 55 percent during the 1970s and to less than 50 percent during the 1980s (table 10.1).

For most of the study period agricultural exports as a group accounted for 70 percent or more of total legal commodity exports (the 1970s average was 78 percent); in the early postwar years bananas came a distant second to coffee,

TABLE 10.1 Composition of exports in Colombia during the twentieth century (percent)

Period	Coffee	Gold	Oil, Fuel Oil, and Coal	Other Primary	Manufactures
1905–9	39.0	19.7	—	← 41.3 →	
1910–19	51.3	12.1	—	36.7	
1922–29	70.6	4.1	9.2	16.0	
1930–39	57.1	12.1	19.8	11	
1940–49	66.4	11.5	14.5	7.7	
1950–59	77.5	2.6	14.0	6	
1960–69	65.0	2.3	14.8	12.1	5.9
1970–79	54.2	2.3	5.4	18.2	19.9
1980–89	42.2	6.9	15.1	← 35.9 →	

SOURCES: Ocampo (1990, 220, table 9.2). Original sources are *Anuario de Comercio Exterior* and the Banco de la República for gold exports over the whole period and for the composition of exports in 1985–89.

while in more recent years a variety of items—including cotton, sugar, and flowers—have attained some importance. Tobacco and beef have long been exported, though never in such quantities as to take on macroeconomic importance. In none of these other commodities did Colombia have the large comparative advantage with which coffee was endowed; it could be produced competitively and in quantity, so large rents were generated. One of the notable costs of depending on coffee as the main source of foreign exchange, however, was that the economy became vulnerable to macroeconomic fluctuations; the price of coffee has been notorious for its volatility, and this behavior has substantially complicated the management of the economy and probably slowed its growth over the long run.

Although coffee, and to a lesser degree the other agricultural exports mentioned, earned the foreign exchange Colombia needed to modernize the economy, the rest of the sector has provided such a wide range of food items and inputs for industry that the country has never had to depend extensively on imports for either of these purposes. Most of the food needs of the population, both urban and rural, have traditionally been met by relatively small family farms, while a high share of beef is produced on the country's larger farms. International price comparisons show that food is relatively cheap in Colombia. Trade does not loom large in the supply of food; in the period 1970–83, for example, imports averaged 4.1 percent of real gross output and exports 6.1 percent (García and Montes 1988, 16). Although the country is thus a net exporter not only of agricultural goods as a whole but also of food products, the manufacturing sector had a negative net trade balance equal to 18 percent of the sector's real gross value of output.

The share of capital formation financed out of agricultural income has likely been substantial, and the transfer process has probably been both facilitated and rendered more efficient by the intraportfolio nature of a good part of it, as discussed in the next section. The extent of agriculture's contribution to the rest of the economy through other linkages is less clear. The agricultural market for manufactured goods has of course been substantial; as of 1950, more than a third of national income was generated in agriculture. Since Colombia has a high level of income inequality, both in agriculture and in the economy as a whole, the demand effects of agricultural growth would not be expected to fall as heavily on wage goods as in more egalitarian countries. This unequal distribution, the correspondingly limited rural demand for locally produced nonagricultural commodities, and the modest supply of savings looking for a local investment outlet probably help to explain the low density of nonagricultural activity in Colombia over most of the postwar period, at least by the standards of Asian countries. Preliminary analyses suggest a rather marked increase in these rural nonagricultural activities over the past decade or so, however, and therefore raise the question of whether agriculture-nonagriculture linkages have changed in character during this recent period.

Many features of Columbia's socioeconomic system are typical of the countries of Latin America: they have a relative abundance of natural resources per person, certainly in comparison with the countries of Asia, and probably those in Sub-Saharan Africa as well; they all have a middle-income level; they tolerate a highly unequal distribution of income and of land; and they pursued import-substituting industrialization in the post–World War II period. Country-specific features include Colombia's marked regionalism, as reflected by the presence of several important urban centers, each dominating a hinterland that earlier in the country's development was isolated from other similar regions by distance and difficult topography; the history of political violence between the two major political parties, centered for the most part in the rural areas; and the country's relatively conservative monetary and fiscal policy, which has kept its inflation rate low by the standards of the region and its public sector moderate in size in comparison with the public sector of some other Latin American countries.

In assessing the contribution of agriculture to economic development in Colombia, one is not primarily concerned with how fast it grew itself (highly subsidized growth, for example, could be unhealthy) but with how much it helped overall growth. A strong contribution to overall growth could be the result simply of a favorable resource endowment, but it would always benefit from effective policy, including the provision of infrastructure; research and extension to improve the level of technology; the provision of credit or inducement to the private financial system to do so; the maintenance of appropriate price incentives, which may or may not involve extensive intervention in product or factor markets but always involves exchange rate management; and other aspects of the tax and subsidy system. Since trade policy helps shape the environment in which agricultural performance takes place—because of its effects on relative prices, market size, and stability—the policies applied in that domain in Colombia must be examined briefly before the evolution of the agricultural sector itself can be fully understood.

The Macroeconomic Environment

Colombia's postwar economic policy was fairly typical of the region. It included a heavy dependence on agricultural exports; a significant episode of import-substituting industrialization, having its roots in the experience of the Great Depression and the associated traumatic drop in the terms of trade, and normally involving some degree of "discrimination" against agricultural exports (via lower relative prices); and a tendency during the more inward-oriented phase to favor an overvalued exchange rate, as a result of internal inflation combined with a fixed exchange rate system kept in place by a political unwillingness to devalue except in extreme circumstances.

Colombia's incentive system, however, appears to have been somewhat less heavily oriented toward import-substituting activities than the incentives of many other Latin countries. The pivotal step toward a more efficient regime, which urged the adoption of a floating exchange rate, came relatively early (1967) and heralded a decade or more of rapid growth. Because Colombia's monetary and political system was on the conservative side, at least in the context of Latin America, inflation was low up through the 1960s, except for periodic bouts following on significant devaluations. Both the size of the public sector and the fiscal deficit were of modest proportions.

A protectionist trend that began in the mid-1880s grew stronger in the wake of the Great Depression, which ushered in a period of major structural transformation in the economy. Since that time, exchange controls have been a permanent feature of public policy, accompanied by an active exchange rate policy and a variety of protective devices (Ocampo 1991, 134). Protection was increased by the tariff reforms of 1950, 1959, and 1964, the latter two of which were induced by the collapse of coffee prices; extensive use of nontariff protection reinforced the effects of the tariff regime. These moves toward import substitution were accompanied by a set of policies designed to promote export diversification, beginning with preferential exchange rates for nontraditional exports in 1948, a drawback system in 1957, and tax incentives and subsidized credit. Decree 444 of 1967 imposed some order on these varied components of the system and guaranteed a stability not previously present.

After the short recession of 1957–58, which followed the collapse of coffee prices, this "mixed" policy package (the term is from Ocampo 1991, 135) coincided with a period of good average growth (4.9 percent over 1959–67; see table 10.2), despite severe foreign exchange bottlenecks and unstable capital flows. Diversification of the manufacturing sector and of exports was by

TABLE 10.2 Growth of GDP and GDP per capita, 1965–1986

Year	GDP Deflator (1980 = 100)	GDP (billions of current pesos)	GDP (billions of 1980 pesos)	Annual GDP Growth Rate (%)	Population (thousands)	GDP per Capita Growth Rate (%)
1965	8.97	60.80	678.14	3.62	16,425	12.57
1970	14.40	132.80	922.22	6.91	21,266	3.80
1975	33.20	405.10	1,220.18	2.19	23,502	1.35
1980	100.00	1,579.00	1,579.00	4.38	25,892	2.30
1985	277.50	4,881.00	1,758.92	2.88	28,418	0.98
1986	344.10	6,362.00	1,848.88	5.11	28,961	3.14

SOURCE: World Bank (1987).

then under way. The post-1967 period saw a trend toward import liberalization, intensified in 1979–81 to stabilize prices that were then under pressure from the large public works program implemented by the administration of President Julio Cesar Turbay (1978–82) and the large fiscal deficit financed by borrowing abroad and by monetary creation; after 1982 the liberalization was drastically reversed. The economic slowdown of the early 1980s was associated with the revaluation of the peso and the restrictive monetary policy designed to offset an expansionary fiscal policy.

Colombia's real exchange rate has gone through several long cycles since the early twentieth century. The Great Depression forced a large devaluation, after which the nominal exchange rate was held constant for 14 years. Next came a major appreciation, which ended with the crash of the coffee price in the mid-1950s and the ensuing devaluation. No clear trend emerged during these stop-go cycles, which ended with the adoption of the floating exchange rate in 1967 and an associated real devaluation in the early 1970s. The reversal that followed brought the rate back to about the level of the pre-1967 decade. The terms of trade for agriculture followed a similar long-run pattern, with positive movements coinciding with real exchange rate appreciation and vice versa (figure 10.1).

Fluctuations around the GDP growth trend have been related to the country's international trade cycles, although the economy did reasonably well even when the foreign sector was not booming. The gap in the growth rate between the periods of "strong" and of "weak" trade performance has not been dramatic. The share of exports of goods and services in GDP (measured at constant 1975 prices) trended down from 24 percent in the late 1930s to a low of 14 percent over 1980–84, but the trend was reversed in the past few years (table 10.3). In the first rapid expansion after the war, during 1945–55, the growth rate reached a little more than 5 percent per year. This expansion was fueled by the running down of foreign exchange balances built up during the war and by

FIGURE 10.1 The exchange rate: terms of trade link, 1925–1985.

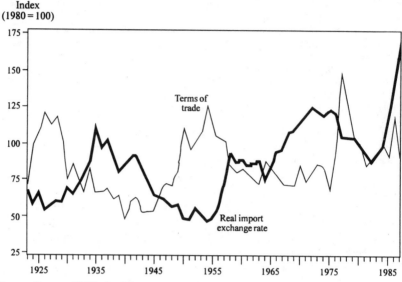

Source: Ocampo (1991), fig. 9.3.

the high price of coffee. When the coffee price fell, growth slipped to 2.3 percent over 1956–58 and to an average of 4.4 percent over 1955–67. The average growth of 5.7 percent in the second boom period, 1967–80, was helped along both by a marked improvement in the terms of trade and by the reforms of the trade incentive system mentioned earlier. The dynamism up to the mid-1970s is commonly attributed to the improvement in export performance wrought by this policy reform and the high growth in the late 1970s to the combination of record high coffee prices and the influx of income from the export of illegal drugs.[1] Export quantum grew at an undramatic 6.4 percent over 1966–75 and then slowed markedly; in this subperiod nearly half of the increased international purchasing power from which the economy benefited was the result of the positive shift in the terms of trade (see World Bank 1987, 100–101). Toward the end of this period the abundance of foreign exchange had Dutch disease effects on the other tradable sectors and, together with a burst of government borrowing abroad and spending at home, paved the way for the balance of payments crisis of the early 1980s. The crisis was finally precipitated

1. The official national account figures used here understate growth for a period beginning in the mid-1970s. Therefore true figures for 1974–80 and 1965–80 would be somewhat higher than those given here.

TABLE 10.3 Export growth, 1900–1988

Period	Coffee Exports (thousand bags)	Quantum Indices (1970–74 = 100)		Purchasing Power of Exports (1970–74 = 100)	Exports of Goods and Services as Percentage of GDP (1975 prices)
		Primary Products	Total		
1900–04	542				
1905–09	604	8.8	7.2	7.4	
1910–14	837	12.8	10.5	13.2	
1915–19	1,244	17.2	14.1	12.8	
1920–24	1,906	27.1	22.2[a]	23.1[a]	
1925–29	2,451	34.3	28.0	38.3	24.0
1930–34	3,149	43.0	35.2	33.1	24.4
1935–39	3,972	53.6	43.8	34.8	24.0
1940–44	4,370	57.5	46.9	31.2	20.4
1945–49	5,429	68.4	55.9	47.1	21.0
1950–54	5,337	72.6	59.3	78.0	18.4
1955–59	5,523	74.1	60.5	70.3	17.2
1960–64	6,139	84.7	70.1	68.1	16.0
1965–69	6,076	92.3	80.9	73.6	15.6
1970–74	6,656	100.0	100.0	100.0	14.9
1975–79	7,990	113.5	123.8	162.7	15.1
1980–84	9,685	139.2	147.8	169.1	14.1
1985–88	10,613	180.8[b]	229.0	268.0	17.3[c]

SOURCE: Ocampo (1991), table 1. Original sources are cited there.
[a]1923–24.
[b]1985–86.
[c]1985–87.

by the recession in the world economy, the high interest rates, and the return of coffee prices to more normal levels (García and Montes 1988).

It is difficult to determine the periods in which Colombia's incentive system was significantly biased against international trade. As in most developing economies, the transportation and trading systems were geared to international trade and biased *against* internal trade.[2] What is clear is that throughout its history the republic continued to search for new exports and to protect import substitutes, these substitutes often a by-product of the need for tariff revenues. Accordingly, it is hard to assess the efficiency of the import substitution that accompanied (or produced) the structural transition of the postwar period.

2. Londoño (1989a and 1989b) has analyzed Colombia's structural change in the light of the cross-country patterns identified by Kuznets and Chenery and concluded that in the early twentieth century the economy was more agricultural and less industrial than "normal," as well as being more export-oriented. It remains to be seen whether further analysis will prove this interesting proposition valid.

Growth during the height of that phase was acceptable and was achieved with modest savings and investment rates, typically in the range of 17–20 percent, which suggests relatively good marginal output-capital ratios (0.31 for the 1970s) by comparison with other countries (0.24 for Latin America as a whole) (see ECLA 1985:224–25; Berry 1987a:11). This phase also contributed in a variety of ways to the modernization of the agricultural sector.

Colombia departed from its long tradition of monetary and price stability (the average rate of inflation was not much above 10 percent since almost the turn of the century) following the 1967 boom. The growth of the money supply suddenly jumped from 16 percent per year over 1966–72 to 26.4 percent over 1972–82, and in the short span of 1971–74 the inflation norm shifted up from its former modest level to about 25 percent per year, where it has remained since then.

Agricultural Growth

What have been the key ingredients of agricultural growth in Colombia and how well has agricultural policy been conceived and applied? It is important to understand both the proximate (supply-side) sources of growth (increases in the level of inputs and improvements in efficiency/technology) and their determinants, which include input and output prices and such nonprice factors as the opening up of new lands and technological change resulting from government efforts in research. Demand affects the growth of output by influencing capacity utilization in the short run, but its more important role is to act as a determinant of the rate of growth of capacity. In what follows, I look at the proximate sources of output growth and then the underlying role of demand and prices. First, however, it is important to have some idea of the components of Colombia's agricultural sector.

Structural Features of the Agricultural Sector

Colombia's agricultural sector consists of several significant subsectors. For more than a century coffee has been the main export commodity; it is produced in important quantities both by small farms and by large ones. Another sector consists of small-scale operations that are dedicated mainly to the production of food crops for domestic consumption and that in the past relied on traditional-technology. Livestock is a third sector. It used to be composed mainly of fairly traditional cattle haciendas, but more and more of them are becoming modern and heterogeneous operations. There is also a modern, large-scale crop sector consisting of sugar (for refining), cotton, rice, soybeans, and several other crops. The relative weights of these subsectors in production and their technological features have changed over time, sometimes significantly. Though there are grey areas between these categories, most farms fall clearly in one or another. Note, too, that Colombia is not a country of primarily "mixed" farms that strike a balance between crops and livestock or between exportables and traditional food crops.

This range of farm types can be traced to the country's varying topography and ecology, as well as to its social structure. The high Andean regions, with their difficult terrain and limited flatlands (mostly in river valleys), were the first to be heavily settled because the health risks there were not as great as in the lowlands. The area eventually became densely populated, with the agrarian structure ranging from some combination of *latifundia* and *minifundia* (e.g., in the region near Bogota) to virtually total *minifundia* (e.g., in the southern department of Nariño). The settlement of new lowland areas added many large farms, most of which focused on cattle ranching. The highly broken terrain in some of the coffee zones opened up in the late nineteenth and early twentieth centuries gave rise to a small producer sector, partly because wealthy absentee owners or would-be owners would have difficulty maintaining control over lands that took weeks to reach by mule. The large-scale, modern crop farms found their home in the few accessible regions with good-quality land and level terrain.

The small noncoffee farms probably have the most complicated product mixes. The main annual crops are corn, beans, potatoes, and yuca, while the main permanent ones are *platanos* (green bananas) and sugar for *panela* (the traditionally consumed block brown sugar). About 65 percent of noncoffee output corresponds to nontradables, almost entirely food for direct consumption (MEDSA 1990, 355). Together with their cropping land, these small farmers currently control a little less than a quarter of the land under pasture. Their share of production is greatest in dual-purpose cattle and in small animals (especially hogs), but it is now low in the case of chickens (5.3 percent) because of the large capitalization of this industry over the past few decades (MEDSA 1990, 359).

As might be expected in a heterogenous agriculture, yields tend to vary widely in most crops, both across regions and by type of farm (MEDSA 1990, 130). Smaller producers tend to have below-average yields on a crop-by-crop basis, but performance varies widely among both small and medium-large producers.

The sector's heterogeneity is also related to the wide range of farm sizes in the country. As 1960 agricultural census data make clear, (table 10.4), the distribution of land was extremely unequal; the smallest 63 percent of farms (those with less than 5 hectares) worked less than 5 percent of the land, whereas the 9 percent with 100 hectares or more worked 65 percent of it.[3] Further contributing to income inequality was the fact that many of the small units were

---

3. These data must be interpreted with caution because of the variation in land quality; the unadjusted data tend to exaggerate the concentration of land.

TABLE 10.4 Aspects of Colombia's agrarian structure, 1960

Size of Farm (hectares)	Farms (%)	Area (%)	Farms Rented (%)
Less than 5	62.55	4.5	28.83
5–10	13.98	4.3	19.32
10–20	9.44	5.9	15.15
20–50	7.17	9.7	10.55
50–100	3.30	9.8	7.08
100–500	2.98	25.5	5.56
500–1,000	0.42	10.0	3.91
1,000 and up	0.28	30.4	3.11
All	100.00	100.00	23.34

SOURCE: DANE (1964), 42.

rented, and that about half of all renters were sharecroppers. The smaller farms were far more labor-intensive operations: the ratio of labor to "effective" land (i.e., amount of land adjusted for quality differences) was about eight times higher on the farms less than 5 hectares than on those greater than 100 hectares (Berry 1973, 219). As a result, labor productivity was much higher on the larger farms, and land productivity greater on the smaller ones. Total factor productivity did not appear to vary greatly across the size classes of farms; if anything, it appeared to be a little higher in the middle-sized farms (5–50 hectares) (Berry 1973, 220), but since such estimates are prone to error, any such conclusion must be viewed as tentative.

The Process of Agricultural Growth

The main proximate sources of growth over the period under consideration have been capital formation and increased productivity, although the available estimates on capital formation and capital stock (especially for the crop subsector) are rather tenuous. The average annual output growth over 1950–80 was 3.95 percent, and of that figure productivity growth accounted for about 2.15 points (a considerable part of which was associated with the shift from low-value to higher-value crops), capital formation for about 1.3 points, area expansion (at 1.5 percent per year) for about 0.25, and the labor force increase for a similar amount (table 10.5). The land/labor ratio rose nearly 1 percent per year, for a significant increase of about 35 percent over the period as a whole, while estimates of the capital/labor ratio imply an increase of 125 percent, or somewhat more than 2.5 percent per year. The labor share of value added fell from close to 50 percent in the first half of the 1960s to less than 40 percent by the early 1980s, while that of capital rose from 35 percent in 1960 to nearly half by 1982, and that of land fell from 19 percent to 15 percent (Romano 1987).

With total factor productivity gains probably accounting for about half of

TABLE 10.5 Sources of agricultural growth, 1950–1987 (percent)

Period	Average Rates of Growth				Contribution of Total Growth				
	Agricultural Output	Area	Capital	Labor	Area	Capital	Labor	All Factors	Factor Productivity
1950–65	3.29	1.05	1.10	0.99	0.19	0.37	0.47	1.03	2.26
1965–80	4.61	1.95	5.38	0.00	0.36	2.22	0.00	2.58	2.03
1980–87	2.01	1.23	1.37	0.70	0.18	0.66	0.26	1.10	0.91
1950–80	3.95	1.50	3.22	0.49	0.27	1.29	0.23	1.80	2.15

SOURCE: Calculated on the basis of data presented in MEDSA (1990), cuadro 1.12.

the output growth over the period 1950–80, and for more than 2 percent per year in absolute terms, it is clear that technological improvements were an important component of growth. Their effect also reflected in the striking yield increases for many crops. In the crop sector as a whole, value added per hectare rose at an average rate of about 2.44 percent, owing to yield increases for the specific crops and to a shifting from lower-value to higher-value crops. Productivity increased in the livestock sector as well. The increase in land in use should not be downplayed, however, since it may have been sufficiently complementary to capital formation to make it more important than this accounting exercise gives it credit for. Expansion at 1.5 percent per year, reaching about 2 percent during the phase of fast output growth in 1965–80, reflects a considerable amount of colonization, as well as a pushing back of the "interior frontier."

The expansion of land in use during the postwar period was accompanied by a marked change in the structure of Colombian agriculture. Immediately after the war, agriculture was a relatively unproductive sector, except for coffee. Much of the best land in the rich river valleys was in large farms with extensive modes of production (e.g., cattle raising) and low land productivity, while small farmers scratched a meager livelihood from inferior land on the mountainsides (IBRD 1950). The most striking change since that time has been the increasing intensity of land use in the large farm sector and the resulting growth in output. Much land previously dedicated to cattle production was converted to commercial crops (cotton, sugar, soybeans, corn, rice, and other products) while land in less productive crops was converted to more productive ones. Over 1950–80 production grew at an impressive average of about 9 percent in this "commercial" or modern noncoffee sector, which many analysts singled out for comparison with the "traditional" sector. Since the commercial crops (the big three being cotton, rice, and sugar) have for the most part been produced on large capitalized farms, the expansion of the sector created only a modest number of jobs. A notable, albeit recent, exception is the cut-flower industry, which began to develop fast in the 1970s and which employs a large number of workers on a small hectareage.

The primary emphasis in the country's research program was on the discovery of new and better varieties of modern crops (some of this research was carried out in private programs of the producers' associations), and the effort paid off well. A new breed of commercially oriented farmers emerged: some rented land from large owners; others bought land; and still others, who represented a younger and better-educated generation than their more traditionally minded elders, modernized the family's agricultural operations. One might guess that the impact of this process on income distribution in the rural areas and in the country as a whole was negative, since (with the exception of flowers) there is no clear evidence of positive spinoffs onto either wage workers in agriculture (beyond the lucky ones who found good jobs in this new type of agriculture) or onto smaller farmers. The bulk of food production was still in the hands of the small farm sector, so the expansion of commercial production did not have a major impact on the cost of food for the rural or urban poor.

Although the timing may not have been quite the same, the livestock industry also underwent a significant modernization during this period. Traditionally, and up until the 1960s, cattle dominated the sector and were mainly produced in a land-intensive way, sometimes on fertile soil with the potential for higher productivity in crop production. Since then the sector has been modernized: better grasses and new breeds and strains have been introduced, and management has become more scientific. As a result, the industry's average productivity has increased substantially, even while the average quality of the land it uses has probably gone down. The production of hogs and chickens has expanded rapidly in response to a shift from traditional small-scale activity to modern, specialized, large-scale production; the resulting fall in the relative price of hogs and chickens has led to a corresponding increase in their share of meat consumption.

Some authors argue that the rapid growth of the commercial crop sector from the 1950s to the early 1970s not only failed to contribute to the modernization of the small-scale *campesino* sector but weakened it by the competition it created in the product and land markets. The ingredients of agricultural modernization were apparently beyond the scope of the *campesino* sector at this time; it may even have suffered a decline in the productivity of land over part of the period (MEDSA 1990, 337). The dualism in the agricultural sector became more prominent during this stage of modernization. Despite its relative lack of dynamism at this time, the *campesino* sector remained important; as of 1960, it accounted for about half of total agricultural production. It remained the source of much of agricultural employment and of the supply of food to urban areas. Meanwhile, the medium and large producers focused on exportable food items and on importable and exportable raw materials.

From about the mid-1970s on, the *campesino* sector began showing substantial increases in land productivity, while growth in the capitalist (large-scale) sector slowed down. Between 1950 and 1972 yields of traditional crops appear to have been stagnant, sometimes even falling (MEDSA 1990, 133–34), whereas the commercial ones racked up major increases. By 1973–76 the gap between the smaller and the medium/large producers had probably reached its peak. Between that time and 1988, however, the gap seems to have been reduced, with productivity rising sharply on the smaller units, but little if at all on the larger commercial ones. The increase in the use of modern inputs by small farms was particularly notable in sugarcane for *panela*, potatoes, beans, *platanos* for export, vegetables, and fruits. Livestock production in the small-scale sector also did well. As of 1984, 66 percent of the *campesinos* in eastern Antioquia had cattle and 30 percent had pigs. The reasons for this striking turnaround are discussed in the next section.

Another major source of growth in Colombian agriculture in recent decades has been coffee. Important technical advances in this sector contributed to a substantial increase in output at a time when—because of the absence of quotas in the international market—it was possible to increase sales rapidly. As of 1988, about 43 percent of the coffee area and about 56 percent of the output came from the farms employing the new varieties and associated production practices (MEDSA 1990, 182). In 1970 small producers accounted for 30 percent of coffee output. Since then, and especially since the coffee bonanza of 1975–77, coffee growers of all sizes, especially those in the central coffee zone, have modernized their production. This move has increased the demand for temporary (seasonal) workers, who now constitute 55 percent of coffee employment and many of whom reside in urban centers, especially municipal *cabeceras* (county seats).

Infrastructure, Investment, and Technological Improvement

The available figures suggest a rather low ratio of gross investment (public plus private) to value added in Colombian crop production. Over the study period it averaged perhaps 10–15 percent, (table 10.6), but the data are too imprecise to draw any firm conclusions.[4] They do suggest a strong cycle in public investment, which jumped to a peak in the late 1960s and early 1970s and then in 1978–82 fell to less than two-thirds of the 1968–72 average (see MEDSA 1990, 325). Private investment in machinery and land improvements, meanwhile, showed strong growth (about 8 percent per year) until 1981, after which it dipped sharply as the economic and social problems of the 1980s made their influence felt.

There appears to have been a considerable increase in public expenditures in the key areas of research and extension from the 1950s up to the early 1970s (in line with an overall increase in public expenditure on agriculture). This was followed by a sharp decline over most of that decade and then a recovery in the early 1980s back up to the level of the early 1970s (tables 10.7 and 10.8). If it is assumed that total research expenditures (or expenditures on research and extension, whichever is more relevant) increased at a good clip until the early 1970s and then fell back, this pattern could help to explain the slowdown in the growth of the yields in the modern sector in the second half of that decade.

At about the same time, however, technological improvements apparently accelerated in the small-scale or *campesino* sector, in large part because of favorable public policy, which gave the small *campesino* improved access to modern technology. As of the early 1970s the technological packages that the Instituto Colombiano Agropecuario (ICA) offered small farmers were criticized for being inappropriate for these farmers and the constraints under which

---

4. Some recent estimates for public expenditure, however, show a similarly sharp downward trend in agriculture's participation in the total budget—from 25.1 percent in 1970 to 7.1 percent in 1982 (Thomas 1985, 238–39).

TABLE 10.6 Estimates of gross annual investment in agriculture, 1965–1987, and its relation to sectoral value added and to total investment (millions of 1975 pesos)

Year/Period	Private Sector[a] (1)	Public Sector (2)	Total[a] (3)	Agricultural Investment[a]/ Agricultural Value Added (4)	Agricultural Investment[a]/ Total Investment[b] (5)
1965–66	2,577	3,272	5,849	4.76	8.11
1967–69	5,793	7,149	12,062	5.80	9.04
1970–74	13,865	13,636	25,369	6.18	8.79
1975–79	17,753	9,679	27,495	5.54	8.51
1980–84	19,161	9,840	29,001	4.93	6.19
1985	2,691	2,392	5,083	4.07	5.45
1986	3,146	4,183	7,329	5.59	7.62
1987	3,360	3,766	7,126	n.a.	n.a.

SOURCE: Columns (1) and (2) are from MEDSA (1990), tables 4.22 and 4.25, respectively. The former includes only machinery and equipment and land improvement. The precise inclusion of the latter series is unclear. MEDSA cites H. Sisa, *Gasto Público en la Producción Agropecuaria,* cuadro 111.1, and notes that the investment figures for 1965–69 and 1985–87 were estimated assuming the same ratio of investment to total public expenditure in the sector for the succeeding and prior years.

NOTE: The sum of columns (1) and (2) should not include any overlap, unless some land improvement undertaken by the public sector somehow got into the figures of the first column. But they do not, it appears, include increases in the value of stands of permanent crops. Livestock is also not included. They seem, nonetheless, consistent with those cited in Ministerio de Agricultura, *Plan de Desarrollo Agropecuario y de Inversiones,* 1987–1990, 11–26, which claims to include both of those items, though it may refer to total investment in the economy, including inventories.

n.a. Not available.

[a]Column (4) indicates private sector investments in machinery and in land improvements, plus public sector investment in value added in the whole sector. As a measure of the true ratio, the figures are low because they fail to include increases in the stock of animals and probably also the value of crop stands. Since most of this investment probably relates to the crop sector, the ratio it bears to value added in crops may be a more meaningful one. It would be approximately twice as high as the series shown, since crop output is about half of total value added in the sector (which includes that for items other than crops or livestock). Partial—does not include all components of investment.

[b]Investment in fixed capital.

they worked. In about 1976, the Programa de Desarrollo Rural Integrado (DRI) began to channel a significant flow of resources to smallholder agriculture (the program gave considerable emphasis to technological development—an average of 10 percent of its expenditures and a peak of 14 percent in 1978/79). After identifying the typical crop combinations and systems of cultivation and production in a region, ICA developed new technological packages that helped farmers adapt experimental results to local conditions and take advantage of group transfer of technology. A substantial increase in institutional credit made it easier for *campesinos* to adopt the new recommendations. And, for the first time, technical assistance was systematically provided to a group of small

TABLE 10.7 Estimated nonprice transfer to agriculture, 1961–1983 (millions of 1978 pesos)

Period	Public Expenditure (1)	Research and Extension (2)	Credit Subsidy (3)	Total (4) = (1) + (2) + (3)
1961–64	4,311.1	1,788.3	2,027.6	8,127.1
1966–69a	4,836.5	1,693.0	2,777.7	9,307.4
1970–74	19,432.6	3,860.3	7,576.3	30,869.5
1975–79b	17,449.1	2,205.2	11,952.7	31,627.1
1980–83	17,378.6	3,468.0	15,014.6	35,881.1

SOURCES: García and Montes (1989), 349. Column (1) is government expenditure (current and investment) in the agricultural sector carried out by the central government. It includes the expenditures by INCORA, ICA, INDERENA, and HIMAT; the transfer to IDEMA, Caja de Crédito Agrario Industrial y Minero, and the rural development program (DRI). It also includes expenditures made by other public agencies in health, electricity, rural roads, education, and wells. The information was derived from Contraloria General de la República, Informe Financiero, Annex II, several issues. Column (2) corresponds to (a) government expenditures through ICA, Caja Agraria, INCORA, and DRI derived from Contraloria General de la República Informe Financiero, several numbers and (b) expenditures on research and extension in the coffee sector carried out by the National Coffee Fund. Column (3) derived from table 3.1.
NOTE: The information was deflated by the implicit price deflator of agricultural GDPA base year 1975 = 100.
aExcluding 1968.
bExcluding 1977.

farmers, the users of the DRI program, to facilitate and complement the process of technological change (MEDSA 1990, 140).

Although the program still needs some ironing out, much progress has been made since the mid-1970s, as is suggested by the fact that farmers taking advantage of the DRI subprogram have obtained yields well above the national average (the unweighted average differential is 53 percent) for the main *campesino* crops (MEDSA 1990, 380). The surpluses gained as a result of higher productivity increased investment capacity, no doubt helped finance the new technologies, and contributed to increased incomes in other ways (e.g., by permitting investment in animals and physical improvements).

The Role of Demand, Prices, and Other Incentives

The more responsive agricultural output is to relative prices, the more important it is that those prices be set at appropriate levels. Most countries, Colombia included, have elected to protect many manufactured goods and have intervened to raise their relative prices. This action has the effect of lowering the relative price of many agricultural products, though some of them may have received protection as well. Overvalued exchange rates, once nearly ubiquitous in Latin America, have the effect of raising the relative price of nontradables in relation to tradables. Determining whether and when the relative price of agri-

TABLE 10.8 Basic data on government expenditures in the agricultural sector of Colombia, 1950–1976 (millions of current Colombian pesos)

Year	Direct Expenditures of the Central Government and Decentralized Agencies	Direct Expenditures of the Central Government	Direct Expenditures on Research and Extension	Direct Expenditures on Irrigation	Indirect Estimates on Expenditures on Education	Indirect Estimates of Expenditures on Health
1950	n.a.	25.4	7.8	n.a.	15.7	9.9
1953	n.a.	57.2	12.4	n.a.	22.5	15.6
1958	n.a.	111.5	22.4	n.a.	56.1	22.5
1960	n.a.	103.7	26.1	n.a.	87.7	30.5
1961	1,004.9	362.5	38.9	n.a.	120.3	n.a.
1965	2,010.5	804.1	50.8	n.a.	281.4	59.1
1970	7,314.0	2,329.5	167.6	2,821.0	652.9	348.6
1973	10,710.7	2,782.0	n.a.	1,430.9	1,464.5	519.0
1975	14,119.8	2,796.0	n.a.	1,915.7	2,304.3	803.8
1976	15,604.0	2,752.0	n.a.	2,003.1	n.a.	n.a.

SOURCE: Elias (1983), 52–53.
NOTE: The figures for 1950–71 imply a 3.4-fold increase (if current prices are deflated by the GDP deflator), and an increase from 0.28 percent of agricultural value added in 1950 to 0.56 percent in 1971.
n.a. Not available.

cultural items has been too high or too low in Colombia boils down to assessing the appropriateness of the protection given to both manufactured and agricultural activities, *and* the management of the exchange rate; this exercise, in turn, requires an assessment of the extent of learning by doing in the protected activities and their success at graduating from the category of "infants" after a reasonable amount of time. Such an assessment is well beyond the scope of this discussion, and in any case there has been little empirical analysis of the extent of such learning by doing in Colombia thus far. But it is important to bear in mind that any conclusions reached with respect to agricultural pricing policy are simultaneously conclusions about the appropriate degree of protection of selected manufacturing and agricultural activities.

Since relative price is only one of several variables by which public policy affects the incentive to produce the item(s) and the income levels of the producers, the other relevant factors—credit subsidies, taxes, and sector-specific infrastructure expenditures—need to be taken into account as well. An effective system must provide each sector with about the right average incentive over the longer run, while having the capacity to make needed adjustments in the face of the serious shocks (e.g., terms of trade fluctuations), which are an important part of the macroeconomic setting. The right combination of incentives must also be present.

Protection and Other Incentives

Agriculture may fail to make its potential contribution to development if it is sufficiently discriminated against in relation to manufacturing tradables, if nontradables are in general favored over tradables, or if the wrong activities in agriculture are favored through protection or subsidies. The available empirical studies suggest on the whole that if there has been a significant policy bias against Colombian agriculture, it has been the result of below-equilibrium exchange rates (e.g., García and Montes 1989, 147).

Although import-substituting industrialization was a principal goal of the postwar period, or a good part of it, some agricultural activities also received a fair amount of protection, in keeping with a long tradition that was earlier concerned with self-sufficiency in important food and raw material products (García and Montes 1989, chap. 2). From the end of World War II until 1967, Colombia suffered recurrent balance of payments crises owing to the combination of a (temporarily) fixed exchange rate and domestic inflation well above that of its main trading partners. By 1969, the year with the most reliable figures on effective protection of manufacturing, any overvaluation that remained was of modest proportions. Effective protection of manufacturing (which in principle includes the impacts of quotas, subsidies, currency overvaluation, and other government interventions in trade, though it is not usually possible to evaluate them all in practice) appears also to have been moderate: it averaged about 19 percent in comparison with the -18 percent for agriculture and 2 percent for that sector excluding coffee.[5]

The figures for manufacturing are low in comparison with contemporary figures for most other developing countries (see, e.g., Krueger et al. 1981). They are probably also lower than in previous years. While the usual cascade effect was manifest to some extent—with lower protection being provided to simpler processed foods, construction materials, and the like, and higher levels to intermediate goods and consumer durables—the only figure above 40 percent was that for transportation equipment. A more recent study indicates a sharp increase in the rate of real effective protection of noncoffee tradables between 1980 and 1988 (MEDSA 1990, 608) and an even sharper increase in the level of real nominal protection since the mid-1970s. (In 1980 the protection of noncoffee agriculture was only 8 percent lower than for other tradables, and by 1985 the gap was down to zero.) This pattern would be consistent with a fairly serious attempt to shield the domestic producer from the recent negative trend of agricultural prices in the world markets.

Other incentives and support that were subject to some quantification include agricultural credit and taxes and subsidies unrelated to trade, as well as, infrastructure expenditures. In most years between 1960 and 1984 below-market interest rates on agricultural credit constituted a subsidy of between 1 and 3 percent of the gross value of agricultural output (García and Montes 1989, 52), an amount comparable to the value of public spending in agriculture (table 10.7). The interest rate charged on agricultural loans (see table 10.9) was typically 60–80 percent of the "market" rate, the latter being defined for different subperiods by the return on stock yields, Certificado de Abono Tributario (CAT) yields, and certificates of time deposits.[6] One might guess that the income tax system (and the related wealth and profits taxes) was biased in favor of agriculture through a lower level of tax compliance than in other sectors, while the rest of the tax/expenditure system was on balance biased in the other direction, as indicated by the heavy urban-specific infrastructure expenditures that were not fully covered by urban-based taxes. Depending on how coffee taxes are treated, the total tax burden on agriculture in the mid-1960s amounted to 8.5–12.5 percent of agricultural income; meanwhile public current and investment expenditures on agriculture and on the families who earn their living

5. There appears to be some discrepancy, however, in the interpretation of the figures from the usually cited source, Hutcheson and Schydlowsky (1982, 131). These authors describe the level of protection as "quite low," but García and Montes (1989, 261) present a figure of about 50 percent for the manufacturing sector excluding sugar, citing Hutcheson (1973), whose work was the basis for the Hutcheson-Schydlowsky study. Note that the estimates in question refer to protection on domestic sales and were calculated using the Corden method.

6. The assumed market rates in the early 1960s look low in relation to inflation, but this and any other credit-related subsidies were probably not large in relation to the estimates made by García and Montes.

TABLE 10.9 Agricultural credit, by institution, 1965–1986 (millions of 1975 pesos)

Year	Caja Agraria	FFAP	Banks	Cattle Funds	INCORA	FNC	Total Credit	Ratio of Agricultural Credit to Value Added	Ratio of Agricultural Credit to AVA
1965–69	n.a.	n.a.	n.a.	n.a.	n.a.	n.a.	77,740	333,067	23.3
1970–74	49,971	11,883	34,206	9,893	6,622	2,609	115,185	406,583	28.3
1975–79	41,817	41,811	21,346	9,706	5,147	3,644	123,473	508,844	24.3
1980–84	52,927	68,828	32,248	7,356	5,510	3,872	170,743	590,617	28.9
1985–86	26,275	32,311	12,956	2,780	3,363	1,984	79,567	251,541	31.6

SOURCE: MEDSA (1990), cuadro 4.18.

NOTE: FFAP = Fondo Financiero Agropecuario (Fund for Agricultural Financing); INCORA = Instituto Colombiano de Reforma Agraria (Colombian Institute for Agrarian Reform); FNC = Fondo Nacional Cafetero (National Coffee Fund); and AVA = agricultural value added.
n.a. Not available.

there appeared to be about 12.5–16.5 percent of agricultural income (Berry 1974, I-17). The estimates of the resource transfer through the tax/expenditure system are still too imprecise, however, to draw any firm conclusions about the overall bias in the system of public sector interventions.

Some analysts believe that on balance the system of trade cum price-related interventions strongly discriminated against agriculture. The most thorough study to date suggests that the negative transfers due to direct price interventions were a little more than offset by the nonprice transfers to the sector (credit subsidy and public sector expenditures on the sector), but that the indirect price effect through the overvaluation of the exchange rate accounted for a substantial net out-transfer of 12 percent of sectoral value added over the period 1965–83 (García and Montes 1989, 154). This can be thought of as an upper-limit estimate; the benchmark exchange rate used is the one that would put international payments in balance with no trade barriers and with a zero net capital inflow. Also, the estimated level of protection in 1969 in the study is higher than that reported by others and implies a high estimated overvaluation of the exchange rate. If any net protection of manufacturing were appropriate, then the resource transfer would be smaller. Thus, any attempt to judge whether the incentive system gives on balance too little or too much to Colombian agriculture cannot be conclusive because (a) there is a serious lack of empirical information with respect to the sectoral incidence of taxes and public expenditures, and (b) it is not clear whether a significant level of protection is defensible for some economic activities. Since the level of protection does appear to have been modest in Colombia, and since the growth rate of the sector was creditable over most of the postwar period, it is plausible to conclude that Colombia does not fall among those developing countries in which an antiagriculture bias has been one of the big mistakes of economic policymaking.

The important question that remains, however, is how successful policy has been in confronting the income fluctuations accompanying the volatile price behavior of Colombia's agricultural exports.

Price Trends over Time

Between 1950 and the late 1970s, there was no discernible trend in the relative price of agricultural value added (see table 10.10); even the fluctuations around the average appear to have been rather muted. (Though some alternative estimates suggest more volatility, e.g., García 1985, 75). But over 1977–88 the relative price of value added fell by nearly 30 percent, leaving it low in relation to the postwar norm.[7] Whereas in earlier times the value-added prices of coffee and noncoffee products had now and then moved in different directions, at this

---

7. When the focus is on relative product price (García and Montes, 1988, 28), this result is less clear since the mid-1970s prices (in relation to that of value added in the rest of the economy) were somewhat above the longer-run average. In principle, the former figures are more relevant to the question of the relative profitability of agricultural activities.

TABLE 10.10 Relative price of coffee and noncoffee agriculture, 1950–1976 (1975 = 100)

Year	Coffee	Noncoffee Crops	All Crops	Livestock	All Agriculture
		Price in Relation to Value Added in Nonagriculture			
1950	101.2	97.6	98.5ᵃ	57.7	98.4
1951	116.1	89.1	93.1	58.9	100.5
1952	121.9	76.1	85.6	87.5	100.2
1953	123.8	82.0	89.1	108.8	104.3
1954	157.0	92.4	105.8	100.9	117.3
1955	133.3	83.4	93.2	85.3	108.8
1956	167.0	88.7	105.9	75.0	115.3
1957	158.0	90.6	104.5	69.9	114.0
1958	133.0	84.1	93.0	78.0	105.2
1959	98.3	84.5	85.7	108.7	102.0
1960	98.8	80.7	82.6	106.6	101.6
1961	96.0	87.1	88.2	91.3	100.0
1962	86.8	79.4	80.0	81.1	94.9
1963	87.1	88.6	88.3	61.9	94.7
1964	97.3	108.1	105.9	73.8	106.0
1965	88.3	94.6	93.6	93.5	101.6
1966	89.9	93.2	93.4	115.4	100.9
1967	85.4	86.6	86.8	115.2	100.1
1968	86.3	84.7	86.0	93.2	98.5
1969	88.5	82.0	83.8	87.2	98.2
1970	105.7	77.3	81.6	73.7	97.4
1971	92.8	79.9	83.8	81.3	96.0
1972	99.7	88.0	88.4	77.1	99.1
1973	109.2	92.9	96.0	86.2	105.2
1974	100.6	91.6	93.3	94.5	106.9
1975	100.0	100.0	100.0	100.0	100.0
1976	165.7	90.3	104.1	94.9	100.5

sources: The price deflators for agriculture and nonagriculture are calculated from the national accounts, as reported in Banco de la República, various publications covering the period 1950–70, and DANE (1985a). Complemented by figures for recent years presented in the *Revista del Banco de la República*. The producer price indices, covering the period 1950–76, for the product categories are from Kalmanovitz (1978, 337). Their original source, not cited with the table, was presumably the tables underlying the national accounts.
note: The national accounts figures on sectoral output used to calculate the sectoral price index for value added in nonagriculture refer to value added at price to the purchaser.
ᵃ As originally calculated from the source, this figure was 89.4, making it inconsistent with the other two, since the value for "all crops" must lie between those for its only two components. This figure was therefore adjusted to the value shown.

time they both fell, in response to the general decline in agricultural prices at the international level.

The recent decline in the relative price is, of course, due at least in part to trends in international prices. As noted above, agricultural tradables have been increasingly protected since the mid-1970s; this trend would be expected to partly offset the international price trends. Between the mid-1970s, when domestic prices were farthest below their international counterparts, and the mid-1980s, the average domestic/international price ratio for 11 products rose from 0.69 (for 1972–76) to 107.6 (1985–87) (MEDSA 1990, 280). The greatest price decline since the mid-1970s (and even more so since the early part of that decade) appears to have been suffered by the nontradables—it amounted to almost 30 percent between 1970–72 and 1982/83 (see García and Montes 1988, table 20). The two most favored groups over that period were the noncoffee exportables, with a decline of just 10 percent, and the importables, with an increase of 4 percent. For this recent period, at least, if government price policy did not adequately support agriculture, this failure related mainly to the nontradables, which are not controlled by the same instruments as tradables.

Agricultural exports were discouraged in the late 1970s and early 1980s by exchange rate movements. The real effective exchange rate was allowed to appreciate considerably at that time, after being held roughly constant for about a decade after the change in exchange rate regime in 1967. By 1981 it was about a quarter below the 1975 level, according to one estimate (García and Montes 1988, 23). As a result, the growth rate of the leading agricultural exports declined markedly in the 1980s. Only flowers continued to grow fast (at 7 percent), but the increase was much less than during the 1970s.

Policymakers in Colombia have had chronic problems managing the exchange rate in the face of the great fluctuations in the country's international terms of trade (related mainly to fluctuations in the price of coffee). Whenever prices have been atypically high or low, the tendency has been to shift too many resources into the production of coffee (in the upswing) or of nontradables (in the downswing), a pattern of resource allocation that is inappropriate for the longer run. Furthermore, when incomes were high, absorption habits developed that could not be sustained, but that would only be given up through inefficient readjustment to the once again lower absorption potential of the economy. The taxation designed to sterilize part of the income boom tended to be imposed mainly on the boom sector, although the government has varied the tax to suit its macroeconomic purposes, subject to the outcome of the political push and pull between the government and the powerful and well-organized Coffee Growers Federation. In any case, government intervention in the sector has steadily increased since 1950.[8] During the coffee price boom of the mid-1950s, the coffee tax rate was still low, at about 10 percent (see table 10.11), and the government had less flexibility in dealing with the crisis on the downside of the cycle because of the fixed exchange rate system. Colombia's coffee tax policy cannot perhaps be greatly faulted for trends since the early

8. A considerable share of the "tax" is returned to the coffee sector via the Federacion de Cafeteros. From the point of view of macroeconomic sterilization, the important thing is that it not be returned to the expenditure stream while the boom is still in progress.

TABLE 10.11 Indicators of taxes and subsidies on traded goods, 1910–1914 to 1985–1987 (percent)

Period	Tax on Coffee Exports[a]	Subsidy for Nontraditional Exports	Average Tariff Rate	Proportion of Imports under the Prior Licensing Regime	Proportion of Import Licenses Rejected	Prior Import Deposits as a Percent of Imports
1910–14			47.4			
1915–19			30.3			
1920–24			24.5			
1925–29			30.6			
1930–34	2.6[b]		41.5			
1935–39	4.3		22.5			
1940–44	13.6		16.8			
1945–49	0.0	44.6[c]	11.1			
1950–54	7.1	32.5	18.3	21.0		4.8
1955–59	12.2	19.2	12.0	29.5		16.2
1960–64	24.7	29.3	14.2	50.4	15.5[d]	21.2
1965–69	33.3	28.8	16.0	78.1	32.3	24.9
1970–74	32.2	28.9	14.3	70.0	8.8	13.7
1975–79	44.9	14.1	13.5	57.8	1.1[e]	5.7
1980–84	33.1	18.9	15.0	55.9	10.4	6.4
1985–87	41.2		16.7	65.4	25.7	10.2

SOURCE: Ocampo (1990), table 6.
[a] Ad valorem tax, differential exchange rate, and retention quota.
[b] 1932–34.
[c] 1948–49.
[d] 1959–63.
[e] 1979.

1960s, when the tax rate was pushed beyond the 20 percent level. It cushioned the effects of the sharp price boom of the mid-1970s (when the rate reached 45 percent), although by itself it was not adequate to the task. The country engaged in massive foreign borrowing to build up infrastructure just when foreign earnings needed to be sterilized, and this decision certainly reduced its ability to stabilize the economy.

Linkages and Voluntary Transfers

The contribution of agricultural development to industrialization and economic development in Colombia can best be assessed by examining the channels through which agricultural development occurred and the subsequent direct and indirect effects. The onset of modern industrialization was directly related to the export success of coffee and other primary products. That first wave of modern industrialization had a regional focus owing to the distribution of coffee production and other agricultural activates. And it may be hypothe-sized, though it is hard to substantiate, that the fact that Colombia's income distribution was less inegalitarian than Brazil's may reflect in part the less skewed distribution of coffee land in Colombia.

Along with supplying the great bulk of the foreign exchange used to fuel the processes of industrialization and modernization, agriculture has met the need for foodstuffs at reasonable prices. The other contributions of agriculture to overall growth are harder to pin down quantitatively, especially in the case of demand linkages with nonagricultural activities in the rural areas and smaller urban centers. Evidence from the coffee zones during the expansion of coffee exports points to important positive interactions or linkages. The ties between industry and agriculture in Colombia have been fairly strong, however; agro-industry is important and may become more so if the economy shifts toward a more outward-oriented focus. And the past decade or so seems to have wit-nessed a considerable increase in rural nonagricultural employment.

Rural Manufacturing and Development: The Longer Run

Like most developing countries, Colombia once had a large rural manu-facturing sector with important linkages to agriculture; in 1870, for example, the rural manufacturing labor force was about five times larger than the urban one (Berry 1987b, 298). From about 1920 to the 1960s, such employment declined in absolute as well as relative terms, leaving the impression that rural manufacturing did not in the end contribute directly or significantly to the evolution of a modern manufacturing sector, as it had in many European coun-tries and some newly industrializing economies like Taiwan.[9]

In view of the isolation between regions, for which Colombia before the twentieth century was justly famous, a substantial amount of manufacturing activity directed to local consumption was to be expected in rural areas and small towns. But there was also considerable regional specialization in certain traditional items and a fair amount of interregional trade. One center of such activity was the municipality of Socorro in the department of Santander, which in the eighteenth century was known for its cotton textiles (Ospina 1955, 69). It was a relatively prosperous region in which smallholders dominated agricul-ture, and textile production, based on the part-time employment of farmers and their families, was symbiotic with agricultural activities. Small-scale rural manufacturing was also common around Pasto in the south of the country, another region of mainly small farms (Berry 1987b, 299).

Although some regions have retained their manufacturing specialization up to or near the present (as in the case of Pasto, which, however, is one of the poorest regions in Colombia), most of these rural centers of activity came under

9. An important interpretation of the European experience with rural manufacturing goes under the term "proto-industrialization" (see especially Mendels 1972, 241–61).

pressure from imports and domestic factory production and lost ground over the course of the present century, or in some cases earlier. The regions that were hotbeds of textile production in these earlier stages of development did not become the centers of the industry in its twentieth-century manifestation, nor did they seem to supply many of the inputs (human skills or capital) for the modern sector. The twentieth-century development of modern textile production in Medellin appears to be related to the accumulation of capital from other industries (mining, and especially coffee and the import-export trade that flourished as the coffee era began), the availability of entrepreneurial skills (which, like capital, were based on earlier experience in other activities), and perhaps the city's status as the major importer of textiles, which meant that the existing demand was more clearly apparent there than in most of the other regions of the country (Berry 1987b, 311). Artisans and small-scale producers apparently did not generate much of the capital ultimately used in the early growth of modern manufacturing or many of the risk-taking enterprises. One hypothesis in the latter regard is that the Colombian class system, with its strongly demeaning attitude toward manual labor, posed a special obstacle to such "graduation." But there are other plausible explanations as well.

Symbiosis around the Coffee Sector

Although rural industry or artisanry could not be called the forerunner of modern manufacturing, it did play a supportive role in the twentieth-century expansion of coffee exports; some activities were a by-product of the growth of exports, and others expanded as a result of the income increases associated with export-led growth.

In the western part of the country there was a striking symbiosis between the burgeoning coffee sector, transportation improvements, and local small-scale industry. Coffee had become an important export before the end of the nineteenth century, with production concentrated in the semifeudal coffee *haciendas* of the eastern region. But coffee production suffered a severe crisis at the turn of the century as a result of civil war and the simultaneous collapse of the international price of coffee. After the return to peace and subsequent price recovery, the coffee supply showed little improvement, however, because of the inefficient organization of the labor force under the existing labor regime (Ocampo 1991, 220). Agrarian unrest, which has plagued the industry right up to the present, was another impediment to production in this region. The boom came, rather, in the western departments of Antioquia, Caldas, Valle, and Tolima, where output grew by 10 percent per year between 1900 and 1932, by which time about 60 percent of Colombia's coffee was coming from small- and medium-size coffee plantings of 12 hectares or less (Machado 1977). Coffee thus brought the first real stability to what had formerly been mainly slash-and-burn agriculture; it was profitable even under the depressed prices of the first decade of the century. But, as Ocampo (1991, 221) puts it, "The consolidation of coffee as the dominant staple of Colombia could not have been possible without the development of a series of subsidiary activities that generated the external economies necessary to make the expansion self-sustaining." The sector expanded quickly into a large component of the economy that warranted an extensive commercialization network; coffee growth interacted both with the modernization of the transportation infrastructure and such manufacturing activities as jute bags, pulping machines, and other coffee-related machinery and inputs. The small-scale coffee farm had demonstrated its ability to compete, and it has remained important ever since.

Infrastructure

The extremely uneven topography of highland Colombia has continued to thwart efforts to integrate rural regions and hinterlands with population centers. Most students of Colombian economic history are aware that cost-lowering transportation investments have played an important role in the periods of economic progress. Railroad investment, for example, was instrumental in the expansion of coffee and the takeoff of the economy beginning in the late nineteenth century (McGreevey 1971, chap. 10). In the past 60 years or so, the road network has been the key to lowering the costs of shipment. It has grown from a tiny system in 1930 to one with more than 100,000 kilometers of roads, 10,000 of which are paved (table 10.12). The 1950s saw a burst of investment in highways in an effort to link the principal cities with each other and with the ports. By 1960, about 31,000 kilometers were listed under the national or departmental authorities (Ministerio de Obras Publicas 1962, I-22); by 1986, these two levels were responsible for about 79,000 kilometers. The inadequate supply and low quality of the feeder roads has long been a concern. By the 1970s, paved national roads were increasing at the rate of about 10 percent per year, as compared with only about 2 percent for all national roads.

More recently, greater attention has been directed to the serious problem of maintenance, and it appears that the feeder road system has been substantially extended. The World Bank and other international agencies have contributed to the financing of the feeder roads, partly in the context of integrated rural development projects. Such improvements have no doubt played a role in the growth of the *campesino* sector.

Current Demand Linkages and Rural Nonagricultural Growth

The more easily measurable linkages between agriculture and manufacturing in Colombia are found in modern agroindustrial operations. This important industry is for the most part located in the larger urban centers. Rural nonagricultural employment has grown significantly in recent years, from about 15–19 percent of the rural labor force in the 1950s and 1960s to close to 30 percent in the late 1980s (table 10.13), but it is not known whether or in what

TABLE 10.12 Road network, by level of government responsible, selected years

Year	National			Total	Departmental			Community	All	
	Total	Paved	Other		Paved	Other	Total	Total	Paved	Other
1986	104,106	9,617	16,316	25,933	636	52,488	53,124	25,049	10,253	93,853
1978				21,000					7,780	
1960	30,728			15,877			14,851			

SOURCES: The 1986 data are from Departamento Nacional de Planeación (1987, 442). Those for 1978 were obtained from the Ministerio de Obras Públicas, and those for 1960 are from Ministerio de Obras Públicas (1962, 1–22).

NOTE: The 1960 figures may be incomplete in relation to those for 1986, because of only partial reporting of the local roads. For 1978, the figure obtained is about 51,000 kilometers for the total size of the network, but again it seems probable that the figure understates the facts. This is partly a matter of definition, and none of the sources is explicit about the definitions used in the data collection.

TABLE 10.13 Evolution of rural nonagricultural employment, selected years

| | Percentage Distribution of Employment or Population | | | | |
Year	Agriculture	Manufacturing	Construction	Commerce	Transportation
1951 (population)[a]	81.1	3.53	1.15	1.40	0.89
1971 (employment)	74.5	8.80	2.17	5.07	1.49
1988 (employment)	71.3	6.09	1.76	8.29	2.12

SOURCES: The 1951 data are from the population census of that year, DANE (1959, 162–65). The 1971 figures are the average from three household surveys taken that year and reported in DANE (1976, 90, 256, and 408). Those for 1988 come from MEDSA (1990): see p. 388, for an estimate of the total share of nonagriculture methodologically comparable to those for the earlier years, and p. 168 for the distribution of nonagricultural employment by sector.
[a]Population by sector on which economically dependent.

sense, this trend has been a response to the growth of agricultural incomes.[10] Some clues may be provided by the sectoral distribution of the nonagricultural labor force. Commerce and services clearly dominate, accounting for 23 percent of rural employment and nearly 60 percent of the nonagricultural component of that employment in the late 1980s, while manufacturing activities account for 7 percent of rural employment (table 10.13). Although nonagricultural activities are naturally less prevalent among the dispersed rural population, even there they accounted for more than 20 percent of employment (as defined by principal occupation). More than 14 percent of employed persons had more than one job, and 18 percent of those were in the dispersed population. Of all persons engaged in agriculture (either as a principal or a secondary activity), about 7 percent were also engaged in a nonagricultural activity; the comparable ratio for families was much higher, at about 20 percent. Although no direct evidence is yet available on this point, it seems likely that the apparently rapid increase in rural nonagricultural employment since 1970 has reflected a variety of linkages with agriculture, both on the demand side and the factor supply side.

Modern Agroindustry

Comparative data suggest that agroindustry has been relatively more important in manufacturing in Colombia than in most of the other middle-level developing countries of Latin America. A little less than half of manufacturing value added (and about 10 percent of GDP) corresponds to agroindustry, which broadly includes textiles (except knitwear), leather and its products, and wood

10. This hypothesis is difficult to explore because there are few data on rural consumption and absorption patterns. The only sample-based data on "rural" consumption of which I am aware pertain to the rural parts of seven mainly urban municipalities (DANE 1972, 175), but the product categories are too broad to be useful and the respondents were not typical of rural Colombia.

TABLE 10.14 Share of agroindustry in manufacturing value added, and in GDP, 1975

Agroindustry	Share of Value Added in Agriculture (%)	Share of GDP (%)
Branch food processing	36.83	8.55
Coffee processing	13.62	
Meats	3.42	
Cereal processing	5.05	
Milk products	1.63	
Sugar	2.67	
Beer	4.02	
Wine	0.14	
Malt	0.77	
Processed tobacco	2.88	
Oils, margarines, and lards		1.21
Fruits and vegetables	0.17	
Candy	0.61	
Miscellaneous food products		0.63
Other agroindustry	10.13	2.35
Textiles, except knitwear	5.66	
Cordage	0.90	
Leather and products	0.66	
Treated wood	0.68	
Pulp	0.78	
Paper and cardboard	1.45	
All agroindustry	46.96	10.91

SOURCE: MEDSA (1990), cuadro 7.9.

and its products (table 10.14); about 37 percent of manufacturing added corresponds to the food industries. By far the most important food-related industry is the processing of coffee, which in 1975 accounted for 13.6 percent of manufacturing value added. Other significant categories were cereal processing, textile production, beer manufacture, meat processing, and sugar refining. The individual activities are numerous and varied, and range from relatively simple to complicated. Agroindustry tends to have a high level of backward linkages in comparison with other branches of manufacturing, but a low level of forward linkages. The causal links between industrialization and agricultural development have perhaps been most evident in the impact of the beer industry on the production of barley, of textiles on cotton, sugar refining and panela production on sugarcane, and animal concentrates and oils on a variety of inputs used in their manufacture (MEDSA 1990, 530).

Between 1965 and 1975, when manufacturing was growing at an annual average of 7.2 percent, the food-related sector grew at a somewhat slower but still respectable pace of 5 percent. In 1975–86, manufacturing grew at just 2.6

percent, while the food-related activities grew at 4 percent, to provide some degree of stabilizing impact (MEDSA 1990, 518). During the heart of the crisis (i.e., 1982–84), however, the food sector's share of total value added in manufacturing was essentially unchanged (MEDSA 1990, 514).

Several factors contributed to the considerable growth of agroindustry during the period 1965–86. Although the evolution of coffee processing was uneven, and its share of manufacturing value added fell rapidly from 1968 to 1977, it then recovered to contribute significantly to the growth of the next decade. Rising per capita incomes and urbanization led to a robust demand for processed foods. The production of food concentrates and oils and fats accelerated from the 1970s on, and sugar exports led this sector to double its share of manufacturing output over the twenty-year period.

With the exception of coffee, sugar, and, in much lesser degree, textiles, exports have not been a major source of demand for the agroindustry sector; overall, they have in recent decades accounted for not much more than 15 percent of the total, compared with about 55 percent for domestic consumer demand and a little less than 20 percent for intermediate goods (MEDSA 1990, 521). During its slow growth phase in the 1980s, the sector depended almost exclusively on the domestic market for increases in demand. Since the income elasticity of demand for food products is typically low, this implies a modest growth rate of output at best.[11] Some products, however, most of them conserved foods, have faced buoyant demands. In a number of cases unexpected growth may have been due to considerable income growth over the past decade or so among the poorer groups whose income elasticity for the items is relatively high.

To the extent that agroindustry locates near the regions in which its agricultural inputs are produced, it has the potential to spread industry to smaller urban centers. In the Colombian case, to judge from the statistics on manufacturing, this has not been a frequent outcome; rather, manufacturing has concentrated in the large centers of consumption and of industrial production in general (though the regional distribution of the small manufacturers is less concentrated than that of the large ones). In 1983 the three largest metropolitan areas—around the cities of Bogota, Medellin, and Cali—accounted for nearly 64 percent of the total (see DANE 1985b, 49, 373). The 1987 figures for the concentration of value added in agroindustry indicate almost exactly the same pattern (MEDSA 1990, 545). Agricultural dynamism *was* the major source of the extraordinary population growth of the city of Cali in the first half of this century, which averaged about 8 percent per year. The region has excellent

11. According to a recent cross-sectional household survey, the income elasticity of demand for food, drinks, and tobacco taken together is 0.59 (see Sociedad de Agricultores de Colombia 1988, 125). Output growth rates for some of the categories suggest that the cross-sectional estimates are too low, although for agroindustry as a whole they tend to confirm that the elasticity is less than 1 (MEDSA 1990, cuadros 7.17, 7.18).

natural resources, and its opportunities to trade with other parts of the country and the rest of the world were greatly expanded when the Cali-Buenaventura road was opened. Cali readily acquired a specialization in the agroindustrial branches of manufacturing. And although the smaller urban centers of the region did certainly share in the spinoffs from agricultural growth, Cali was the main beneficiary.

Some agroindustrial activities *are* located close to the raw materials, as with milk products (high share in Cundinamarca), milling (Huila), animal feeds (Cundinamarca), and a few others. Such cases do not, however, appear to have been frequent or strong enough to outweigh the powerful centripetal forces toward concentration in the few largest cities. This concentration may have limited the positive externalities between industrial development and agriculture to rural areas near the larger urban centers, where most of the recent increase in rural nonagricultural employment may be located. A hypothesis suggested by the Colombian experience is that the total benefits from agriculture-industry linkages are smaller, manifest themselves later, and are less dispersed regionally in countries with an unequal distribution of land and of income than in countries where those distributions are more or less equal.

Transfer of Savings

There is some evidence to suggest that, for given nominal income levels, savings tend to be higher out of agricultural than nonagricultural income and also higher in rural than in urban areas. Part of those savings are, of course, invested in agriculture, but in view of the usually modest investment rate of the sector and the considerable flow of savings from the rest of the economy into agriculture (especially since the acceleration of modernization in recent decades), it is evident that a significant gross flow moves to other sectors. Tentative estimates for the 1950s and 1960s suggest that the rate of savings out of agricultural income lay in the range of 6–8 percent, that there was a private gross transfer of 6–12 percent of agricultural income to finance investment in the rest of the economy, and that the gross inflow of credit and investment out of nonagricultural income was about 5–8 percent, leaving a net private outflow of 1–4 percent (Berry 1974b, I-16).

Apparently a defective capital market seriously impedes the effective transfer of savings out of agriculture, or from one subsector to another, in many countries. While Colombia's capital market is far from perfect, it probably outperforms those of many developing countries. Colombia has had the advantage of being a low-inflation country, at least by the standards of Latin America; until the 1970s, the average rate of inflation was in the neighborhood of 10 percent per year, although since that time it has been closer to 25 percent. The Caja Agraria, the public agrarian bank, has many branches around the country, and they probably facilitated the savings process even though the interest they paid was traditionally low. It is also possible that the intersectoral transfer of resources has been facilitated by the concentration of land and of agricultural income. A correlate of this concentration is that a significant share of agricultural income accrues to people who reside in urban areas and are also engaged in nonagricultural activities. The "Intraportfolio" transfer of resources between sectors has long been a standard part of the modus operandi of the Colombian economy: it dates back to times when coffee incomes financed the expansion of commerce and later of industry (textiles and other industries made Medellin the manufacturing center of the country) (Berry 1974b, chap. 4). This intraportfolio transfer goes in both directions, as the strong flow from non-agriculture to agriculture in recent years attests. A considerable amount of new money has been flowing into the sector from the urban professional and business classes, some of them having family backgrounds in agriculture. Most recently there has been a large flow of narcodollars into agriculture, especially into the cattle sector. A considerable movement of resources may also be taking place between the sectors of the smaller-scale economy as well. The recent rather marked expansion of rural nonagricultural activity probably indicates an increase in such flows; rising incomes in the smallholder sector would facilitate them.

Nonagricultural Growth

In the transition from Colombia's dependence on import substitution to a more outward-looking policy, 1967 stands out as a particularly important year. During 1950–67, while agriculture grew at just over 3 percent per year, manufacturing averaged 6 percent, the service sector 5.3 percent, and GDP (at factor cost) also 5.3 percent (table 10.15). Over the period 1967–80, agriculture registered an impressive average growth of 4.3 percent, while two quite different patterns emerged in the nonagricultural sector. During the heart of the

TABLE 10.15 Sectoral output growth rates, 1950–1986, by subperiods

Period	Agriculture	Industry	Manufacturing	Services[a]	GDP[b]
1950–60	3.06	6.24	6.60	5.07	4.64
1960–67	3.24	5.25	5.49	5.50	4.59
1967–74	4.42	7.45	8.26	7.04	6.62
1974–80	4.53	3.63	4.01	5.69	4.91
1980–86	2.46	3.84	2.30	2.02	2.63
1950–80	3.71	5.80	6.20	5.75	5.13

SOURCE: For 1950–80, directly from the national accounts of Colombia. For 1980–86, World Bank (1987).
[a]Including public utilities.
[b]At market prices.

postreform boom (1967–74) the economy grew at 6.6 percent, manufacturing at 8.3 percent, and services at 7.0 percent. Growth was fast and well balanced among the sectors. The real exchange rate rose (i.e., devalued) by about 20 percent during the first four years of the period and remained well above its 1967 level until 1977, while the relative price of exports (in relation to the implicit price of the gross value of nonagricultural production) rose by 44 percent and the terms of trade by 62 percent (World Bank 1987, 102). In contrast, the ratio of exports to GDP in constant 1980 prices fell from 18.4 percent in 1967 to 16.6 percent in 1974, while the current price share rose from 12.7 percent to 16.9 percent. If the production of tradables contributed significantly to the growth of this period, it was not reflected in an increase in the share of exports.

In the second subperiod of fast agricultural growth, from 1974 to 1980, the rest of the economy did less well, especially manufacturing, whose growth slumped to 2.8 percent, before ceasing entirely in the early 1980s. The economy as a whole maintained an acceptable average of 4.3 percent over this period only because the service sector kept growing at more than 5 percent. More telling was the decline of the goods-producing sectors, which presaged the recession of the early 1980s. This period of "Dutch disease" saw Colombia's policymakers wrestle unsuccessfully with the problems caused by a sharp upturn in the price of coffee and the upward pressures this created for the exchange rate, as discussed above. The turnaround between 1967–74 and 1974–80 was particularly dramatic in the manufacturing sector. In the first subperiod, the productivity and the incomes of persons engaged there rose rapidly, as output grew at more than 8 percent per year. In the next six years output grew at 4 percent, but then stagnated, while labor productivity declined; this, coupled with a decrease in the relative price of coffee, led to a sharp decline in the income generated per worker.

Although, as noted, the overall export quantum performance after 1967 was not impressive, manufacturing exports did make something of a breakthrough (see table 10.1), which led many to believe that Colombia was about to become a major exporter of such goods and thereby gain access to a more reliable source of foreign exchange revenues. As the performance of manufacturing faded, analysts debated the maladies of the sector and the degree to which they were the result of unwise macroeconomic policy.

Trends in Poverty, Income Distribution, and the Rural Standard of Living

With Gini coefficients of 0.5 or higher, Colombia has ranked among the more inegalitarian of the developing countries. Inequality has certainly long been evident in the distribution of land. An additional concern in recent years has been the inequality in the distribution of education and the lack of coherent and strong public sector intervention in the economic system to alleviate poverty and inequality (e.g., by a satisfactory system of health care, access to good-quality primary education, and housing). Considerable improvement has occurred over time, however.

It seems likely that the degree of income inequality increased between the 1940s and the 1960s, as urbanization proceeded apace but real wages rose little. The picture is unclear for the decade or so before the mid-1970s. Since that time a significant decrease in inequality may have taken place. If so, one reason may be a fall in the rate of return to education, whose unequal distribution has contributed greatly to the inequality of labor income. Levels of productivity in the *campesino* sector and the agricultural wage rate are on the rise, and rural dwellers now have greater access to nonagricultural incomes.

A variety of studies have pointed to a declining level of inequality in the urban areas over the late 1970s, but show no clear trend for the 1980s. Rural inequality also seems to have declined between 1971 and 1978: the Gini coefficient fell from 0.53 to 0.48 (Londoño 1989b).

Increases in rural income are likely to be based on increases in the value of agricultural output, which reflect trends both in output and in prices. Between 1950 and 1980 the average productivity of persons employed in agriculture rose nearly 3 percent per year (table 10.16), which is considerably faster than the rates in either manufacturing or services, and also faster than the average for the economy as a whole, even though that figure is affected positively by the transfer of employment from the low-productivity sector (agriculture) to the higher-productivity ones. As of 1980, labor productivity in agriculture was 70 percent of that in the rest of the economy (values expressed in 1975 prices), up from 66 percent in 1950. More striking, between 1950 and 1980 it increased from 54 to 69 percent of the level in manufacturing and from 44 to 71 percent of the level in services.

The extent to which increases in a sector's relative labor productivity show up in increases in the relative income of its workers depends in part on changes in the relative prices among sectors and on changes in the share of sectoral incomes accruing to owners of capital who do not work in the same sector (or perhaps in any sector at all). On the first count, agriculture fared less well, as reflected in an average income growth of 1.7 percent per year compared with the 2.9 percent increase in productivity.[12] Over the first two subperiods distinguished, the terms of trade for agriculture improved; income growth was especially rapid over the boom period 1967–74. Since then, however, income per worker in the sector has barely increased, since productivity gains having been offset by price declines.

12. When agricultural income is deflated by the price index of private consumption or by the national cost of living index corresponding to blue-collar workers, the trend in purchasing power is more positive, in the latter case reaching about 2 percent per year.

TABLE 10.16 Evolution of labor productivity and average income per worker, by broad economic sectors, 1950–1986 and subperiods

Period	Labor Productivity			
	Economy	Agriculture	Manufacturing	Services
Ratio of 1967 to 1950	1.474	1.259	1.760	1.311
AGR	2.31	1.35	3.38	1.61
Ratio of 1974 to 1967	1.256	1.218	1.319	1.092
AGR	3.31	2.86	4.04	1.27
Ratio of 1980 to 1974	1.067	1.257	0.828	1.012
AGR	1.09	3.88	−3.06	0.20
Ratio of 1986 to 1980	1.017	1.105	1.077	0.935
AGR	0.28	1.68	1.25	−1.12
Ratio of 1980 to 1950	1.975	1.928	1.922	1.450
AGR	2.60	2.86	2.02	1.25

SOURCES AND METHODOLOGY: Sectoral growth figures are from the national accounts for 1950–1980 and from World Bank (1987) for 1980–1986. Sectoral weights are based on 1975 prices; this was the base year for the Colombian national accounts for many years from 1970. Growth rates over 1950–67, however, being based on the earlier national accounts series, have the base year 1958. The labor force figures are based on a piecing together of data from Reyes (1987, 84–85), and Berry (1978, 223–34). At the sectoral level, there are likely to be considerable inaccuracies, as suggested especially by the erratic movements in labor productivity in manufacturing in the last two subperiods distinguished. The total figures may also be somewhat off the mark, but the full period growth rates should be fairly accurate. Unfortunately, neither of the two population censuses since 1964 has provided good information on the employment structure of the economy.

The figures on average income per worker are based on the figures for labor productivity, adjusted for changes in the relative price of value added by sector over the periods in question. Price figures are taken from the national accounts over 1950–80 and from World Bank (1987) for 1980–86. These figures do not quite represent the trends in real purchasing power per worker, since they do not take into account the international terms of trade. They do refer to changes in purchasing power if all of the purchasing was done domestically.

NOTE: AGR is average growth rate.

The small farm sector has had considerable success in raising output and productivity, especially since some time in the 1970s. Its performance has clearly helped push up some of the incomes at the lower end of the rural distribution. In addition, the distribution of land appears to have improved, perhaps significantly, between the agricultural census of 1960 and the agricultural sample taken in 1988; the share of land in the top 10 percent of farms fell from about 82 percent to 68 percent and that in the bottom 50 percent rose from about 2.5 percent to about 4 percent.[13] Moreover, the frequency of tenancy fell sharply, both on the smaller farms and in general; for farms of less than 10 hectares, for example, the share owned by the operator rose from 60 percent

13. The results of the recent survey have yet to be analyzed carefully, however.

to about 81 percent. For all farm sizes together, the share cultivated by the owner rose from about 75 percent in 1960 to about 88 percent in 1988, while the shares corresponding to rental and untitled land fell sharply, from 8 to less than 3 percent of the total area for the former and from about 12 to 6 percent for the latter. In the rental category, sharecropping also declined.

Factors that probably contributed to the decrease in the concentration of landholding include the process of colonization and the division of large land-holdings through inheritance. Titling of public lands was an important source of new farms of 50 hectares or less (MEDSA 1990, 352–53). As a result of these various changes, farm size has begun to increase at the lower end of the size scale, increasing the share of families who are more or less secure "farmers" rather than that of the precarious *campesinos*. The trend over the 1980s may differ from that of the longer period, however, since drug dealers are known to have accumulated large tracts of land in some parts of the country.

The period 1975–88 did see a substantial fall in the relative price of the products of the *campesino* economy as a whole, especially for those not inten-sive in inputs. (The appreciation of the peso lowered the price of purchased inputs.) This decline appears to have offset most of the increase in productivity then occurring. The market for food products of the *campesino* economy is essentially domestic and hence dependent on an increasing demand within the national economy; international trade is important only in the case of wheat and cacao. During the period 1960–75, the 3 percent growth rate in food production was insufficient to prevent a price increase of just over 3 percent per year. But with demand growing more slowly from the late 1970s on, prices subsequently trended downward.

The main direct indicator of income trends for the bulk of the agricultural labor force is the daily wage rate; it tells a modestly positive story, with the increase for the entire study period probably lying between 49 percent (1.3 percent per year) and 83 percent (2.0 percent per year).[14] A best guess might be 1.5 percent, which is virtually identical to the estimate of the average increase in income generated per worker in the sector. The similarity between the two figures suggests that income gains were shared in about the same proportions between workers and other factor owners. There are some intriguing hints that the distribution of wage income may have improved over the latter part of the period (see Reyes 1987, 87). Household survey data suggest much greater wage increases (about 50 percent between 1978 and 1988) than do the agricultural

14. Between 1949–51 and 1969 wages grew about 14 percent in total (Berry 1974a, 298–99). After 1976, when a new wage series was initiated, they increased about 25 percent in the cooler regions and 14 percent in the warmer ones. The sharp increase was clearly associated with the coffee boom and has been interpreted in some quarters as a signal of the end of Colombia's labor surplus phase. The economic slowdown of the 1980s, however, saw real wages slip back again, in agriculture at least, and perhaps in some other sectors, though this is not clear. For further discus-sion on this subject, see Urrutia (1985, 12–13) and Berry (1978, 10–11).

daily wage series, perhaps because of an increase in the number of days worked and/or an increase in the share of income from nonagriculture; the former, while preliminary, do add to the presumption of a considerable increase in the wage income of persons involved in agriculture (for further details, see Londoño 1989b, MEDSA 1990, cuadro 3.39). One of the striking phenomena of the intercensal period 1973–85 was the sharp increase in the female participation rate in rural areas (from 13.7 percent to 32.4 percent). Presumably this increase mainly reflected an increase in the number of female workers hired. This phenomenon has yet to be studied in detail, but may have played an important role in the increases in family incomes over this period.

Useful indicators of rural living standards include data on housing and related services, which show a fairly continuous improvement since the early 1950s (and before). The share of occupied family dwellings with electricity rose from 5.6 percent in 1964 to 13–15 percent in 1973 (there is some discrepancy among sources) before jumping to 41 percent in 1985 (table 10.17). Over the same interval, the urban access to this service, which as in rural areas had not risen significantly if at all during 1951–64, climbed from about two-thirds to about 95 percent. Running water, available in only 7 percent of rural dwellings in 1964, was found in more than a quarter by 1973; apparently its frequency did not rise between that time and 1985 (although the 1973 figure may be upward biased). The presence of an earthen floor, which generally implies the lack of economic resources for something better, fell from 52 percent in 1973 to 41 percent in 1985, suggesting gains for the middle-income group of rural families. For the bottom few deciles, however, not much can be deduced from these housing-related data. The 1985 rural figures were in no instance as high as those for urban areas in 1938 in any of the dimensions considered here, but there is no denying the rather rapid advance that has been taking place in the rural areas.

The share of the rural population of 10 years and up that is illiterate fell from 41 percent in 1964 to 23 percent in 1985; the corresponding figures for the age cohorts just passing through their schooling period fell from more than 30 percent to not much more than 10 percent. By the latter year the share of youth (proxied by the 18–24 age group) with some secondary schooling had reached 21.5 percent, up from probably no more than 3 percent in 1964.[15] Whether this sharp increase in the number of people with some secondary (only a minority had completed it) played a role in the broadly based productivity growth discussed above is a matter warranting closer attention.

Despite a number of positive indications with respect to rural incomes, the concentration of household income in the rural areas remains striking (as of

15. The 1964 census does not provide a breakdown by age of persons who had taken technical programs, many of which would be the equivalent of secondary or higher school programs. But a reasonable guess as to the size of this group leads to no more than 3.5 percent with secondary or higher.

TABLE 10.17 Housing services and characteristics in rural Colombia, 1951–1985

Service/ Characteristic	1951			1964			1973			1985		
	Colombia	Cabeceras	Resto	Colombia	Cabeceras	Resto	Colombia	Cabeceras	Resto	Colombia	Cabeceras	Resto
Sanitary												
Toilet, sewer	21.0	52.4	3.3	30.5	58.0	4.9	50.6	47.6	8.4	59.5	80.7	11.3
Toilet, septic tank	n.a.	n.a.	n.a.	n.a.	n.a.	n.a.	6.3	6.7	5.6	10.1	7.8	15.4
Latrine	n.a.	n.a.	n.a.	n.a.	n.a.	n.a.	10.8	9.7	12.6	7.4	5.1	12.7
None	n.a.	n.a.	n.a.	n.a.	n.a.	n.a.	32.3	8.7	73.3	23.0	6.4	60.6
Electricity[a]	>25.0	>64.9	4.2	34.5	65.4	5.6	57.6	87.0	14.9	78.5	95.1	40.8
Piped water	24.4	60.3	5.1	30.1	54.9	6.8	62.7	86.8	27.6	70.5	89.2	28.0
Floor materials, earth	n.a.	n.a.	n.a.	n.a.	n.a.	n.a.	34.3	22.3	51.8	17.1	6.7	40.8

SOURCE: The population/housing censuses of the four years in question.

NOTE: It is not always clear whether the definitions applied for these various services are the same in each year.

n.a. Does not imply that the figures were not collected, but simply that we do not have access to them.

[a] The greater than sign (>) results from the fact that in the cases indicated the data exclude Bogota and Cundinamarca, whose inclusion would push them up somewhat.

1988), as reflected in the Gini coefficient of 0.465 (MEDSA 1990, 233). But, if the Mision's figures can be trusted, there was a sharp decline in the incidence of poverty over the decade 1978–88, from 80 percent of families to about 62 percent (MEDSA 1990, 251). Those in "critical poverty" fell from 52 percent of all families to 32 percent, a striking improvement. The main source of these substantial reductions in the incidence of poverty was the growth in average income over the decade; although the figures imply a slight decline in inequality (the reported Gini coefficient fell from 0.486 in 1978 to 0.465 in 1988 in rural areas, excluding municipal seats), this would not be large enough to have much impact on poverty in the absence of an increase in average income.

The Pattern of Urbanization

From the end of World War II to the present, the share of population found in rural areas fell from about two-thirds to less than one-third. Colombia has been noted among the countries of Latin America for its "healthy" dispersion of the urban population among several major centers. This dispersion has been due at least in part to the regional isolation wrought by the difficult topography in the Andean region of the country. As of 1973, there were four cities with more than a half million people—Bogota, Medellin, Cali, and Barranquilla; their total population of 5.6 million was 25 percent of the country's total population and 42 percent of the urban population (approximated as the population living in municipal seats). As expected, these ratios have been rising over time.

More important in the context of this discussion is the distribution of the urban population by size class. Effective linkages between agriculture and other sectors are most likely to be forged in the context of numerous and fairly small urban centers. As of 1964, when 47 percent of the population was rural (by the Colombian definition, a rural center consists of up to 1,500 people), 21 percent lived in centers of 1,500–50,000 people, 15 percent in centers of 50,000–500,000 people, and 16 percent in the three cities larger than that (see DANE 1967, 32). Apart from not being dominated by a single, very large city, the rest of the urban structure appears to be more or less normal, with many centers of a size to interact in a close and mutually beneficial relationship with agriculture. Over the period 1964–73, at least, the growth rate of the small and medium-sized cities, although not quite as fast as the largest ones, was nonetheless striking.

Conclusions

Between 1950 and 1980 Colombia's agricultural sector grew at a creditable rate of 3.7 percent per year. It generated the great bulk of the foreign exchange that fueled the growth of the rest of the economy. Output increased mainly through a combination of capital formation and productivity improvements, with land and labor expansion playing smaller roles. The large-scale sector underwent a striking modernization, concentrated especially between the 1950s and the 1970s, with rapid increases in yields due to more intensive use of modern inputs and to new varieties. The small-scale or *campesino* sector also achieved important productivity gains, starting somewhat later and probably continuing on into the 1980s. Coffee, the single most important crop both because of its share in agricultural output and because of its preeminent position among exports, underwent a price boom in the 1950s and a price and output boom in the 1970s; in the latter case the resulting income bonanza brought Dutch disease problems to the economy. The 1980s have been a problematic decade for agriculture as a whole, as for the rest of the economy.

Apart from its obvious contributions to overall development through the production of nearly all the food consumed in the nation, the generation of nearly all of the exports (until quite recently), and the provision of most of the savings that fueled the growth of the other sectors, several other aspects warrant attention. Nearly half of manufacturing value added as of the mid-1970s took place in branches that could be classified as agroindustry. The comparative advantage of coffee and of sugar, for example, was the source of the processing industries built up around them. In turn, the expansion of manufacturing during the import substitution phase created inducements for the modernization of several activities within the agricultural sector.

The land and income concentration that have characterized Colombian agriculture may help to account for the absence, at least until recently, of a strong rural nonagricultural sector. There have been examples of strong symbioses between agriculture and local manufacturing, including coffee and sugar processing activities, but these have not been the norm. Some of the strong intersectoral linkages have involved ties between large-scale agriculture and urban nonagricultural activities, a natural enough outcome when the large farmers are urban residents. Another factor explaining the relative weakness of the rural nonagricultural sector may be the lower population densities in many regions of rural Colombia and the more difficult terrain than is found in some of the countries with a well-developed nonagricultural sector.

Although Colombian agriculture has not coaxed into existence a systematically dynamic rural nonagricultural sector, it has clearly contributed to a reasonably successful national development, one whose main flaw has been the inequality of income distribution and the associated social maladies. But there is evidence that the distribution of income, both in rural areas and in the country as a whole, has become somewhat less unequal since the mid-1970s; that rural nonagricultural activates, important historically and always significant in some regions of the country, have become important more generally; that the small-scale *campesino* sector has achieved significant increases in productivity and incomes; and that living standards have in general improved in the rural areas.

These patterns raise the possibility that even though the positive reinforcement between growth and equality through strong symbiosis between agriculture and rural nonagriculture has appeared only recently, it may still make an important contribution in the later stages of Colombia's socioeconomic development.

References

Banco de la Republica. *Revista del Banco de la Republica.*

Berry, R. Albert. 1973. "Land Distribution, Income Distribution, and the Productive Efficiency of Colombian Agriculture." *Food Research Institute Studies in Agricultural Economics, Trade, and Development* 12 (3).

———. 1974a. "Changing Income Distribution Under Development: Colombia." *Review of Income and Wealth.* Income and Wealth Series 20 (3):298–99.

———. 1974b. "Resource Transfers between Agriculture and Nonagriculture in Colombia." Mimeo.

———. 1978. "A Positive Interpretation of the Expansion of Urban Services in Colombia." *Journal of Development Studies* 14 (2).

———. 1987a. "Aspects of Savings and Investment during the Economic Crisis in Latin America." Mimeo.

———. 1987b. "The Limited Role of Rural Small-Scale Manufacturing for Late-Comers: Some Hypotheses on the Colombian Experience." *Journal of Latin American Studies* 19.

Departamento Administrativo Nacional de Estadistica (DANE). 1959. *Censo de Poblacion de Colombia 1951: Resumen.* Bogota.

———. 1964. *Directorio Nacional de Explotaciones Agropecuarias (Censo Agropecuario) 1960: Resumen Nacional (Segunda Parte).* Bogota.

———. 1967. *XIII Censo Nacional de Poblacion: Resumen General.* Bogota: Imprenta Nacional.

———. 1972. *Bolentin Mensual de Estadistica* 252 (July).

———. 1976. *Encuesta Nacional de Hogares, Etapas, 3, 4, y 5 Fuerza de Trabajo.* Bogota.

———. 1985a. *Cuentas Nacionales de Colombia 1970–1983.* Bogota.

———. 1985b. *Anuario de Industria Manufacturera 1983.* Bogota.

Departamento Nacional de Planeacion. 1987. *Plan de Economia Social: Planes y Programas de Desarrollo Economico y Social, 1987–1990.* Bogota.

Economic Commission for Latin America and the Caribbean. 1985. *Statistical Yearbook for Latin America and the Caribbean.* Santiago, Chile.

Elias, Victor J. 1983. *Government Expenditures on Agriculture in Latin America.* Washington, D.C.: International Food Policy Research Institute.

Fei, John C. H., and Gustav Ranis. 1964. *Development of the Labor Surplus Economy.* Homewood, IL: Richard D. Irwin.

García, Jorge García, and Gabriel Montes-Llamas. 1988. *Coffee Boom, Government Expenditure, and Agricultural Prices: The Colombian Experience.* Research Report 68. Washington, D.C.: International Food Policy Research Institute.

————. 1989. *Trade, Exchange Rate, and Agricultural Pricing Policies in Colombia.* Washington, D.C.: World Bank.

Hutcheson, Thomas. 1973. "Incentives for Industrialization in Colombia." Ph.D. diss., University of Michigan.

Hutcheson, Thomas L., and Daniel M. Schydlowsky. 1982. "Colombia." In *Development Strategies in Semi-Industrial Countries,* ed. Bela Balassa and associates. Baltimore, Md.: Johns Hopkins University Press.

International Bank for Reconstruction and Development (IBRD). 1950. *The Basis of a Development Program for Colombia.* Washington, D.C.

Kalmanovitz, Salomón. 1978. *Desarrollo de la Agricultura en Colombia.* Bogota: Editorial la Carreta.

Krueger, Anne O., Hal B. Lary, Terry Monson, and Narongchai Akranasee. 1981. *Trade and Employment in Developing Countries,* Vol. 1. *Individual Studies.* Chicago: University of Chicago Press.

Londoño, Juan Luis. 1989. "Income Distribution in Colombia: Turning Points, Catching Up, and Other Kuznetsian Tales."

————. 1989a. "Agricultura y Transformacion Estructural: Una Comparacion Internacional."

————. 1989b. "Income Distribution in Colombia, 1971–88: Basic Estimations." Report to the World Bank. Washington, D.C.

Machado, Absalón. 1977. *El Café: de la Aparceria al Capitalismo.* Bogota: Punta de Lanza.

McGreevey, William Paul. 1971. *An Economic History of Colombia, 1845–1930.* Cambridge: Cambridge University Press.

Mendels, Franklin. 1972. "Proto-Industrialization: The First Phase of the Industrialization Process." *Journal of Economic History* 32.

Ministerio de Obras Publicas. 1962. *Estudio del Transporte Nacional.* Bogota: Ministerio de Obras Publicas.

Mision de Estudios del Sector Agropecuario (MEDSA). 1990. *El Desarrollo Agropecuario de Colombia.* Bogota: Ministerio de Agricultura y Departamento Nacional de Planeacion.

Ocampo, José Antonio. 1984. *Colombia y la Economia Mundial, 1830–1910.* Bogota: Siglo Veintiuno de Colombia.

————. 1991. "The Transition from Primary Exports to Industrial Development in Colombia." In *Diverging Paths,* ed. M. Blomstrom and P. Mellev. Washington, D.C.: Inter-American Development Bank.

Ocampo, José Antonio, and Santiago Montenegro. 1984. *Crisis Mundial, Proteccion e Industrializacion.* Bogota: CEREC.

Ospina, Luis Vasquez. 1955. *Industria y Proteccion en Colombia, 1810–1930.* Medellin: Editorial Santa Fe.

Republica de Colombia, Ministerio de Agricultura. 1990. *Primera Encuesta Nacional Agropecuaria: Total Departamentos.* Bogota.

Reyes, Alvaro. 1987. "Tendencias del empleo y la distribución del ingreso." In

El Problema Laboral Colombiano: Informes e la Mision Chenery, Vol. 1, ed. José Antonio Ocampo and Manuel Ramirez. Controleria. General de la Republica. Bogota.

Romano, Luis. 1987. "Economic Evaluation of the Colombian Agricultural Research System." Ph.D. diss., Oklahoma State University.

Sociedad de Agricultores de Colombia. 1988. *Revista Nacional de Agricultura* 882 (March).

Thomas, Vinod. 1985. *Linking Macroeconomic Policies for Adjustment with Growth: The Colombian Experience.* Baltimore, Md.: Johns Hopkins University Press.

Urrutia, Miguel. 1985. *Winners and Losers in Colombia's Growth in the 1970s.* London: Oxford University Press.

World Bank. 1987. *World Tables 1987.* 4th ed. Washington, D.C.

11 Conclusion

JOHN W. MELLOR

How agriculture grows, the pace at which it grows, and the impact it has on growth of the nonagricultural sector, on poverty and urbanization, and on the quality of the physical environment are highly complex issues. As the preceding chapters demonstrate, many factors influence the pattern of growth in any given country: its physical conditions, public policy, institutions, and, above all, its economic and cultural history. Although it is therefore difficult to draw simple generalizations from the eight case studies in this volume, they illustrate a myriad of interesting relationships that have profound implications for the contribution that agriculture could make to development and that give powerful hints as to how the process might proceed in other contexts.

Many of the broad generalizations that follow are simply points on which all the authors seem to agree. The most complex issue, which is discussed at the end of the chapter, is the central one of this book: What stimulus does agricultural growth provide to nonagricultural growth?

How Does Agriculture Grow?

One of the clear conclusions emerging from the case studies is that agricultural growth may be induced by an expansion of the area farmed, increased intensity of the output mix, and yield-increasing technological change. The output mix is in turn influenced by export markets and rising per capita income. A change in the cropping pattern may bring about increased intensity, and yield-increasing technology becomes increasingly important as incomes rise and sophistication in tapping export markets increases. Although the relative importance of each of these factors varies from case to case, they can collectively be called the engine of agricultural growth.

Area Expansion

Thailand, Argentina, and Costa Rica depended primarily on area expansion to achieve their agricultural growth. Note, however, from table 1.1 that of the eight countries examined, Argentina is the only country to have experienced growth in arable land per capita of the total population, although Thailand was close to neutral on that account, while all the other countries show a rather rapid decline, ranging from about 2 percent to somewhat more than 3 percent per year.

In each of the cases of area expansion, factor productivity was increased, except possibly in Argentina, whose macroeconomic policies were unfavorable to agriculture. At least in Thailand and Costa Rica the emphasis was not on driving out to the margins of area expansion, but rather on mobilizing resources to bring land into production of superior quality, as measured by the value of output per unit area, and to utilize it in a superior manner. Thus area expansion made some contribution to rising factor productivity.

In the case of both Argentina and Thailand, the potential for further expansion of the land area has just about run out. In that sense, they are only 30 years behind India, which as late as the 1950s relied mainly on area expansion to achieve growth. In recent years, Argentina has been putting more emphasis on increasing yields per acre through rapid development of the institutional structure for agricultural research.

It was suggested in the Thailand case that comparative advantage in agriculture was lost because the potential to expand the land area was exhausted. In general, however, countries that have expanded production by enlarging farm areas have a particularly large potential for increasing yield through technological change. Thailand has among the lowest crop yields in Asia, yet its underlying resources have the potential for high productivity. With the appropriate institutional structure, Thailand could achieve output growth comparable to the growth other countries have reached in that manner, and well above the rates Thailand achieved largely through area expansion. Indeed, Thailand's agricultural growth rate has been below that of all but two of the eight cases. Put simply, agricultural research systems and ancillary policies create comparative advantage, and Thailand seems to be missing the boat.

The case of Argentina should be instructive to Thailand—since it, too, was faced with a land area that was losing its potential for further expansion, a growing view that agriculture has or will soon lose its comparative advantage (although the reasons behind this view differ), and the prospect of protectionism (mentioned explicitly in the Thailand case). Furthermore, it failed to recognize, until recently, that yield-increasing technological change could improve factor productivity and preserve or even increase comparative advantage.

An important point to mention before going any further in this discussion is that the physical conditions underlying agricultural production vary so greatly from one country to another that to say a country "gains" or "loses" comparative advantage in agriculture is not quite accurate. The gain or loss is more properly defined as the proportion of agriculture that will lose or gain comparative advantage in the dynamic context of technology and demand shifts.

Thailand's land-based agricultural growth owed a great deal to technological and infrastructural inputs. Much of the area expansion was devoted to increasing maize production. Thailand was unusually fortunate in that maize varieties that had been developed in Guatemala turned out to be highly suitable for the conditions in Thailand. By opening up a new production area with highly productive soils and introducing an improved maize technology farmers increased the average productivity of the incremental resources brought into agriculture beyond expected levels. Thus, as population growth added more numbers to the labor force, the land area expanded more than proportionately. Since the productivity of that land was already innately high, it was increased further by the improved maize varieties. Naturally, average labor productivity rose in those circumstances. With the land expansion there also came increased mechanization.

Another important development for Thailand was the extensive road-building program, which continually opened up new areas to cultivation. That road building may well have been prompted more by international and national security considerations than agricultural growth. Nevertheless, agricultural growth was an important by-product. Thus, a sound expenditure policy and good fortune in identifying an appropriate technology, when combined with expanded land area, stimulated agricultural growth.

How did Thailand manage to attain an agricultural growth rate nearly twice that of Argentina? Surely not because of a better land base. Thailand also taxed its agriculture somewhat heavily during much of the period analyzed. Rather, Argentina's main problem lay in its public policies. A good many of them offered no incentive to expand agricultural production, and they promoted a development strategy that favored large-scale industries. Nevertheless, as the Thai case and especially the Philippines case demonstrate, agriculture can grow quite rapidly in the face of unfavorable macroeconomic policy as long as sectoral policies for technology and infrastructure are right. If, however, negative macroeconomic policy is combined with public expenditure patterns inimical to growth, as reflected in poor infrastructure, agriculture will indeed suffer. The point is that although Thailand taxed agriculture, its macroeconomic policies were basically favorable, including its regime for exports, whereas Argentina's policies were basically unfavorable. In the case of Thailand, even the taxation of rice, a principal export, was varied against international prices and thus provided greater certainty not only to rice growers but also to employers, whose workers therefore enjoyed relatively stable prices for their major expenditure item.

All three of the countries that relied largely on area expansion for their agricultural growth used the bulk of that expanded area for producing for export—for Thailand, it was maize; for Argentina, cereals and livestock products; and Costa Rica, traditional tropical commodities. Thus, the nature of the trade regime, as explained in a later section, was critical to their success or failure.

Intensified Output Mix

Another important finding from these cases is that high rates of agricultural growth cannot be sustained without eventually changing the composition of output. Land expansion and technological innovation certainly play a vital role in the early stages of agricultural development, but once the land area is fully utilized, it becomes necessary to strive for long-term growth through technological change, which also has its limitations. However, these constraints can be offset by intensifying the output mix. In fact, intensification is a natural by-product of growth, for as incomes rise expenditure patterns swing toward agricultural commodities with a high income elasticity of demand, which also tend to be labor intensive in production, provide high yields per unit area of land, and lend themselves to increased factor productivity. Livestock, vegetable, and fruit production are good examples. Export markets may also provide elastic demand for intensively produced crops.

Once again, it seems that if agriculture is to play a major role in economic development, it must be seen as a dynamic sector, and the interplay of its various forces must be facilitated by appropriate public policy. Take the case of traditional tropical exports such as tea, coffee, and bananas. Typically, they have much higher factor productivity than the traditional cereals and roots in the areas to which they are suited. Thus, a shift of resources to those export commodities raises factor productivity, as was the case in Kenya, where specialized agencies played an important role in providing the necessary institutional support. Land reform, which opened up these commodities to indigenous farmers, was also critical.

Expanded production of export commodities by small farmers was also a driving force in the rapid agricultural growth of both Costa Rica and Colombia. Improved technology was a necessary condition of this shift in output mix, and in Costa Rica it also contributed to the expansion of land. Private sector research played an important role in Costa Rica as well.

In sum, a change in product mix made a significant contribution to production and factor productivity in a majority of the cases. In Argentina it was largely irrelevant because of adverse policy, but it was central in Costa Rica, Colombia, and Kenya, where it was driven by exports, as well as in Taiwan and Punjab, where it was driven by both domestic demand and trade. It was probably not very important in the Philippines, in part because of unfavorable trade policies. The Philippine case provides one more example of why an expansionary trade policy allows agriculture to play an important role in development. Indeed, more and more developing countries themselves are driving the demand in international trade for agricultural exports, especially for cereals and for tea and coffee. The effect, of course, is to raise the demand elasticities for those commodities.

It is well to remember, however, that if specialized exports do well as a result of favorable trade policies and technological initiatives, agricultural growth may be restricted to that export sector, and other sectors may be left out for lack of effective institutional support. That is a relevant concern for both Kenya and Costa Rica. The point is not that the private sector or a specialized agency cannot handle these commodities adequately, but that those benefits should be broadened to the agricultural sector as a whole.

Technological Change

Agriculture contributes to growth through increased factor productivity. In the Kenya study, that contribution is said to depend on technical progress, although the likelihood of such progress is not discussed at length. Technological change is considered vital in the other cases as well, especially as it relates to the expansion of land area and changes in output composition as a means of raising agricultural output and factor productivity.

In three cases—Taiwan, Punjab, and the Philippines—major technological improvements were introduced to increase the productivity of commodities produced on the existing land base, largely for domestic consumption. In Taiwan, this effort, along with substantial development of the appropriate institutional structure, had been under way for some years before the period under consideration in this book. Thus, there was very little potential for catching up in technology and so the growth rate in agriculture in general, and in factor productivity in particular, was considerably lower in Taiwan than in Punjab or in the Philippines. Nevertheless, because Taiwan's population was growing at a modest rate, the agricultural output per capita of the total population increased. Of course, the land area in Taiwan was by then tightly constrained and even the potential to expand area through irrigation had largely been realized.

In Punjab, factor productivity rose rapidly. Yields increased because of new varieties, and their use was strongly reinforced by the greatly accelerated development of small-scale irrigation and the use of fertilizer and pesticides. These changes were reinforced once again by the relative growth in area for the commodities receiving the technological improvements. The rate of growth first provided by the new wheat varieties was sustained by the somewhat later development of greatly improved rice varieties. That experience underlines the importance of an institutional structure that provides a flow of technological change. Because the object is to accelerate the rate of growth, the rate of technological change is the important consideration here. In other words, the objective is not a once-and-for-all "green revolution," but a continuous process.

Rapid growth is difficult to achieve in the basic food staples and almost certainly requires considerable governmental attention. The system of production and the income levels in this sector at the outset of development generally do not lend themselves to having either the private sector or producer organizations provide the technology package. Furthermore, the institutional support required for such a task is large and complex.

The Taiwan and Punjab case studies provide rich detail as to how such institutional support can be amassed. One of the central lessons of these two studies is that an institutionalized infrastructure is vital for carrying out the necessary research and for disseminating the results. Farmer organization is also important, along with a massive investment in physical infrastructure, rural education, and the integration of rural financial markets. The process is complex and poses difficult issues of what to do when, given the limited capacity of governments.

The technological success in the Philippines, although confined to one commodity, certainly merits attention because of the importance of that commodity—namely, rice. Again, a catching up was possible. There was a period of particularly rapid technological change, reinforced by rapid growth in input use. But there was apparently less scope for the development of well-controlled irrigation through private initiatives, in response to the increased factor productivity. Also, the growth rate in the agricultural sector was clearly slowing down, which was not the case for Punjab. The explanation probably lies in their different methods of institutionalizing the research process.

The rapid technological change in the Philippines grew directly from the research breakthroughs at the International Rice Research Institute (IRRI), located in one of the country's most productive rice areas. The Philippines made an explicit decision to downplay its own rice research in view of the large resources in the international institute. However, the IRRI made little progress in its maximum-yield trials following the initial breakthrough, since, at the urging of its donor community, it began to give more emphasis to areas less well suited to producing rice in an effort to alleviate poverty. The Philippines lacked the research capacity to develop ways of identifying and meeting its own specific needs, and its research system was not extensive enough to provide nearly the degree of improvement achieved in the succession of technological innovations in Punjab and in Taiwan. Thus, the Philippines sends a clear message underlining the importance of developing a capacity for technological change and of building an indigenous capacity to articulate national needs.

Population Growth

From the point of view of structural change, the relevant variable is not aggregate agricultural growth, but agricultural growth per capita of the total population. That is what determines the course of wage goods prices and the potential to support the nonagricultural population and is the driving force behind expenditures for nonagricultural goods and services, as well as for income-elastic, labor-intensive agricultural commodities. Thus, the rate of population growth is an important variable in the discussion of how agriculture grows. Agricultural growth per capita can be significantly increased by restraining the rate of population growth.

Kenya stands out on the negative side. Its rate of population growth has been considerably faster than that of any of the other countries studied and thus has offset its rapid agricultural growth, pushing it to a position in the middle in the group of eight. Add to that Kenya's strong regional concentration of growth, and the outcome is a relatively small impact on economic transformation in Kenya as a whole. Its subregions did register high rates of growth in their nonagricultural sectors, however, as discussed further below.

In contrast, Argentina, which had a very low rate of population growth, converted a dismal rate of agricultural growth, particularly in relation to its resource base, into a record that was at least positive per capita, although it was still the worst of the eight cases and hardly sufficient to give a strong drive to overall economic growth. In most of the eight cases, eliminating a percentage point from the population growth rate would seem a feasible proposition and equivalent to adding a percentage point to the agricultural growth rate. That is an important relationship to keep in mind when considering scarce public sector resource allocations, particularly for institutional development.

Trade and Agricultural Growth

Trade is so important to agricultural growth that it needs special attention. Here, it is treated in a descriptive manner, as it adds to the agricultural growth rate. The topic arises again in the discussion of macroeconomic policy in the broad sense, as well as in the context of linkages and public policy.

Since trade varies greatly in the specific form it takes, its policy links also vary. Three of the eight cases built their accelerated agricultural growth largely on traditional tropical export. Three depended heavily on exports of basic food staples, particularly cereals. And in the remaining two, agricultural exports were important to growth, although less so than in the others.

Taiwan tells a particularly interesting story. In the period 1960 to 1975, when its structural transformation was almost complete, the share of exports in agriculture dropped from 71 percent to 17 percent, while the nominal value of exports rose by a factor of 7.5. The Taiwan study also drives home the point that comes through in several of the other cases. To determine how to increase the production of "nontraditional exports," it is necessary to consider the potential increases in agricultural production. The base of production and export is so immense that a modest shift of agricultural resources to nontraditional products represents a large aggregate. Taiwan's agricultural exports are highly dynamic. They shift with changing internal forces and thereby affect comparative advantage and external markets. Trade policy should be more specifically oriented to diagnosing these potential interactions and to establishing the institutional structure needed for this purpose.

The rapid growth of the agricultural sector in Kenya, Costa Rica, and Colombia was an outcome of a change in the commodity mix toward export commodities, and hence the growth of agricultural exports was critical to overall growth. Each of those case studies emphasizes the role of macroeconomic policy, particularly as it affects the real exchange rate, and notes that restrained fiscal policy is essential.

The Kenya study illustrates the difficulty of practicing such restraint. On the one hand, commodity exports require stable macroeconomic policy; on the other hand, when those exports represent a major portion not only of trade but of overall growth and of GNP, they tend to precipitate much of the observed instability. When Kenya's government let the benefits of increased export prices in short-lived boom situations run back to the farmers, it appeared to have avoided the problem typical of virtually all other developing countries: their governments usually treat transitory income as though it were permanent and build it into the expenditure stream. Farmers know transitory income when they see it, and Kenyan farmers behaved according to the textbook, saving and spending on durable products. Even so, after a lag, much of the income did flow back to the government, which then built it into patterns of current expenditure just in time for the inevitable bust. The point is not Kenya's irresponsible behavior. Quite the contrary. The government tried to act in a stabilizing way but found the temptations and difficulties too great. Thus, stable macroeconomic policy is important and difficult to achieve. This point is best made by the success stories in which correct policies were attempted. They succeeded only in part, but that partial success was quite enough to provide substantial growth. None of the success stories are paragons of the application of the 1990s fashion of unadulterated neoclassicism.

Kenya is important in another respect. It did very well in its overall agricultural growth but increased its imports of basic food staples, particularly maize, at a rapid rate. Why was that? Three factors were at work. Its population was growing very rapidly, as was its large agricultural sector, which therefore provided broad participation in increased income and hence pushed up the per capita demand for food. The agricultural growth, which occurred mainly in export commodities, had two further effects. It did not add as much to domestic supplies of food as if the growth were in a dominant food sector (although remember that net food imports have tended to increase in countries that have done well in food production), and it provided rapid growth in foreign exchange to finance food imports. The point was made earlier that food imports can quickly grow to the point of affecting the real exchange rate. Agricultural exports are the dominant exports for most low-income countries, so it is only through rapid growth in agricultural exports that rapidly growing food consumption can be supplied significantly from imports. In practice, Kenya financed a high proportion of its food imports from foreign aid in the form of food aid. But it is doubtful if Kenya would have countenanced the food price increases implicit in not allocating foreign exchange to finance food imports if the food aid had not been available. Its growing agricultural exports not only made the food imports necessary, but they would have facilitated financing them if foreign aid had not been available.

That leads to the three cases for which basic food staples, particularly cereals, were the primary export. This is an area in which the sample is decidedly biased. Thailand and Argentina are the only two significant developing countries participating in the international cereals market in a substantial way. Together, they alone represent two-thirds of developing-country cereal exports. Punjab's cereal-exporting activity is a special case, since the state is part of a large country.

For low-income countries, exporting basic food staples is contrary to gaining the full favorable effects of agricultural growth on nonagricultural growth. That is because the optimal growth strategy necessarily involves spreading capital thinly over the labor force and increasing the total wage bill through increased employment and slowly rising real wages. Marginal propensities to spend on food are high and remain high as incomes rise, particularly as livestock products, and hence feed cereals, increase their weight in the diet. This is a neoclassical argument in its essence, except for the fact that labor as an input and food as a wage good are so large as to have major macroeconomic effects on the economy in themselves.

In view of these complex relations, it is worth pursuing further the analysis of the three major cereals exporters. Thailand, of course, has a large, rich, land resource that is able, even with relatively low capital inputs, to produce a substantial surplus of food beyond what the rural population consumes. And since it has a small urban population, it naturally generates a surplus. Thailand has historically followed a policy of stable rice prices, which are favorable to agriculture as well as to urban consumers and their employers. It has done so by regulating the "export premium," a euphemism for export tax. Thus, policy kept rice prices on average somewhat below world prices and reduced the fluctuations in relation to international prices. These were both favorable to employment growth and also to government revenues, a significant part of which were deployed in building rural infrastructure and thereby reduced the cost structure of agriculture. In addition, a major portion of expanded production was in the form of corn, which was not consumed heavily in Thailand, and for which there needed to be a "vent for surplus."

But the striking feature about Thailand is that cereals exports are now declining rapidly, led by maize, which is increasingly being used as livestock feed domestically. Maize exports will probably end within a few years. Domestic rice consumption will obviously not increase much, and even livestock consumption (but not livestock exports) seems to be leveling. (Note that livestock consumption in Thailand seems to be leveling off at much lower levels of income and of consumption than is typical in developing countries. Thus, one wonders if the demand picture presented will hold up over the long run.) Rice exports will presumably continue unless large areas are diverted to oilseeds, which are imported in large quantity, or to livestock feed.

Low-cost feed has given particular encouragement to the livestock industry, which is expanding rapidly for exports. Thus, another point emerges here, namely, that developing countries are well suited to labor-intensive livestock production if feed is relatively cheap.

Punjab, too, is a special case. Its unusually productive agricultural resource, large capacity for expansion of small-scale irrigation, and a period of rapid catching up in productivity combined to provide an unusually high growth rate. Naturally a vent for surplus was needed, and the large Indian market provided that. However, the rate of growth of Punjab's nonagricultural sector, stimulated by agricultural growth, was significantly smaller than might have been expected. If that faster nonagricultural growth had occurred, it seems likely that considerably more of the accelerated agricultural growth in Punjab could have been absorbed through increased demand from the laboring classes within the state. In particular, the demand for livestock products would have grown even more rapidly. The land is well suited to the production of livestock feed, particularly high-quality roughage, and so there would have been an even larger diversion of area to such roughage. It is notable that most parts of the developed world with an agricultural resource such as that of Punjab do not produce cereals to any great extent. Thus the vent for surplus was more important to Punjab than would have been the case under a full realization of the potential for nonagricultural growth.

Nevertheless, it is important to note the potential for limited agricultural areas to experience unsustainably high rates of growth when they are in a particularly rapid period of catching up in their stage of technological change. It is during such a catching-up period that trade must take up a good deal of the excess production if prices are to be maintained at a level that provides the stimulus that takes full advantage of the technological advances.

Argentina's exports of food are readily understandable. First, it is not really a low-income country in either its income levels, consumption patterns, or employment structure. Its superb land resource and low population density naturally make Argentina an exporter. But it is the one example among the eight cases of a country with highly productive agricultural resources and with a domestic policy that kept agriculture growing at a low rate. Moderately poor performance in agriculture, despite an extraordinarily productive agricultural base, can be attributed largely to the negative impact of an unfavorable price regime that emanated from heavy import duties and their impact on the prices of exports and tradable goods generally.

The moral to be learned from this brief review of the agricultural trade experience of these countries is that high degrees of protectionism for the nonagricultural sector wreak havoc on agriculture. That point is dramatically illustrated in the case of Argentina, and somewhat less so in the case of the Philippines. Notably, Taiwan, Punjab (as a part of the larger Indian entity), and Thailand benefited from quite open trading regimes.

A final question on trade is what does all the emphasis on agriculture indicate beyond the message that the trade economists and neoclassicists have been sending all along—that is, get the macroeconomic policy right? The answer to that question is very important to development policy. Yes, do what the trade economists say. But that is not enough, because agricultural growth plays a vital role in the economy as a whole, and that growth depends on public policy for the generation of technological change and for the provision of other public goods such as infrastructure and education.

The preceding pages give a heavy weight to trade policy. That is sensible given the recent historical damage to the agriculture of many countries. Of the cases, fully half give a central place to trade policy and the exchange rate. Yet when so many dimensions of government policy serve to weaken intersectoral linkages, it becomes clear that trade policy alone cannot be the principal explanation.

The Effects on Poverty

The eight cases examined here are notable for the decline in absolute poverty reflected in all of them, although they were not selected because of that effect. Of course, accelerated agricultural growth should reduce poverty drastically. But, given the strength of the logic behind that statement, perhaps what is striking from the cases is the clear message, to use the title of the Philippines chapter, that agricultural growth is not enough. The expected poverty-reducing associates of accelerated agriculture growth are a reduction in relative food prices as a result of expanded food supplies, or an increased capacity to import food financed by agricultural exports; increased employment in agriculture itself; and increased employment in nonagricultural employment, particularly in rural areas.

Of the eight cases, the Philippines is the extraordinary outlier, and has the most to tell. The evidence could not be more clear that the Philippines has had an unusually good record in agricultural growth, particularly rice, the most important and dominant food crop. Nevertheless, the evidence is unequivocable that the real wage rate has declined steadily over time, and the numbers of people, and in all likelihood the proportions of people, in poverty have continually increased. That evidence has accumulated from a variety of sources and covers a considerable period of time, including the extended period of rapid agricultural growth.

Concurrently, there is ample empirical evidence to suggest that the rice breakthroughs did result in a substantial increase in farm employment, that lower-income people benefited from that, and that the real price of rice fell, further benefiting the poor. Thus, the direct effects of the technological changes in agriculture were clearly and substantially favorable to reducing poverty. Poverty would undoubtedly have been greater without the improvements in agriculture. What went wrong in obtaining positive improvements? Note that in Thailand, with a slower growth rate in agriculture, poverty reduction was substantial.

In the Philippines, two contrary forces were at work. First, population growth was rapid, at least for a Southeast Asian nation. But too much should not be read into that alone. The Philippines population growth is not a complete outlier, and the agricultural growth per capita was still impressive. More than population growth was at work.

Second, and related to the first point, agricultural growth did little to stimulate nonagricultural employment. To put it bluntly, the linkages and multipliers were not there. They are essential to poverty reduction if population is growing significantly, let alone rapidly.

This suggestion is corroborated further by the wealth of empirical evidence on labor absorption from high-yielding crop varieties. In aggregate, it is substantial. However, as a percentage of the growth of production, it is modest. That is, the elasticity of employment with respect to output is certainly no higher than 0.6 and is more normally on the order of 0.3. With agriculture the dominant source of employment growth, rapid growth in population was extraordinarily onerous, for it pushed real wage rates down and increased poverty. Thus, the unavoidable conclusion that simply increasing agricultural production, even when it brings about some decline in the real price of food, does not bring about sharp reductions in poverty unless it is associated with rapid growth in nonagricultural employment. The Philippines case explains why this was so. For the moment, however, remember that direct government efforts to accelerate growth in the nonagricultural sector have increased employment in that sector by very little, and certainly not by enough to solve the employment and, hence, the poverty problem. Evidence from all the cases is pulled together in a succeeding section to draw some broader generalizations on this important issue.

Thailand is a notable contrast to the Philippines on the question of poverty reduction. Poverty declined sharply, particularly in the fast agricultural growth period of the 1970s. It slowed in the 1980s, when agricultural growth slowed; and, as a corollary, the real wage rate in the country as a whole and certainly in the agricultural sector rose throughout the period of rapid agricultural growth. The growth rate in agricultural production was significantly slower than that of the Philippines, and even though the population growth rate was also considerably slower than that of the Philippines, the growth in per capita agricultural production was also lower than in the Philippines. In reading the two cases, one can hardly assume that Thailand mechanized its agriculture less than the Philippines! Thus, the difference in poverty reduction must lie with differences in the growth of nonagricultural employment.

Thailand had a much higher proportion of its population employed in agriculture, and it was still higher than in the Philippines at the end of the period (table 1.1). (Remember that different periods are chosen for each country to catch periods of rapid agricultural growth, but in the case of Thailand and the Philippines the offset is only seven years.) On the whole, however, Thailand remains much more rural than the Philippines. The Philippines, of course, had a very strong pro-industrialization and urbanization policy, but with low-employment content. Clearly, Thailand's more open economy favored more employment-intensive export industries in the greater Bangkok area in comparison with Manila in the Philippines. On simple arithmetic grounds, however, the difference cannot be fully or even largely explained by the employment difference between Manila and Bangkok. The difference must lie with the difference in the increase in and the productivity of rural employment in the two countries. There is a strong implication that the large increase in the rural nonagricultural population in Thailand was more and more productively employed and certainly provides indirect evidence of a favorable effect from rural expenditure patterns. Unfortunately, the data base in Thailand is too poor to measure the growth and the sources of growth of nonagricultural employment in rural areas.

In view of the Thailand case, however, one must wonder if these small firms in the countryside are headed for a life of their own, as in Taiwan, or if Thailand is in effect pursuing a more dualistic policy: the future lying with the more modern firms in Bangkok and the rural firms at a dead end. Indeed, the comparative analysis leads one to expect some future problems in regard to both poverty reduction and growth in Thailand—a clear slowing of agricultural growth, owing to its apparent failure to make the shift from land-based expansion to technology-based expansion; a concentration of modern industry in Bangkok; and failure to exploit the growth potential from the expansion of highly selected (self-selected by market forces) entrepreneurs in the rural areas.

Finally, Thailand must address the problem that poverty has largely disappeared in the better agricultural areas and is now concentrated in the agricultural areas of lower technological potential. Lessons from other parts of the world suggest this to be the intractable part of the poverty problem. Continued agricultural growth will increase employment more rapidly than other approaches to growth, but migration is still likely to be a major part of the poverty answer for countries that have progressed to Thailand's stage in development. Fortunately, this case documents rather ready migration of all kinds in Thailand—which is what the conceptual framework of this discussion would lead one to expect.

With the particularly useful comparison of Thailand and the Philippines in mind, consider now the record of Taiwan on poverty reduction. Most striking is the substantial decline of the Gini coefficient, throughout the period of modern development. That may not be the norm in development, but it does show that such a decline is possible and urges examination of the factors at work. Certainly, much more than a redistribution of assets through land reform is at work here, although that was an important part of the background to the story. By the standard measures, absolute poverty has virtually disappeared from Taiwan. Clearly, the pattern of development has been very favorable from all aspects of equity and poverty reduction. In comparison with the Philippines record, the Taiwan record must be saying something very important about the role of labor-intensive, dispersed, small-scale industry.

The record in Punjab is what one would expect from the Taiwan example: drastic reduction in absolute poverty, despite a substantial in-migration of labor from poorer parts of India. The preceding analysis indicates that the exemplary record on poverty must have come by and large from the vigorous expansion of the small- and medium-scale rural industry.

In Kenya, the situation is made more complex by extraordinarily rapid population growth and the consequence that a high agricultural growth rate has provided only rather modest growth in agricultural production per capita of the total population. Nevertheless, that rate occurred during the period of rapid growth comparable to that in the Philippines and Thailand. Since it was concentrated in the smallholder coffee and tea areas, the effect on poverty reduction in those areas should have been substantial. Casual observation would suggest the situation is like that in Punjab, with booming market towns and a great deal of small-scale nonagricultural activity. The case study also alludes to such development.

In Costa Rica and Colombia, poverty has declined, as expected from the agricultural record. In Argentina, neither the agricultural nor the industrial record should lead to an expectation of poverty decline or improvement in income distribution.

To summarize, where there has been a marked increase in agricultural production per capita of the total population and where nonagricultural growth has occurred rapidly, poverty has experienced a rapid decline, as in Taiwan, Punjab, and Thailand, but also regionally in Kenya, and in Costa Rica and Colombia. Where accelerated agricultural growth has not been accompanied by accelerated growth in employment in the nonagricultural sector, poverty has not declined. But one must not be misled on that. The direct approaches to industrialization along the lines followed in the Philippines and Argentina have been disastrous from the point of view of poverty reduction. Those two countries went straight for industrialization—in one, this was to the absolute detriment of agriculture; and in the other, agriculture did well for a period despite the unfavorable policies.

Urbanization

One of the major problems of contemporary developing countries is the unhealthy structure of urbanization—a tendency for the urban population to concentrate in one or a very few of the major population centers. That was not a characteristic of developed countries when they were at similar stages in development. Their urban centers were more numerous and the urban population more diffused over those centers.

A growing concern about the future of already unhealthy urban concentrations has led foreign assistance communities to devote more and more attention to the urban sector and less to agriculture. Yet, on the surface, it would appear that an important manifestation of accelerated agricultural growth in the eight cases is a healthier, more economic pattern of urbanization, except for the Philippines, where urban growth has been substantial and heavily concentrated in one city, Metropolitan Manila. The Philippines case contains a particularly trenchant discussion of this issue, as well as comparative data on other Southeast Asian countries, and some broader comparisons as well. Note, in particular, that the Philippines, with about two-thirds the per capita income of Thailand, has nearly three times as high a proportion of its population in urban centers but only a 30 percent higher share of manufacturing in its GDP (but the small urban population in Thailand certainly does not equate with more rural underemployment or lower productivity of labor in agriculture).

Argentina is very much like the Philippines, but with a poorer record in agricultural growth. Its city problem is not as onerous as that of the Philippines because of a very low rate of population growth and a much higher per capita income.

It would seem logical that, where agriculture is not playing its stimulative role, efforts to industrialize would involve a move toward import substitution and industrial protectionism and the development of large-scale industry of a capital-intensive nature. It would be logical to expect major externalities in locating such industries near each other, and of course near the center of governmental power, which determines the licensing and other rules that enable innately uneconomic industries to survive. Even if exports are fostered to provide nonagricultural growth, the same points apply. That is why Thailand has its "modern" industry concentrated in Bangkok. Thus, one can see a logic for a number of unhealthy elements here: the concentration of industrial growth in a large-scale capital-intensive sector located in the seat of government in the single metropolitan area.

One of the basic aspects of the relationship between agricultural growth and the diffused pattern of urbanization that needs to be understood is that accelerated growth in agriculture accelerates the growth rate in the nonagricultural sector even more. The result one would expect is at least faster growth of the nonagricultural sector, and at least implicitly of urbanization. If the agricultural growth is diffused over a substantial portion of the geographic area of the country, however, one would expect a demand-led stimulus to result in the development of broadly diffused nonagricultural activity. At least initially, that nonagricultural activity might occur in virtually every small market town. It would not be surprising if eventually some externalities caused some concentration, but perhaps initially in increasingly larger market towns. Once the agricultural stimulus developed many small firms, one would expect some of them to show a highly effective entrepreneurship and therefore to spread their activities to find demand outside of their immediate rural area. The firms still might stay in that rural area because of familiarity, capital availability, and a labor force with which they are comfortable. It is endlessly asked, are these relationships causal? The sensible response is to turn the question around. Why would small- and medium-scale industry develop in rural areas that are agriculturally stagnant—that offer no prospect of an increase in income, effective demand, or, for that matter, raw materials. Would one locate there solely because of cheap labor? Probably rarely, if ever so. In any case, is infrastructure needed, and if so why not put it where agriculture, too, can develop? The point is, dispersed urbanization, but not slower urbanization, has strong ties with agricultural growth.

This process is well illustrated in Taiwan. An extraordinarily high proportion of total nonagricultural output takes place in small firms. Indeed, 60 percent of all exports come from firms of less than 100 employees. Those firms are broadly distributed through the previously rural areas. They would seem to have been initially stimulated by growth in agricultural demand, both for producer goods and consumer goods. But they clearly now accrue most of their demand from outside the rural sector in Taiwan, and indeed from the world as a whole. Taiwan developed a myriad of small firms with effective flexible entrepreneurs who could shift their activities with changing market conditions. There was considerable concern in Taiwan that, as real wages rose rapidly and the currency was valued upward, its small-scale firms would not be able to adjust as readily as the much larger, ostensibly more sophisticated firms of the Republic of Korea. In the event, the small entrepreneurs have, if anything, proved themselves to be more flexible and, to use a term correctly, "entrepreneurial." Thus the Taiwan lesson is doubly valuable.

The pattern described for Taiwan is clearly the case for Punjab. There is no single dominant city in Punjab. There are large numbers of equally important major centers and a host of others running down to smaller and smaller centers that still are important sources of nonagricultural employment. One notes the similarity with Taiwan, which features broad participation in agricultural growth across farm sizes and across the state; all villages with all-weather roads and electricity, and excellent communications with all the towns; and immense numbers of small businesses growing from an agricultural stimulus and then many taking on a life of their own. The disadvantages of locating a business in a rural area are small. The Punjab case provides data mostly for the large firms that have already graduated to being outward looking.

In many respects, Thailand is the most intriguing case with respect to urbanization. Clearly, labor productivity in agriculture has been rising, as have rural incomes, while poverty has been declining. Those favorable trends by and large disappear with the slowdown in agricultural growth in the 1980s, but then the primary interest here is the periods of good rates of agricultural growth. The case emphasizes, correctly, the centrality of Bangkok as an urban center, but perhaps in the sense of Paris always having been central in France, at the same time that many other urban centers existed and urban population was widely dispersed. In the case of Thailand, one must ask, what do all those "nonurban" people do, who seem not to be poor and not to be working in agriculture? One cannot help but think that they are servicing a multitude of rural needs. Construction was given attention in this case; perhaps transportation has more local input than was assumed, particularly with a tendency for vehicles never to be retired and hence eventually rebuilt in the countryside. And, then one must ask the same question raised in another context earlier, "Is Thailand prepared as was Taiwan for those rural firms to grow and gain a life of their own?" Is that the appropriate course, rather than pushing existing firms out of Bangkok? Are financial markets, trade policy, and even agricultural policy facilitating that transition? From the case, it would seem not.

The Kenya case, like the Thailand case, emphasizes Nairobi as the single metropolitan center. And, as in Thailand, a very high, and perhaps increasing, proportion of modern industry is located there. Perhaps Thailand and Kenya are pursuing industrial strategies that favor import substitution more than is generally made out, and also favoring industries for export that have little connection with the countryside, at the same time that a vigorous nonagricultural development is occurring in the countryside, stimulated by the growth in agricultural income. This description suggests a somewhat dualistic development. In any case, Nairobi has not grown at the expense of other commercial centers. Its share of the urban population has declined from half to one-third in the 20 years from 1959 to 1988. In fact, the share of urban population in the four largest cities has fallen substantially. The secondary centers have indeed grown rapidly. One sees that clearly illustrated in the areas of most rapid agricultural growth where market towns are vital, vibrant areas. In the case of Kenya, accelerated agricultural growth occurred particularly in the highland areas producing tea and coffee and adjacent dairy production areas.

Colombia's pattern of urbanization reminds us once again that history is important. The urban dispersion has powerful historical roots. Colombia also raises the question of the relation between good communications and centralization, a question that could also have arisen for Kenya, the Philippines, and perhaps others. In the case of Colombia, poor communications provided economic protection to dispersed urban centers, but that is a dangerous basis for building an economy, because eventually that form of protection disappears. One sees the deleterious effect of that in Colombia. Where nonagricultural activity is fomenting the growth of secondary urban centers, the better the modern communications the better these firms can compete and look outward. That is the lesson from Taiwan and Punjab, and it needs to be taken to heart in Kenya and other countries with considerably poorer physical infrastructure.

Costa Rica seems to be very concentrated, but it is difficult to judge, since there is some separation between the cities that make up the major metropolitan area, and they are all located in the main coffee-producing region, which is the center of increasing small farmer income. Thus, the pattern may be less divergent from the other success stories than appears on the surface.

Structural Change and Linkages

The time has now arrived to pull together some key bits of information from the cases to fit into the conceptual framework presented in the introduction. It needs to be clear at the outset that the conceptual framework is well understood. The empirical data are the missing pieces of the puzzle. Economists, too, are prone to look for their car keys under the street light—rather than in the dark where they no doubt dropped them—and point out that it is useless to look in the dark even if the keys are somewhere there. Thus, all the case studies, particularly the two dealing with Punjab and Thailand, focus on the larger firms for which there are data. There is scope for detective work even in this dusky environment. In chapter 5, Ammar Siamwalla presents consumption data that spotlight transport and construction expenditure. Is that the first step from agriculture on the road to industrialization? What is the process in the steps after that? No one seems to know. It may be valuable to know if, for example, credit is not important to getting started, but is critical to growing to the next step.

The path of detective work is pursued in this chapter by taking up poverty reduction and urbanization before this treatment of linkages. Of course, it is the economic linkages that provide the poverty reduction and urbanization patterns. But, the light is on poverty and urbanization patterns. And, the link can be made with agricultural growth. So now that evidence can be used to establish the link between agricultural and nonagricultural growth.

Finally, much of the problem in establishing the link between agricultural and nonagricultural growth arises from the same prejudices against small-scale nonagricultural activities as against agriculture on the part of urban people. It is only the kind of activities that locate in Bangkok, Nairobi, and even Taipei that are seen as modern. It is difficult to see agriculture as the first step on the road to industrialization, and rural, small-scale service and goods-producing firms as the second step—and way down the road, maybe a tea factory or an automobile factory.

One reason for the paucity of data on these key issues is that for policy one needs only to know that the enterprises are there, and to act on the association between physical infrastructure and key institutions such as education, on the one hand, and the growth of employment and rural small-scale industry on the other.

The thrust of this examination of the relation between agricultural growth and structural change and their linkages in the process of economic development— or as it is put in the title, agriculture on the road to industrialization—focuses attention on the domestic aspects of development. Professor Gustav Ranis of the Economic Growth Center has turned our attention once more to "domestically-oriented development as between agriculture and nonagriculture, a truth which has sometimes been lost sight of in the wake of the oil crisis of the 1970s and the debt crisis of the 1980s, which drew away too much of our attention to the international dimensions of successful economic development."

The cases in this book all emphasize the importance of agricultural exports and how they are hurt by closed-economy processes. International trade is clearly important to the growth process in many other ways as well. That point comes up repeatedly and is strongly represented in this chapter. Professor Ranis is not urging a return to thinking in terms of closed economies, but rather is suggesting that the core around which the international fits is the set of domestic policies and issues. In addition, one does have to worry not just about the economics but also the implicit social policies if the effective demand for growth of output in developing countries comes largely from foreign sources.

Three key elements of this discussion set it apart from much of the mainstream of development economics. First, *technological change* is the most important driving engine of growth—the emphasis then is on the agricultural sector for two reasons. It is initially such a large sector. It has well-proven immense potentials to absorb factor productivity increasing technological change. Second, given the large increase in net national income from technological change in agriculture, the emphasis is on *domestic effective demand*, particularly for consumption goods and services as a driving engine for additional growth. Third, and following from the first two, is a concern with respect to the characteristics and requirements for growth of the *rural, small- and medium-scale nonagricultural sector,* and particularly the potential for that sector to graduate into playing a major role in the industrialization of the economy.

The approach also assumes substantial market imperfections in low-income countries, particularly in the labor market, but also with respect to the elements Bruce Johnston and Albert Park emphasize in their illuminating chapter on Kenya, such as a whole host of factors under the rubric of scale economies.

The authors of the two cases, Kenya and Thailand, reach clear conclusions of at best a little link between agricultural growth and industrial growth and effectively strike hard against the heart of the argument. The Johnston and Park chapter deals effectively with the arguments in both of those chapters, while concentrating on Kenya. One must understand that labor markets are imperfect in poor countries, that nontradables are critical in labor absorption, and that scale economies in institutional development play an important role. With that understanding, in essence, however, both Kenya and Thailand turn out to illustrate much that is positive with respect to the agriculture-nonagriculture relation. Nevertheless, it is well to first look at the surface message of little link.

First, the Kenya and Thailand studies confirm, and I think without legitimate counterargument, that there is not a strong link between growth in agricultural incomes and the industrial firms of the major metropolitan centers. That is very important. It states that the kind of growth and stimulus desired is not particularly consistent with the kind of industrial growth stimulated even in countries with quite liberal trade regimes. In the Thailand case, the budget share that rural people allocate to the major urban-based consumption goods industry is very small. As an aside, one should point out that the same is roughly true of the mass of urban people also, and that even for those industries the total rural market is some multiple of the urban market (in India, market surveys by large-scale private firms, for their own products, suggest $2^1/_2$ times as large). But that is not the point, the point is that if output is to be led by domestic demand it has a *very* different structure than if it is led by exports. Of course, export industries led by domestic demand have a similar structure for foreign and domestic demand.

Second, their analysis confirms that if one is truly interested in this set of demand-led relationships one needs to develop the data sources. It is striking that, in the Punjab case, the point is made that the data for the small-scale rural enterprises are completely inadequate and that the author then goes on, inadvertently, to show how superior the Indian data base is in these areas in relation to virtually every other developing country! But the analysis suffers greatly from the data darkness.

Both the Kenya and Thailand cases emphasize the importance of the construction industry, substantially for rural housing, and the Thailand case mentions locally made furniture. Both industries have the potential to expand through learning by doing. Transportation bulks large, and the local component is probably understated, as is the potential to expand repair enterprises into metal working shops, small industries, and eventually larger firms. But this whole approach of starting with a service orientation, evolving to manufacturing, and then growing is alien to the modern approach to stimulating industry at a much larger scale.

The Kenya case remarks on the poor links of rural nonagricultural activities outside the rural area—but the question that now needs to be asked is about the dynamics. One can look to Taiwan for some hints and note that in general the consumer goods industries in urban areas are not producing goods of interest in rural areas. That suggests incorrect industrial policy, along the lines of misguided import substitution. Why is it that in Taiwan so much of even export industry is small scale and located in the countryside? Perhaps the reason for the sharp contrast with the Republic of Korea is that Taiwan's initial steps concentrated on agricultural and domestic demand and substantial domestic capital, whereas Korea was foreign-demand led, and substantially foreign financed, from the start.

In all of these cases something important is clearly going on out there in the countryside. Poverty and urbanization were discussed early in this chapter because the consensus is much clearer on those points than on the linkages argument, and those two areas indicate without doubt that something important is going on. It is apparent from the Kenya and Thailand analysis that what is going on is very different from what is normally thought about in industrialization. Yet it is the Taiwan example that takes us to the most interesting turns.

Three further additional bits of information gleaned from the cases shed light on these issues of structural changes and agricultural linkages. First, the Philippines case documents that the share of nonagricultural income in agricultural households is lower in the Philippines than in the other countries compared. At the opposite end of the same argument, the Colombia case demonstrates the rapid growth of rural nonagricultural employment.

Second, in the Philippines case, some multipliers are computed, analogous to the cross-sectional relations between agricultural and nonagricultural growth rates presented at the beginning of the introductory chapter. The multipliers for most countries are surprisingly similar. But, the Philippines multiplier— agriculture to nonagriculture—is much lower than that of other Southeast Asian countries, again confirming that something is at work between agricultural and nonagricultural growth and that it has been interfered with in the Philippines.

Third, there is an almost gratuitous remark in the Costa Rica case about domestic markets being too small for domestic industrial production. But is that not a function of what is produced? Although scale economies are reached with rising rural incomes, the scale is very low. The rural market provides a demand for goods that reach scale economies at the low levels that are within the grasp not only of small economies but also of small producers within those small economies.

Among the most important issues raised in nearly all of the cases was the effect of the distribution of income and assets, or more specifically of land, on the growth of agriculture and its effects on other sectors. In every case in which it was raised, land reform played a major role in the processes at hand wherever land reforms had occurred, or acted as a continuing barrier where it had not. (As an aside, note that what Punjab considers quite a bad tenure situation would be seen in a number of the other cases as a great improvement.)

Land tenure is explicitly cited as a major problem in four cases: Colombia,

Costa Rica, Kenya, and the Philippines. It is probably a problem in Argentina as well. Two of the remaining three experienced major land reform. Thailand seems to have been all right and remained that way. In each of these four cases close to half the production falls in the large-scale sector and about half in the small-scale sector. Thus, the favorable effects of agricultural growth are greatly diluted in each of these cases if land tenure is a problem.

The land tenure issue has two important implications in the structural transformation context: it influences both production and consumption patterns, and hence the nature of the links to nonagricultural production. Most land tenure literature emphasizes the former. Admittedly this sample is biased toward cases that did well in agricultural production. Nevertheless it is striking that the problem with land tenure does not seem to be on the production side. In general, the large-scale systems in the four countries in question performed well from a production point of view. In Colombia, perhaps, the bimodal structure has been responsible for what was noted as a slow response of the smallholder sector to improved production possibilities. The land tenure problem does seem to produce less favorable linkages with the domestic economy, particularly the rural economy. This was noted explicitly in the Colombia case.

Land reforms were carried out in both Taiwan and Punjab. In Punjab the percentage of land in owner cultivation went from 61 percent to 88 percent, and in Taiwan from 60 percent to 74 percent. Two aspects of these changes are striking. First, the proportion in smallholder farming was higher before the land reform than at present in four of the cases. Second, in the Punjab case, the land reform was thought to have not gone nearly far enough, whereas in Taiwan it is seen as highly successful, and yet the difference between the two is not very great. The difficulties of instituting land reform are without doubt immense. Even the two successes were probably possible primarily because the landed group were out of favor politically at the time of reform. Even so, they were handled quite carefully.

Conclusion

This discussion of linkages concludes with four reminders. First, it is not important to understand the linkage process in detail. Because of the very complexity and flexibility of this process, all that is required, once technology has increased rural purchasing power, is that markets function as they are supposed to and that small- and medium-scale private firms respond to market signals. Second, with rare exception, rapid growth in the agricultural sector is associated with an increase in employment that is sufficiently rapid to raise real wage rates in the relatively short run. Third, employment increases arising from accelerated agricultural growth are broadly distributed throughout rural regions—that is, they are not concentrated in the capital city. And fourth, the employment intensity of the firms stimulated by agricultural growth tends to be fairly high, either because of generally high employment elasticities or sufficiently high cross-elasticities of demand, and thus it is eventually able to shift consumption to employment-intensive activities for which demand is elastic.

Interestingly, several readers of drafts of this manuscript, particularly Hsi-Huang Chen, have asked why countries would want to pursue bad development policy to begin with. Richard Sabot raised the same question in a different guise in response to chapter 4, on the Philippines, when he noted that "the distorted trade regime may only be a symptom rather than the underlying cause of the failure by the Philippines to capitalize on rapid agricultural growth." Surely that answer must give us all pause to reflect about the recent round of macroeconomic policy conditioning by the foreign assistance donors.

In Argentina, the "bad" policies seemed designed to strengthen organized labor, and probably the landed aristocracy found an acceptable way to live with a bias against agriculture as long as their asset positions remained undisturbed. In the Philippines, a wealthy elite felt suited to running a large-scale, capital-intensive industry in Metro Manila. Again, the landed interests could accommodate if their assets were left undisturbed. If favorable policies for such interests are removed, will those interests be able to think up new favorable policies faster than foreign aid conditioners can think of the means to remove them? When will the weight of political influence swing to growth? What can be done to assist that shift? Can policies be devised that will meet the minimum acceptable needs of the powerful and still provide growth? Perhaps in Argentina the system got so bad that everyone wanted change. Perhaps developing countries are becoming more democratic and providing at least an opportunity to debate policies in support of growth. Perhaps the changes will come innocuously—through the efforts of institutions for technological change in agriculture, expansion of rural infrastructure, the processes described in this book, and a gradual change in political structure. Some bad policy must surely be the result of ignorance. We are at least better at vanquishing ignorance than reforming skewed power structures. Moreover, examples of the economic take-off of the type described here seem to be growing. Like the best of the cases reviewed in this volume, they, too, are all covered with warts. But that is the best news of all. Perfection seems unnecessary for processes and rates of growth that cut poverty in half every 15 years.

Above all, it is important to remember that in-depth analysis is the only way to understand these processes. As mentioned throughout this chapter, the processes are complex and interact with underlying diversity. Broad generalizations are possible, but successful growth requires detailed application. The hope is that this book provides enough hints to move those processes forward.

Appendix: Economic Development of the Republic of China on Taiwan

SHIRLEY W. Y. KUO

This discussion focuses on several topics: Taiwan's past economic performance, the main policies that have contributed to its success, current issues of concern, and the economy's future prospects.

Taiwan's Past Economic Performance

Economic development in Taiwan over the past four decades has been characterized by rapid growth, export expansion, stable prices, full employment, and fairly equitable income distribution. In the natural course of its development, the economy underwent significant long-term changes in terms of production, trade, and employment. Although the two oil crises of the 1970s had short-term impacts on price movements and growth rates, Taiwan recovered from the crises quickly, and the economy was promptly brought back on track.

Since the beginning of the 1970s, Taiwan has experienced a massive export surplus, a high saving rate, low tax rates, a sound government budget, and an increase in real wage rates. The essential long-term characteristics of the Taiwan economy are given in table A.1. The main features of its performance in the period since 1950 are outlined in the following sections.

Growth and Industrialization

Immediately after World War II, per capita GNP in Taiwan was about US$70. This figure increased rapidly, reaching US$7,500 by 1989. Between 1952 and 1989 real GNP grew at an annual rate of 8.9 percent, and real per capita GNP grew at 6.4 percent.

Rapid industrialization caused the economic structure to change appreciably. Statistics show that in terms of production, trade, and employment, the economy moved from an agricultural to an industrial orientation. During 1952–89, the share of agriculture in gross domestic product dropped from 32 percent to 5 percent, while the share of the industrial sector rose from 22 percent to 44 percent. The rapid expansion of the industrial sector was caused primarily by the rapid growth of three manufacturing industries: food processing, textiles, and electrical machinery. Throughout most of this period, the value added by these three industries contributed more than a third of the total manufacturing expansion. Reflecting the structural changes in production and trade, the

TABLE A.1 Characteristics of the Taiwan economy, 1961–1987 (percent)

Item	1961–71	1971–81	1981–88	1989
Production				
GNP (% real changes)	10.0	9.5	8.5	7.2
Unemployment rate (%)	2.9	1.6	2.2	1.6
Gross domestic investment				
rate (% GNP)	22.3	30.4	22.4	22.0
Gross national savings rate (% GNP)	21.8	31.8	34.0	31.3
Balance of payments				
Exports (% GNP)	18.4	42.0	48.9	44.0
Imports (% GNP)	21.0	40.0	36.9	35.0
Current account balance (% GNP)	−0.5	1.4	11.6	9.3
Debt service ratio	—	3.8[a]	4.3[b]	3.2[c]
Fiscal				
Public sector expenditures (% GNP)	23.6	24.1	23.5	34.1
Fiscal surplus (% GDP)	2.4	6.7	5.2	6.2
Total change in monetary base (% GDP)	1.4[d]	2.6	2.8	6.8
Money and prices				
M2/GDP (%)	34.1	57.9	100.7	146.5
Annual change in CPI (%)	3.3	11.6	2.9	4.4
Annual change in WPI (%)	1.8	10.4	−0.5	−0.4
Annual change in real wage				
rate of manufacturing	6.2	8.0	6.9	9.7
Staff	1.3[e]	5.6	7.4	7.3
Worker	11.9[e]	9.7	6.5	9.4
Exchange rate (NT$ = US$1)	40.0	37.8	36.7	26.4
Real effective exchange rate index (trade				
weighted, 1979 = 100)	108.9	104.0	99.2	106.7

SOURCES: Taiwan, DGBAS (1981, 1986, 1987, 1988, 1989a, 1989b, 1989c); Taiwan, Department of Statistics (1989); and Central Bank of China (1990).
NOTE: Figures are period averages.
[a] 1974–81.
[b] 1962–71.
[c] 1969–71.
[d] 1981–87.
[e] 1987.

manufacturing sector provided the majority of new job opportunities. In the 1970s more than half of all newcomers in the work force were absorbed by the manufacturing sector. The rapid expansion of labor-intensive light manufacturing up until 1970 characterized a specific pattern of industrialization in Taiwan. After 1971, this trend changed. The share of the three industries in manufacturing expansion started to decline, mainly because of a rapid decrease in the share of food processing and a gradual decline in the share of textile expansion. Instead, a relative increase was observed in more capital- and skill-intensive industries such as petrochemicals, metals, and machinery. With this development, the center of gravity shifted from agriculture to industry and, within industry, from labor-intensive light manufacturing to more capital- and skill-intensive manufacturing.

The development of labor-intensive light manufacturing made many important contributions to the economy, particularly to the reduction of unemployment, to more equitable income distribution, and to a higher standard of living.

Labor Allocation and Labor Absorption

The structural change in the economy was accompanied by substantial growth and structural change in employment. Employment in agriculture decreased from 56.1 percent of total employment in 1952 to 12.9 percent in 1989, while employment in the industrial sector increased from 16.9 percent to 42.2 percent during the same period.

The labor force in Taiwan was absorbed successfully, particularly during the 1960s. The unemployment rate decreased from 6.5 percent in 1952 to less than 3 percent in 1971 and has been maintained at less than 3 percent ever since then. In other words by 1971 Taiwan's economy had successfully achieved full employment after a period of extensive labor absorption. Unemployment rates from various sources, some of which have been adjusted or estimated, are presented in figure A.1. These rates give a general idea of the level of and changes in the rate of unemployment during the period from 1953 to 1989.

The rapid outmigration of agricultural labor after 1965 was possible only because of rapid labor absorption in the nonagricultural sector. In the 1950s the economy failed to absorb all the newcomers. As a result, the number of unemployed increased during this period. In the 1960s, however, employment opportunities were successfully provided that absorbed not only all the newcomers but also some of the unemployed.

Foreign Trade

Exports and imports have played a crucial role in the development of Taiwan. Being a small-scale economy with limited domestic resources, it has depended heavily

FIGURE A.1 Unemployment rate, 1953–1989

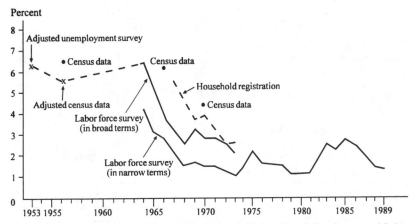

Sources: Unpublished data from Thailand Agricultural Workers Population Census and Labor Force Survey.

334 Shirley W. Y. Kuo

on the expansion of foreign trade to promote sustained growth. Between 1952 and 1989 the value of exports increased from US$0.12 billion to US$66.2 billion, and imports rose from US$0.19 billion to US$52.2 billion. At the same time, Taiwan's trade dependency increased greatly.

With the transformation of the economic structure, the composition of exports showed a marked change. Exports of agricultural products decreased from 92 percent of total exports in 1952 to 5 percent in 1989, while exports of industrial products increased from 8 percent to 95 percent. In 1952 rice and sugar accounted for 74 percent of total exports; however, rapid industrialization in the 1960s brought the share down to 3 percent by 1970.

Overall Improvement of Living Standards Over Time

Table A.2 shows clear improvements in living standards over time in terms of advances made in education, sanitation, transportation and communications, and housing.

TABLE A.2 Quality-of-life indicators, selected years

Indicator	Years	
Education	*1966*	*1989*
Literacy rate (of population 6 years old and older) (percent)	45.0 (1946)	92.9
Percentage of those 6–11 in primary schools	78.6 (1946)	99.9
Percentage of those 12–14 in junior high schools	48.3	94.5
Percentage of those 15–17 in senior high and vocational schools	28.3	74.5
Percentage of those 18–21 in junior colleges and universities	11.3	28.9
Sanitation	*1952*	*1989*
Crude death rate (per 1,000)	9.9	5.1
Life expectancy (years)	58.6	73.5
Per capita daily calorie intake	2,078	3,070
Per capita daily protein intake (grams)	49	91
Transportation and communications	*1952*	*1989*
Automobiles (per 1,000 population)	1	129
Motorcycles (per 1,000 population)	0.2	379
Telephones (per 1,000 population)	4	390
Correspondence posted (per capita)	49	91
Housing	*1952*	*1989*
Percentage of households with electric lighting	33.0 (1949)	99.7
Percentage of population with piped water	28.8	82.7
Living space per head (square meters)	4.6 (1949)	23.8
Dwellings investment/GNP (percent)	1.0	3.1

SOURCES: Council of Economic Planning and Development, Executive Yuan, 1990, *Economic Development, Taiwan, Republic of China;* Manpower Planning Committee, Council for Economic Planning and Development, Executive Yuan, 1989, *Social Welfare Indicators, Republic of China; DGBAS, 1986, Statistical Abstract;* DGBAS, 1989, *National Income of the Republic of China.*

Although some education was available to the people of Taiwan when the island was under Japanese occupation, it was usually limited to the primary level. Advanced education was rare and almost always limited to medical science. After Taiwan was restored to Chinese sovereignty in 1945, the government of the Republic of China made strenuous efforts to promote education. Not only was a large portion of the government budget spent on education, but equal opportunity in education was also emphasized. As a result, the level and rate of education increased greatly.

The literacy rate of persons six years of age and older increased from 45.0 percent in 1946 to 92.9 percent in 1989. Over the same period, the percentage of school-age children in primary schools increased from 78.6 percent to 99.9 percent. In 1968, nine years of education was made compulsory. Over the 1966–89 period, the percentage of those 12–14 years old in junior high schools increased from 48.3 percent to 94.5 percent; the percentage of those 15–17 years old in senior high and vocational schools increased from 28.3 percent to 74.5 percent; and the percentage of those 18–21 years old in colleges and universities increased from 11.3 percent to 28.9 percent. The promotion of education on the island greatly contributed to the rapid growth of the economy by providing higher-quality labor for advanced production.

The crude death rate and life expectancy are considered to be two typical indicators of the level of sanitation. The crude death rate in Taiwan decreased from 9.9 per thousand in 1952 to 5.1 per thousand in 1989, and life expectancy increased from 58.6 years to 73.5 years over the same period.

Transportation in Taiwan has become an increasing problem because of Taiwan's scarcity of land and population density. In the 1960s, the speed of industrialization greatly exceeded the rate of highway and harbor construction. However, transportation construction was intensified during 1974–78 through the implementation of the government's "ten major projects." Transportation has been greatly facilitated since then, although the situation is still far from satisfactory. As the economy grew, the number of automobiles, motorcycles, and telephones also increased rapidly.

Housing construction during the past three decades has been quite successful. About 90 percent of the houses in Taipei City and 80 percent of those in Taiwan Province were built after World War II. Living space per capita increased from 4.6 square meters in 1949 to 23.8 square meters in 1989. The share of dwelling investment in GNP increased from 1 percent in 1952 to 3.1 percent in 1989. One particular welfare item, the widespread diffusion of public utilities, brought benefits to even the poorest and most isolated families. The percentage of houses equipped with electric lighting increased from 33 percent in 1949 to 99.7 percent in 1986. In sum, industrialization and urbanization have brought significant social welfare benefits to Taiwan.

Main Government Policies Contributing To Success

Many factors contributed to Taiwan's success. The first prerequisite was political and social stability. A free economic system was also crucial. The government policies involved promoted a free economic system, anti-inflation policies, outward-looking strategies, efficient utilization of resources (particularly labor and capital), balanced growth, and flexible adjustment of government policies beginning in the 1970s.

Adoption of a Free Economic System

The economic system of Taiwan is based on private ownership. After the late 1950s the institutional environment left entrepreneurs free to seek their own profits and workers free to seek their own wages. This free economic system developed a dynamic that led the economy to grow rapidly.

The access to managerial positions is now entirely open. Entrepreneurial talent forms the basis for the recruitment of business managers. As a result, business executives are drawn largely from the middle and lower-middle classes. The strategy of more liberalized externally oriented policies allowed entrepreneurs to play a more active role in exploring the internal and external markets. An environment characterized by rapid development and price stability will strengthen the market mechanism and help increase entrepreneurial efficiency.

Anti-inflation Policies

Price stability has been a historical concern in Taiwan. The government has long promoted "growth with stability," a doctrine that emphasizes political and socio-economic considerations. Although prices on the whole have been stable over the past four decades, the Taiwan economy experienced severe inflation immediately after World War II and during the oil crises. The government's policies for curing inflation are noteworthy.

Outward-Looking Strategies

Appropriate government policies are considered to have been essential to rapid export expansion. In the early 1950s, policies stimulated import substitution. A multiple exchange rate system, an overvaluation of the new Taiwan dollar, and the maintenance of higher prices for import goods versus export goods during this period were all in favor of import substitution.

From the late 1950s, however, export expansion was emphasized and various export promotion schemes were implemented. The 19-point economic and financial reform and the statute for the encouragement of investment emphasized carefully designed outward-looking trade policies. Nominal rates of protection, exchange rates, investment policies, tax rebates, and trade loans all provided a favorable environment for export promotion. Thus, outward-looking government economic policies and measures contributed greatly to a successful transition in Taiwan.

Efficient Utilization of Resources

With limited natural resources, an efficient utilization of resources—land, capital, and labor—constituted another important factor contributing to rapid growth.

LAND REFORM. Land reform in Taiwan was carried out in three stages: rent reduction, the sale of public land, and a program that returned land to the tiller. The rent reduction program implemented in 1949 legally limited the amount of farm rent on private tenanted land to 37.5 percent of the harvest, down from the original 50 percent. The public land sale program and the land-to-the-tiller program were implemented in 1953. The land bought by tenants through these two programs amounted to 71 percent of the total area of public and private tenanted land. After land reform, tenancy conditions were altered significantly. The ratio of owner-farmers to total farm families increased from 36 percent to 60 percent. Owner-farmers and part owner-farmers owned more than 83 percent of the total farm land in 1957.

Following land reform, there was a strong incentive to put extra effort into cultivation. After rent reduction, the tenant not only benefited from lower rents but also from increased production. The advantages of an owner-farmer system over a tenancy system were obvious, as seen from an increase in per family, per person, and per hectare incomes. The incomes of the tenant in all three categories were less than three-fourths those of owner-farmers and part owner-farmers. Therefore, significant changes in tenancy conditions provided a strong incentive for production increases, and facilitated a more efficient utilization of the land and the agricultural labor force.

U.S. AID, FOREIGN INVESTMENT, AND DOMESTIC SAVINGS. In an open economy, investment can be financed by domestic and foreign savings. Foreign savings correspond to a trade deficit that, when financed by foreign aid or capital inflow, can make up for both the trade gap (i.e., the import-export gap) and the savings-investment gap. The success of the Taiwan economy can be attributed to the availability of foreign capital and domestic savings, which augmented its import and investment capacity.

The savings ratio in the GNP increased from 5 percent in the 1950s to more than 10 percent in 1963. This made it possible for the economy to reach the "takeoff" stage and to continue sustained growth after the termination of U.S. aid in 1965. Savings as a percentage of GNP amounted to 22 percent on average in the 1960s and 32 percent thereafter. This achievement of a high savings rate was a decisive factor in the successful development of Taiwan. Government policies contributed to the high savings rate in various ways: they stabilized prices, helped maintain positive real interest rates, and provided attractive incentives to savings such as tax exemptions on interest earnings while none were offered on interest payments. In addition, sound government fiscal policies provided a considerable portion of domestic savings. Thus, the generation and efficient utilization of both foreign and domestic capital greatly contributed to import and investment capacity.

LABOR UTILIZATION. With limited natural resources and a dense population, the success of the Taiwan economy can be said to depend largely on the efficient utilization of its labor force. That is, the abundance of labor can be a negative or positive factor, depending on whether it is inefficiently or efficiently utilized. Fortunately, Taiwan followed the latter. Various government policies contributed to the efficient use of labor.

Emphasis on education. As mentioned earlier, when Taiwan was under Japanese occupation, education was limited to the primary level. Advanced education was rare and almost always limited to medical science. After Taiwan was restored to Chinese sovereignty, the government made a concerted effort to promote education. A large portion of the government budget was spent on education, and equal opportunity in education was emphasized. As a result, the level and rate of education increased greatly. The emphasis on education greatly contributed to the rapid growth of the economy by providing higher-quality labor for advanced production.

Competitive labor market. The conditions in Taiwan's labor market are close to perfect competition. Wages are flexible and labor mobile. The existence of a competitive labor market has been most beneficial to the efficient reallocation of the factors of production, particularly in the course of rapid growth and speedy industrialization. The labor force in Taiwan seems to have been guided by an invisible hand—the wage rate— urging it to take up new activities with new technologies. For example, during the era of labor-intensive production, wage rates reflected an increase in demand and a shortage of labor supply by rising significantly. Wage rates rose much faster for unskilled labor than for skilled labor, and this was an important contributing factor in achieving a more equitable income distribution in Taiwan. However, in response to the weaker compet- itiveness of unskilled labor products and exports in comparison with skilled labor products in the 1980s, the increase in wages for unskilled labor started to lag behind the wages for skilled labor. Flexible wage rates and a liquid movement of the labor force were thus an essential factor in the efficient utilization of labor in the past. Also note that because of the expansion in higher education, the labor structure was upgraded rapidly. The proportion of the work force with a secondary or higher education increased consid- erably to meet an increasing demand for skilled labor in production.

IMPORTANCE OF MARKET EXPANSION. The creation of job opportunities is concerned with two essential factors: labor productivity and output market. On the one hand, given a certain quantity of production, an increase in labor productivity will reduce job opportunities. On the other hand, with labor productivity held constant, an expansion of the output market will create job opportunities by increasing production opportunities. Therefore, the number of real job opportunities a society can create actually depends on the algebraic sum of the above two elements, namely, the num- ber reduced by the advancement of labor productivity and the number increased by market expansion. In other words, in the course of increasing productivity, market expansion for production is a necessary condition for achieving and maintaining full employment.

Fortunately, labor demand due to market expansion was more than enough to compensate for the labor released by increasing productivity in Taiwan. The increment of labor demand due to export expansion constituted approximately one-third of the labor demand due to market expansion.

Labor utilization by export business calculated by input-output tables shows that export business utilized 41.3 percent of total employment in 1985, with 3.9 percent in agricultural exports, 25.4 percent in industrial exports, and 12.0 percent in service exports. Here again, the importance of outward-looking policies to labor absorption and utilization is clear.

Emphasis on Balanced Growth

With two-thirds of the island being mountainous and most of the arable land located along its west coast, economic activities in Taiwan are heavily concentrated in one-third of its total area. The four largest cities—Taipei, Taichung, Tainan, and Kaohsiung—are rather evenly spaced, to form balanced urban centers. The government advocated balanced growth, and the interdependence of agriculture and industry was strongly emphasized. Government policies aimed at improving equity between rural and urban regions through an emphasis on rural irrigation, electrification, education, trans- portation, and other forms of rural construction.

As a result, the irrigation system was diffused over most of the cultivated area. Electrification was extended to every home. Education was promoted and spread to males and females alike. Excellent road and rail networks spread throughout the island.

The mileage of rural roads increased rapidly. Technical assistance through the Joint Commission on Rural Reconstruction and through farmers' associations was enhanced, and thus sound foundations were laid for a marked spatial dispersion of economic development. Past industrial development was rural oriented and designed to make it easier to acquire raw materials, rural laborers, and cheaper land. As a result, industrialization in Taiwan became dispersed.

Current Issues

The general environment of the Taiwan economy changed significantly after 1973. Internationally, the new environment was characterized by expensive oil, the threat of inflation, expanding protectionism, financial disorder, financial innovation, the need for liberalization, and keen competition from newcomers.

Domestically, the basic concerns had to do with production, the trade imbalance, and environmental awareness.

Issues Related to Production

In the post-1973 era, the economy passed the surplus labor stage of development. Unskilled labor became fully utilized, and wages began rising. Taiwan had also moved beyond the stage of the easy acquisition of raw materials, rural laborers, and cheaper land. Technological progress has begun moving at a slower pace. The economy has begun expanding its scope horizontally and vertically as it moves toward the production of sophisticated products with more complicated processes. Greater liberalization and internationalization are therefore being called for.

Trade Imbalance and Excess Savings

Continuous trade surpluses have created a massive amount of foreign exchange reserves. Although the central bank has exercised sterilization intensively, the accumulation of foreign exchange reserves has generated heavy pressure on the money supply. These trade surpluses are also reflected in a large amount of excess savings and a shortage of investment. Excess liquidity, which has continued for several years, has created financial problems.

Desire for Improved Environment

As a result of economic development, people in Taiwan have started to demand a better environment, housing, transportation, communications, education, sanitation, and other amenities of life. Also, a new system of values has turned to public opinion to guide social and political behavior. Although this is a natural course of development, much more efficient government management and careful planning are needed to ensure that development continues to evolve in the desired manner.

Future Prospects

Since the 1970s, policymakers have been aware of the direction in which future development should proceed in view of these new conditions, and some appropriate adjustments have been progressing successfully since the 1980s.

Restructuring of Production and Exports

Taiwan's current growth strategy is particularly concerned with conserving energy and upgrading industries.

ENERGY POLICIES. Since Taiwan depends heavily on imported petroleum, it must make efficient use of petroleum if the economy is to continue its vigorous growth. Thus an important goal of energy policy is "to achieve a certain economic growth rate with a minimum consumption of energy." Accordingly, energy policies are designed to promote energy conservation through the use of energy-efficient machinery and equipment; to improve the industrial structure by expanding the output shares of energy-efficient, skill-intensive, and high value-added industries; and to save oil through the diversification of energy utilization, particularly in the generation of power.

UPGRADING INDUSTRIES. The nation's industrial development strategy was carefully planned some 10 years ago, with emphasis on the following points in the development of future industries: low-energy intensiveness, high-technology intensiveness, high value added, high labor intensiveness, good marketability, strong defense, and high domestic linkage.

Among the manufacturing industries, machinery and electronics best fit all these conditions. Computers are also climbing fast in importance. Upgraded textiles are an important industry for the future. Some results of restructuring can be detected from the change in the composition of exports. The share of "strategic industries" in the industrial structure increased tremendously in the 1980s, and this increase is expected to continue. In the service sector, banking and finance have become more important in recent years. Development of the service sector will not only generate value added but will also provide benefits for other industries, especially manufacturing. All these are considered strategic industries for future development.

Advancement in Technology

The rate of technical progress measures the speed of increase in output that is not caused by an increase in inputs but by an advancement in the efficiency of production. Technical progress contributed greatly to the growth of the Taiwan economy, accounting for about 50 percent of the growth of all sectors in the 1950s. Technical progress began slowing down in the 1960s, however, and it took a turn for the worse in the 1970s. In order to provide for a more effective utilization of resources, efforts are being made to upgrade management, emphasize research and development, improve vocational education, encourage automation and standardization, and introduce legal and regulatory reforms.

Trade Imbalance and Excess Savings

Taiwan's trade surpluses have given rise to two kinds of problems in particular. It now has large foreign exchange reserves that exert pressure on the money supply, and it has a huge excess of savings as a result of insufficient investment.

Measures have been taken to adjust the trade imbalance, mainly through liberalization and internationalization. To reduce the export surplus, Taiwan will endeavor to eliminate or reduce export subsidies and encourage import liberalization. Tax rebates for exports have been gradually reduced. Import liberalization has been implemented through the lifting of import restrictions and the lowering of tariff rates. In February 1988, for example, tariff rates were reduced by an average of 50 percent on 3,523 items. These changes constitute the largest cut ever on a single round.

Also, foreign exchange controls have been relaxed to allow greater capital movement and to allow foreign exchange rates to be influenced more by market forces. In July 1987, most foreign exchange controls were relaxed to allow direct capital outflows; the amount of purchase of foreign exchange for outward remittance was relaxed to a maximum of US$5 million per adult per year. This was a significant step toward liberalization. After the new Taiwan dollar was stabilized, the ceiling on inward remittance was increased gradually to US$2 million.

The slowdown in investment has received great attention, and more emphasis is now being put on active implementation of public investment. As a result, the share of investment in the GNP increased from 17 percent in 1986 to 20 percent in 1987 and 22 percent in 1989. Thus, the ongoing adjustments have had some results.

Desire for Improved Environment

Now that the economy has become much more affluent in terms of material production, people have begun to demand better environmental conditions rather than more consumer products. Industries that in the past paid a minimum in social costs have been asked to increase their investment in environmental controls. All aspects of the infrastructure—including the MRT system, transportation, telecommunications, education, and sanitation—are inadequate to meet public needs and certainly require immediate expansion. More rapid public construction will not only provide a better environment, but will also be an efficient means of reducing excess savings and the trade surplus.

On the whole, the adjustments made in the 1980s seem to have been on the right track and have given Taiwan hope for the future. If Taiwan is to achieve the national goals of a suitable rate of growth, stable prices, full employment, and improved welfare, however, much obviously remains to be done.

References

Central Bank of China, Economic Research Department. 1990. *Financial Statistics Monthly, Taiwan District, The Republic of China.* January.
———. *A Supplement to Financial Statistics Monthly, Taiwan District, The Republic of China.* 2d ed.
Taiwan, Department of Statistics, Ministry of Finance. 1989. *Monthly Statistics of Exports and Imports, The Republic of China.* December.
———, Directorate-General of Budget, Accounting, and Statistics, Executive Yuan (DGBAS). 1989a. *National Income of the Republic of China.* Taipei.
———, DGBAS. 1989b. *Quarterly National Economic Trends, Taiwan Area, The Republic of China,* November.
———, DGBAS. 1981, 1986, 1987, 1988, 1989c. *Yearbook of Labor Statistics, Republic of China.* Taipei.

Contributors

Romeo M. Bautista is a research fellow in the Trade and Macroeconomics Division, International Food Policy Research Institute (IFPRI). He has worked extensively on international trade, economic development, and Asian economies. Before joining IFPRI in 1983, he was a professor and chairman of the Department of Economics at the University of the Philippines and served as deputy director-general for policy of the National Economic and Development Authority in the Philippine government.

Albert Berry is professor of economics at the University of Toronto. His main areas of interest have been agriculture, small and medium industry, labor markets, and income distribution in developing countries, with special reference to Colombia and other Latin American countries. He has been an adviser to the Planning Commission and most recently acted as international director for the Agriculture Mission to review the agricultural sector in Colombia.

G. S. Bhalla is professor emeritus, Jawaharlal Nehru University, New Delhi. He has worked on regional agricultural development, the impact of technological changes on agrarian structure, and problems of agricultural policy. He was formerly a member of the Planning Commission and chairman of the Commission for Agricultural Costs and Prices, government of India. He has also been a consultant with the Food and Agriculture Organization in Rome and a research fellow at the International Food Policy Research Institute in Washington, D.C. He served for many years on the faculty of the Jawaharlal Nehru University and acted as the dean of its School of Social Sciences for two years.

Arne Bigsten is professor of Development Economics in the Department of Economics, Göteborgs University, Sweden. His primary research area has been African economic development, focusing on issues of regional development, income distribution and poverty, labor market behavior, smallholder agriculture, and macroeconomic stabilization. He has been a visitor at the Institute of Development Studies, the University of Nairobi, and the Institute of Economics and Statistics, Oxford University. He has been a consultant to the World Bank, United Nations, International Labour Organization, and International Fund for Agricultural Development. He is a member of the board of the Swedish International Development Authority and of the Scandinavian Institute of African Studies.

Rafael Celis is a resource economist and director of ProDesarrollo Internacional al Limitada, based in Costa Rica, and is working on sustainable development issues. He has been a member of the board of directors of the Organization for Tropical Studies, director of the Sustainable Agricultural Program at the Tropical Agricultural Research and Training Center, research fellow at the International Food Policy Research Institute, and lecturer at the University of Costa Rica and Rafael Landivar University in Guatemala.

Paul Collier is a professor at Oxford University, where he directs the Centre for the Study of African Economies, a designated research center of the Economic and Social Research Council. He is a visiting scholar at the Kennedy School of Government, Harvard University, and at the Centre d'Étude et de Recherché sur le Développement International, Université d'Auvergne, and is managing editor of the *Journal of African Economies*.

Roberto A. Domenech is an Argentine economist, at present serving as a vice-president of Banco de la Nación Argentina and as an adviser to the minister of economy of Argentina. He is a professor (on leave of absence) of macroeconomics at the University of Córdoba. Most of his professional career has been as a researcher at the Institute for Economic Studies of the Fundación Mediterránea, where he is the editor of an international newsletter.

Bruce F. Johnston is professor emeritus at the Food Research Institute, Stanford University. An early article, "Agricultural Productivity and Economic Development in Japan," published in the *Journal of Political Economy* in 1951, was followed a decade later by a joint article with John Mellor and a 1975 book with Peter Kilby, which broadened the analysis of agriculture's role in structural transformation. Since 1954 he has focused much of his attention on Sub-Saharan Africa. His most recent book, *Transforming Agrarian Economies: Opportunities Seized, Opportunities Missed,* a joint effort with T. P. Tomich and Peter Kilby, is being published by Cornell University Press.

Shirley W. Y. Kuo is the chairman of the Council for Economic Planning Development and was formerly deputy governor of the Central Bank of China.

Eduardo Lizano is an economist with Consultores Económicos y Financieros S.A., based in Costa Rica. He is professor emeritus of the University of Costa Rica and a professor at the Universidad Autónoma de Centroamérica. He has been president of the Central Bank of Costa Rica; visiting professor at various universities in Latin America, the United States, and Europe; adviser to two Costa Rican presidents on economic matters, and governor of the International Monetary Fund. He has published extensively on issues related to social and economic integration in Central America and on policy reform for the agricultural sector.

Yu-Kang Mao is a counselor with the Council of Agriculture, Executive Yuan, Taiwan. He was formerly a professor in the Department of Agricultural Economics, National Taiwan University, and director of the Rural Economics Division, Sino-American Joint Commission on Rural Reconstruction. He has also served as director of the Department of Planning and Economics, Council on Agricultural Planning and Development, Taipei.

John W. Mellor is President of John Mellor Associates, Inc., a policy consulting firm. He is author of *The Economics of Agricultural Development,* and has won several prizes for quality of research in that area. He was chief economist of the United States Agency for International Development; built the International Food Policy Research Institute into the premiere institute in its field; won the Wihuri International Prize (Finland) and the Presidential Award (United States) for his contribution to the reduction of hunger; and is a fellow of the American Academy of Arts and Sciences, American Association for the Advancement of Science, and American Agricultural Economics Association. He served for many years on the faculty of Cornell University.

Yair Mundlak is F. H. Prince Professor of Economics at the University of Chicago and Ruth Ochberg Professor Emeritus of Agricultural Economics at Hebrew University of Jerusalem. He was formerly a research fellow at the International Food Policy Research Institute. He has published widely and won awards in Israel, including the Rothschild Prize, and numerous awards from the American Agricultural Economics Association. He is a fellow of the Econometric Society and of the American Agricultural Economics Association.

Albert Park is a doctoral candidate at Stanford University's Food Research Institute. His research focuses on rural development in China, where he has worked with the Rural Development Institute of the Chinese Academy of Social Sciences. He has also lived and worked in Kenya and Korea.

Chi Schive is vice chairman of the Council for Economic Planning and Development, Taiwan, and professor of economics at National Taiwan University. His research areas include foreign investment, technology transfer, trade, industrial research and development, automation, public enterprises, small- and medium-size businesses, industrial policy, and Dutch disease in Taiwan.

Ammar Siamwalla is president of the Thailand Development and Research

Institute, Bangkok. He was formerly a lecturer on the Faculty of Economics, Thammasat University; an assistant professor and research staff economist in the Department of Economics, Yale University; a visiting professor at the Food Research Institute, Stanford University; and a research fellow at the International Food Policy Research Institute.

Index

Farmers' Training Center, Kenya, 235
Fei, John C. H., 46n, 54
Fertilizers: Argentina, 182; Kenya, 198,
203; Philippines, 124, 137; Punjab, 79,
98; Punjab seed, 67, 59, 76
Fields, G. S., 142, 208
Fleming, M., 234
Food Corporation of India, 68
Food crops. *See* Colombia; Costa Rica
Foodgrains: Argentina, 179; Costa Rica,
248–49, 252; Punjab, 94, 95
Food Stabilization Fund, Taiwan, 58, 59
Forests: Punjab, 70; Taiwan, 28
Foster, J. E., 142

Galenson, Walter, 46, 54, 55
Garcia, Jorge, 255, 264, 269, 280, 281,
283, 285
GDP. *See* Gross domestic product
Gerchunoff, Pablo, 178, 180
Gibbs, A., 137
Granger test, 221–22, 232
Great Britain, legislation relating to Punjab
land system, 71–72, 72n
Great Depression: Argentina and, 176, 187,
193; Colombia and, 266, 267
Green revolution
—benefits from, 125, 144
—India, 67
—Punjab, 67; development strategy for,
108; factor development gains from, 83
Gregorio, R. G., 131
Gross domestic product (GDP), country
comparison of growth rate, 113. *See also*
individual countries
Gulati, Ashok, 96

Harris, J. R., 208
Hazell, Peter B. R., 159, 163, 234, 249,
255
Health: Costa Rica, 252; Philippines, 121–
22
Herdt, R. W., 126
Hermoso, V. P., 134n
Herr, J. R., 222, 225, 227, 228
Herrin, A., 141
Hiemenz, U., 43n
Hirashima, Shigemochi, 70
Hirschman, Albert O., 13, 136
Ho, Samuel P. S., 42, 46
Holazo, V., 142
Holleman, Cindy, 255
Hooley, R., 129, 130, 132

Hossain, M., 255
Housing: Colombia, 300, 301; Kenya, 326;
Taiwan, 335; Thailand, 159, 162–63,
326
Hsieh, S. C., 241
Hsing, Mo-huan, 47
Hsu, W. F., 36
Human Settlements Commission, Philip-
pines, 141
Hutaserani, Suganya, 170
Hutcheson, Thomas L., 281n
Hyami, Y., 82

Income distribution: Costa Rica, 258–59;
Philippines, 114, 126; Punjab, 73, 83.
See also Colombia; Taiwan
India: green revolution, 67; independence
and land reform, 72; intersectoral resource flow, 96; manufacturing sector,
90; national policies influencing Punjab
development, 109; net domestic product
at factor cost, 68; per capita income, 67;
plans for rural infrastructure investment,
84–85; subsidies to agriculture, 96; value
added, 80–81
Indonesia: gross value added in agriculture,
113; linkage between agricultural and
nonagricultural growth, 138
Industrial Incentives Act of 1967, Philippines, 133
Industrialization: Argentina, 177, 182, 183,
184; Costa Rica, 245, 251, 256, 327; dynamic view of, 234; Kenya, 196, 198–
99, 223; Rosenstein-Rodan Big Push
Theory of, 234, 240. *See also* Taiwan
Inflation: Argentina, 175, 180, 181, 183;
Colombia, 265, 266, 270; Costa Rica,
250, 256; Taiwan price stabilization poli-
cies to fight, 35–37, 336
Instituto Colombiano Agropecuario (ICA),
276, 277
Instituto de Desarrollo Agrario (IDA), Costa
Rica, 245
Instituto Nacional de Technologia, Argen-
tina, 182
Intal, P. S., 120
Integrated Agricultural Development Pro-
gram (IADP), Kenya, 204
International Coffee Agreement, 254
International Food Policy Research Insti-
tute, 99
International Monetary Fund, 154, 181, 250

Library of Congress Cataloging-in-Publication Data

Agriculture on the road to industrialization / edited by John W. Mellor.
    p. cm.
   Includes index.
   ISBN 0-8018-5012-6
   1. Agriculture—Economic aspects—Developing countries. 2. Agricultural
innovations—Developing countries. 3. Agricultural productivity—Developing
countries. 4. Farm income—Developing countries. I. Mellor, John Williams, 1928–
HD1417.A478 1995
338.1'09172'4—dc20
                                 94-39359
                                   CIP